The Early Modern Papacy

LONGMAN HISTORY OF THE PAPACY

General Editor: A.D. Wright

This ambitious new series will cover the history of the Papacy from early medieval times through to the present day in five substantial volumes. Each, written by a leading scholar in the field, is designed to meet the needs of students and general readers, as well as those of the specialist.

Already published is:

The Modern Papacy since 1789
Frank J. Coppa

The Early Modern Papacy

From the Council of Trent to the French Revolution, 1564–1789

A.D. Wright

LONGMAN

An imprint of **PEARSON EDUCATION**

Harlow, England · London · New York · Reading, Massachusetts · San Francisco · Toronto · Don Mills, Ontario · Sydney
Tokyo · Singapore · Hong Kong · Seoul · Taipei · Cape Town · Madrid · Mexico City · Amsterdam · Munich · Paris · Milan

Pearson Education Limited
Edinburgh Gate
Harlow
Essex CM20 2JE
England

and Associated Companies throughout the world.

Visit us on the World Wide Web at:
www.pearsoned-ema.com

First published 2000

ISBN 0-582-08748-1 CSD
ISBN 0-582-08747-3 PPR

British Library Cataloguing-in-Publication Data

A catalogue record for this book is available from the British Library

Library of Congress Cataloging-in-Publication Data

A catalog record for this book is available from the Library of Congress

Set in 10/12pt Bembo by 35
Produced by Pearson Education Asia Pte Ltd.
Printed in Singapore

Contents

General Editor's Preface

As one millennium ends and another begins, according to the reckoning of the Christian tradition, the papacy probably remains as prominent as ever in the public mind, not only in Europe, East and West, but in the non-European world too. A work on the history of the papacy which presents to readers in English the most recent scholarship is thus timely. While shorter volumes, organized on a biographical basis, certainly exist, there has been lacking hitherto a more extended survey, covering the whole history of the papacy and originating in the English language. This series is thus intended to supply the deficiency. To achieve the greatest coherence of interpretation and argument which might reasonably be expected, an initial decision was taken that each volume should be written by a single scholar, expert in the period covered. Similarly, to ensure the best possible clarity of analysis, it was decided that all the authors should be scholars who naturally wrote in the English language, avoiding the difficulties which can arise from the need for translation. The series will examine in five volumes, of unequal chronological coverage, the history of the papacy from the earliest centuries of evidence for the bishopric of Rome to the close and consequences of the Second Vatican Council in the twentieth century, where the argument of the final volume concludes.

Preface

As the Introduction to this volume suggests, the period covered raises questions about the history of the papacy not only within the two and a quarter centuries treated here but also more widely over the whole evolution of the papal office. The dates chosen for this volume do not correspond precisely to the end dates of pontificates. For the argument of this work concerns the development of the papacy as affected by events of overwhelming influence, the conclusion at the end of 1563 of the Council of Trent and the outbreak of the French Revolution in 1789. In this volume it is argued that the impact of the decrees of the Council was indeed major, as far as the exercise of papal responsibilities was concerned. Yet the closure of the Council, while proving to be the prelude to a long period, until the later nineteenth century, in which no further General Council met, was for that very reason also the end of an era for the papacy. The popes since the beginning of the fifteenth century had had to fulfil their role alongside a sequence of such Councils, a sequence in that sense terminated at Trent. Thus in a series which is the history of the papacy, not of the Church as a whole, it seemed fruitful to approach the Council of Trent from a fresh perspective, allowing the third volume to review the whole period from the early fifteenth century to the Council of Trent inclusive. Similarly, the impact of the French Revolution on the exercise of papal office was obviously vast, and therefore its outbreak was clearly of more importance than the subsequent death of the last pope of the eighteenth century, in whose pontificate the Revolution began. The epoch of papal history considered here was thus bounded by major events, rather than by biographical specifics. For reasons suggested in the Introduction, the volume is also organized on an analytic, not a biographical or chronological basis.

Chronological Table

December 1563	Conclusion of the Council of Trent
1559–65	Pius IV (de' Medici)
1566–72	Pius V (Ghislieri)
1572–85	Gregory XIII (Buoncompagni)
1585–90	Sixtus V (Peretti)
1590	Urban VII (Castagna)
1590–91	Gregory XIV (Sfondrati)
1591	Innocent IX (Facchinetti)
1592–1605	Clement VIII (Aldobrandini)
1605	Leo XI (de' Medici)
1605–21	Paul V (Borghese)
1621–23	Gregory XV (Ludovisi)
1623–44	Urban VIII (Barberini)
1644–55	Innocent X (Pamfili)
1655–67	Alexander VII (Chigi)
1667–69	Clement IX (Rospigliosi)
1670–76	Clement X (Altieri)
1676–89	Innocent XI (Odescalchi)
1689–91	Alexander VIII (Ottoboni)
1691–1700	Innocent XII (Pignatelli)
1700–21	Clement XI (Albani)
1721–24	Innocent XIII (Conti)
1724–30	Benedict XIII (Orsini)
1730–40	Clement XII (Corsini)
1740–58	Benedict XIV (Lambertini)
1758–69	Clement XIII (Rezzonico)
1769–74	Clement XIV (Ganganelli)
1775–99	Pius VI (Braschi)
Summer 1789	Outbreak of the French Revolution

CHAPTER 1

Introduction

The history of the papacy between the end of the Council of Trent (1563) and the outbreak of the French Revolution (1789) has often been seen as a period of decline. The supposed stagnation of papal policy, after the splendours of the Middle Ages, the excitement of the Renaissance and the vigour of the early Counter-Reformation, has not attracted much appreciative interest among historians writing in English. Even among art historians the attention paid to the glories of the high Baroque in Rome has not been equally sustained for the eighteenth century, except in distinctly specialist studies. Yet the papacy, together with Western European Catholicism, was to emerge from the sub-sequent trials of the French Revolution and tribulations of the Napoleonic period with renewed energy. However much that may be attributed to the salutary shock of those decades, a capacity for survival and thus a residual strength must also be allowed. For such reason alone the 'quiet' centuries of the papacy, between 1564 and 1789, would deserve reconsideration. But in fact, as this volume will suggest, the evolution of the papacy during this period of the 'long Counter-Reformation' represented more than a conservation of vestigial authority, after the challenge of the Reformation and consolidation of Protestantism in Western Europe.

The vitality of the papal office was, on the contrary, demonstrated by the pursuit of defined but difficult programmes, which were not confined to defence of political sovereignty or a compensatory ostentation in visually dramatic art. The popes of these centuries largely succeeded in their aim of maintaining unity of doctrine among Catholics, based on the clarifications of the Council of Trent. Not only was formal schism substantially prevented, despite the prolonged disputes over alleged or actual Jansenism, but the con-solidation of lay knowledge of the faith was achieved by the extension of catechism. Secondly, a measure of internal reform of the Catholic Church was still pursued by most popes of this period, representing at least a partial real-ization of the Tridentine disciplinary ideals. Thirdly, these first two goals had to be pursued in the face of undiminishing assertion by secular rulers, Catholics included, of enlarged authority in religious affairs. The eventual suppression

1

of the Society of Jesus by the papacy itself was the eighteenth-century climax of the tensions generated by the pursuit of such policies in these pre-Revolutionary conditions. But the popes of the post-Tridentine era could not restrict their vision to Europe: Catholic overseas mission created its own problems on a global scale.

In the absence of other sustained treatment in English of the post-Tridentine papacy, readers have previously been able to turn to the volumes of von Pastor's *History of the Popes*. The impressive research on which that series is based is evident enough in the English translation of the work, published between 1891 and 1953. But the need for a new review of the popes in the period covered by this present volume does not derive solely from the further progress of historical research. The later volumes of von Pastor's great enterprise were not fully completed by his own hand at the time of his death. They remain partial both in the sense of what they treat and in the imperfect balance of their discussion of contentious questions like the suppression of the Jesuits. Opportunity certainly remains for a reassessment of the popes of the period between the Council of Trent and the French Revolution.[1]

AN INFLUENTIAL MODEL

A challenging new perspective has in any case been offered to English-language readers in more recent times. In 1988 the English translation appeared of Paolo Prodi's *The Papal Prince*, which argued for a distinctive interpretation of the papacy in the period under discussion here and hence of the whole history of the papacy as well. The centuries between 1564 and 1789 thus take on a further interest, when they are seen as the key to a revaluation of the entire history of the popes. For this reason also it would seem vital for a new English-language history such as the present series to give critical attention to those centuries. The account offered here will attempt a more comprehensive survey of the papacy as an institution than Prodi's extended essay in interpretation was intended to be; and in so doing will make critical analysis of that interpretation, with consequences for the whole of papal history as well as for the two centuries immediately in question. But it is important to note initially that English readers, among whom Prodi's model has become a received opinion, may not all be aware of the development of Prodi's own views. While the Italian original of his book was published in 1982, his contribution of 1986 to the *Annali*, Volume 9 of the Einaudi *Storia d'Italia*, represents a modification of his argument, qualifying it in ways which seem more convincing. The analysis of the present volume offers a response to that qualified form of Prodi's argument.

1 L. von Pastor, *The History of the Popes, from the Close of the Middle Ages* (Engl. trans., 40 vols, London 1891–1953). Concise biographies of popes (under their pontifical not family name) are gradually appearing as volumes are published of the *Dizionario biografico degli Italiani* (Rome 1960 onwards). A recent resource is the *Dictionnaire historique de la papauté*, ed. P. Levillain (Paris 1994).

It is obviously of first importance to set out as simply as possible the basic line of that argument, precisely because of its implications for the whole history of the papacy. The starting point is the observation, long accepted by most historians, that the medieval papacy developed a precocious skill in centralized administration which challenged the secular rulers of Western Europe. They in turn gradually responded by refining their systems of government, until the later medieval schism gave them an opportunity of gaining from rival popes considerable degrees of control over the local Church in their territories.[2] Prodi's point of departure from received interpretations, however, is the history of the Renaissance popes. The territorial ambitions of the popes of that period, still evident for example in the pontificate of the Farnese pope Paul III (1534–49), he sees not as a deviation in papal history but as a continuation of traditional aims by modified means. The attempts to consolidate and extend the central-Italian papal states thus emerge as a reaction to the political pressure of the 'New Monarchies' and 'Nation States' traditionally regarded as developing in early modern Europe. Increasing dependence on the political and above all financial foundation represented by the papal states was of course furthered by the consequences of the Protestant Reformation, especially the loss of ecclesiastical revenues from considerable parts of Western Europe.

It will be noted that this interpretation does not otherwise accord a traditional degree of importance to the challenge of Protestantism, nor even directly to the Council of Trent (1545–63). If anything, the Italian Wars of the late fifteenth and early sixteenth centuries would seem of more significance, as marking the transformation of papal priorities, in response to a challenge from secular rulers who had now digested the earlier lessons taught by the model of papal power. But if this competition with secular authorities in directly territorial terms was thus part of a continuous evolution in the institution of the papacy, the supposed reaction to Protestant Reformation, the so-called Counter-Reformation, has also been misunderstood, according to Prodi, as far as it concerns the papacy at least. That next stage of papal history, from the mid-sixteenth century onwards, he would rather see as part of the same long-term consolidation as a territorial principality, not as a specific religious response to doctrinal innovation or even to rival spiritual leadership. The attempt, however, to maintain claims to all traditional manifestations of papal authority naturally placed growing but ultimately disproportionate and destructive pressure on the resources of the papal states. The erosion of the economic strengths of the various territories within those states, not least by the burdens of taxation, was the logical outcome, marked as early as the end of the sixteenth century by the increase of banditry for example. To this extent the evidence on which Prodi's argument is based may readily be agreed, while the papacy's

2 P. Prodi, *The Papal Prince. One Body and Two Souls: the Papal Monarchy in Early Modern Europe* (Cambridge 1987), an unreliable translation of *Il sovrano pontefice, un corpo e due anime: la monarchia papale nella prima età moderna* (Bologna 1982). But see Prodi's revised views in *Annali*, Vol. 9, of the *Storia d'Italia*, ed. R. Romano and C. Vivanti, pp. 198–216 (Turin 1986).

further dependence, already by that same period, on Sicilian grain to provision the city of Rome can equally well be recalled.[3]

But Prodi would go still further, and argue that within the papal states themselves religious priorities, such as the pursuit of Tridentine reform among clergy, religious orders and laity, were gradually but decisively subordinated to the necessities of secular government, in the popes' own name of course. The insufficient foundation, in the form of temporal rule, for the continued claims of the papacy as a European principality therefore reduced not only the prosperity of central Italy but also the ability of the papacy as an institution to resist the Revolutionary attacks in Rome itself and more widely in Europe in and after 1789. Such an interpretation of papal history thus turns out, even if unintentionally, to resemble a traditional strand in Italian thinking, arguably visible from at least Machiavelli to the Risorgimento and beyond, which deplores the political and economic consequences of the preservation of papal temporal government. But such a similarity is not exactly accidental, because much of Prodi's extended argument turns on events within the papal states themselves. Even if the evidence as to those internal developments were to be entirely agreed upon, which it is possible to question, the insistence on that local history of central-Italian territories is open to challenge. To see it as the key to the whole cycle of papal history before, during and after the period considered here, suggests a doubt. For the preoccupations of papal temporal government, though undoubted and pressing, were surely only partly a priority of the popes between 1564 and 1789.

In this volume, by contrast, a comprehensive understanding of papal policies during that period will be urged. It will be argued that even those popes, such as the Borghese pope Paul V (1605–21), the Barberini pope Urban VIII (1623–44), or the Pamfili pope Innocent X (1644–55), for example, for whom the consolidation of family property and revenue indisputably remained a central concern, simultaneously retained a sophisticated and complex set of priorities, in pursuit of which 'nepotism' was a coherent and ordered part, not a distraction. In the case of so-called 'reforming' popes, especially in the late seventeenth century, such as the Odescalchi pope Innocent XI (1676–89) or the Pignatelli pope Innocent XII (1691–1700), there is even less case for some supposed divergence from universal concerns into an exclusive care for the maintenance of a papal principality. The interest of the period between 1564 and 1789 for the whole history of the papacy is thus undoubted, but its excitement rather derives from considering the efforts of various popes to pursue a whole range of aims from a position of unalterable political disadvantage. Far from being a dull interlude of steady decline, this era in papal history

3 Archivio Segreto Vaticano: Segreteria di Stato: Spagna [hereafter A.S.V. Spagna]: vols XXX ff.: e.g. XXX, 446r ff., 484r ff.: 13 Aug., 26 Nov. 1584; Archivo General de Simancas, Spain [hereafter A.G.S.]: Estado: Negociación de Roma, Legajos 947; 968; 981; 1855; Sicilia, Legs 1149, fo. 34; 1161, fos 273, 285; 1162, fo. 128; 1885, fos 12, 69, 186, 321; 1887, fo. 251; Consejo de Italia, Secretaría Provincial, Sicilia: Varios: Legs 1453, 1454; Napoles: Visitas y Diversos, Libro 96 *passim*: 1580–1631; cf. J. Delumeau, *Vie économique et sociale de Rome dans la seconde moitié du XVIe siècle* (2 vols, Paris 1957–59), II, p. 634 ff.

is indeed crucial for the variety of ways in which different popes tried to exercise an impressive sequence of traditional and revived roles, not only in the city of Rome or the papal states, but throughout the Italian peninsula, in Catholic Europe and even in the rest of Western and Eastern Europe more generally, and more widely still beyond Europe. To the responsibilities of the bishop of Rome was added, precisely during this period, a fascinating attempt to display a clearly metropolitan jurisdiction in the Roman province, and to perform the part of an Italian primate in the rest of the peninsula. The institution of that effectively primatial authority is acknowledged by Prodi himself, in his *Storia d'Italia* contribution, as a part of post-Conciliar papal achievement after Trent.

The task of promoting beyond the peninsula an essentially patriarchal authority in the Western Church was more difficult, for obvious political reasons rather than because of the obscurity of that dimension of papal power in theoretical terms. The extension of European Catholicism overseas led eventually to new initiatives for more direct Roman intervention by the supreme pontiffs there. If then the argument to be advanced here is that the popes of the post-Reformation era did indeed pursue an ambitious programme, of universal scope, during the two centuries of the 'long Counter-Reformation', it may be most clearly set out by analysing each manifestation of papal authority in turn, and examining its practical exercise in each case. Papal sovereignty in its temporal application will thus be treated in its proper place, and not assumed to have an overriding importance to which all other papal activity was subordinate.

The papacy had emerged from the stormy debates of the Council of Trent over the relationship between papal and episcopal jurisdiction with an authority unexpectedly confirmed and even strengthened. But this restored power was potential rather than secure, not least because of the ambiguities involved in the resolution of the Council's business, especially at its swift conclusion in the last months of 1563. The potential for reasserted Roman control was nevertheless present in the wording of many of the Conciliar decrees, the Council's explicit request for papal confirmation prior to the publication of those decrees, and the influential nature of the 'unfinished business' (especially liturgical revision and catechism, rather than the Index of prohibited literature) left by the Council to the pope.

Contemporary criticism from within the Catholic world itself, as in the case of the Venetian dissident Sarpi, concentrated on the relative success with which the immediately post-Conciliar popes of the late sixteenth and early seventeenth centuries realized that potential, by extending Roman supervision of local Church affairs. In fact, however, such application of Curial oversight was hardly easy or rapid even in the Italian peninsula, let alone beyond its confines. The example of the offshore islands of Sicily and Sardinia is an immediate reminder of the more serious obstacles in the way of reimposing papal direction of ecclesiastical life. They derived not from episcopal independence or the insubordination of a dissident friar so much as from the political might of secular rulers, in the case of the Italian lands at this date that of Spain specifically. Catholic governments, whether Habsburg or subsequently Bourbon, just like the lesser powers of the Venetian Republic or Tuscany under the restored Medici dukes, pursued their own ambitions to influence in one degree or another the local life of the Church. Such policies were effectively Erastian, even if that term was itself derived from the articulation of state claims to religious supremacy within the Protestant world.

The political as well as purely military impotence of the papacy, by contrast, was already a commonplace soon after the Council, and was not substantially affected by momentary concern aroused for instance by the addition of Ferrara to the papal states at the end of the sixteenth century. Neither Venetian nor other commentators needed to await the Peace of Westphalia in 1648 in order to discern this impotence. Yet the papacy's at least partial commitment to the Tridentine ideal of Church reform contributed to that weakness, in as much as secular revenue raised in the papal states was increasingly to replace some relinquished sources of ecclesiastical income which had previously supported the work of the Roman Curia for example.[4] The revised form of Prodi's interpretation of papal history accepts that in early modern Europe secular rulers, including Catholic rulers, were successfully inverting earlier papal claims when they in turn asserted supremacy within their states in all things spiritual as well as temporal. Yet on this interpretation the papacy's response to such a tendency was already distinctive, when the incipient separatism evident both in the evolution of Conciliar theory and in other ways in later medieval Western Christendom was met by an increasing clericalization of the papacy's central administration. Here a need for greater clarity might be felt, for it might be asked just when exactly that clericalization became evident, and whether it appeared in the offices of the Roman Curia generally or precisely in the government of the papal states.

That papal ambition in the wake of schism and the related development of Conciliarism was to recover a firm territorial basis in central Italy may more readily be agreed. The constitutions for the March of Ancona devised by Cardinal Albornoz in 1357 were confirmed for the whole of the papal states by the revisions of Sixtus IV, especially those of 1478. In the form revised by Cardinal Pio da Carpi on the eve of the Tridentine era they were confirmed in 1544 by Paul III. But while the achievements of Albornoz can be viewed as a new start in papal rule, rather than as just one step in its evolution, his constitutions already used legatine authority to legislate on secular and essentially ecclesiastical questions alike within the territories concerned: that was not an innovatory clericalization effected by Pio da Carpi, whatever the complaints of bishops at the Council of Trent about the interference of papal governors in

---

4 A.D. Wright, '"Medievalism" in Counter-Reformation Sicily', in *Church and Chronicle in the Middle Ages. Essays Presented to John Taylor*, ed. I. Wood and G.A. Loud (London 1991), pp. 233–49; A.D. Wright, 'The Venetian View of Church and State: Catholic Erastianism?', *Studi Secenteschi*, XIX (1978), 75–108.

diocesan management. Detailed work on the constitutions, which in theory were to remain in force for centuries, despite Revolutionary and Napoleonic interruption, has suggested that they were never in fact applied with perfect uniformity throughout all parts of the papal states however, and this Prodi's revised views allow.[5] They also accept that this imperfect application was in part the result of papal concern to avoid giving further examples, to secular rulers elsewhere in Catholic Europe, of the reduction of ecclesiastical rights and especially of clerical immunities in the interests of temporal government. Instead of a perfect subordination of ecclesiastical priorities to the necessities of temporal rule in the papal states, then, Prodi discerns a 'mixed' result, in which the move to centralized government was halted and gave way to greater clericalization of that government.

Clericalization of office was thus not a symptom and fulfilment of central-ization after all, but a paradoxic mutation of papal evolution. That this was as 'anachronistic' as is asserted may yet be doubted, for cardinal ministers of state and clerical diplomats were not exactly conspicuous by their absence from other parts of Catholic Europe, whether in seventeenth- and early eighteenth-century France and Spain, or the seventeenth-century vice-regal administration of Naples and Sicily for example. All the same, the rise of lay *letrados* in Spain might also allow a doubt as to whether the clericalization of papal bureaucracy in the period from Trent to the French Revolution was so simply or certainly a block to the creation of a lay middle-class, capable of wealth generation, in central Italy. The evolution of the papal principality was, it can be argued, anomalous, and contained internal contradictions. But that clericalization in this context can therefore be identified with the 'secularization' of the Church because of the peculiar nature of the popes' office may still be doubted.

The same doubts therefore arise over the interpretation of Rome in the age of the Enlightenment, more recently offered by a non-Italian scholar, accord-ing to which papal policy after the immediately post-Conciliar era was diverted from ecclesiastical reform. Here the 'post-Tridentine syndrome' unusually describes the abandonment not the pursuit of the Tridentine programme, and the institutional history of the papacy during this period is seen as just one part, however peculiar, of the 'Ancien Régime'.[6] An elective monarchy, as the papacy may be described, could never in any case be perfectly equated with other supposedly 'absolute' governments in Europe. Prodi's revised views make room for such an objection; and can also accommodate the recent research on popular disorder and competing manifestations of authority, tem-poral and ecclesiastical, in Rome itself *sede vacante*, during the vacancy of the papal throne which followed each pope's death and accompanied the duration of each conclave. Such events do not alter the fact that during each pontificate

5 C. Hoffmann, *Kardinal Rodolfo Pio da Carpi und seine Reform der Aegidianischen Konstitutionen* (Berlin 1989).
6 H. Gross, *Rome in the Age of Enlightenment. The Post-Tridentine Syndrome and the Ancien Regime* (Cambridge 1990).

of this period the nominally civic administration of Rome was in reality dominated by papal officials.[7]

But the multiplication in the same era of venal offices at the papal Court, for the usually nominal performance of bureaucratic or personal services, was again not a perfect parallel to 'declericalization' in other states of the Ancien Régime. This multiplication, and the related creation of *monti* as investment funds by which the papacy raised revenue, certainly benefited lay as well as clerical investors. Yet the governors and other officials in the papal states who intervened in religious as well as in temporal affairs were hardly an example of a precocious 'laicization' of the state, precisely because of their clerical status to which Prodi himself draws attention. His revised 'hypothesis' would rather see the creation of a clerical 'aristocracy', of initially bureaucratic or career origin rather than of birth, emerging between 1620 and 1650. He acknowledges that the erection in 1620 of a new Congregation among the administrative departments of the Roman Curia, that of Immunities, for the defence of ecclesiastical rights had implications for the papal states themselves, affecting any potential dominance by the Curial machinery for the temporal government of those states. Clerical liberties which were being reasserted in the face of secular government in the states of Catholic Europe could thus not be wholly marginalized under papal rule, lest a fatal precedent be set for suppression of such liberties elsewhere. The definitive revision in 1627 of the post-Tridentine form of the traditional papal Bull *In Coena Domini*, the annual publication of which represented the post-Conciliar papacy's claim to maintain ecclesiastical immunities intact, could only therefore enhance such immunities within the papal states as well as elsewhere.

Thus in fact the defence of clerical immunities in one part of those states, the Romagna, was followed by the successful reduction of lay patronage rights and reimposition of the episcopal court's authority in 1690 in a further enclave of papal rule, at Benevento: this was the achievement of the Dominican archbishop, Cardinal Orsini, subsequently Pope Benedict XIII (1724–30). In the Marches, again, the reassertion of episcopal and clerical rights, in the supervision of charitable institutions, for example, extended a precisely Tridentine programme into the eighteenth century.[8] In Bologna, never in any case a perfect paradigm for developments in all parts of the papal states, the late eighteenth century did see some reduction in clerical immunities, just before the Revolution; but this subordination to the necessities of temporal government concerned the clergy's legal immunities rather than their fiscal interests. Elsewhere in Catholic Europe secular rulers in the eighteenth century were increasingly demanding not just papal suppression of the Jesuits. The other general demand was for papal abandonment of the Bull *In Coena Domini*. Within the papal states themselves, by contrast, the continued growth of central Roman control over

---

7 L. Nussdorfer, 'The Vacant See: Ritual and Protest in Early Modern Rome', *Sixteenth Century Journal*, XVIII (1987), 173–89.
8 A. Turchini, *Clero e fedeli a Rimini in età post-tridentina* (Rome 1978).

appointments and the local working of temporal government created a career and salaried bureaucracy which was, however, clerical and therefore privileged.

If there was a transformation in the papacy's relations with the Catholic population of Europe generally during the period under discussion here, it is perhaps better seen in the evolution of the nunciatures. One means by which the post-Tridentine popes maintained and increased their influence beyond Rome and the papal states was by the establishment of permanent delegations at the Courts of Catholic rulers. In the immediately post-Conciliar decades and into the early seventeenth century the nunciatures were usually held by Italian diocesan bishops, seconded for such tours of duty in a commonly brief rotation. Despite objection to such a formal breach of the Tridentine insistence on the personal duty of bishops to reside in their see, expressed for instance in Clement VIII's pontificate (1592–1605) by the Jesuit Cardinal Bellarmine, this system had real pastoral advantage. For the diocesan experience of these Italian prelates enabled them to support and encourage bishops elsewhere, in Spain for example, in beginning the often difficult local application of the Conciliar reforms. Clement VIII justly considered that his own daring coup, reversing papal diplomatic policy and recognizing the Bourbon, Henri of Navarre, as a legitimate Catholic occupant of the French throne, in 1595, proved his commitment to the ideal of a Church free from political domination by secular interests. For this reversal was made only in the face of fierce Habsburg opposition and protest, since Spain had entertained hopes of securing the French succession for its own royal line.

Clement's brave decision however did not remove the difficulty subsequently facing the popes, as competing claims escalated between Habsburgs and Bourbons to exercise influence at Rome as well as superiority in Europe generally. Following the outbreak of warfare, in what was to prove the Thirty Years' War (1618–48), the correspondence of the papal nuncios in Catholic Europe became swiftly dominated by political rather than pastoral affairs. This changed reality was recognized by the alteration, at one nunciature after another, of the nature of the pope's representation. Career diplomats, from among Curial clerics, came to replace diocesan bishops. This certainly reflected the distraction of papal attention, but not in fact the abandonment of all commitment to ecclesiastical reform.[9] The pontificate of Urban VIII was to see a revival of certain concerns of Clement VIII, for the ecclesiastical supervision of confraternities and charities or the greater Roman control of saints' cults and canonizations for example. The papacy was able to encourage a real, if gradual, improvement in the quality of royal nominations to French bishoprics between the late sixteenth century and the start of the personal reign of Louis XIV.

The prolonged wars of the later seventeenth century, dragging on into the early eighteenth century during Louis's reign, prompted a succession of

9 P. Brezzi, *La diplomazia pontificia* (Milan 1942); cf. P. Blet, *Histoire de la Représentation Diplomatique du Saint Siège* (Vatican City 1982).

reforming popes, intent on pastoral priorities, some of whom had ascended not so much by diplomatic experience as by crucial involvement in the Church's chief instrument for doctrinal direction, the Roman Holy Office. The pontificates of Gregory XV (1621–23) and Urban VIII also saw important initiatives taken by these popes to enable Rome to intervene more directly in the Catholic overseas missions. But the pontificate of Clement VIII had also demonstrated the need for attention to maintaining doctrinal unity among Catholics. Despite the clarification provided by the Tridentine decrees, which made it possible to draw up coherent catechisms after the Council, some doctrinal questions remained in dispute among Catholic theologians, which were not easy to resolve. Clement's own formation as a canon lawyer did not equip him particularly well for the role of arbiter in such contested issues, and the attempt of Paul V to impose silence on the rival theological parties did not achieve much long-term success. While this contributed to the caution with which subsequent popes approached the continuing doctrinal disputes within the Catholic Church, it also ensured that the preservation of doctrinal unity necessarily had to remain a papal priority. But Catholic unity was also potentially threatened by political division in Western Europe, as the rivalry between Habsburgs and Bourbons became more bitter.

The danger that schism might arise from unresolved conflict at a papal conclave was always present, for recognition of Roman authority remained one sure measure of unity. Hence arose the efforts of various popes to make better regulation of the conduct of conclaves, so as to diminish political pressure on the cardinal electors and enlarge their freedom of choice. After Clement VIII's attempted provisions on this matter, an important step was taken by Gregory XV to reduce precisely the opportunity for political manipulation of the system for choosing a pope in conclave which Spain especially had made use of in the past. Despite predictable Spanish hostility, the next conclave saw the emergence of Urban VIII as a beneficiary of the better regulation of papal election, which he subsequently confirmed as pope.[10] Urban's own preoccupation with demonstrating his authoritative guardianship of doctrinal orthodoxy, precisely when Spanish political and financial attack on his supposed pro-Bourbon partiality alleged that he was tolerant of the heretical allies of the French, was a major factor contributing to his notorious withdrawal of protective favour from Galileo. But immediately after Trent the need to balance political pressure and doctrinal precision was already involved in the papal supervision, for nearly a decade to 1576, of the Roman investigation of the primate of Spain, Carranza, accused by the Spanish Inquisition of heterodoxy.[11] The pontificate of Clement VIII saw the execution of Bruno as a condemned heretic, whereas the Calabrian rebel against Spanish authority, Campanella, despite suspicions of heterodoxy, survived beyond that same period into old

10 Biblioteca Apostolica Vaticana [hereafter B.A.V.], MSS Vaticani Latini [Vat. Lat.] 10714, fos 51r–54v; 10841, fo. 204v; cf. Barberiniani Latini [Barb. Lat.] 1251.
11 J.I. Tellechea Idígoras, *El proceso romano del arzobispo Carranza 1567–76* (Rome 1988).

age under Urban VIII. Friction between the Spanish viceroys and the popes over affairs in the kingdom of Naples, which was a papal fief, was not just political competition between territorial states.

On temporal issues, such as campaigns against banditry, common interests could rather allow co-operation. It was partly financial interests but also a clash over ecclesiastical immunities and the promotion of Tridentine reforms which led to conflict. The confrontation between Paul V and the Venetian Republic, which produced the celebrated Interdict of 1606–7, was again not directly the result of secular disputes, even allowing for Venetian sensitivity after Clement VIII's annexation of Ferrara in 1598. It rather concerned the maintenance of ecclesiastical immunities, economic certainly but also judicial. For in Venetian territory as in most states of mainland Italy, including Spanish-ruled Lombardy, the local tribunals of the Holy Office, subject ultimately to Roman direction despite procedural variations demanded by secular government, were symptomatic of a fundamental agreement on the priority of securing peninsular orthodoxy.[12] Even where this instrument of a virtually primatial supervision of the Italian dioceses by the popes was not permanently established, as at Lucca or Naples, other means were found to allow Roman intervention in inquisitorial business. The Tridentine papacy had agreed in the end that the all too independent Spanish Inquisition would not be established at Naples or Milan.

PAPAL OFFICE AND HOLY OFFICE

A new interpretation of the papacy's direction of the Catholic Church, from this period onwards, has indeed now been put forward. In the most recent historical debate this new model has arguably become even more influential than that proposed by Prodi. But as yet that debate has not been widely evident to an English, as opposed to an Italian, readership. In the view of the Italian historian, Adriano Prosperi, there was certainly a fundamental shift in the exercise of papal authority from the mid-sixteenth century, eclipsing the implications of the Tridentine decrees for the evolution of Catholicism. But the transformation was not the result of a concentration on the governing of the papal states, as in Prodi's understanding of the case. The key, according to Prosperi, must rather be sought in the foundation in 1542 of the revived Roman Inquisition. This immediately pre-Conciliar decision, in the pontificate of Paul III, reflected the personal programme of Carafa, who as pope Paul IV (1555–59) subsequently consolidated the Holy Office in Rome and developed its activity throughout the Italian peninsula.

The policies of Paul IV thus prepared the way for the related foundation of the Congregation of the Index, for the control of publication, in 1571, while

---

12 *Nunziature di Napoli*, ed. P. Villani et al., vols 1–3 (Rome 1962, 1969, 1970); A.D. Wright, 'Why the *Venetian* Interdict?', *English Historical Review*, LXXXIX (1974), 534–50.

the original Inquisitorial programme was further advanced by Carafa's disciple, Ghislieri and then by the latter's follower, Peretti. These two became pope in turn, as Pius V (1566–72) and Sixtus V (1585–90) respectively. The personal direction of the Roman Inquisition by such popes, at the head of the cardinals appointed by them to administer the affairs of the Holy Office, thus established a lasting identification of the pope's authority with that of the supreme Inquisitor. So absolute was this, in Prosperi's view, that the essential function of the pope, his defining office, was recategorized as inquisitorial: the papal office was the Holy Office. For Prosperi, this was to affect the whole working of the Catholic Church, not least with respect to the sacrament of penance and confession, for centuries thereafter. It also had an even more enduring impact on Italian society, according to this interpretation.

Some of the difficulties for this line of argument have been noted by Prosperi himself, however. In the first place, the papacy never secured effective control of the substantially independent Inquisitions of Portugal and of Spain, the latter operative not only in the peninsular kingdoms themselves but also in Sardinia, Sicily and ever more widely in the Spanish territories overseas. Secondly, the Roman Inquisition was not in fact established in other major territories of Catholic Europe, neither in France nor in the Holy Roman Empire, let alone in the family lands of the Austrian Habsburgs or in Poland. It might be added that the post-Tridentine papacy lamented its lack of control over the Inquisition in the Spanish Netherlands, and that the precisely Roman Index was not, in practice, directly effective outside the Italian peninsula. Prosperi's model, therefore, cannot really be considered as applicable to conditions outside Italy. Even in the Italian states, moreover, as he readily acknowledges, the tribunals of the Roman Inquisition did not operate with absolute uniformity of procedure, despite the powerful direction of the Holy Office in Rome. In so large an area of the peninsula as the kingdom of Naples, indeed, no permanent tribunal of the otherwise common type was established.

In the present volume, on the other hand, a different understanding is suggested. It has earlier been accepted that the Holy Office remained an important route by which some prelates became pope, even in the later seventeenth century. The argument that the Roman Inquisition was one mechanism, but not the only one, by which, to the end of that century at least, the papacy developed an effective primacy over the Church in the Italian peninsula will be developed further in Chapter 4. But it will also be seen, in due course, that the popes of the period after the Council of Trent were conscious of the wide range of their functions and responsibilities, well beyond Rome, Italy and even Europe. Gregory XV (1621–23) was indeed to claim the propagation of the faith, beyond Christendom as well as within, as the chief duty of the pope.[13]

13 A. Prosperi, 'Una esperienza di ricerca nell' Archivio del Sant' Uffizio', *Belfagor*, LIII, iii (1998), 309–45.

Within the papal states themselves it is certainly possible to detect an import-ant shift, concentrating temporal power in the hands of the popes, by reduction of the remaining power of baronial families. This may indeed be a resumption of earlier ambitions, not least those of the Renaissance popes. Arguments have been advanced for the claims of the immediately post-Tridentine popes as the chief champions of this extension of internal temporal power, possibly not secure until after the pontificate of the Buoncompagni pope, Gregory XIII (1572–85). City planning and monumental edification in Rome under Peretti, Pope Sixtus V (1585–90), certainly promoted an image of the papal imposi-tion of order, temporal as well as spiritual, but of course family display in palaces or chapels did not for that reason cease in Mannerist and Baroque Rome. A modification of the means by which the family relations of popes themselves saw their collective and individual interests advanced is never-theless visible.[14] For the Aldobrandini relatives of Clement VIII and those of Paul V were hardly attempting to create a territorial inheritance in the same sense and on the same scale as the Farnese, whatever the accumulated wealth of Cardinal Scipio Borghese in particular. Ferrara was recovered for the papal states, not recreated as an Aldobrandini principality, though the case of the Barberini in the mid-seventeenth century is more ambiguous.

But the move to providing for at least the male clerical relatives of popes by ecclesiastical promotion and revenues reserved from other ecclesiastical appointments and foundations is arguably decisive in the long term. Though the surviving interests of the Farnese were to continue to trouble the papacy into the eighteenth century, the history of the papacy between 1564 and 1789 is thus not simply a stage, albeit a key one, in a continuous evolution of the papal office towards territorial principality above all else.[15] For in the first place the active involvement of popes in the pastoral responsibilities of the bishopric of Rome remained impressively constant. After special efforts by the immediately post-Conciliar popes for the reform on Tridentine lines of the Roman diocese as well as the papal Court, this pastoral commitment was still very much evident under Clement VIII, who initiated a canonic visitation of the see. Participation in liturgical acts remained characteristic not only of Gregory XV and Urban VIII but of Paul V too. Throughout this period, to the mid-seventeenth century, episcopal oversight, very much on Tridentine lines, of charitable institutions such as hospitals and pilgrim hospices in Rome was not forgotten either. Papal commitment to the expansion of educational provision in the city and diocese of Rome, for local as well as universal needs, continued in the pontificate of the former diplomat, the Chigi pope, Alexan-der VII (1655–67).

14 G. Carocci, *Lo Stato della Chiesa nella seconda metà del secolo XVI* (Milan 1961); cf. M. Caravale and A. Caracciolo, *Lo Stato Pontificio da Martino V a Pio IX* (*Storia d'Italia*, ed. G. Galasso, vol. 14) (Turin 1978).
15 C. Robertson, *'Il Gran Cardinale': Alessandro Farnese, Patron of the Arts* (New Haven, CT 1992).

Similarly, the use of the visual and dramatic arts for didactic purposes, making the city of Rome a sacred theatre of buildings and ceremonies, was a constant complement in these pontificates to initiatives such as Alexander's reform of the University of Rome. Thus his successor Cardinal Rospigliosi, Clement IX (1667–69), was famous already as the author of a sacred music drama first triumphantly staged as part of the Roman celebrations for the former Protestant queen, Christina of Sweden, after her reception at the papal Court as a convert to Catholicism, in 1656.[16] The popes of the later seventeenth century and early eighteenth century were again prominently pastoral, not only in fulfilment of liturgical duties, but in new attempts to improve charitable care, as for example under Innocent XI. The commitment to pastoral work of Benedict XIII, in the first half of the eighteenth century, was such that he exceptionally retained his beloved archbishopric of Benevento in addition to his responsibility as bishop of Rome. Even more striking than his personal devotion to liturgical functions was his attempt to assert a distinctly metropolitan authority by means of a Roman provincial council. The erudite tastes of the Corsini pope, Clement XII (1730–40), and of the famous Lambertini pope, Benedict XIV (1740–58), did not exclude pastoral care of Rome. For Lambertini, like Gregory XV before him, had knowledge of such practical questions from his previous experience as archbishop of Bologna.

On the wider stage of the Italian peninsula, an effectively primatial solicitude was pursued once again not only by immediately post-Tridentine popes, whether the Medici Pius IV (1559–65), Ghislieri Pius V (1566–72) or Peretti Sixtus V (1585–90) for example, but very much still by Clement VIII with his attempts to enforce Roman examination of candidates for at least mainland Italian dioceses with reference to the standards specified at Trent. This care for the Italian sees can equally be demonstrated by the efforts of Gregory XV to use papal power, such as it was, to protect the peninsula from the disasters of foreign invasion. The damage in fact caused by foreign troop movements, not only as they affected the papal states themselves, was again a preoccupation of the Albani pope, Clement XI (1700–21) at the beginning of the eighteenth century. The reception and deployment of ex-Jesuits within the peninsula were the melancholy concerns of Ganganelli, Pope Clement XIV (1769–74), and of Braschi, Pius VI (1775–99).[17] So in this sphere it is hardly convincing to seek artificial limits to the post-Tridentine era, in the history of the pre-Revolutionary papacy, whether such a break be envisaged *c.* 1590 or *c.* 1605 or *c.* 1623 or *c.* 1644, or indeed any later date.

OUTSIDE ITALY

When one turns from the Italian peninsula to the undoubted attempts of the post-Conciliar popes to recover and reactivate an authoritative leadership of

16 G. Rospigliosi, *'La Vita Humana'* or *'Il trionfo della pietà'* (with Engl. trans.), ed. K. Brown and W. Edwards (from 1st printed edn of score [Rome 1658], Glasgow 1990).
17 M. Batllori, *Cultura e finanze: studi sulla storia dei Gesuiti* (Rome 1983), pp. 263–340.

the Western Church on a wider scale, at any rate in those parts of Europe which remained Catholic, it is obvious that certain internal watersheds do appear in papal history. But these may best be measured in terms of achievement rather than aim, counter-balancing expanded action beyond Italy against restrictions on the papacy within the peninsula after 1700. The relative weakness of the Buoncompagni pope, Gregory XIII, or that of his eventual successor Sfondrato, Gregory XIV (1590–91), in the face of political pressure applied by Spain did not mean that they had abandoned the ideal of ecclesiastical independence, as specific acts of their pontificates demonstrate. Defence of the immunities of the Church in areas of Spanish rule, whether in Spain itself or its Italian possessions, in Portugal after the Spanish succession there in 1580, or to some degree in Spain's overseas territories, continued not only under Sixtus V but also under Clement VIII. The pontificate of Paul V was marked by the same struggle to defend ecclesiastical immunities reasserted at Trent, even if its results, which included a prolonged exclusion of the Jesuits from Venetian territory, were ambiguous in the case of the Republic of Venice. The insistence of Gregory XV that the papacy should be free to supervise more directly the affairs of the Catholic Church beyond the confines of Western Europe offended both the Spanish monarchy and the Venetian Republic.

The policies of Urban VIII led the Habsburgs to accuse him of prejudice in favour of France, but these policies and that reaction were both part of the long-term legacy of Clement VIII and his attempt to establish greater papal autonomy within Catholic Europe, by balancing an independent France, once again officially Catholic, against the influence of the Habsburg powers. Popes from Gregory XIII onwards had equally sought to preserve the interests of the Church in Portugal under Spanish rule. The prolonged struggle for the recovery of Portuguese independence, from 1640, gave a new edge to papal difficulties in confronting Spanish assertions on this front. Urban VIII and his immediate successors only gradually resolved the problem of interrupted relations with a Portugal once again independent, and this arguably contributed to the great condescension of later popes, into the eighteenth century, towards the demands of the Portuguese monarchs. Though these concessions were in fact largely ceremonial, they were not sufficient to prevent the subsequent Portuguese lead in the expulsion of the Jesuits from Catholic states in Europe and overseas. Such an internal watershed in the exercise of papal leadership in the Western Church thus reflected an originally more local and limited problem.

In just the same way, the terms on which Clement VIII finally granted Roman recognition of Henri IV's reconversion to Catholicism and consequent legitimacy as king of a Catholic France were supposed to ensure the kingdom's commitment to the decrees of the Council of Trent. Though political policies diverged considerably in fact, including those of Philip II of Spain himself, most Catholic powers had made formal acceptance of the decrees a relative priority, always allowing for pre-existing political realities, such as those in the Holy Roman Empire. But the long history of difficulties between

French Bourbon monarchs on the one hand and popes of the seventeenth and eighteenth centuries on the other turned as much as anything on the failure to achieve a full and unchallenged reception of the Tridentine decrees in France. The non-reception of the decrees by the royal courts, even after the end of the Valois monarchy, was often of greater consequence than the periodic profession by the French clergy of their own commitment, while in any case clerical behaviour did not make such affirmations consistently credible. It was not merely that the Tridentine marriage legislation, for example, was incapable of enforcement in its own right, whatever parallels French authority in fact sanctioned.[18] More crucially, for papal exercise of an effective supremacy within the Western Church, the French lawyers gave no recognition inside the kingdom to the jurisdiction asserted by such papal instruments as the Roman Holy Office or Index of prohibited literature. Yet though the great doctrinal disputes within the Catholic Church of the seventeenth and eighteenth centuries might draw their origin from conflicts in Spain, Italy and the Netherlands, and continue to find expression in those areas and in the German lands too, they came to be predominantly domiciled in France.

So the resolution of such prolonged contests by the papacy, as supposed arbiter of any future disagreements over the Tridentine foundations of a restored faith and practice, was severely hampered. The revival of a conscious Gallicanism, reflecting in large measure late-medieval French Conciliarist theories, was a reaction, from the late sixteenth into the seventeenth century, against the previously protracted papal support for the ultra-Catholics of the League, even when, at the end of the French Wars of Religion, this necessitated Spanish patronage. The diplomatic reversal effected by Clement VIII came too late to alter manifestations of French mistrust among the Catholic population itself, typified by the temporary expulsion of the Jesuits from a large part of the kingdom of Henri IV. The danger represented by revived Gallicanism was evident not so much in moments of clerical disaffection from strict Roman obedience, in the dissidence of individual bishops or fluctuating coalitions of prelates, or in the clerical adoption at royal prompting of the Four Gallican Articles during Louis XIV's reign; but rather in the path opened by such actions for the royal and *parlementaire* manifestations of Gallicanism, to the death of Louis and beyond. Neither the Paris *parlement* nor the Paris theological faculty of the Sorbonne accepted the Tridentine theory of the papacy's sole as well as ultimate arbitration in the post-Conciliar Church of all potential questions about the Council's doctrinal or disciplinary decrees. Despite the undoubted conflicts between the monarchy and the *parlement* and the uncertain relations of the Sorbonne with either, the net result was to make papal pronouncement on specific controversies, supremely the various issues aroused by the evolving phenomenon of Jansenism, nearly impossible. For

18 J. Bernhard, C. Lefebvre and F. Rapp, *L'époque de la Réforme et du Concile de Trente* (*Histoire du Droit et des Institutions de l'Eglise en Occident*, ed. G. Le Bras and J. Gaudemet, vol. 14) (Paris 1989), pp. 409–10.

even when the turns of royal policy produced a request for clear papal con-demnation of certain positions allegedly held by Jansenists, the papacy had to confront the additional problems of avoiding open schism and preventing explicit rejection of its rulings by self-proclaimed Catholics. The caution with which popes after Clement VIII approached doctrinal determination was indeed logical.[19]

Such practical conservatism is arguably more important than the exposi-tions of a high theory of papal indefectability and inerrancy advanced on occasion by Curialists during this period. The Council of Trent had of course produced no definition of personal papal infallibility and had avoided any positive promulgation of the Marian doctrine of the Immaculate Conception. While post-Tridentine popes resisted Spanish, Habsburg and other pressure to supply a bindingly positive pronouncement on this dogma, the practical limitations to the papal exercise of superior authority within the Western Church remained clear enough. Popes such as Paul V, Gregory XV or Urban VIII did not hesitate to criticize the Austro-Imperial branch of the Habsburg family in defence of ecclesiastical as against dynastic interests. But papal pro-test was unavailing against the Peace of Westphalia, concluding the Thirty Years' War in 1648, in which Catholic and non-Catholic states made an inde-pendent settlement of religious as well as political allegiances.

FURTHER EUROPEAN CONTRASTS

The constitution of the Holy Roman Empire continued after 1648 to allow the greatest of the prince-bishops to conduct themselves with the large degree of independence, in ecclesiastical affairs, which was natural, given their ter-ritorial authority. This was true not only of the three electoral archbishops of Mainz, Cologne and Trier, but also of other great ecclesiastical rulers within the Empire, such as the prince-archbishops of Salzburg. By the eighteenth century occasional friction between German prince-bishops and Rome pro-duced an explicit articulation of German ecclesiastical 'rights', in the theories of Febronianism. But Roman influence was not lacking in reality, at any time in this period, in the affairs of the Catholic Church in German-speaking Europe. The training at Rome of a clerical elite for ecclesiastical office in the German and Hungarian lands had in time its own effect, despite the inevitable political implications, involving French interests as well as rivalry between Protestants and Catholics within the Empire itself, of the succession to major Imperial sees. For this nevertheless gave potential ground for papal inter-vention by essentially diplomatic means. The necessary papal permission for

---

19 V. Martin, *Le Gallicanisme et la réforme catholique* (Paris 1919); V. Martin, *Le Gallicanisme politique et le clergé de France* (Paris 1929); V. Martin, *Les origines du Gallicanisme* (2 vols, Paris 1939); P. Blet, *Le clergé de France et la monarchie: étude sur les Assemblées Générales du Clergé de 1615 à 1666* (2 vols, Rome 1959); P. Blet, *Les Assemblées du clergé et Louis XIV de 1670 à 1693* (Rome 1972); P. Blet, *Le clergé de France, Louis XIV et le Saint-Siège de 1695 à 1715* (Vatican City 1989); P. Broutin, *La réforme pastorale en France au XVIIe siècle* (2 vols, Tournai–Paris 1956).

the representatives of Catholic dynasties within the Empire to hold sensitive dioceses in plurality, even after Trent, in the interests of excluding Protestantism, was arguably more effective than the often contested intervention of nuncios on other Imperial issues.

The exercise of effective papal jurisdiction in the family lands of the Austro-Imperial Habsburgs was difficult for the opposite reason. The recovery of parts of Hungary for Habsburg and in that sense Catholic rule was delayed until the end of the seventeenth century. But in Austrian and Bohemian lands themselves it was the relative weakness of the diocesan structure which hampered the application of the Tridentine decrees, which presumed and reasserted the local responsibility of the diocesan bishop. The religious orders which did so much in the Catholic restoration in these lands looked naturally enough to the patronage of the Court, since regulars were by definition more concerned to confine than extend episcopal supervision of their own activities; and the dynasty gave an increasing coherence to a network of lands which still lacked any logic in terms of diocesan organization. For all the proclaimed and indeed conspicuous Catholicism of the Austro-Imperial Habsburgs, then, reaching glorious heights for example in the reigns of the Emperors Leopold I and Charles VI, it is not entirely surprising that the policies subsequently adopted by Joseph II so alarmed the papacy.[20] The extraordinary journey of Pius VI beyond the confines of the Italian peninsula, as far as Vienna, demonstrated the extent of that alarm, however meagre the results of this Roman condescension.

But the papacy at many times after the Council of Trent proved capable of bold gestures in the assertion of a headship of the Western Church aiming not merely to preserve but even to regain Catholic allegiance. At the end of the sixteenth century the papacy had been involved in perfectly serious negotiations for the restoration of the Catholic faith in Sweden under the new Vasa dynasty. Although, for ultimately political reasons, such negotiations failed there, as in the rival state of Denmark, the Polish kingdom provided a contrasting arena in which papal authority in Western Christendom was successfully exercised. The peculiar constitution of Poland, in which the elective character of the monarchy was asserted from the later sixteenth century, gave greater scope for the influence of papal nuncios and their encouragement of the Polish kings to restore a Catholic predominance in their territories, not least in the face of Swedish and Russian attack. It was indeed in the Polish lands that the pontificate of Clement VIII registered one of the greatest triumphs of the post-Tridentine papacy. The adherence to Roman obedience of the Eastern-rite Christians there, by the Union of 1596, allowed a recognition of papal jurisdiction which enlarged the visible role of the popes, at the head of a substantial number of European Christians who were not of the Western rite.

The post-Tridentine popes in fact took care, despite Spanish governmental or Italian episcopal intransigence, to preserve evidence that papal authority was wider than the headship of the Latin rite alone: the Greek-rite clerics and

20 R.J.W. Evans, *The Making of the Habsburg Monarchy 1550–1700* (Oxford 1979).

monasteries of central and Southern Italy and Sicily during this period also acknowledged Roman supremacy. Less secure, after all, as a symbol of such universal jurisdiction, were the Greek-rite subjects of the Venetian Republic, in the city of Venice but more importantly in the Dalmatian enclaves and the islands of Corfu, Crete and the other insular possessions. Not only was the loss of Cyprus in the late sixteenth century followed by that of Crete in the further extension of Ottoman power in the later seventeenth century, but the theory that the Republic's Greek-rite subjects acknowledged papal authority was often glaringly at odds with the known reality of local conditions, and for obvious political reasons the Republic was always anxious to prevent Inquisitors, nuncios or Latin-rite archbishops and bishops testing this distinction between theory and practice too precisely.

Brave attempts in the post-Tridentine period to establish a relationship between Roman authority and Ethiopian Christianity led to little more in the end than new opportunities for Jesuit martyrdom. The Roman claims upon the St Thomas Christians discovered in the Indian Malabar produced chronic schism rather than united obedience, though complicating factors, such as Portuguese political power, also intervened here. The serious attempts of popes at the end of the sixteenth century and beyond to resume or establish relations with Christians of the ancient Oriental and Orthodox Churches, with some success in the case of the Maronites for example, are certainly a reminder that the post-Conciliar papacy did not confine its attention to duties lying clearly within an effective patriarchate of the West. A more dramatic indication of this were the attempts to inaugurate relations with the Russian Church, even if these essentially collapsed with the end of the so-called 'Time of Troubles' and reassertion of Russian independence after 1613 and even more after 1618.[21]

THE NON-CATHOLIC WORLD

Within Western Christendom of course the great question of non-Catholics remained throughout the two centuries under discussion here, and it is this dimension of papal policy, during the period, of which many English-speaking readers will doubtless be most readily conscious. In the first place, it may be noted, the popes after the Council of Trent achieved some limited but real success in encouraging the survival of Catholic communities under proscriptive regimes. This was true in the Dutch Netherlands, after they had gained first *de facto* then temporary then permanent independence, and remained the case despite the subsequent Jansenist schism of the Church of Utrecht in the eighteenth century. It was certainly true in Ireland in the long term, but in Wales only substantially in the short term, until much later developments. In Scotland it remained true enough, despite the political disability further

21 O. Garstein, *Rome and the Counter-Reformation in Scandinavia*, vol. 2 (Oslo 1980); cf. *Acta Nuntiaturae Polonae*, ed. H.D. Wojtyska, vols I ff. (Rome 1990 onwards).

added by an attachment supposed, rightly or wrongly, to link Catholicism and the Jacobite cause, after the Hanoverian succession to the British throne especially. The Huguenot diaspora which was the unintended consequence of French royal policy under Louis XIV, in his revocation of the Edict of Nantes, contributed to the well-preserved sense of certain Protestant regimes elsewhere in Europe that they were under constant threat of subversion from papal policy. This cannot have failed to perpetuate such sensitivities in England for example, long after the Armada of 1588 or the Gunpowder Plot of 1605.

The realities of papal policy, however, need examination in such notorious cases. The degree of financial commitment, even to an enterprise such as the Armada which the papacy may be shown to have made, might revise confident opinions about the centrality of such events to papal plans. The immediately post-Tridentine popes, including Clement VIII at the end of the sixteenth century, were arguably much more concerned to raise resources, financial, military and naval, against the common enemy of Christendom, the Ottoman Turks, whose progress in the Mediterranean seemed still pressing, despite the victory of Lepanto in 1571, as witness the loss of Cyprus and the near-loss of Malta. The ultimate goal of a Christian alliance against the Turk remained a priority of papal diplomacy even in the seventeenth century, as in the painfully protracted negotiations involving Habsburgs, Bourbons and their allies, both during the Thirty Years' War and during the further period of prolonged Franco-Spanish hostilities to 1659. The preoccupation with the Turkish threat proved its necessity when Vienna was besieged in the later seventeenth century, and the need to encourage Polish participation against the Ottomans was well demonstrated then, as Louis XIV refused to abandon France's traditional encouragement of Turkish pressure on the Habsburgs. The Austrian lead in the subsequent campaigns of the early eighteenth century to push back the frontiers of the Ottoman empire with Christian Europe, specifically in Hungary, was some comfort after the earlier loss, by France's other traditional ally, the Catholic Republic of Venice, of the island of Crete.

But none of this affects the arguably counter-productive aspects of papal policy towards certain Catholic populations under penal Protestant circumscriptions. The English Catholic community was perhaps adversely affected not so much by the views of Pius V or Paul V on English monarchical sovereignty as by the failure during the earlier part of these two centuries, on the papacy's part, to make clear and practical provision for the local direction of all the Catholic clergy working in England. The division of responsibility for their various ministries was one reason why the internal disputes, not unnaturally produced in a clandestine and proscribed community, became both so disruptive, even of perfect obedience to Rome, and so fruitful a ground for governmental intrusion in the interests of subverting allegiance to Catholicism itself. That virtually all Western European states still conceived unity of religion to be an internal prerequisite for stable government as late as the mid-seventeenth century cannot be overlooked. In fact, it enhanced the consolidation of Catholicism in non-Protestant territories of the Empire after

1648, by the very terms of the Peace of Westphalia to which the papacy objected, both on the grounds of the inevitable corollary that Lutheranism and Calvinism respectively were confirmed in other territories of the Empire and because of the unacceptable reassertion of a secular prince's right to determine local religious obedience itself. But the persistence of the assumption that religious unity was a necessary foundation for a state's integrity can also be seen, it has been suggested, in the desperate appeal of the Protestant Charles I of England, faced by Scots rebels against his religious and political authority and incipient English dissidence on both these grounds, for Catholic assistance, not only from his Catholic subjects but later even from the pope.[22]

The later sympathy shown for a while by the popes to the Jacobite pretenders in exile did not however preclude the subsequent cautious reopening of links with Hanoverian Britain in pursuit of Catholic interests. Similarly, the refusal by the later seventeenth-century popes to accept all the policies and demands of the Catholic ruler of France, Louis XIV, even when the papal enclave based on Avignon was on occasion occupied, reflected the continued papal programme of attempting independence of Catholic rulers, whether Habsburg or Bourbon, whenever necessary. This indeed helped to account for the ironies and difficulties of papal alliance or non-alliance during the War of Spanish Succession in the early eighteenth century. This war arguably demonstrated that hostility between European powers was now as much a rivalry for overseas empire as a contest for continental supremacy. Such competition beyond Europe, already experienced on a smaller scale within the Mediterranean during the seventeenth century, as the French challenged English and Dutch traders there, affected the conditions in which the supreme pontiffs tried to exercise a global authority over the expansion of Catholic Christianity.

BEYOND CHRISTIAN EUROPE

The preconditions for such an attempt were in one sense distinctly unfavourable, because of the substantial and largely unrecoverable delegation of powers made by the Renaissance popes to the Iberian monarchies for the control of the Church in areas overseas newly discovered and subsequently to be discovered. The immediately post-Tridentine popes experienced the difficulty of altering the practical results of this delegation, when, for example, in Spanish America Jesuit designs for a native priesthood met the opposition of Spanish government and friars.[23] On the other hand, in the case of the Portuguese overseas empire, not so much in the coastal Brazilian settlements but rather in the trading enclaves of the Indian and Far Eastern spheres of activity, the practical limitations of European power were unaffected by the interlude of the personal union of the Iberian monarchies between 1580 and 1640. For

22 C.M. Hibbard, *Charles I and the Popish Plot* (Chapel Hill, NC 1983).
23 A.S.V. Spagna, XXX, 387r ff.: 15 Mar. 1584.

while the overseas possessions of Portugal, their ecclesiastical affairs included, remained under separate royal supervision from those of the Spanish Indies during these decades, the support which missionaries could receive beyond the boundaries of those trading enclaves, once admitted to the interior of China or to Japan in particular, was obviously limited. The papacy also experienced a fatal failure to make effective at such a distance its own theoretic resolutions of the dangerous competition between Spanish missions and Portuguese missionaries, overlapping in China and Japan and contributing in the latter case to the suspicion of all Catholic presence and its virtual extermination by violent repression. Yet the further decline of the Far Eastern Portuguese empire, even if it represented in part the successful intrusion of the Protestant Dutch in the East Indies or Ceylon for example, seemed to leave greater room for direct papal supervision of Catholic expansion in those parts.

But the example of China showed the other difficulties facing distant papal direction of conditions in non-European civilizations. The papal arbitration attempted on the disputed 'Chinese Rites' which, with partial parallels contested in India, involved a clash between different missionary methods in non-European cultures, was in one sense a response to European competition between rival religious orders, particularly Jesuits and friars, and between parties to internal Catholic controversies over doctrine and practice which constantly threatened schism. But papal intervention, difficult enough to enforce locally in any case, had the wholly counter-productive effect of determining the Chinese imperial authorities to resist all such 'barbarian' intrusion. The severe limitation of Catholic missionary achievement was the chief result, in the case of China rather more than in India, of the papacy's pronouncements by the early eighteenth century. That limiting action affecting missionary expansion in an extra-European culture can certainly be taken as some kind of watershed in the post-Tridentine papacy's programme for directing the course of Catholic Christianity.

In other parts of the overseas territories being opened up by European conquest and colonization over the two centuries under discussion here the results of new papal intervention, after the creation of Roman mechanisms to attempt this more direct involvement in the first half of the seventeenth century, were also ambiguous. For the Iberian possessions in America remained largely under monarchical control, in religious as much as temporal affairs, despite occasional papal intervention to try to resolve disordered relations between bishops and secular clergy on the one hand and the regular missionaries on the other for example. The inquisitorial authority eventually established in such areas was not that of the Roman Holy Office but, naturally enough, offshoots of the Spanish and Portuguese Inquisitions. The papacy was unable to maintain supervision of bishops in such territories by the means and on the terms which it wished. The eventual termination of the partly independent Jesuit presence in the overseas Iberian territories, in the eighteenth century, consolidated royal control of the Church there still further.

Further North, in America, the French monarchy eventually gave some support to Catholic expansion there. But though the French Crown in the seventeenth and eighteenth centuries lacked a formal grant of patronage rights over the Church in its overseas acquisitions, such as the Iberian Crowns enjoyed, it came to exercise *de facto* a comparable degree of control; and this was true of eventual French gains in the West Indies too. Nor was this remarkable, since the French Church came to provide much of the manpower and hence financial resources for Catholic mission not only in North America but in the Far East too in fact, as effective Portuguese power gave way in India and further East to Anglo-French rivalry for empire. This degree of French dominance in the second stages of Catholic mission beyond Europe was thus one of the greatest limitations on the papacy's ability to realize its explicit claims to direct control of Catholicism overseas, by means of the Roman Congregation De Propaganda Fide. The complications engendered by Catholic controversy centred in France were indeed a major factor in the papacy's slow but in the end uncompromising course towards condemnation of the innovatory missionary methods employed by Jesuits in China. A rare but relatively independent Catholic community beyond Europe, as established in North America by Lord Baltimore, again owed little in practice to papal programmes. For the ultimate limitations during this period on the ambitions of the popes to exercise an effectively global authority as supreme pontiffs were substantially those of money and manpower, compounded by the problem of communications. This did not preclude, however, great activity by the Congregation De Propaganda Fide, inspired by the first conception among clerics in early seventeenth-century Rome of the need for a supply of mission priests, distinct from the existing religious orders, available for missionary work under direct papal authority.[24]

Beyond the Christian community, though inside Catholic Europe, the policies adopted by the popes of this period towards Jewish communities were of limited effect. That a more negative attitude towards Jewish communities was evident during the pontificates of the later sixteenth century may well be true, but the capacity of the popes to influence governmental policies elsewhere, outside the city of Rome, where a ghetto was maintained throughout the period under discussion here, and beyond the confines of the papal states, was

---

24 *S. Congregationis de Propaganda Fide Memoria Rerum*, vols Ii–IIIii, ed. J. Metzler (Rome 1971–76). O. Chadwick, *The Popes and European Revolution* (Oxford History of the Christian Church) (Oxford 1981), provides an introduction to part of the period covered in the present volume, with the added perspective of Revolution and Restoration. A useful resource is the annual bibliography in the *Archivum Historiae Pontificiae* (vols 1 ff., Rome 1963 onwards). An introduction to the resources of the Vatican Archives, not in fact relating only to the Medieval period, is L. Boyle, *A Survey of the Vatican Archives and of its Medieval Holdings* (Toronto 1972). See also now the monumental volume edited by F.X. Blouin, Jr, *Vatican Archives. An Inventory and Guide to Historical Documents of the Holy See* (New York 1998). Most recently, the distinct historical archives, partially conserved, of the Holy Office have finally been made accessible to some scholars, making possible a new type of publication, such as P.-N. Mayaud, S.J., *La Condemnation des livres coperniciens et sa révocation à la lumière de documents inédits des Congrégations de l'Index et de l'Inquisition* (Rome 1997).

clearly limited. Venetian or Tuscan governments, or the Spanish rulers of Lombardy, for example, conducted their own policies towards local Jewish communities irrespective of whether or not these perfectly coincided with papal wishes. In other ways, however, it has been seen how broad was the scope of papal aims and plans of action, in Europe and beyond. Not every part of this programme was wholly or even partly successful, but the established priorities were surely pursued with reference to larger goals than a preponderant attention to the government of the territorial papal possessions or an obsessive concentration on inquisitorial control. If that is true it has further implications for the whole history of the institution of the papacy and not solely for the two centuries considered in this volume.

CHAPTER 2

The Bishop of Rome

Attention to pastoral duties as bishop of Rome was a constant feature of the pontificates from 1564 to 1789. Thus the conspicuous pastoral preoccupations of the late seventeenth- and early eighteenth-century popes, from Innocent XI to Benedict XIII in particular, were not an innovation but the resumption of a priority evident immediately after the Council of Trent and even into the first half of the seventeenth century. Pius IV had promised critics at the Council who denounced Curial abuses that reform of the papal Court would be pursued by the direct action of the pope himself. Reform of the papal household, and of the Roman Court more generally, was indeed implemented, as by his successors Pius V and Sixtus V for instance, and such programmes were renewed at the start of later pontificates such as those, once again, of Innocent XI and Benedict XIII. But in a way more important, for the evidence it gave of serious commitment to the ideal of Tridentine reform, based on the diocesan model, was the repeated intervention of popes to improve the life of the Roman diocese itself, beyond the confines of the Court, in the city and its rural margins.

A striking initial symbol of this commitment was visible in the employment, immediately after the Council, of Ormaneto to inaugurate a canonic visitation of the diocese. He had been the Italian assistant in Marian England to Cardinal Pole, during the short-lived Catholic restoration there, and he had represented the Cardinal's plans for internal reform of the Catholic Church during the later stages of the Council in 1562–63. His personal representation of such a reform programme also led to his being chosen by the nephew of Pius IV, Cardinal Charles Borromeo, to precede the latter to Milan and prepare for the reform of that North Italian diocese, to which Borromeo himself was to move as resident archbishop, in conspicuous application of the Tridentine decrees.

Ormaneto was subsequently to fulfil similar aims himself as bishop of Venetian-ruled Padua and to encourage Spanish bishops to begin the implementation of the Conciliar reforms in their own dioceses during his secondment as nuncio in Spain. After Ormaneto's first efforts in Rome, there were other reform commissions established during the remaining decades of the sixteenth century, involving clerics who were equally noted for their devotion to the improved standards of Church life envisaged at Trent: Cardinal Agostino Valier, himself a post-Conciliar reforming bishop of Verona, within the Venetian Republic, was one such example. Such efforts culminated in the major canonic visitation of the Roman diocese launched by Clement VIII at the start of his pontificate in 1592. The pope visited not only the major basilicas but other churches and convents in Rome in person, and ordered that confraternities and other charitable institutes also receive a formal inspection by his assistant visitors.[1] This initiative led to the creation of a more permanent Curial commission for visitation of the Roman diocese, established before the end of the seventeenth century as one of the Congregations of the Roman Curia.

A TRIDENTINE DIOCESE

The pope as bishop in his diocese

That the popes during the next two centuries of the 'long Counter-Reformation' personally performed certain spectacular ceremonial duties is hardly unexpected. To the coronation of each new pope and to his solemn procession to take possession of his cathedral, St John Lateran, were added the lengthy canonization ceremonies and the special offices for the inauguration of Jubilees, such as that of 1600 under Clement VIII for instance. Nor is it surprising that popes also participated in ceremonies to mark outstanding events, such as signal victories of Catholic arms, like the Battle of the White Mountain in which Catholic Habsburg forces defeated Bohemian rebel supporters of the Elector Palatine early in the Thirty Years' War. But it may be noted that such occasions were not just ceremonial, but usually specifically liturgical, commonly involving celebration of Mass by the pope in person; and that they did not always take place at the papal basilicas alone. A pope might for such a purpose visit some other church relevant to the event, such as one of the 'national churches' in Rome, like the German church of S. Maria dell'Anima. Most of the popes were continuously visible to the citizens of their see: even the annual cycle of the liturgical year might ensure this, when a pope toured the 'stational' churches for specific feasts and solemnities. Few popes of the period under discussion here became so physically decrepit as to cease this liturgical round which marked Roman life and withdraw from sight.

What indeed may be less well known than papal participation in ceremonies of exceptionally conspicuous spectacle was the constant involvement of popes in personal celebration of public liturgical functions, especially the sacraments. Benedict XIII's addiction to liturgical duties did not quite make him the only pope of the period to perform a public baptism. For the display afforded to the baptism of converts from the Jewish community in Rome was not confined

1 D. Beggiao, *La Visita Pastorale di Clemente VIII (1592–1600). Aspetti di riforma post-tridentina a Roma* (Rome 1978). Important studies on the Roman diocese are to be found in the volumes of *Ricerche per la storia religiosa di Roma*, vols 1 ff. (Rome 1977 onwards).

to the annual incorporation of such celebrations in the ceremonies of Holy Saturday conducted at the papal cathedral of the Lateran or in some other major festival of the Church's year. When a particularly prominent Jewish family was received into the Christian faith Clement XI performed the baptism himself. The hearing of confessions by popes in person was also not unknown, whether in a Jubilee year, as in the case of Clement VIII for example, or more regularly each Holy Week, as was the practice of certain other popes, not only Benedict XIII but also for instance Clement IX. The popes of these centuries also renewed the provision of confessors serving the major basilicas, such as the Dominican penitentiaries at S. Maria Maggiore. For the universal Church they reformed the office of the Cardinal Penitentiary, to remove alien bureaucratic features in the supervision of the penitential system of the Church, banish the suggestion of financial profiteering and regulate relations with the Holy Office's supremacy in matters of faith.

The sacrament of marriage had been the subject of Tridentine legislation, intended to clarify the conditions of valid sacramental union in the future and reduce the dangerous ambiguities and oppressively multiplied obstacles previously surrounding marriage in Catholic society. When royal or princely dynasties were linked by marriage in the post-Conciliar Church, popes were occasionally present in person to preside over the administration of the sacrament, when the ceremony took place in Rome or exceptionally elsewhere in Italy. Once again Clement VIII, Urban VIII and Benedict XIII provide immediate examples. Virtually every one of the popes during these post-Tridentine centuries, in addition to public celebrations, said a daily private Mass, or alternatively heard Mass every day, for all the popes in question were in priest's orders at the time of the papal election which made them bishop of Rome, even if priestly ordination had occurred only just before entry to the conclave, as was the case with Cardinal Albani, who emerged as Pope Clement XI in 1700. The administration of extreme unction by a pope was not unknown: it is not surprising that Benedict XIII managed to set an example here.

The Western tradition that the sacrament of confirmation was ordinarily reserved for episcopal administration had been reaffirmed at Trent. The Roman diocese maintained the usage that confirmation was normally administered at the Lateran, as the cathedral of Rome. Under Clement VIII one of the canons of the chapter of that basilica who was in episcopal orders was specially delegated to supply this function of the diocesan, and did so at regular intervals. Later arrangements were equally well ordered as part of the responsibilities, under the Cardinal Vicar of Rome, of the episcopal vicegerent of the diocese. On those occasions when public baptism, as of adult converts from Judaism or more rarely from Islam, was incorporated in a major ceremony such as the Holy Saturday rite, it was easy for confirmation to be supplied immediately by the presiding prelate if in episcopal orders, as was normally the case with a cardinal pontificating at the Lateran. But in the exceptional case of a public adult baptism by the pope in person, he obviously could proceed to administer confirmation himself as bishop of Rome; and Clement VIII personally confirmed a convert from Protestantism, before Alexander VII's confirmation of Christina of Sweden.

Ordination was the other sacrament reserved for episcopal administration. The presence in Rome of many bishops, both those who were titular and those who should more properly have been resident among the faithful of their see, made it easy for ordinations to be performed, but popes could and did ordain in person, more usually conferring the episcopal ordination of new bishops than the ordination of priests. But the examination of ordinands was part of the duty of the Cardinal Vicar and his subordinates; and though only some cardinals during these centuries were in episcopal orders, among the total body of the college of cardinals, enough resided in Rome to ensure an adequate supply of co-consecrators in episcopal ordinations, quite apart from the other bishops present in the city at any one time. All the popes of this period who were not yet in episcopal orders at the time of their election received immediate episcopal ordination before their coronation, as for example did Clement XIV and Pius VI. Some, like Gregory XV, Benedict XIII or Benedict XIV for example, had previously held important bishoprics or archbishoprics in any case.

The administration of the Rome diocese

The Council of Trent had prescribed that in the years following its own conclusion the reforms decreed should be treated further, at stated intervals, in provincial councils and diocesan synods, for the specific application of improvement at local levels. In post-Conciliar Italy, and in certain other areas such as parts of Spain and Portugal, there were examples of provincial councils and more commonly of diocesan synods. In the view of Cardinal Agostino Valier, one particular occasion, during the personal visitations conducted by Clement VIII from 1592, on which he assembled all the secular clergy, though not regulars, of the city, amounted in practical terms to a diocesan synod.[2] But it remains true that this gathering lacked not only the presence of the regular clergy or their representatives, but also the canonic status of a synod. The diocese of Rome in fact during these post-Conciliar centuries was not directed by means of synods, but rather by occasional regulations issued in the pope's name. The chief responsibility for the ordering of diocesan life was that of the pope's Vicar, who by papal decree, made even before the last sessions of the Tridentine Council, was to be always precisely a Cardinal Vicar, emphasizing the centrality of the episcopal role of each pope within Rome. Under Clement VIII the Cardinal Vicar had not only deputies for the conduct of criminal and civil justice in the Church courts of the diocese, but also, already, a crucial figure, the vicegerent, who from this period onwards was invariably a bishop. The duties of the episcopal vicegerent under the Cardinal Vicar of Rome thus in some ways approximated to those in other

2 Beggiao, *La Visita*, p. 80 n. 7.

dioceses of the Vicar General under the diocesan bishop. The vicegerent was especially charged with the oversight of the clergy and of the regulars in Rome.

The ancient sees proximate to Rome, the Suburbicarian Sees held by the Cardinal Bishops, the inner group of senior cardinals who headed the whole college of cardinals and were themselves invariably in episcopal orders, already, as in more modern times, could also use the Rome Vicariate for the examination of their candidates for ordination. This degree of integration between the administration of the Rome Vicariate and that of the Suburbicarian Sees did not, however, in the early modern period, preclude pastoral provision made independently in those sees, for the creation of a diocesan seminary for example, as in the post-Conciliar work of Cardinal Paleotti as Cardinal Bishop of the dioceses in turn of Albano and Sabina. A later example of active pastoral care in the Suburbicarian See of Frascati was provided by Cardinal Henry Stuart, the eighteenth-century Duke of York and last of the direct Jacobite succession. Other Cardinal Bishops, in the seventeenth century, might insist on their own Vicars residing in such a see, in fulfilment of the duty of pastoral oversight, and appoint a prelate in episcopal orders to act as Vicar. But given the proximity of the Suburbicarian Sees it was conventionally understood that the city of Rome could properly be the normal residence of the Cardinal Bishops; though Paleotti again set an example in restoring an episcopal palace for his use when literally in residence in his see.[3]

In the diocese of Rome itself the Cardinal Vicar had the services of an episcopal police force at his immediate disposal, distinct from other agencies of supposed law enforcement under papal authority. In this the bishopric of Rome did apply the Tridentine provision for just such a force, to make effective the authority of the episcopal courts, in a way which bishops elsewhere in Catholic Europe, even in the states of the Italian peninsula, often found very difficult to achieve in practice. In other ways too the Roman diocese saw the implementation of parts of the Tridentine reform programme, such as the reorganization in the later sixteenth century of the parochial network in the city, to make more adequate pastoral provision for the population. This involved reducing, for a recovering population, the number of parish churches with full baptismal rights, in order that a better control of registration could be maintained. This indeed could find parallels in other dioceses in the post-Conciliar Church, such as Naples, for instance. Orders were similarly issued in Rome, as in the model dioceses of the post-Tridentine period, such as the archbishopric of Milan under Charles Borromeo, for the regular meeting of sections of the parish clergy of the city to discuss cases of conscience, reflecting the new emphasis placed on frequent confession in the post-Conciliar Church.

---

3 Biblioteca Vallicelliana, Rome: MS E.48; cf. *Istruzzione per li Predicatori destinati alle Ville, ò Terre, composta da . . . Gabriele Paleotti per . . . la Diocese di Sabina* (Rome 1678); *Constitutiones Synodales Sabinae Dioecesis editae ab Hannibale Cardinale S. Clementis Episcopo Sabinorum . . . 1736* (Urbino 1737).

The regulation of the regulars

As bishops of Rome the popes had one clear advantage over all other diocesans, however much the latter benefited by special delegations of power for longer or shorter periods. Beyond the carefully conditioned Tridentine provisions for episcopal intervention in the affairs and above all the pastoral work of the religious orders and regular clergy and beyond any privileged delegations of authority to individual prelates in such matters, the popes obviously had the ability to intervene in any aspect of the life of the regulars within Rome. After such interventions by immediately post-Conciliar popes, especially in the case of Sixtus V, himself a friar, Clement VIII continued detailed regulation of religious houses, male and female, in Rome, often in connection with personal visitation. Subsequent popes were free in the same way to intervene as and when they wished in all facets of regulars' activity in the Roman diocese. This was not confined to the type of control typified by insistence on strict enclosure of female convents, in the city as elsewhere in the post-Tridentine Church. New Orders of the period with specialist skills and purposes were authorized to establish themselves in Rome, such as the Ministers of the Sick, who nursed the terminally ill in particular, or the Clerics of the Pious Schools who extended education to male children of the middle and lower social orders. Such additions to the comprehensive presence in Rome of canons regular, monks, friars and other orders, congregations and societies, in all their varieties and sub-species, continued into the eighteenth century; until the age of the suppression of the Jesuits under Clement XIV, himself a friar of the Franciscan Conventuals.

The enclosed regime of female convents was further applied by post-Conciliar popes to new or reorganized foundations for unfortunate females, some for the care of female orphans and others for the custody of former prostitutes. The attempts to reduce prostitution in Rome were repeated under the popes of the later sixteenth century, and such attempts were renewed at intervals by later popes. A virtually consistent policy of the popes throughout this period was to prohibit female singers and actresses in public performances in Rome. The theatrical and musical representations spectacularly staged in the households of cardinals raised the question of what constituted a public performance, while high-voiced male singers available in Rome were not confined to the *castrati*. But on at least one occasion when a music drama was staged in such circumstances using a female performer in the premiere, papal intervention forced the substitution of the male voice as a condition of subsequent repetition. On the other hand, the annual attempts of the popes to limit the licence traditionally allowed to clerics as well as laity during the pre-Lenten Roman Carnival showed little substantial success over the decades. Admonitions to the cardinals to regulate their own behaviour during the festivities suggested the size of the task involved in moderating vices more generally during Carnival.

City improvements

Pilgrims to Rome, however, particularly in Jubilee years, could be encouraged in more pious occupations and attracted by more than usually conspicuous celebrations of Catholic ritual. From the Jubilee of 1600 onwards the popes made special efforts to ensure that the physical as well as spiritual needs of pilgrims were catered for. The papal programmes for improving the city of Rome were not just directed to fountains and obelisks. The improved road system carved by Sixtus V enabled pilgrims to progress more conveniently between the major basilicas and other particularly sacred spots in the city. The popes of these centuries not only superintended the long evolution of St Peter's, the changing completion of its structure and exterior, and long-term embellishment of its interior. While the mid-seventeenth-century creations of the colonnaded piazza in front of St Peter's, and the *Cathedra Petri*, symbol of Petrine authority as the terminal focus of the interior, complemented Bernini's baldacchino over the papal altar under the dome, the same century saw papal activity beyond that basilica alone. Its structural completion and consecration were eventually to be followed by the addition of large sacristies.

But more important than that, in a way, was the attention paid to the Lateran basilica as the cathedral of Rome. The personal visitation of Clement VIII had begun the improvement of its ancient structure and fittings, and at intervals his successors renewed their restoration. New sources of revenue, from papal income directly gathered and also paid by Spain as part of seventeenth-century adjustments to the financial concessions granted by the papacy to the monarchy, were allocated to the fabric of the cathedral. An artist of the stature of Borromini was commissioned in the seventeenth century to make the interior more impressive, and subsequently a great exterior loggia for papal benediction was added. This was similar to papal embellishments of the interior and exterior of the basilica of S. Maria Maggiore, provided by popes from Sixtus V and Paul V onwards. Individual cardinals were encouraged by the popes not only to continue their patronage of family chapels in some of the new or rebuilt churches of Mannerist and Baroque Rome, but furthermore to restore their own Titular Churches in the city.

The archaeological exploration of the catacombs began with a new systematic purpose in the pontificate of Clement VIII, and provided more than evidence for controversialists arguing the historic continuity of Catholic faith and practice against Protestant charges of innovation. The bodies and lesser relics of supposed saints from the catacombs supplied new objects of devotion for churches not only in Rome itself but more widely in Catholic Europe, not least in German-speaking areas. This development was well established by the time of the subsequent publication of Bosio's previously prepared survey of the catacomb discoveries, *Roma Sotterranea*. Prior to the codification by Clement X in 1672 of rules concerning relics from the catacombs, already by 1669 the commission set up by Clement IX to study in particular the debated martyr status of those in certain catacomb niches had developed into the regulatory Congregation of Indulgences and Relics.[4]

The care of pilgrims

In the physical care of pilgrims the pontificate of Clement VIII again saw important initiatives for their housing, feeding and medical as well as spiritual assistance, administered by the foundation of SS. Trinità dei Pellegrini. This continued its work, not only in Jubilee years, under succeeding popes, and represented an important fusion of the traditional services offered by some of the Roman confraternities, with their lay and not necessarily solely clerical membership and officers, on the one hand, and the work of the new congregations, such as Philip Neri's Oratorians, on the other. While the Council of Trent had intended to eradicate previously criticized abuses, above all financial abuses, in the granting of indulgences, the post-Conciliar popes made carefully controlled grants of indulgences to the Roman archconfraternities. This not only encouraged continued membership within the city, but allowed a Roman influence on confraternities elsewhere, in Italy or beyond, which by association with a particular Roman archconfraternity might share some of the spiritual benefits of the latter under certain conditions. This selective encouragement of traditional devotion under more precise diocesan control in Rome was matched by the regulations provided in Jubilee years for the conduct of pilgrims to the city wishing to gain the spiritual privileges offered for pious visitation of specified basilicas and other sacred locations. The care of the sick and those incapable of work by reason of age or disability in Rome also received repeated attention during the pontificates of these two centuries. Different popes, however, adopted individual policies towards social welfare.

Hospitals, in the modern sense of institutions to care for the sick, were certainly maintained throughout this period, and their number increased, often by the munificence of cardinals and other prelates.[5] But the popes also had an important role in ensuring the efficient administration of such hospitals, whether in this medical work, or in their more traditional mixture of purposes, in many cases, for the care not only of the sick but also for other categories such as orphans or the aged. From the Conciliar period itself the popes instituted canonic visitations of the Roman hospitals, and the results, as at the major foundation of S. Spirito in Sassia, were to promote a clearer specialization of functions, each organized apart, or even a separation into distinct institutions, as was evident in the reforms of 1563, 1635, 1725–29 and 1737–48 for example. This increasing specialization of social care was also encouraged by the papal

4 A. Bosio, *Roma sotterranea* (Rome 1632) [1634]; cf. S. Ditchfield, *Liturgy, Sanctity and History in Tridentine Italy. Pietro Maria Campi and the Preservation of the Particular* (Cambridge 1995).
5 Gregory Martin, *Roma Sancta*, 1st edn from the MS by G.B. Parks (Rome 1969), pp. 105 ff.: The Second Booke, Principally Concerning the Charitie of Rome.

approval given to the new foundations of specialist New Orders, as in the hospices for the terminally ill or the contagious, and specifically for the syphilitic, under Benedict XIII for instance. Public approbation was given by the visits of popes to such foundations in their diocese, and lay support was encouraged once again by the selective grant of indulgences and spiritual benefits which such institutions could convey to their patrons and benefactors.

The Tridentine provision for episcopal supervision of charitable institutions and audit of pious bequests, to ensure the fulfilment of testators' intentions and maintenance in return of Masses for the repose of their souls, was certainly realized in the Rome diocese. The efficient administration of other bequests, for example for the provision of marriage or convent dowries for honest girls of slender means, whether brought up in orphanages or otherwise, encouraged further donations for similar purposes throughout this period, as did the more centralized control of all charitable foundations in Rome from 1742 onwards.

Relief of poverty

It was in the treatment of poverty more generally, however, that the policy of different popes most conspicuously varied. The provision on a large scale of entirely new foundations, such as the great orphanage-cum-workhouse for otherwise unemployed boys, created on the edge of Trastevere in the late seventeenth century, was an eventual solution to part of the problem. The occasional attempts of late sixteenth-century popes to banish beggars from Rome did not, however, provide a structural solution to Roman poverty. A more fruitfully discriminating policy was adopted by some seventeenth-century popes, especially in preparation for Jubilee years when the crowds of the poor and unemployed in the city always naturally swelled: this involved the registration by parish priests of the truly resident beggars of each parish. Such control had the further advantage that parochially administered relief, in the form of a bread ration for example, could be made conditional on fulfilment of other Tridentine aims, like attendance at catechism. But none of these measures was totally successful in limiting the rise of urban poverty or the numbers of beggars on the streets of Rome. A more drastic paternalism was attempted under Innocent XII, who followed the aims already outlined under Innocent XI and attempted to order beggars off the streets and into a 'general hospital', in the sense of the large hostels confining the aged, the unemployed and the disabled, in distinct wings, for a totally enclosed and quasi-conventual residence, and adherence to a workhouse regime.

Such institutions, starting from precocious Netherlandish examples found even before the consolidation of religious divisions of sixteenth-century Europe, were established during the seventeenth century and into the eighteenth century in French, Italian and some Spanish cities, despite the residual criticism of more conservative Catholics, who argued that the prevention of begging for casual alms and the removal from public circulation of these representatives of Christ-like poverty dangerously, if inadvertently, confirmed Protestant positions. Such a revolution in social relief supposedly denied Catholics the opportunity for that Work of Mercy which brought to the benefactor spiritual returns in Catholic but emphatically not in Protestant theology, and even allegedly gave credence to Protestant attack on the whole existence of the religious orders and the purpose of the mendicants above all.

It was not, however, such remonstrances, from Spanish friars for example, which led to the collapse in Rome of an experiment in social welfare successfully made in many cases elsewhere, but already without lasting success by Gregory XIII and Sixtus V. The numbers of beggars and unemployed in Rome were simply too vast to be accommodated in even the most ambitious edifice, and above all the vital financial support, to supply the necessities of life and the materials for work for example, was not available on an adequate scale, despite the tradition of personal alms-giving maintained by popes as well as cardinals throughout this period. In the case of this failure to reorganize poor relief on a systematic basis in the diocese of Rome, episcopal initiative was clearly not enough, as was still evident in the reaction of Clement XIII to the influx of beggars to Rome in the food shortage of 1764. The structural problems of poverty and underemployment in the city of Rome were singular, and greater by far than those of other dioceses. In such an instance the complicating factor of the papacy's role as also a temporal regime certainly becomes relevant; and further consideration of larger problems, of the economy of Rome and the papal states, which were beyond the ability of popes merely as bishops of the city to resolve, deserves to be made as part of later treatment of papal government.

The provisioning of Rome with an adequate and affordable supply of bread was, however, seen, by the popes of the late sixteenth and early seventeenth centuries still at least, as part of their properly pastoral duties. Such provision certainly became more difficult, not only in Jubilee years or in years of particular harvest failure in the Roman countryside, as the agricultural yield of that area alarmingly decreased. Such decrease was related to increasing taxation levels and a corresponding increase in banditry, factors which will be included in subsequent discussion of the policies pursued by papal temporal government. But regulation of the weight and price of the Roman loaf, as part of papal administration in the city of Rome, was not the limit of the popes' intervention. In a less purely temporal role, the late sixteenth- and early seventeenth-century popes included in their negotiations with the Spanish monarchy under Philip II, Philip III and Philip IV more than the defence of ecclesiastical rights and the promotion of Tridentine reform in Spanish-ruled territories in Europe and overseas. Responding to the Spanish preoccupation with preserving financial concessions renewed or extended from time to time by the papacy, to support Spanish confrontation with Islam as well as with European heresy from essentially ecclesiastical sources in Spain itself and increasingly in its other possessions, the popes countered with requests for

Sicilian grain to relieve Rome's shortfall; and such applications were often met, though not necessarily on the tax-free basis which Rome hoped to achieve.

A more lastingly successful policy of the popes of the Tridentine era within the city of Rome was the maintenance of a new source of credit for the temporary relief of poverty, rather than for the removal of structural poverty. This was the Roman *Monte di Pietà*, created by the beginning of the sixteenth century, on the model of the similar *Monti* established first by friars in central and Northern Italy, then in Venetian territory above all, in the pre-Tridentine era, and subsequently elsewhere in Northern and central Italy under varied patronage, including that of diocesan bishops. The papal initiative in encouraging such a loan bank, with its characteristic employment of pawned goods as security, was thus not original, but nevertheless vital for the adoption of this new system within the Rome diocese, which still had a crucial need of it in 1764 for example. The popes as the bishops of Rome had the further advantage that they were the undisputed authority for the regulation of those low rates of interest paid by the borrowers, but also, increasingly in the operation of Italian *Monti di Pietà*, paid to depositors, to encourage their investment in the necessary capital of the loan bank not for the eternal reward of spiritual benefit alone, but also for the more immediate expectation of a small monetary return. Interest in all senses thus spurred participation in such a Christian Work of Mercy. But the regulation of the tolerated rate of interest was sensitive, and outside papal territory the management of such *Monti*, even in the jealously guarded lay boards of administration in Venetian territory, might feel safe in their consciences only after securing papal permission for a small increase in the carefully moderated rate when this proved necessary.[6] What of course is immediately obvious, should it be necessary to reassert the point, is that the papacy had no absolute objection to the operation of interest as such, but pursued its policies within the framework of Catholic debate throughout this period on just what low rates of interest were within the permitted bounds. As will subsequently be seen, in consideration of the financial and economic conditions of papal temporal administration, the employment of interest was indeed vital in the development of venal office at the papal Court and of *monti* in the sense of investment funds, as the post-Conciliar papacy sought to make up its revenues from a range of secular sources, over and above the sale of alum to clothworking areas such as those of Protestant Elizabethan England.[7]

The relative success of the Roman *Monte di Pietà* as a source of Christian credit did not at first alter the papal acquiescence of money-lending by members of the Jewish community in Rome. The regulation of such activity, as of the whole conditions of life in the increasingly confined and strictly enclosed Roman ghetto, became certainly more stringent under the popes of the late sixteenth century. But whatever the mania of suspicion and hostility occasionally

6 Archivio di Stato, Venezia [A.S. Ven.]: Collegio: Relazioni 51 (Rettori, Vicenza): 1598, 20 Oct.: Relatione di Benetto Correr Podestà.
7 A.S.V. Spagna, CCCXX, especially fo. 122v: 13 Apr. 1594.

evident, in the case of Pius V for instance, the Roman Jewish community in fact continued in existence throughout this period. The popes indeed remained reliant on the community as an additional source of revenue, since varied levies were not easily resisted. Other conditions were imposed, of a different sort, such as compulsory attendance at Christian sermons on specific occasions. Conversions were encouraged, but those refusing to follow relations into Christianity, where part of a family converted, were allowed to return to the ghetto. What was eagerly hoped for was genuine not forced conversions, and the Roman foundation for the reception of converts, mainly though not exclusively from Judaism, operated with papal approval as part of the network of specialist charitable institutions for different purposes established in the diocese.

The degree of success which the Christian credit of the Roman *Monte di Pietà* had achieved, however, by the time of Innocent XI persuaded him to make a further alteration in the total provision for social welfare in the city. His closure of the Jewish loan banks in Rome in 1682 should thus be seen as part of the comprehensive plans, already noted, to redraw the pattern of relief for different categories of need in his diocese. In all aspects of his social policy, but also that of other popes before and after him, practical success was not always forthcoming. But the popes throughout these two centuries adhered to the image reformulated at Trent which saw personal almsgiving as only one part of a dutiful bishop's responsibility: care for Christ's poor also required, in changing social conditions, renewed attention to the direction of charitable institutions and audit of pious bequests to ensure the efficient relief of corporal needs as well as the fulfilment of spiritual conditions prescribed by testators and benefactors. 'Roman Charity' was not just a Baroque conceit, embodied in sculptural form on papal tombs; its practical manifestations in the diocese allowed Catholic apologists to laud the ever-extending number and variety of charitable foundations in the city, in defence of the theology of Good Works. Visitors to Rome from other parts of Europe, including Protestants, on occasion recorded a spontaneous appreciation of the extent of this relief provision throughout the period considered here. Not all the institutions functioned with constant efficiency, nor were the persisting problems of structural poverty and unemployment removed even by the more innovative experiments in social welfare; but the number of general and specialist 'hospitals' and other hospices, orphanages and almshouses was undoubtedly impressive. During the sixteenth and seventeenth centuries over 130 new confraternities were founded in Rome, including, for example, one for the relief of imprisoned debtors in 1579, while a new focus, the ransom of Christians from Islamic captivity, was provided in 1581 for the venerable confraternity of the Gonfalone by Gregory XIII.[8]

---

8 E.P.d.G. Chaney, 'Giudizi inglesi su ospedali italiani, 1545–1789', in *Timore e Carità. I Poveri nell'Italia moderna*, ed. G. Politi et al. (Cremona 1982), pp. 77–101; P. Simoncelli, 'Note sul sistema assistenziale a Roma nel XVI secolo', in ibid., pp. 137–56.

Rural poor relief

The Roman poor, however, were not all strictly urban, even when the seasonal influx of the rural poor to search for alms, there as in other great cities in early modern Europe, is taken into account. The diocese of Rome contained rural margins, even before the contiguous territory of the Suburbicarian Sees was reached. The gangs of unskilled labour, in harvest season above all, who worked in these areas included women and adolescents whose conditions were devoid of anything beyond bare subsistence. The system of gang labour indeed produced servile submission to armed foremen and enclosure at night in what can only be described as labour-camps. By the end of the eighteenth century and even before the end of the seventeenth, these virtually penal conditions seemed shocking to contemporaries themselves. In addition to the papal judge who was delegated especially to conserve the basic rights of the rural poor of the territory, in a policy pursued by the central organs of papal government into the 1780s themselves, a new campaign to bring pastoral care to these subjects on the peripheries of the diocese was begun under the popes of the early eighteenth century. A parochial structure adequate to providing for these dispossessed camps of agricultural labourers was lacking.

The internal mission

But the concept of internal mission, first developed in the post-medieval Church by Jesuits in central and Southern Italy and parts of Spain during the sixteenth century, and furthered in France in the seventeenth century by Vincent de Paul and others, was revived in the Rome diocese at this date, as it was to be during the rest of the century both further south and elsewhere in the Italian peninsula. In the Roman case, papal encouragement of teams headed by secular priests from the city brought at least occasional catechism and sacraments to these agricultural camps, and short-term relief in the form of alms.[9] Such seasonal initiatives complemented the more settled pattern of catechizing in the urban core of the Rome diocese from the later sixteenth century onwards. Parish priests in the city were repeatedly reminded of their duty to ensure the teaching of catechism, and this provision was complemented by the catechetical work of other individuals and agencies, and the distinct instruction of the Roman Oratory, to take perhaps the most famous example. The Schools of Christian Doctrine, in which lay teachers of both boys' and girls' catechism classes were involved under clerical supervision, were systematically reorganized by the end of the sixteenth century, first in Northern Italy and then increasingly elsewhere in the peninsula. By means of parochial and other

9 J. Coste, 'Missioni nell'Agro romano nella primavera del 1703', *Ricerche per la storia religiosa di Roma*, II (1978), 165–223; G.F. Rossi, 'Monelli e monelle dell'Agro Romano: un proletariato agricolo del Settecento nelle visite pastorali del card. Rezzonico', in ibid., III, 315–51; cf. A. Turchini, *Sotto l'occhio del padre. Società confessionale e istruzione primaria nello Stato di Milano* (Bologna 1996).

similar classes not only catechism but also the rudiments of literacy and numeracy, or occasionally even basic trade and domestic skills too, were taught to children, usually of the middle and lower social orders.

This pattern was reflected in Roman educational provision during the period considered here, and papal regulations sought to use the existence of the Roman University to monitor the daily work of schoolmasters in the city's schools, as opposed to the catechetical classes of Sundays and holydays. The development of the Pious Schools in Rome added to the educational opportunities for male pupils at least; and from the seventeenth century there was, relatively, but more than in many other places, increased female schooling. Neither educational nor specifically catechetical provision in the Rome diocese was entirely systematic, but the episcopal duty reasserted at Trent, to see that Christian education was maintained and the faith expounded, was certainly performed under all the popes of this period. The 1624 diocesan visitation begun by Urban VIII recorded over eighty catechism schools in Rome. The papal privileges accorded to the Collegio Romano, run by the Jesuits, enabled that expanding institution, newly housed from 1582, to function both as a selective secondary school for male pupils from families of means and simultaneously as a college of higher education, of virtually university level, for male students who were not all necessarily destined to be clerics.

Those enrolled at the Collegio Romano, as its fame rapidly increased, were not all from families resident in Rome of course, whereas the diocese of Rome was in need of secular clergy to staff its parishes. Such clerics needed adequate training, even if they were not from families of substance. Within two years of the Council of Trent's conclusion in 1563, after it had made clear and quite detailed provision for the creation of diocesan seminaries, as a new and systematic form of vocational and professional training for the parochial clergy, a Roman seminary had already come into existence, partly as a result of prelatical benefaction. The popes as bishops of Rome did not thus face the very real and often overwhelming practical difficulties, financial and otherwise, encountered by diocesan bishops elsewhere in post-Tridentine Catholic Europe as they sought to create a seminary. Such problems obstructed the erection of these new institutions in parts of Italy, in much of Spain, and elsewhere in the post-Conciliar Church. The expansion of a network of precisely diocesan seminaries was long delayed in France, parts of Spain, and throughout much of seventeenth- and eighteenth-century Catholic Europe. But in Rome the necessity for the popes was merely to ensure the efficient running of the Roman Seminary and its adequate funding, which was indeed secured.

The question of the staffing of diocesan seminaries, especially at their first creation in each see, was another area where post-Conciliar bishops elsewhere found difficulty. For until the general level of the secular clergy's attainments had begun to improve, not least as a result of better training, suitable manpower was not always easy to find, or of course to fund. Some bishops, at various dates, sought Jesuit expertise in first staffing a seminary; but this experiment was not always successful, if the Society was seen to be subverting the whole process of improving the diocesan clergy by encouraging the most promising seminarians to join its own membership. Such a problem confronted the papacy in its wider role as patron and guardian of special seminaries in Rome designed to train clergy for areas where, because of Protestant proscription or otherwise, local seminaries were an impossibility: the troubles at the English College partly reflected this, as will be seen, but Jesuit direction of the Greek College in Rome was not without its difficulties either, for instance. As bishops of Rome, however, the popes did not seem to find difficulty in overriding opposition to Jesuit direction of the Roman Seminary, until the suppression of the Society. The Jesuits in Rome had, after all, their own novitiate and other famous institutions which could manifest the attractions of the Society to those who might wish to join it. The Roman Seminary contributed its own part to the range of institutions in the city offering education or clerical training and benefited precisely the diocesan body of secular clergy.

The provision of pastoral care

Pastoral provision available to the faithful of the Rome diocese was not confined to the parochial structure, though parochial recording of the laity's duties was tightened from about 1614. The parish churches had their rights in such matters as baptism or Easter communion, or by Tridentine prescription in the sacrament of marriage, but preaching and confession, for example, in Baroque Rome as much as in the pre-Tridentine Church, were widely available. Cardinals superintended the pastoral care of the members of their own households, however. The older religious orders, especially the friars, and the New Orders, including the Jesuits as well as the Oratorians, continued throughout this period to provide some pastoral services on a large scale, not only to papal courtiers and Curialists or to temporary pilgrims and visitors, but to the laity of Rome as well. The large number of female convents in the city, relative to the levels of vocation, even allowing for membership of their communities drawn from beyond Rome, meant that any female able to provide a dowry of a suitable level could find a place in one or other convent as a choir-sister, if she wished; while the opportunities for those without such resources to find a place as a lay-sister were commensurate, despite the economic difficulties of many houses.

Lay confraternities in papal Rome were not all under the supervision of religious orders, despite the elegant composition of some of the Jesuit-run confraternities, eventually famed for their elite membership or the musical standards of their confraternity devotions. Some were still related to specific crafts or trades, while the 1624 diocesan visitation ordered confraternities devoted to the Reserved Sacrament to be founded in parishes still lacking such a confraternity. Others had the new, outwardly directed, spiritual and charitable characteristic of confraternities founded or reorganized in the Tridentine era. These could contribute a specific role in the administration of Rome, as in the care of prisoners and the accompaniment and subsequent burial of those condemned to public execution, or provision for the employment of poor girls.

Papal approval of the New Orders which established their headquarters in Rome, as with the Theatines and Jesuits, ensured noble as well as more popular attendance at the special ceremonies from time to time mounted at the churches of these orders. The favour shown by Clement VIII to the new foundation of the Roman Oratory ensured the success of the distinctive occasions presented there for the consolidation of the faith of the laity above all. The devotions and informal instruction of the Oratorians, which evolved into the musical and eventually also dramatic presentation of sacred themes, provided another facet of the unusual variety of encouragements to piety in the Rome diocese. Papal approval of certain forms of sacred music outside the confines of the liturgy thus allowed musical life in the city to continue even during the extended seasons of the year when secular opera, after its later development as a distinct genre, was prohibited. This also complemented the stricter and indeed relatively conservative regulation of precisely liturgical music in the churches of Rome, more particularly the papal chapel and basilicas, by the popes throughout this period. Papal control of the official Roman artists' academy, of St Luke, made a general supervision of artworks placed in the city's churches, as opposed to secular locations or private places, implicitly possible, despite the very real importance of the determining patronage of individuals and families.

The pope as resident bishop

The popes between 1564 and 1789 were above all, in one very obvious sense, resident bishops of their diocese. With infrequent exceptions, from Clement VIII's journey to Ferrara to Pius VI's visit to Vienna, this was supremely a prolonged period of stability in the papal presence in or near Rome. By the mid-seventeenth century the use of a retreat in the Roman hills, as at Castel Gandolfo, was becoming known on occasion, but not even then on a regular basis or for the whole of the summer months necessarily. What was becoming more standard, from the late sixteenth century onwards, was the tendency to use the papal residences within Rome in a seasonal rotation. Though most popes of these centuries used the elevated Quirinal Palace as a residence during the longer and warmer part of the year, the Vatican was not unused, and most popes resided there for parts of the year, or at least on occasion. The Lateran palace was no longer a normal residence for the popes in person, despite its sixteenth-century and again eighteenth-century rebuilding. But the papal Court, in any case, was not confined to any one set of buildings at a given time. It was also housed in official residences such as the Cancelleria or in the additional residences of a Cardinal Nephew for instance. As an institution, indeed, it could be said to have spread across the city of Rome.

The papal household, on the other hand, was a more distinct and carefully guarded entity. Some popes took their episcopal duties, urged by Trent's decrees as by earlier theorists, to include as a central concern the regulation of behaviour among members of their household. Such oversight was not necessarily confined to morals or to sumptuary prescription, but could extend to the demonstration of spiritual care, for instance by the distribution of General Communion to the assembled household on some special occasion. This foundation of the bishop's duties in his domestic sphere was very much in line with pre- and post-Tridentine discourse on episcopal office. It accounts for the extraordinary care taken in the arrangements for Christina of Sweden's brief reception in the Vatican before her official entry into Rome and before her establishment of a separate household of her own in the city, in conditions which did not then always match papal expectations of decorum.

Beyond the papal household

Such concern also extended from the truly domestic to the public sphere again when popes officiated at the marriage of their nieces or other relations with conspicuous solemnity. It also explains the genuine scandal caused by the access which the female relations of Innocent X, his sister-in-law especially, were known to enjoy and to exercise with frequency. The precise cause of scandal was not so much the pope's visits to his female relatives, for popes through-out this period moved about their diocese as they wished, and etiquette in no way confined them to their palace or the major basilicas. Indeed, a few popes took more private, that is less official, exercise in the city or the surrounding countryside, riding out to the latter or being driven in the city in a simple carriage with a very reduced entourage. The objection to Innocent X's ways derived from his permitting a female visible access to the systems of influence and therefore of course to patronage.

The physical access to the pope within his household was as strictly regu-lated as in any monarchical Court of the early modern period. In most pontificates during these centuries one of the most important functions of the Cardinal Nephew or later of a Cardinal Secretary of State was as the ultimate regulator of such access. When a pope granted a truly private audience to an individual other than such a cardinal, the conditions were supposed to be known to all. A French ambassador who pressed an unwelcome point on the pope by allegedly touching his arm very properly incurred immediate warn-ing of excommunication. Furthermore, the pope could terminate any audience by ringing the bell to summon attendance. The more personal sense in which the aged primate of Spain, Carranza, was reconciled, after hearing final Roman sentence read on him in the pope's presence, after the years of his inquisitorial process, involved him being nevertheless permitted to approach and perform the ceremonial kissing of the pope's feet, on his formal submission.

Like any other conscientious bishop, the pope naturally included domestic spiritual advisers in his household, especially his confessor. Though that was a more truly domestic office than, say, the Mastership of the Sacred Palace, held by the Dominican charged with official theological advice to the pope as well as with certain duties as censor within Rome, a few confessors had an influence which clearly affected papal policy. An outstanding example was the Oratorian Baronius, confessor to Clement VIII, who did much to encourage the pope in his determined and innovatory defence of ecclesiastical independence. The office of Papal Preacher, by contrast, pertained more to the routine of the papal Court than to the intimate workings of the household when exercised at certain seasons within the papal liturgy. But outside those occasions it was traditionally exercised by a regular, often a friar, though indeed many papal confessors were regulars too.

The domestic chapel of a pope during these centuries was not necessarily so simple an affair however. The Tridentine devotion to the Reserved Sacrament, the Quarant'Ore, as systematized in Northern Italy before the end of the sixteenth century, was celebrated in Rome at intervals regulated by the pope, often in connection with prayers for a public need, such as a Catholic victory, or delivery from some pressing threat or misery. By command of the pope it might be celebrated in one or more or all of the basilicas, churches and convents of his diocese; but the Baroque apparatus for this Forty Hours' Devotion was on occasion created in one of the papal chapels, with some degree of access for at least the privileged. Such temporary manifestations of Baroque staging for religious purposes, as equally in the monumental catafalques temporarily erected for the obsequies not only of popes themselves but also of cardinals, rulers and princes, were an important part of the work of even the most eminent artists, such as Bernini. The lengthy ceremonies at canonizations also required the staging of costly apparatus according to very detailed prescription, which put a premium on the efforts of rulers, religious orders or dioceses wishing to promote the canonization of a particular saint. The conspicuous devotion accorded to the Reserved Sacrament was also maintained as part of the annual liturgical cycle, when popes, as in previous periods, participated in the Corpus Christi procession. But since popes were of course not simply bishops of Rome, the ceremonies at and after the death of each, prescribed by traditional ritual, were as distinctive and elaborate as ever, and naturally different from those surrounding the death of bishops elsewhere.

The quest for liturgical uniformity

The revision by the post-Conciliar popes of the liturgical texts of the Roman rite meant, however, that in the city the new Missal was to be followed from the later sixteenth century onwards, despite the initial nostalgic yearnings for older, more local usages among members of the English College for example. This new Roman rite applied, papal ceremonies themselves apart, in the churches of the diocese, except for those religious orders still permitted distinctive liturgies during this period. The degree of liturgical uniformity sought by the post-Conciliar papacy, with however imperfect success, throughout all dioceses but a few privileged sees of Catholic Western Europe, was thus more easy to impose in the pope's own bishopric. The standardization in the administration of the sacraments, equally aimed at by the papal revision of the Rituale after Trent, was similarly applied with immediate effect within the Roman parishes already by the time of Gregory XIII. For the secular as opposed to many of the regular clergy of Rome, the papal revision of the Breviary, after the Council, again had immediate implications, however much, among regulars, the New Orders (specifically Theatines and Jesuits) had differed in their views on such revision. But that revision, aimed at uniformity among at least the secular clergy of the whole Church just as much as in the case of the other liturgical books, proved troublesome to the popes themselves. Even after the revision of both the Breviary and the Martyrology had been in a sense completed, by the end of Clement VIII's pontificate, the desire of Urban VIII to use his poetic talents for the tasteful improvement of the Breviary's Latin hymnody caused much later successors further work, as they were less convinced of his gifts in this sphere.

Other action initiated in the diocese of Rome might not always have implications or repercussions limited to that area. The condemnation of Molinos by Innocent XI, to take a notorious example, had wide implications for the Quietists everywhere, yet in the most immediate sense it was the priestly conduct of Molinos in Rome itself, his activity as spiritual director there, which provided the basis for his arrest in 1685. In the more immediately post-Conciliar period, the revision of the ceremonial of the papal chapel itself caused diplomatic difficulties in relations with Catholic states.[10] Similarly, the revised codification of canon law, begun under Pius V and issued in a definitive, if partial, text under Gregory XIII, had obvious importance for more than the diocese alone. In the Rome diocese a papal edict of 1622 regulated the observance of holydays, a matter in which later popes were to agree to some moderation, on a universal basis or at least for Italian sees.

Rome compared with other dioceses

Within the Rome diocese, more frequent lay communion certainly advanced during this period, whatever the disputes over this in the Catholic Church more widely. The condemnations pronounced by Clement XII and Benedict XIV, by contrast, did not prevent the establishment of freemasonry in Rome itself, even if confined to expatriate antiquarian circles and those of political exiles. This result certainly differed from the firmness with which the suppression of Jesuit communities was imposed in the city and diocese of Rome in the summer of 1773. Prior to the suppression of the Society of Jesus Clement XIV had allegedly urged Cardinal Stuart to end the educational and catechetical work of the Jesuits in his Suburbicarian See of Frascati. The suppression affected not only the Collegio Romano but also other institutions in Rome under Jesuit direction, such as the Irish College. Yet though internal

10 Fondazione Cini, Venice: Microfilmoteca [F.C.M.]: Archivio Segreto Vaticano: Segreteria di Stato: Nunziatura in Venezia: filza 266, fos 96, 104, 117: 16 Apr.–14 May 1575.

missions, for popular catechizing and conversion in the margins of the diocese and the Suburbicarian Sees, had been the work not only of Jesuits but of other regulars and secular clerics too, the Jesuits had continued them in the eighteenth century at Palestrina and Albano as well as Frascati. Another of the famous internal missioners during that century, the Franciscan Leonard of Port Maurice, also worked in Rome as well as elsewhere in the Italian peninsula. The special devotions and indulgences of the Jubilees continued from 1575 to 1775, at the traditional quarter-century intervals, nevertheless set Rome apart.

The reform of the calendar by Gregory XIII, in 1582, affected the ordinary sequence of the liturgical year not only in Rome, but throughout Catholic Europe, even though the change was long resisted by Protestant states and with even more perseverance in Orthodox Russia. The organization of the Vatican Press by Sixtus V similarly had a universal importance, well beyond that of initiatives by other, seventeenth- and eighteenth-century Italian bishops who established presses for diocesan use. But the impact of papal censorship in Rome itself, whether under the Master of the Sacred Palace in person or by means of the Congregation of the Index, arguably had a limiting effect on the work and eventually the viability of other learned printers there, in the late sixteenth century and for a while longer at any rate. The monopoly rights asserted by Rome in certain forms of liturgical printing, then, did not represent simply a mercantilist measure; this was also primarily intended to ensure the accuracy of the newly revised texts for use beyond the Roman diocese alone. Such an aim did not, notoriously, prevent Clement VIII's having to publish an emended version of the Latin Vulgate Bible which Sixtus V had issued in a supposedly authentic revision. Of a Roman but not merely diocesan importance, again, was the major renovation of the Vatican Library by Sixtus V. So too was the new organization of the papal archives, first planned and constituted by Clement VIII and Paul V, and provided both by Urban VIII and by some of his successors.

Diocesan bishops resident in Rome without good reason were from time to time ordered to depart for their own sees. This was a concern not only of immediately post-Conciliar popes of the later sixteenth century, but of others too, as for example Paul V on his election in 1605. For while some popes might share the educational background of other Italian bishops, it must not be assumed that all the popes prior to Clement XIV were *ex officio* favourable to the Jesuits, for example. Gregory XV showed a sympathy for the Society of Jesus which derived not least from his education at the Jesuit-run Collegio Romano. But his attitude was not shared by his successor, Urban VIII, while Clement VIII had not been particularly positive in his view of the Society, and had varied in his opinion of individual Jesuits, including Bellarmine. The brief inclusion of the latter's work in an edition of the Roman Index of prohibited literature had been the result of a previous pope's objection to the qualified basis on which he had defended the supreme authority of the papacy and its application in temporal affairs. Sixtus V had not had an affection for the Society, though he was a Franciscan friar and not a member of the Society's chief rivals, the Dominicans. Clement VIII seemed increasingly to favour the Dominicans in their doctrinal disputes with Jesuit theologians, but his pontificate was also conspicuously the era when the chief influence on the pope, his policies and important figures at the papal Court was that not of the Jesuits but of the Roman Oratorians.[11]

The visitation system

The pastoral tradition of the popes as bishops of their see was continued, after the visitation of the diocese by Clement VIII, by the visitation ordered by Urban VIII in 1624. By order of Innocent XII, at the end of the century, records of Clement VIII's visitation were carefully collected, in relation to Innocent's creation in 1696 of a special Congregation to reform the Rome diocese. Even before Clement's activity, a report on the Roman Seminary had been made to Sixtus V in 1585. The visitors delegated by Clement, in his diocesan visitation begun in person, included another figure associated with the exemplary application of Conciliar reform in post-Tridentine Italy, the Welsh former assistant to Charles Borromeo in Milan, Owen Lewis. Another former assistant to the Borromean archbishops at Milan, Seneca, was also subsequently involved. Such direct interventions by the popes in person were the more important because of the relative limitation of the authority of a Cardinal Vicar, represented by the fact that each cardinal was in a sense master in the affairs of his own Titular Church, while religious houses and 'national' churches were under the more than formal patronage of the Cardinal Pro-tectors of different religious orders and states. His authority was similarly limited by the fact that at the papal basilicas the chapter was presided over by a Cardinal Archpriest; while at that of St Paul Outside the Walls, the monastic chapter was headed by an abbot enjoying prelatical status and rights. Clement VIII's personal intervention meant that restoration of his cathedral at the Lateran, with a view to the Jubilee of 1600, provided an example for Innocent X's improvements there, made similarly with the 1650 Jubilee in mind; the post-Tridentine papacy had indeed reconfirmed the preeminence of the Lateran among the Roman basilicas.

The long experience of the Tridentine and post-Conciliar Cardinal Vicar Savelli, between 1560 and 1587, was vital in introducing reformed standards in the diocese. It was he who ensured the existence of the Roman Seminary, on the pattern decreed by the Council for all sees, in addition to the diocesan visitations he made in person, as well as by means of other delegates during the pontificate of Pius IV. When Ormaneto was delegated by Pius V to con-tinue the reform of the diocese, it was with the papal household itself that he began in 1566. This diocesan delegation was again the more important because Pius V's personal visitations extended only to the three basilicas of the

11 A.D. Wright, 'Bellarmine, Baronius and Federico Borromeo', in *Bellarmino e la Controriforma*, ed. R. De Maio (Sora 1990), pp. 323–70.

Lateran, St Peter's and S. Maria Maggiore, and the substantial hospital of S. Spirito with its adjacent church. While Sixtus V planned a more extensive visitation of his diocese, at the beginning of his pontificate, his choice of a new Vicar to succeed Savelli was arguably more obviously effective, for Cardinal Rusticucci was again to provide stability in diocesan management, as Savelli had done, across several pontificates, in this case from 1587 to his death in 1603.

A similar if less active continuity in the office of Cardinal Vicar covered the mid-seventeenth century, for a new pope did not necessarily appoint a new Vicar. Ormaneto's thorough procedure had extended to the device used also in other sees under zealous diocesans, of making confidential enquiry among the laity of respect and standing about the conduct of parish clergy. This pastoral tradition as a whole was consolidated for the diocese when Alexander VII instituted a new Curial Congregation in 1656 for the maintenance of Apostolic Visitation. This therefore built on the plan formed as early as 1592 by Clement VIII for a commission of cardinals charged precisely to oversee visitation of the Roman diocese. In fact, one of the cardinals delegated by Clement also became, though briefly, his successor, when Cardinal Alessandro de'Medici was elected pope in the first conclave of 1605.

The pastoral image promoted by Clement at the start of his pontificate at least was emphasized by the charge to the delegated visitors to include in their attention the provisions for the sick and the poor of Rome, even though not all hospitals were in fact visited. The pope's role as bishop of Rome was strikingly demonstrated at the cathedral of the Lateran, when his personal visitation included not only the celebration of a pontifical Mass, not in itself unusual, but also the distribution of General Communion to the clergy of the basilica, from the Cardinal Archpriest downwards. A second personal visit was even made to the same basilica, for the examination of the penitentiaries, who, at the Lateran, were Franciscans by the provision of Pius V. Canons appointed to any of the papal basilicas and other capitular churches of Rome during Clement's pontificate might find the pope present in person at the examination of their competence in theology. The hospital of SS. Salvatore adjacent to the Lateran also received a personal visitation, in which Clement applied Tridentine priorities in ensuring that catechism as well as physical care was provided there. A review of all the charitable institutions of the city was then begun by the Cardinal Vicars during the first half of the seventeenth century, since only a few hospitals, as has been seen, in fact received visitation under Clement VIII.

This complemented canonic visitation of Roman churches carried out by the Cardinal Vicars after 1600. Since the regular clergy of the city were also required, like the seculars after 1567, to hold systematic discussions of cases of conscience, by papal regulations of Pius V in 1571, Clement VIII in 1592 and Cardinal Gaspare Carpegna in 1682, the frequent employment of regulars as confessors, at Rome as elsewhere, could be viewed with more confidence in the diocese than perhaps in some other sees, where bishops for long struggled to realize Tridentine provisions for episcopal supervision of this essential pastoral function. The revised Roman Ritual issued by Gregory XIII in 1584 had equally demanded the construction and use of confessional boxes, which had its effect in Rome itself, in the case of the hearing of the laity's confessions, and those of females above all, including those of nuns. Urban VIII's diocesan visitation at Rome, begun in 1624 and continued to 1632, produced a vast written report; while between 1636 and 1642 his brother, the Capuchin Cardinal, acted as substitute Cardinal Vicar, strengthening still further Barberini command of Rome.

CONCLAVES

The system by which a bishop was chosen for the Roman see was of course unique, for a papal conclave differed from the various methods by which bishops for other dioceses were selected. The papal conclaves throughout these two centuries were very often prolonged precisely because of the international, not local, considerations involved. The death of elderly popes relatively soon after their election could produce two conclaves within a short space of time, as in 1590 and again in 1605. Even when a pontificate was fairly brief, however, its achievements could be on occasion most important, as with the reform of conclave procedure itself, among other dramatic policies successfully pursued by Gregory XV in his period as pope from 1621 to 1623. Indeed, the importance of the achievements of each pope is not necessarily reflected by the length of his pontificate. Among the popes whose policies produced most obviously major results might be numbered Pius IV (1559–65), Pius V (1566–72), Sixtus V (1585–90), Clement VIII (1592–1605), only the last of whom had an obvious advantage in terms of years as pope. But the list could continue with the long pontificates of Paul V (1605–21) and Urban VIII (1623–44), but could not, as has been seen, omit the few years of Gregory XV.

Both Alexander VII (1655–67) and Innocent XI (1676–89) enjoyed moderately extended periods as pope, while the long pontificate of Clement XI (1700–21) was rather more of a valiant struggle against almost insuperable difficulties caused by war in Europe and its destructive effects in Italy. Benedict XIV was able to exercise his wit and wisdom over a long period in less overwhelmingly unpropitious circumstances, from 1740 to 1758, though the previous, much shorter pontificate of Benedict XIII (1724–30) was arguably more startlingly innovative. Clement XIII attempted to maintain resistance to unwelcome but severe political pressure, with mixed results, throughout the period 1758–69. But Clement XIV succumbed to the intensification of those pressures within the short space of years between 1769 and 1774. By 1789 Pius VI had accumulated considerable experience of the difficulties facing the papacy, since his election in 1775, though he was not to be released from his subsequent tribulations until his death in 1799.

Most of the popes during these two centuries lived to a fairly advanced age, despite in rare cases prolonged years of decrepit health. Considering the mature years of most of them at election as pope, however, the record of physical vigour is impressive. For though the caution of the electing cardinals and the pressures brought to bear by political interests commonly combined to regard an aged rather than a relatively youthful pope as the safest choice, since even the most unwelcome policies might then prove short lived, the latter expectation was not necessarily fulfilled. Urban VIII's election nevertheless came as a surprise not least because of his unusual youth, in relative terms: he was under sixty.

Foreign pressure

Of all these conclaves, it was arguably the first of 1605 which in most dramatic form demonstrated the circumstances in which capable cardinals failed to be made pope. The exercise of an effective veto, the so-called *exclusiva*, was attempted on many occasions, however, by the Catholic rulers of Europe during this period, and in the earlier part of it particularly by Spain. Such intervention by the representatives of Spanish interests, cardinals within a conclave as well as ambassadors awaiting its deliberations without, was the more easy to achieve before the reform of conclave procedure made by Gregory XV, as the conclave of 1592 in which Clement VIII was elected had already demonstrated, for instance. In the first conclave of 1605 the abilities of Cardinal Baronius, the Oratorian adviser of the deceased Clement, were thought by many, even if not by Baronius himself, to make him eminently worthy of the succession. But Spanish intervention ensured that his election did not take place. This was formerly thought to reflect a general Spanish hostility, because of Baronius's defence of ecclesiastical rights wherever he saw them infringed, even if in areas of Spanish rule, and above all his part in persuading Clement VIII finally to reverse papal policy and accept the reconciliation of Henri IV as Catholic ruler of France, in the face of Spanish resistance.

But more recent re-examination of the precise circumstances at the time of the conclave has suggested that the Spanish exclusion was rather more a specific reaction to the publication by Baronius of his attack on the *Monarchia Sicula*, the legatine control of the Church in Sicily claimed by the Spanish monarchs as rulers of the island. That was indeed clearly crucial, though the entire correspondence of the Spanish Court and its Roman representatives concerning the events of the first conclave of 1605 and the alleged intentions of Baronius were he to have become pope reveal a wider sensitivity to other aspects of the cardinal's relations with Spanish power as well. It was similarly for a whole series of reasons involving Church–State relations in Spanish-ruled territory, and the advocacy in the end of the reconciliation of Henri IV, and not only as a supporter of Baronius, in particular during that conclave, that another cardinal, Federico Borromeo, came to be viewed by Spain as an unacceptable candidate for the papacy, if proposed.[12] In the conclave of 1623 in which

---

12 A.D. Wright, 'Federico Borromeo and Baronius', in *Baronio Storico e la Controriforma*, ed. R. De Maio (Sora 1982), pp. 167–82.

Urban VIII was elected, Spain made it clear that Federico, the archbishop of Spanish-ruled Milan, could not be accepted. The revision of conclave procedure ordered by Urban's predecessor, Gregory XV, with the approbation of Borromeo, who was a friend of the Ludovisi as well as sharing scholarly interests with Maffeo Barberini, the eventual beneficiary, had made such intervention less easy but still not impossible; but Spanish resentment of the revision and its supporters was thus also involved.

The Catholic European powers continued to apply pressure to the work of the cardinals in conclave throughout these centuries, in any case, and effective exclusions of otherwise possible candidates were still achieved. This state of affairs in practice was thus distinct from the explicit debate about formal rights to exercise an *exclusiva*, as conducted by Spanish theorists in the later sixteenth century for example. It was also different from attempts by European rulers, with much less evident success during the conclaves of this period, to exercise an effective *inclusiva*, to the extent of securing positively the election of one particular candidate. More common and arguably more productive of a desired result was the influence used, by means of favoured and confidential cardinals within the conclave, to make known which handful of candidates would be acceptable to a given government, and even to indicate an order of preference. The latter, even so, did not necessarily secure the election of the most favoured candidate. For the competing wishes of rival European powers could obviously hinder or at any rate complicate such operations. When in the eighteenth century such pressure became more intense and more difficult to resist as the century progressed, this was chiefly because of the coincidence of governmental wishes in the matter of papal policy towards the Jesuits. Such correspondence of demands, aiming at the suppression of the Society, was beyond doubt of considerable effect in the emergence of the unfortunate Clement XIV.

Habsburg policy had earlier complicated the conclave which elected Gregory XV, before his own reform of conclave procedure, for a commission of cardinals had been forced to devise a special form of warning of the imminent conclave for Cardinal Klesl, reflecting their awareness that he could not in fact attend, having been imprisoned by the Austro-Imperial Habsburgs, just as Cardinal Lerma was for a while imprisoned by the Spanish monarchy.[13] Gregory's own reform of conclave procedure, following considerations put forward not only under Clement VIII but also under Innocent IX, Leo XI and Paul V, included one feature with a wider impact: that all cardinals participating in a conclave must have received at least deacon's orders. Thus it was intended that to exercise this crucial electoral role the participating cardinals should henceforth be in fact and not just in theory of at least the status implied by membership of the third and lowest tier within the college, that of the Cardinal Deacons.

---

13 B.A.V.: MSS Barberiniani Latini 5538: 13 Jan. 1622; Ferrajoli 142, fos 174v–183r: 1621.

Length of conclave

That conclaves could often be prolonged affairs is not surprising given the importance of competing political interests. The very swift conclave of 1572, in which Gregory XIII was elected in only a couple of days, represented a high-water mark of Spanish dominance. A relatively swift conclave also elected Sixtus V in 1585, even if in the event Spanish expectations of his policies were not so perfectly fulfilled. But though Spanish influence remained predominant, the succeeding conclaves were more protracted, although Innocent IX was quite quickly elected in 1591. After his brief pontificate the conclave which elected Clement VIII was only moderately extended, but was noted for the sharp division of the electors and the difficulty which Spanish policy encountered in pursuing its original intentions. The two conclaves of 1605 were, as has been seen, contentious enough, but were also of reasonably confined duration.

The reform of conclave procedure ordered by Gregory XV was thus not aimed directly at reducing the length of conclaves but rather at the more important goal of limiting the opportunities for disruptive political intervention and, above all, at removing as far as possible any doubt as to method and result of election, to avoid the danger of schism. This clarification in a sense benefited Urban VIII, despite a moment of procedural uncertainty in the counting of votes in the scrutiny which finally elected him. Such improvement was not immediately obvious in terms of the length at least of the next conclave, since it took over five weeks to elect Innocent X. Even this looked brief, however, compared with the nearly three months' duration of the conclave required to elect Alexander VII, in the context of Catholic Europe divided still, even after the Peace of Westphalia, by the continued Franco-Spanish war. The succeeding conclave from which emerged Clement IX was less extended, but the following one in which Clement X was elected was once again of more than four months' length. Innocent XI was elected in a conclave of about two months' duration, but Alexander VIII became pope after a conclave of only a little over a month.

The century concluded nevertheless with the longest conclave of all, for it took five months to elect Innocent XII, reflecting the political rivalries in Catholic Europe which were to culminate eventually, at the pope's death, in the war over the Spanish Succession. The conclave of 1700, lasting over a month, was itself in the end encouraged to a conclusion, in the election of Clement XI, by the news of the death of Charles II, the last of the Spanish Habsburg line. The election of Innocent XIII in 1721 was again reasonably swift, achieved in little over a month. But it took more like two months, once again, for Benedict XIII to be elected, and just over four months for the election of Clement XII. This trend continued when it required six months to elect Benedict XIV. Only with the election of Clement XIII in 1758 was this reduced, to a conclave of more like one month.

It was the contentious question of the fate of the Jesuits that dominated the next conclave, and so it is not surprising that a conclave of three months produced Clement XIV. In the subsequent confusion and recriminations following this unhappy pope's death, one of the longest conclaves once again concluded the pontificates of a century, when it took four and a half months to elect Pius VI. At all times, of course, other factors delayed the work of conclaves. The state of communications during this period did little to improve the speed with which cardinals not resident in Rome, whether elsewhere in Italy or further afield in Europe, could make their way to join a conclave. In any case news of a pope's death had first to reach them and then, in the case of cardinals resident in France or Spain, for example, a political decision normally governed whether they should make the journey and exert their influence personally in the interests of the ruler. The care with which Spain from the later sixteenth century onwards, and also other European Catholic powers subsequently, ensured in or near Rome (at Naples for example in the Spanish case) a sufficient presence of cardinals who could vote in even the most unexpected of conclaves was of course logical.

Composition of the conclave

The number of cardinals participating in a conclave was therefore variable, quite apart from those not uncommon occasions when the combination of age, excitement, heat and overcrowded conclave quarters reduced that number in the course of the conclave itself. Indeed, one of the factors which occasionally induced a prolonged conclave finally to reach a conclusion, over and above the more common fear of popular disorder and violence in Rome increasing the longer the see remained vacant, was an outbreak of illness within the conclave itself. This was particularly a risk during the long summer months, when an epidemic in Rome might reach the crowded confines of the conclave itself. The potential number of electors was not even constant however, even allowing for cardinals who did not reach Rome in time or did not attempt the journey at all. For though Sixtus V had fixed the size of the college of cardinals, and his maximum of seventy members was respected by all his successors during this period, the death of cardinals during a pontificate might reduce the number of electors still alive at the next conclave by either a small or large factor. This was so not least because pressure from rival European powers for the creation of prelates to represent their interests as cardinals, with a future conclave in mind above all, grew rather than diminished during these two centuries.

But the consequent attempt of some popes to resist such pressure, either because warmly recommended candidates were patently unsuitable or because of the fear that to accommodate the demands of one ruler would ruin papal relations with rival governments, meant that at such a pope's death the college might be quite depleted. The number of cardinals in fact participating in a conclave thus varied, the figures involved moving from a high sixty-one to fifty-nine, fifty-two, fifty-four, fifty-six and eventually back to sixty-five over a given period, for example. But numbers alone were not the only important

aspect of the composition of a conclave. A short pontificate might be followed by a conclave in which the division of the electors reflected, in addition
to other, often political factors, the high number of previous pontificates
during which the various electors had first been made cardinal. Whereas at the
death of a long-lived pope, the succeeding conclave could include a considerable proportion of electors who owed their creation as cardinals to the one,
deceased pope. Thus in the case of the conclave which elected Alexander VIII
in 1689, forty-three cardinals entitled to vote had been elevated to the college
during the long pontificate of his predecessor, Innocent XI.

In the eighteenth century the number of cardinals participating in a conclave
began by fluctuating from fifty-eight to fifty-five and fifty-three. But the final
scrutiny in a smaller conclave could at least potentially more easily reach the
ideal unanimity (less the one vote of the successful candidate himself), as
demonstrated in the conclaves which elected Benedict XIII and Clement XII,
long though both were. At the death of Benedict XIV only fifty-five cardinals
were even potentially able to vote, and the election of Clement XIII was
relatively swiftly achieved in a conclave in which only forty odd cardinals
participated in fact. The much debated conclave in which Clement XIV was
elected was prolonged for other reasons, as has been noted, but in the end
unanimity (in the sense remarked above) was, for better or worse, achieved in
a conclave not very much larger. Nor did a very similar number of electors
produce a speedy result in the case of Pius VI.

THE POPES' BACKGROUND

Choice of name

During the long evolution from Pius IV and Pius V to Pius VI, the choice of
name by the cardinals elected pope showed only a limited range of variation.
After Paul V no other pope until modern times took the name, but during the
period in question here there was equally no successor of the same chosen
name as Urban VIII, nor in the case of Sixtus V. Of the ancient traditional
names taken by popes, Gregory, Alexander and, in one case, Leo, were all represented during this period. Innocent occurred five times, Benedict twice, and
Clement most commonly, in seven pontificates. The reason for such choices
is often instructive. In some cases veneration for a predecessor of the same
name was implied, or a determination to continue an identifiable papal policy.

Such continuity of policy was not always marked by choice of name however. Cardinal Albani succeeded Innocent XII as Clement XI, though determined to follow the reform programme, specifically against nepotism, on which
he had advised his predecessor. Other determining factors included homage
to a previous pope with whom a newly elected one had closely worked or by
whom he had been particularly favoured. This was particularly true for a
previous pope who had first created his eventual successor a cardinal. The

naming of Benedict XIII also resolved beyond any doubt that the prelate who had employed that title at the beginning of the fifteenth century had been an anti-pope, and not truly in the papal succession.

Age of popes

While most popes of the period were indeed sixty or over at the time of their election, Gregory XIV was only in his mid-fifties, yet his pontificate was of only a few months. When this was followed by the even briefer pontificate of Innocent IX, who was over seventy, a total of four conclaves occurred between 1590 and 1592, starting with the election of Urban VII at the age of almost seventy, who did not live long enough even to be crowned. This sequence changed with the election of Clement VIII, who was under sixty, but threatened to recur when his successor Leo XI, who was seventy, lived only a few days beyond his coronation. The second conclave of 1605 produced Paul V and his longer pontificate, begun when he was in his mid-fifties. This same alternation was suggested by the election of the short-lived Gregory XV who was over sixty and the long subsequent pontificate of the younger Urban VIII. It repeated once more with Innocent X who was over sixty, followed by Alexander VII who was under sixty at election. It was interrupted when the over-sixty Clement IX was succeeded by the octogenarian Clement X, who nevertheless lived for six years as pope, before Innocent XI was elected in his mid-sixties.

The succeeding octogenarian Alexander VIII was indeed short-lived, but though Innocent XII was himself seventy-six at election he lived until he was eighty-five. The new century returned, as a result of the conclave of 1700, to a younger pope, for Clement XI was only a little over fifty at election. His long pontificate gave way, however, to the succession of Innocent XIII who was over sixty and did not enjoy good health as pope, and Benedict XIII, who was over seventy at election. Similarly, Clement XII was nearly eighty at election, and though his pontificate lasted a decade it was one in which the pope's capability was seriously limited, since by 1732 he was blind, though he never became mentally incapacitated. Benedict XIV's long and active pontificate, by contrast, began when he was in his mid-sixties and Clement XIII was only just entering his sixties at election. Clement XIV was again elected when a cardinal in his mid-sixties, though his final illness, as he approached seventy, inspired rumours that the Society of Jesus, which he had suppressed, had poisoned him. A relatively youthful choice brought the last pope of the century to the papal throne, for Cardinal Braschi was not yet sixty when he became pope.

Popes from religious orders

Of the cardinals elevated during this period to the papacy who were members of a religious order, not secular clerics, examples can be found both early and late. The friars include the Franciscan Peretti, Pope Sixtus V from 1585 and the Franciscan Conventual Ganganelli, Pope Clement XIV from 1769, as well as the Dominican Orsini, Pope Benedict XIII (1724–30) earlier in the eighteenth century. But the Dominicans had already provided Ghislieri, Pius V (1566–72). The preponderance of seculars as opposed to regulars who became pope during these centuries is thus clear, but the previous experience of these non-regular cardinals was far from uniform. The minority of the popes who were mendicants, it is true, stood a better chance of theological expertise, yet, as has been noted, Orsini's dedication to pastoral work as archbishop of Benevento was his most outstanding characteristic. The pastoral positions held by some of this majority of non-regulars before their election as pope, on the other hand, may also be remembered, as in the cases of Gregory XV, Benedict XIV, or Pope Clement XIII. The canonist training of many of this majority of the popes did not impede their appreciation of the pastoral priorities of ecclesiastical reform, furthermore, as the case of Clement VIII eminently suggests.

Diplomatic expertise did not limit the activity of Alexander VII within the diocese of Rome either, as has already been noted in Chapter 1 with reference to his reform of the University of Rome. The influential experience of those clerics who were particularly associated in their previous career with the Holy Office could be seen as having stood the popes of the later seventeenth century in a relatively better position for dealing with the endless problem of Jansenism: this would apply to Cardinal Altieri, Pope Clement X (1670–76), and Ottoboni, Pope Alexander VIII (1689–91), as well as Pamfili, Pope Innocent X (1644–55).[14]

Without exception, the popes of these centuries were Italian, but again the variety of peninsular origins is evident. Those Medici from whom Pius IV sprang were Lombard, but the Aldobrandini family of Clement VIII was of Florentine origin. The Buoncompagni of Gregory XIII and Sfondrati of Gregory XIV were from central or Northern Italy but the Pignatelli of Innocent XII (1691–1700) were a noble Neapolitan family. The Ludovisi family of Gregory XV, like the Lambertini of Benedict XIV, were natives of Bologna, within the papal states; but Rezzonico, Pope Clement XIII, was a native of the Venetian Republic.

In terms of purely ecclesiastical eminence, however, the cardinals who were oldest at the time of their election as pope might stand in the highest dignity, because of the tradition of reserving for those members of the college of cardinals who were the most senior, essentially by date of creation, the Suburbicarian Sees of the Cardinal Bishops. These could be enjoyed, if a senior cardinal exercised his option to accept one when a vacancy occurred, in practice whether or not he also held a see elsewhere, since such a position, if occupied, was not necessarily or immediately relinquished. Thus the aged Leo XI, elected in the first conclave of 1605, was not only a Medici of the famous

14 G. Signorotto, *Inquisitori e mistici nel Seicento italiano. L'eresia di Santa Pelagia* (Bologna 1989).

Florentine family, and hence a relation of Henri IV's queen consort, but also Cardinal Bishop of Palestrina, having previously become Cardinal Bishop of Albano. For the Cardinal Bishops often acquired a new Suburbicarian See as their seniority increased, the most eminent of the Sees, that of Ostia, indeed conveying the right to use the pallium.

Such internal practices in the college of cardinals, however, were not what motivated the reaction of Catholic rulers to the prospective election of different candidates. The zealously pastoral Cardinal Valier was regarded by the ministers of the Spanish monarch as in any case axiomatically unacceptable, since as a Venetian he was regarded as favouring Henri IV, whose reconciliation he did indeed urge Clement VIII to accept. This was similar to the raging alarm of representatives of the Spanish interest that even in the second conclave of 1605 the name of Baronius might make some progress.[15]

POPES' MEMORIALS

The death of each pope during these two centuries raised the question of the burial place of a bishop of Rome. The habitual use of the Quirinal Palace as a papal residence for at least a good part of the year during this period meant that the parish priests of the church below the palace, SS. Vincenzo ed Anastasio, acquired certain rights, and a tradition begun by Sixtus V and continued beyond this period led to the crypt burial of the hearts of popes, removed in the embalming process, at this church. A monument erected there by Benedict XIV reflects the singular distinction accorded to this parish church of the popes. But not all popes left this part of their mortal bodies there, for in any case not all died at the Quirinal. Despite the Lateran's status as the cathedral of Rome, the popes of this period were not in the habit of being buried there, unlike bishops of other sees who were often buried in their own cathedrals. Pius V, devoted to the Madonna, was eventually buried at another papal basilica, S. Maria Maggiore. Innocent X, who created the Baroque church of S. Agnese in Piazza Navona, not least as a monument to his family's greatness, was fittingly buried there, although he was one of the popes who had troubled to restore and embellish his cathedral as bishop of Rome. The unfortunate Clement XIV, having suppressed the Jesuits, found burial at the church of his own order, the Franciscan Conventuals, SS. Apostoli.

Monuments

The monuments erected to popes, as in that case, might mark the tomb itself. But the papal monuments of this period had a wider significance, as with the splendid monument to the patron of the Jesuits, Gregory XV, subsequently erected in the newly built church of the Society adjacent to the Collegio Romano, S. Ignazio, a church itself the creation of his nephew, Cardinal

15 A.G.S.: Estado: Roma: Leg. 1870: Nov. 1590.

Ludovisi. That a Jesuit education did not necessarily produce a constant affection to the Society was of course demonstrated by Urban VIII, who took care to secure for his own monument in St Peter's one of the two most conspicuous and honoured locations, rearranging other papal monuments to accord that of one favoured or possibly envied predecessor the corresponding location, opposite Urban's. Many popes, or subsequently their nephews or relatives, saw St Peter's as the natural location for a papal monument, in proximity to the traditional shrine of the Prince of the Apostles and first bishop of Rome. Even this was not universal custom, however, for other connections of family or patronage, such as the location of an existing family chapel, might intervene. Thus Urban VII, after his brief pontificate, was commemorated by a monument in the chief Dominican church of S. Maria sopra Minerva. Clement VIII was memorialized by statues in S. Maria sopra Minerva as well as in S. Maria Maggiore, but the papal cathedral of St John Lateran also acquired a sculptural celebration of his achievements.

Leo XI had a brief pontificate but achieved lasting fame in a monument in St Peter's. Monuments to Alexander VII, Innocent XI and Clement XIII were also placed there, while that of Pius VI was eventually, after the tribulations and removals of the pope and his body in death as well as in life, given a conspicuous place of honour there, in front of the tomb of St Peter beneath the papal altar. The monument of Innocent XII, also in St Peter's, faithfully records his status as the last pope of this period to wear moustache and beard, by his date small, before the pontificates of his clean-shaven successors. The learned controversy about the secular clergy's right to wear a beard, or alternatively their duty to be clean-shaven, conducted in the later sixteenth century among Catholic prelates, thus had a belated reflection. One later pope, within these two centuries, to receive a memorial in the Roman cathedral of the Lateran was Clement XII, who was buried there in the family chapel he had founded. The subjects represented on the papal monuments of this period suggest their wider significance for the history of the popes as more than bishops of Rome alone, however; reflecting not only locally visible virtues, such as Charity, but also events beyond Rome or beyond Italy in which a pope had attempted or indeed managed to play a conspicuous part.

Canonizations

The positive judgement passed by one pope on a predecessor, within this period, is also worth attention, on the other hand, as a further indication of the view of the papal office held by the bishops of Rome. Pius V was beatified by Clement X in 1672 and canonized by Clement XI in 1712. Innocent XI however, though considered for beatification as early as 1714, while his opponent Louis XIV was still alive, was, in death as in life, a victim of accusations that he was favourable to Jansenism. His cause was not continued after the pontificate of Benedict XIV, and only more successfully resumed in the twentieth century. It was, then, during the period in question here, not the pastoral work of Innocent on the local stage of the Rome diocese that was precisely the stumbling-block.

Canonizations successfully made by popes in this period included those, in the pontificate of Gregory XV, of the Jesuit saints Ignatius Loyola and Francis Xavier, as well as the virtual founder of the Roman Oratorians, Philip Neri, in addition to St Teresa of Avila, a female saint of a more than Spanish fame. The canonization by Paul V, on the other hand, of St Francesca Romana involved very much a saint for the city and diocese of Rome. But his canonization of St Charles Borromeo was also important as elevating a model of the resident, reforming diocesan bishop of the post-Conciliar Church. This was understood by other zealous bishops, not only in Italy but beyond, from Spain and Portugal to France and Poland, however much the official iconography established at the canonization ceremony represented Charles as cardinal and an example of penitential austerity. Popular reception of his cult, which was rapid and widespread, in any case concentrated on yet another aspect of the saint, his role as an additional protector against plague, such as that which affected large parts of Italy once again in 1630–31 for example.

The public image of popes

The degree of approval given by Clement XIII to the cult of the Sacred Heart of Jesus, after long papal caution in respect of this devotion, was taken by contemporaries, not incorrectly, to signify some sympathy for the Jesuits as the prolonged doctrinal campaigns of their critics became subsumed in overtly political pressure from their enemies in Catholic states. But the less than positive view which some popes held of the Society of Jesus had at times recurred, and perhaps contributed to the opposition of Innocent XI to laxist positions allegedly held by some Jesuit theologians, despite the concern of the Society's superiors from a much earlier date to prevent the advance of such teachings which might harm its reputation. The early eighteenth-century evolution of papal opposition to the innovatory missionary methods practised by Jesuits in China was certainly affected by such reserve, as in the case of Innocent XIII. By the end of Benedict XIV's pontificate, however, the initiative against the Jesuits was clearly being led by Catholic secular governments, in the first instance that of Portugal, to which Benedict had to begin a papal response. After Clement XIII's resistance to demands for suppression it was no accident that Clement XIV acceded not only to the demand for the Society's suppression but also, significantly, to the Erastian insistence of Catholic rulers that the annual publication of the post-Tridentine form of the Bull *In Coena Domini* be abandoned.

The last pope of the period in question here, Pius VI, was nevertheless a former pupil of the Jesuits; though he was constrained by the Catholic powers of pre-Revolutionary Europe not to reverse the suppression of the Society. The bishop he first approved for the newly independent American Catholics, beyond the reach of the European powers in this respect at least, was, however, a former Jesuit. But in Rome itself, by the end of the seventeenth century and into the eighteenth century, there were occasional suggestions that aspects of Jansenism had found favour at the papal Court and among Roman clerics, on a basis that went beyond mere anti-Jesuit positions. Members of the Roman Oratory, by the later eighteenth century, were believed to be affected. The anti-Jesuit suspicions of Innocent XI led him to be considered pro-Jansenist by some, though his sympathies for Quietists were more certain, unlike the antagonism to the latter of Cardinals Albizzi and Ottoboni, subsequently Pope Alexander VIII.

The reality of popes' experience

While earlier popes also included those with experience of Holy Office affairs, such as Innocent X, as well as Paul V, it is noteworthy that the latter had also been Cardinal Vicar of Rome. A pope's previous experience might also have brought him in one sense even closer to the affairs of a predecessor: Sixtus V had been a close collaborator with Pius V in the latter's attention to Inquisition business. The survey of religious houses in Italy ordered by Innocent X himself, which was to lead to the suppression of some which were found to be incapable of maintaining an adequate existence, did not exclude those in Rome. The more pro-Jesuit attitude of Alexander VII encouraged his negotiations with the Venetian Republic, which was increasingly anxious about the defence of Crete, for the readmission to Republican territory of the Jesuits, who were expelled at the time of Paul V's Interdict from the Venetian state. Though Clement IX's agreement to the suppression of certain other religious houses at Venice represented a continuity with Innocent X's policies, his own most important previous experience in Rome itself had been not as Cardinal Vicar but as papal governor. Clement IX's aid to the Venetians did not in the end save Crete from Turkish conquest, but Venetian help contributed to the election of a native Roman, Altieri, as his successor, Clement X.

Papal intervention could at any time be far-reaching, as religious orders found with regard to their Roman houses, particularly under Clement VIII. His exasperation with the perpetual troubles which seemed to afflict the Society of Jesus during his pontificate, both in Spain and more universally, led to his personal visit in 1594 to the Jesuits' chief house in Rome, to deliver a warning that the Society should remedy its alleged abuses before he himself took action. The Jesuits of *Il Gesù* were to encounter a similar sense of papal displeasure in 1632, when their great patron Cardinal Ludovisi was ordered by Urban VIII to leave Rome and take up residence in his archbishopric of Bologna. Ludovisi's ostentatious visit to the Jesuit house before his retirement from Rome was perhaps of ambiguous help to the Society, associated in Urban's eyes with the disgraced nephew of his own predecessor, but in any case Ludovisi was soon to be dead. Once again Spanish problems had troubled papal–Jesuit relations, however, since the nephew of Urban's pro-

Jesuit predecessor was believed to have supported the outburst of the Spanish Cardinal Borgia against the pope.

PASTORAL TRADITION

Continuity despite differences of policy

Clement VIII had been one of the post-Conciliar popes who made general orders to bishops unnecessarily present in Rome to leave the city and take up residence in their sees. Clement's dissatisfaction with the Jesuits, however, was once again evident towards the end of his pontificate, when in 1604 he removed the direction of the Greek College in Rome, designed to train Greek-rite priests loyal to Roman authority, from the Society, to which it had previously been entrusted. The pro-Jesuit Ludovisi, subsequently Gregory XV, on the other hand, had worked in the service of the Roman diocese from the beginning of his career as a young priest, before he became archbishop of Bologna. Under Clement VIII, he had been one of the two Vicars heading the ecclesiastical courts, under the Cardinal Vicar, and in Paul V's pontificate, before his appointment to Bologna, he had had pastoral experience in the crucial role of vicegerent of the Roman Church. After 1619, release from diplomatic and other duties allowed him to reside in his Bolognese archbishopric, where he implemented reform, before appointing his nephew archbishop after his own election as pope. In Rome itself the pope and his Cardinal Nephew increased their charitable donations, especially in the food shortage and epidemic of 1621–22, when the pope also resumed Paul V's requests for Sicilian grain supplies.

The restoration of the direction of the Greek College in Rome to the Jesuits, in 1622, was a natural expression of Ludovisi policy, but was also followed by a papal order for the visitation of all the colleges in the city, including those training clerics to serve in various parts of the world. While Gregory's solemn reception in Rome of the Madonna of Victory, brought there from the Catholic triumph in Bohemia at the Battle of the White Mountain, was the prelude to the further embellishment and rededication of the Carmelite church near the Roman Charterhouse, the pope was also successful in acquiring for the Vatican the Palatine Library, transported from the war-torn Palatinate itself. Of the New Orders of the Counter-Reformation, the Theatines and their Roman church also continued to receive papal favour. The pope's nephew, Cardinal Ludovisi, gave assistance not only to Roman foundations for female orphans and ex-prostitutes, but also in particular to the poor in the parish of S. Lorenzo in Damaso, the church of which was within the walls of the Cancelleria, the official residence of the cardinal as Vice-Chancellor of the Church. The Roman Oratorians as well as the parish church of S. Lorenzo, and orders specializing in educational and hospital work in Rome, were also beneficiaries, as were ecclesiastical and charitable foundations in Bologna. Much of the cardinal's income from commendatory abbacies in Italy, belonging to older, monastic orders, was thus redirected to new purposes.

Pastoral response to political pressure

Urban VIII, prior to his election, had been as cardinal a patron of the Theatines in Rome too. Having been ordained priest at the time of his appointment to the essentially titular archbishopric of Nazareth, he was subsequently sufficiently free of other major duties between 1609 and 1611 to be able to reside in his new bishopric of Spoleto, where he held both a canonic visitation and a synod. As pope he participated in the final celebrations at Rome of the fall of La Rochelle, celebrating Mass at the 'national' church of S. Luigi dei Francesi, while his holding of a special Jubilee, in an otherwise non-Jubilee year, 1628, was intended to promote prayers for peace, as the spread of European warfare to Northern Italy continued to threaten. But the political pressure which Urban himself felt from Spain at this juncture and the potential danger to the papal states themselves led to his Interdict on the Spanish 'national' church in Rome, S. Giacomo degli Spagnoli, after the Spanish ambassador had resisted a canonic visitation of the church, whose administrator was accordingly excommunicated. The renewal of the Jubilee in 1629, however, marked the intensification of disasters in Italy, as troop movements in the North led to food shortages which in turn contributed to the spread of the epidemic affecting large parts of the peninsula in 1630–31. The prospect of peace, in Italy at least, nevertheless allowed the pope public celebration in Rome, in a thanksgiving Mass.

The renewed need for prayers for peace, however, led to the papal order for the exceptional suspension of the Carnival in Rome immediately afterwards, as the cost of relieving famine and epidemic rose. Another extraordinary Jubilee was understandably held in 1631 instead, in the ceremonies of which Urban took part. The constant need for prayers in this conjuncture resulted in the grant of special indulgences, particularly in connection with a celebration of the Forty Hours' Devotion at S. Maria della Vittoria, in which the pope himself took part, in 1632. The continued pressure on the pope, from the rival powers of France and the Habsburgs, ensured that this was not the end either of special Jubilees nor of public celebration by the pope of select Catholic victories in the Empire. Yet Urban VIII's pontificate had begun with personal papal visitation of the basilicas of the Lateran, St Peter's, and St Paul Outside the Walls; and then and subsequently the Cardinal Priests in their Titular Churches of the city and the Cardinal Bishops in their Suburbicarian Sees were urged to supervise their churches and exercise their duties in person. This had results in the canonic visitation of the Suburbicarian See of Porto in 1626, the visitation of his Titular Church of S. Lorenzo in Damaso by Cardinal Ludovisi in 1625, and, as late as 1640, the visitation by an episcopal delegate of Cardinal Antonio Barberini of his commendatory abbey of Subiaco. The discipline of the clergy, including the regulars, in Rome was reinforced, particularly in the hearing of confessions and the receipt of Mass stipends, from the start of the pontificate too. The Roman Seminary also received a visitation, and in 1636 a special seminary was additionally created at St Peter's to train clerics to serve in that basilica.

After his election, the pope announced a Jubilee for 1625 in which he and his nephew made particular provision for the charitable reception and housing of pilgrims, while Cardinal Ludovisi also contributed to the provision of charity in the city, for the Italians and non-Italians who visited Rome on that occasion. It was also Urban who admitted Allegri, the composer of the famous setting of the *Miserere*, to the papal choir in 1629. The printing of further, corrected issues of the revised Breviary, published in 1631, was entrusted to a Roman firm, in the attempt to maintain uniformity and accuracy of the text. In the annual Corpus Christi procession in Rome, Urban himself carried the monstrance, on foot, until 1639, after which he was borne behind it. At that time, despite events earlier in the pontificate, the pope and Cardinal Antonio Barberini were received at the Jesuits' chief Roman church of *Il Gesù*, during the conspicuous celebrations of the first century of the Society, and the cardinal contributed to the cost of the display and the associated distribution of alms. The pope's lay nephew, Taddeo, paid for subsequent celebrations at the Roman church of S. Ignazio, next to the Jesuit Collegio Romano, to which Urban himself also paid a visit in 1640. The innovative attempt of the English Catholic, Mary Ward, to extend the provision of female education, allowed for a while in the Rome of Gregory XV, was however brought to a halt in the city early in Urban's pontificate. In that context, her degree of association with the ideals of the Jesuits had certainly not helped her, given all the other reasons for male clerical reserve towards her endeavour, despite a later period of years during which she resumed her work in Rome under Urban's supervision.

Papal severity and pastoral provision

The attention given by the pope to the business of the Holy Office was recognized not least by the repairs made to its headquarters in 1626. The condemnation and recantation in 1635 of a group of Romans allegedly involved in necromancy among other things, during Urban's campaign against forms of judicial astrology which he regarded as threatening to him, demonstrated his interpretation of pastoral care as embracing the campaign against magic or witchcraft begun by his predecessor, Gregory XV. Even so, such inquisitorial concern did not exclude adherence to canon law, which prescribed the distinction between ecclesiastical and secular authority in the execution of sentence on condemned laity as well as clerics. Despite the momentary cloud to the reputation of the church of S. Carlo al Corso cast by the activities of this group, that church had however already been honoured by its elevation as an extra Titular Church, among those held by cardinals, in 1627. The number of 'national' churches in the city was similarly increased in 1633, when a church was made over as that of the natives of Lucca in Rome, though this barely helped to resolve the jurisdictional conflict between the papacy and that Republic, which recalled the conflicts between Paul V and various Italian Republics, including Lucca.

Diplomatic restoration of the pastoral ideal

The more diplomatic skills shown by Cardinal Chigi during the negotiations leading to the Peace of Westphalia, and his tact in the very difficult
task subsequently of helping to manage papal policy during the later part of
Innocent X's pontificate, were the great qualifications for his election as pope
on Innocent's death. But he had also nominally had responsibility for the
South Italian see of Nardò, and then held the bishopric of Imola, before his
election to the papacy, and his continuation of the programme of visitation
of the Rome diocese. For despite the scandal, already mentioned, caused by
aspects of Innocent X's pontificate, a more pious example in Rome had been
set by the pope himself and cardinals during the Jubilee of 1650. Some cardinals were prevailed on to preach in person to the fashionable congregations
at S. Marcello. The pope participated in public assistance to the pilgrims, who
came in good numbers still, despite the continuing European warfare between
France and Spain, though such hostility was on occasion reflected among the
Italian confraternities, from different states of the peninsula, which visited
Rome as in previous Jubilees. The usual effect of the Jubilee crowds, of producing price rises in Rome, contributed to the papal decision to provide a
hospice in the borgo for impoverished bishops who came to Rome for the
Jubilee. The Roman archconfraternities were another channel through which
the assistance to pilgrims was organized, which represented an outlay offset-
ting gains made in terms of increased trade, within the economy of the city.
Clement IX began his pontificate in 1667 by completing the late Alexander
VII's plans for the permanent housing of the Banco di S. Spirito, Rome's first
public bank, founded by Paul V in 1605, for Chigi had extended many of the
public and charitable works of the earlier Sienese pope, not least at the related
Hospital of S. Spirito.

The triumph of the pastoral tradition

For the Jubilee of 1675 Clement X renewed papal attention to grain supplies
for the crowded city and assistance for pilgrims. His general contributions to
charitable work in Rome, including intervention in the working of the *Monte
di Pietà*, as well as his patronage of improvements to the structure and décor
of basilicas and churches in the city, reflected his pastoral interests, as did his
care for Camerino where he had formerly been bishop. This was also demonstrated by his choice of an excellent Cardinal Vicar, Cardinal Carpegna. The
pastorally minded Innocent XI had similarly had previous experience as bishop
of Novara, had not held diplomatic appointments nor ever been outside the
Italian peninsula. But his scrupulous conscience, which critics saw as pro-
Jansenist, meant that he celebrated private Mass, as opposed to hearing Mass,
only once a week. Such rigorist leanings led to his prohibition of plays staged
at seminaries in the city during Carnival, but it was economic difficulties in
the papal states rather than just a quasi-Jansenist view on usury which caused

his reduction of the interest rate on the *monti* investments from 4 per cent to 3 per cent. The Turkish threat to Vienna was the context for the special Jubilee to encourage intercessions in 1683.

The relief of that city was celebrated according to orders issued by the Cardinal Vicar, but popular disorder generated by these festivities required the intervention of the other arm of papal authority, that of the Cardinal Governor of Rome. The celebrations of the relief of Buda in 1686, perhaps with this in mind, included prominent papal distribution of alms to the poor of Rome. But Roman assistance had also to follow the effects of earthquake which, as at other times, had damaged the papal enclave of Benevento. Innocent was also insistent that clerics in Rome should be properly dressed in soutane, and that the priests of the city should fulfil their preaching and catechizing duties. The necessity of catechism was recalled to parents also, while by papal provision parochial schooling was extended to benefit destitute girls. The catechizing of ignorant adults, including soldiers, was also addressed. The Franciscan convent of the Aracoeli was subjected to canonic visitation, conducted by the rigorist Cardinal Gregorio Barbarigo, himself an exemplary pastor; and this was ordered without prior reference to the Cardinal Protector of the Franciscans, Cardinal Barberini.

The Cassinese Benedictines, who had removed from the papal basilica of St Paul Outside the Walls on the grounds of malarial infection, were ordered to return to monastic residence there, while a general prohibition, from 1677, of regulars residing in Rome outside the convents of their orders was stringently enforced despite resistance. In the same year a visitation of all the religious houses in the city was instituted. The urging of the pope that cardinals take a personal care of the life of their Titular Churches had some effect, in cases where cardinals renewed their encouragement of catechism classes. The rigour of the pope's own views was indicated by his rebuke to the zealous Cardinal Vicar, Carpegna, for having allowed a musical entertainment during Lent. The importance of the pastoral role of the pope was still emphasized towards the end of the pontificate by the elevation to the college of cardinals of the vicegerent of the Rome diocese, De Angelis. The excessive costs of canonization were also reduced, benefiting devotion rather than conspicuous display. In these ways the pontificate of Innocent XI certainly validated the view that it was a high-water mark in the demonstration of papal commitment to pastoral functions, even if after this the tradition of visitation in the Rome diocese (as opposed to Suburbicarian Sees on occasion) declined.

Innocent also returned to the priorities of immediately post-Conciliar popes of the later sixteenth century in his renewed charge to medical practitioners not to continue attendance on those who refused to receive the sacraments when ill. After these austerities, Alexander VIII relaxed the restrictions on public spectacles, and was one of the popes whose learned tastes encouraged academic activity in Rome, in the sense of learned societies of clerics and laymen, after the disfavour which even the scholarly Urban VIII had allowed to fall in mid-century on the Roman Academy of the Lincei. The Neapolitan

Innocent XII, a pupil in his time at the Collegio Romano, revived aspects of Innocent XI's policies, not least by his attempts to benefit the poor of Rome by innovatory experiments in welfare provision, drawing on French precedents in particular. His pontificate also saw a belated Roman application of the post-Tridentine campaign, pursued elsewhere from an earlier date, to secure ecclesiastical supervision of midwives in each see. The pastorally minded friar, Benedict XIII, though a member of the noble Orsini family, is remembered for his liturgical rigour, and for prohibiting the use of perukes by clerics, especially when performing liturgical functions, as well as reviving the attempt of Innocent XI to dictate more modest female fashions. Clement XII was similar to a number of popes in having studied at the Jesuits' Collegio Romano, but less commonly, he had not at first pursued a clearly clerical career. The pope who was to suppress the Jesuits, Clement XIV, had also had good relations with the Society during his years of study after becoming a friar; but his pontificate was marked not only by the suppression of the Society of Jesus but also by further campaigns of Catholic governments leading to more or less selective dissolutions of other religious houses too.

While disorder was a recurring danger at the death of each pope, and the most unpopular pontificates might end with popular manifestations designed to defame the memory of the deceased, all the popes while alive continued to be a potential target for pasquinades. Papal policing and censorship never permanently interrupted the tradition of critical wit expressed in the placards appearing on Pasquino's statue. In this way too the bishops of Rome had to perform their duties in a distinctive context, not commonly experienced by bishops elsewhere.[16] In Rome itself, however, as has been seen, exemplary devotion to the duties of bishop was neither unusual nor a new direction in the later seventeenth century. It could in fact be found with an impressive constancy throughout virtually all the pontificates of the period examined here.

16 Archivo de la Corona de Aragon, Barcelona: Consejo de Aragon: Leg. 686: 1614: placards against the archbishop of Valencia.

CHAPTER 3

Metropolitan initiative and provincial reaction

In the period from 1564 to the later seventeenth century Innocent XI arguably represents neither a unique case of devotion to pastoral duty as diocesan of Rome nor a new departure in papal policy in concentrating on such episcopal responsibilities. But his undoubted exemplary model was taken up by the first half of the eighteenth century and developed in a dramatic way which was at the time new, when Benedict XIII sought to extend the influence of this Roman model by reviving an explicit and discrete role of the bishop of the city as also metropolitan of the Roman province. As archbishop of Benevento, the see which he was to retain even as pope, Orsini had celebrated a series of diocesan synods, at a time when provincial councils, as called for by Tridentine regulation, had become a rarity, not least in Italy. Benedict's summons of a council of the Roman province, early in his pontificate, was thus a conscious alteration of recent tradition, and was assured of publicity because of its exceptional nature. But his explicit and repeated insistence that he was presiding as metropolitan, not as supreme pontiff, did not resolve profound difficulties in the attempted distinction of these roles.[1]

A PROVINCIAL COUNCIL

The formal sessions of the provincial council, held in the cathedral of St John Lateran in the spring of 1725, a Jubilee year, were dominated by the long interventions of the pope himself. Cardinals who were not bishops of Suburbicarian Sees nevertheless shared a jealous anxiety lest the decisions of the metropolitan with his provincial bishops should be seen to exclude the right of the college of cardinals to advise and be consulted by the pope in potentially all circumstances. This question of the relationship between the cardinals and the pope, even acting as metropolitan, was joined to a concern that the papal prerogatives should not be reduced for his successors by Benedict's actions. In formal terms, the latter point was met by the manner in which

1 L. Fiorani, *Il Concilio Romano del 1725* (Rome 1978).

65

cardinals and bishops eventually signed the decrees of the council. But the rumbling crisis over the exercise of papal authority in doctrinal dispute, still acute at this date as Jansenist opposition continued to the *Unigenitus* Constitution issued by Clement XI in 1713, ensured that a more substantial difficulty remained. For on the one hand, some Jansenists claimed a right to appeal to a future general council; and this was more topical than ever by 1725, following the schism of the Church of Utrecht. Yet on the other, the pope, even in a provincial council, could hardly in these circumstances appear to exercise a limited or non-binding authority if doctrine were touched on, although this would be difficult to avoid.

The definition of the Roman province was also a sensitive aspect of the council. In addition to the Suburbicarian Sees and other dioceses safely within the boundaries of the papal states, some archiepiscopal sees that were without their own provinces and other Immediately Subject dioceses to which summons were sent, lay of course beyond papal territory. In practice, problems arose not so much with sees situated in Northern Italy or outside the peninsula entirely, as with dioceses South of Rome included in the Kingdom of Naples. The long-standing sensitivity at Naples to supposedly unjustified exercise of papal suzerainty over the Kingdom had engendered regalist opposition to Roman directives, renewed ever since the Council of Trent.[2] The determination of the Austrian Habsburgs to demonstrate their hold on Naples, secured in the long struggle over the Spanish Succession, made such anti-Roman policy all the more active at this time. The fact that Benedict retained the see of the papal enclave of Benevento raised the level of suspicion at Vienna still further, quite overwhelming the more conciliatory efforts of the Neapolitan viceroy Cardinal Althann. Regalist challenge to the decrees of the council was given more opportunity because of widespread Jansenist allegations that reference in the published decrees to *Unigenitus* had been altered by Jesuit intrigue, so as to impose obedience to the constitution as a 'rule of faith', in place of the less stringent formula supposedly accepted in the council itself.

The republication of the provincial council's decrees by subsequent popes, by Benedict XIV in 1751 and by Clement XIII in 1764, represented a response to these wider allegations rather than to local conditions in the Roman province. To that extent it might be argued that the experiment of Benedict XIII in attempting to isolate and celebrate his pastoral role as metropolitan had undermined papal authority rather than enhancing it. Yet the positive interest of Benedict XIV himself in the synodical government of the Church reflected an undoubtedly pastoral view of his office. For him, the synodical activity of Benedict XIII at Benevento was worthy of comparison with that of St Charles Borromeo, the heroic post-Tridentine reformer of the Milanese diocese and province. The tradition of provincial as well as diocesan assemblies maintained at Milan both by Charles Borromeo and, into the seventeenth century,

---

2 A.G.S.: Secretaría Provincial: Napoles: Visitas y Diversos: Libros 39, 47, 48, 54, 60, 93, 94, 95, 96, 97, 98, 99, 100, 102, 104, 105, 106, 107, 108.

by Federico Borromeo subsequently had been in clear contrast to the absence of synods at Rome itself. Bologna too, under Gabriele Paleotti immediately after Trent and much later under Lambertini, the future Benedict XIV, set an example of pastoral involvement which other bishops noted, just as they drew on the published decrees of the Milanese archbishops. The achievement of Benedict XIII was thus distinct, despite the prolonged controversy over the formula published in the decrees with reference to *Unigenitus*.

The association of a Roman see with a revival of reform by means of synods was an innovation which produced positive results elsewhere, at least for a while. A series of synods in Italian dioceses succeeded the Roman council of 1725, consciously following the pope's example. For instance, a close collaborator of Benedict XIII, Cardinal Lanfredini, held diocesan synods for Osimo and Cingoli in 1734, 1735, 1736 and 1737. Bonaventura, bishop of Montefiascone and Corneto, promulgated the decrees of the Roman provincial council in the context of a diocesan synod of his own. The diocesan synod held at Naples in 1726 by the rigorist archbishop, Cardinal Pignatelli, who had been represented at the Roman council by a proctor for his Suburbicarian See of Frascati, encountered powerful local resistance, inspired by regalist sentiment. The frequency of synods, even in Italy, declined again after 1730, but those held before that date included one in 1729 for the Suburbicarian See of Palestrina. Even more striking was that Archbishop Borgia's diocesan synod for Fermo in 1728 was preceded by a provincial council held there in 1726.

The influence of Benedict's initiative in reviving an explicitly metropolitan role extended beyond Italy too, when Pierre de Tencin held a council for the Embrun province in 1727. This council could not avoid complications arising from the continued dispute over *Unigenitus*; yet more positively it reflected a moment when traditional Roman reserve towards provincial councils outside Italy, inspired by fears of 'nationalist' independence, particularly with regard to Gallican ambitions in France, could be overcome. As a Dominican himself, Benedict XIII was liable to be the object of special observation by Jansenists hoping for support in their campaign against the Jesuits, given the traditional rivalry between the Dominicans and the Jesuits. The potential revitalization of the provincial structure of the Church effected by Benedict was nevertheless clear, when following the Roman provincial council a number of bishops responded to their Tridentine obligation, newly reaffirmed, by nominating a metropolitan see with which, for certain purposes, their otherwise exempt dioceses would be associated. Such renewal of Tridentine duties, as also with the explicit support given to seminary education for ordinands, was clearly a pastoral initiative quite contrary to an unbroken decline from Trent's standards, in a supposedly 'post-Tridentine syndrome'.

This return to Tridentine objectives can equally be contrasted with the complaint brought to the provincial council by some bishops of the central papal states. In this they did denounce specific obstructions of their episcopal responsibilities caused by the interference of papal temporal government. The parish priests of the Rome diocese equally took the opportunity of the provincial council to accuse confraternities in the city of intrusion into properly parochial functions. But in either case, what is striking is that Benedict's exceptional action as metropolitan allowed such redress to be sought. In this his initiative was entirely concordant with his work at Benevento, demonstrating pastoral solicitude for rebuilding after the earthquake of 1688, and including among his assemblies there two provincial councils in 1693 and 1698. So too in the decrees of the Roman provincial council the priestly duties of preaching and catechizing were emphasized afresh, alongside the reiteration of regulations about clerical dress with which Benedict is often associated. The reforms to which the provincial council renewed attention reflected the pope's own action as bishop of Rome, continuing the diocesan visitation begun by Innocent XII, and his intervention as pontiff in the organization of the Roman Curia, to create a specific Congregation for seminaries. A survey of the resources of charitable foundations throughout the dioceses of the Roman province also emerged from the council.

THE COLLEGE OF CARDINALS

Size of membership

The Roman provincial council, however, raised in emphatic form the problem of the relationship between the papacy and the college of cardinals in the post-Tridentine Church. As the eighteenth century continued, the pressure on the popes from secular rulers wishing to affect the composition of the college became even greater in fact. This in itself suggests a necessary caution about any simple theory of a drastic reduction in the importance of the cardinals' position after Trent. In 1586 Sixtus V stabilized the size of the college at seventy; but depending on papal activity in relation to the mortality rate within the college, this maximum was not at all times reached. Between 1591 and 1700 there were 402 creations; between 1700 and 1799 there followed 343 elevations. From creation to death (or election as pope) the life expectancy of cardinals remained remarkably stable throughout this period. A median term, little affected by rare cases of secularization for instance, of 13 to 14 years established itself between 1592 and 1700, rising to 14 to 15 years between 1700 and 1799.

Because some cardinals, especially papal relatives and members of ruling families, were still appointed when very young (though not all survived to old age), the college could nevertheless include men of considerable experience gained under several pontificates.[3] Those who remained cardinals for twenty years or more formed 35 per cent of the membership between 1592 and 1700, and still 30 per cent from then until 1799. The membership of the college at the time of Sixtus V's limitation of future size stood at sixty-five in fact, which was a reduction from the exceptional post-Conciliar figures of

3 J. Broderick, 'The Sacred College of Cardinals: Size and Geographical Composition 1099–1986', *Archivum Historiae Pontificiae*, XXV (1987), 7–71.

seventy-six in 1565 and seventy-four in 1570. The subsequent variation of size at the time of conclaves, depending on mortality and previous papal creativity, has already been noted. But gradual depletion could produce temporary reductions of momentary importance, as when the figure of forty-three was reached in 1686 and repeated in 1743. The number of cardinals permanently resident in Rome, however, might not necessarily show such dramatic variation, even briefly.

Popes remained determined to control the composition of the college themselves; for by this period no way existed of forcing a pope to abide by any election treaty he might have agreed to while participating in a conclave. Such treaties can be traced at eight conclaves between 1605 and 1676. But the limiting constitution of 1586 issued by Sixtus V on his own authority, while claiming the consent of the existing cardinals, was careful not to specify any limitations on papal freedom in the choice of cardinals. Protests from existing members against new additions to the college, as also against conspicuous exclusions, were still voiced, even under Sixtus V himself, but rarely to much effect. The Council of Trent called for its specification of the necessary qualities in those appointed bishop to be observed also in the selection of cardinals. It also urged that as far as possible cardinals be chosen from the whole of Christendom. But in other respects Roman opposition to Conciliar claims to extend reforms specifically to the college of cardinals had been largely successful at Trent.

Secular pressure

The greatest threat to unfettered papal regulation of the college's membership after the Council proved to come rather from pressure exerted by Catholic secular rulers. Despite the fact that rulers of Italian states sometimes followed the example of major powers elsewhere in this respect, an Italian predominance in the creation of cardinals, continued after Trent, can in part be seen as the result of papal determination to retain freedom of choice and resist such pressure. Between 1566 and 1605, 72 per cent of new creations were Italian, and of these 106 Italians thirty-eight were natives of the papal states. Though other parts of Europe were represented in the creations of this period, particularly the Spanish and French realms, the proportion of Italians among the new creations between 1605 and 1655 further increased to 82 per cent. Of the 152 Italians involved, nearly half, seventy-eight, came from the papal states. Only 4 per cent of the new cardinals originated from areas outside Italy, Spain and France. Other regions were thus represented, but on a very small scale, and this changed only relatively between 1655 and 1799. For even then 80 per cent of new creations remained Italian, and of these 393 Italians a total of 170, rather less than half, were from Roman families or from the papal states.

Such imbalance could in its turn, of course, prove partly counter-productive, in stimulating pressure from non-Italian sovereigns for the creation of more cardinals from among their subjects. Papal resistance to these demands could equally be in part outmanoeuvred, when such intervention was more successful in promoting the claims of an Italian candidate who would subsequently represent the interests of the ruler in question to some degree at least. Italian prelates who served as papal nuncio at a Catholic Court were not beyond temptation, and their nomination as suitable candidates by the relevant ruler caused difficulty for popes intent on obstructing the growth of claims from competing sovereigns that the nuncios to their Courts should be assured of virtually automatic promotion. During the eighteenth century the claims of rival Courts more generally became increasingly strident, as rulers in Poland, Portugal and the Italian states sought to emulate the monarchs in the French, Spanish and Austro-Imperial realms by demanding that their nominations be accepted. Diplomatic pressure could be applied particularly when international hostilities put popes in a potentially compromised position. In exceptional circumstances prelates of Italian birth even became leading figures in the government of non-Italian states, securing their position by virtue of the legal privileges accorded to cardinals in the states of Catholic Europe: notorious examples were Mazarin in seventeenth-century France and Alberoni in early eighteenth-century Spain. Poland's potentially precarious position in European affairs was increasingly clear as Polish monarchs nominated not only Italians but even other non-Polish prelates as prospective cardinals.

In the case of Portugal, dispute over a *de facto* right of nuncios there to be made cardinals, alongside nuncios who served at the Spanish, French and Imperial Courts, escalated to such a degree that the papacy was forced to make an extraordinary concession on a parallel question. A secret clause in the concordat of 1737 allowed that the patriarchate of Lisbon would carry with it assured elevation to the college of cardinals. The confirmation of this in 1766 thus matched the exceptional ceremonial privileges which the patriarchal see of Lisbon was accorded by the eighteenth-century papacy, in an attempt to assuage the troublesome demands for greater recognition made by the Portuguese monarchy ever since the recovery of independence from Spanish rule in the mid-seventeenth century. Even the exiled house of Stuart maintained a claim as Catholic sovereigns to make nominations of prospective cardinals. Monarchs with a more real power, eminently Louis XIV, sought to demonstrate it by nominating French prelates as the 'crown' cardinals of lesser rulers, specifically again those of Portugal and Poland. The diplomatic manoeuvres intended by Louis to secure a succession favourable to France in the electoral archbishopric of Cologne also involved successful nomination of the princely prelate of the Empire, on whom royal hopes rested, as a 'crown' cardinal of France. But just as Louis's real aim here was frustrated, so his demand for the removal of an Italian who was deemed to have offended French sovereignty from the college of cardinals was valiantly refused by the pope. Benedict XIII similarly met French claims to limit his freedom in creating cardinals by threatening rather to resign the papacy and retire to his other see of Benevento.

The explicit claim of France and Spain to an absolute prerogative in naming 'crown' cardinals had equally been rejected by Clement IX in 1667. But the nominees of Catholic rulers continued to be marked by diplomatic and political experience most commonly; and this pattern was in a sense encouraged by papal agreement to the elevation of Italian prelates who served as nuncios, since after the first decades of the seventeenth century these were usually Curialists and career diplomats. But these conditions cumulatively reinforced papal determination to maintain a preponderance of Italians in the college of cardinals, to reinforce such chances of independence from foreign political pressure as existed. Thus, of the thirty-five cardinals created by Clement XII between 1730 and 1740 twenty-eight were Italian, and of these, nine were from the papal states. The procedure by which the pope could make a secret elevation, without revealing the name of the new cardinal *in petto*, could be employed as a device to resist unacceptable secular pressure for public promotion of an unwelcome nominee, while rewarding a more favoured candidate privately. Such a device misfired, however, when Clement XIV sought to use it amid the exceptional political pressure to which he was subject. Unfortunate to the end, he died without having reached a suitable moment at which to make public the extensive list of eleven cardinals named *in petto* some time before.

But prelates whose public admission to the college, in an elaborate sequence of requisite ceremonies, remained unfulfilled, in any case raised the spectre of acrimonious dispute when a conclave met. As political pressure from rival Catholic powers complicated the role of the papacy, it was no accident that the reservation of names *in petto* increased precisely from the pontificate of Urban VIII onwards, being employed on nearly ninety occasions between 1623 and 1799. The specific pressure for the creation of cardinals never ceased, since each major power regarded successful nomination by another monarch as necessitating another demand of its own, to redress or enhance diplomatic advantage, and lesser states, including those in the Italian peninsula, jealously calculated the number of creations of prelates from other second- or third-rank powers. The result nevertheless obstructed any political dominance in conclaves, especially given the numerous presence of less committed cardinals among the Italians. Such composition also of course tended to prevent speedy conclaves, as has previously been observed. Only two of the fifteen conclaves between 1644 and 1775 were completed inside a month; and the average length of conclaves in fact increased, from seventy-four days in the seven conclaves between 1644 and 1691 to ninety-two in the eight between 1700 and 1775.

The shifting balances within the membership of conclaves more easily allowed the obstruction of a cardinal's election as pope than facilitated the successful formation of alliances to promote a candidate. The variety of interests that were represented ensured competitive rather than complementary calculation of the likely policies of a potential pope, including the chances for securing new members of the college of cardinals itself from one prospective pontiff or another. This doubtless contributed to the fact that major Catholic powers continued to exercise at least *de facto* the right of exclusion of cardinals from the papal throne with some success, while failing to make effective their more grandiose claims to an 'inclusive' right of positively determining the outcome. Papal determination to maintain, or if necessary rapidly restore, an Italian predominance in the college of cardinals could in turn be reasonably sure of success, since even the more austere popes usually found it necessary to elevate at least some relations and close associates, by definition Italians in this period, to safeguard and maximize their own independence. At the other extreme, the absence in this period of patriarchs of the Eastern-rite Churches in communion with Rome from the college of cardinals at least avoided delicate questions of precedence within that membership. However, papal pursuit of an independent element in the college of cardinals was rewarded from the second half of the seventeenth century by the emergence of the *squadrone volante* in conclaves, a body of Italian cardinals intent on resisting external pressure and pursuing reform ideals in the election of a pope.

Relations between popes and the college of cardinals

The Dominican Orsini became a cardinal at a relatively young age, in 1672, before being raised to the archbishopric of Benevento in 1686. In his first thirty-eight years in the see, before his election to the papacy in 1724, he developed his fatal reliance on Coscia, whom as pope he in turn made cardinal. The intense hostility to the powerful Cardinal Coscia, which so undermined the authority of Benedict XIII himself, was the prelude to the trial of the cardinal in the subsequent pontificate of Clement XII. Such formal proceedings against a cardinal were exceptional at Rome, but not without partial precedents and parallels. Action taken by Innocent X after the death of Urban VIII led to the flight of the Barberini cardinals to France. Under Innocent XI Cardinal Petrucci was forced to make a private retraction of suspect opinions, and even the pope could not prevent the inclusion of the cardinal's writings in the Index of prohibited literature. His successor, Alexander VIII, further deprived the Oratorian cardinal of his see of Jesi to which he was only restored under the following pope, Innocent XII.

To consider the popes of this period not only as bishops of Rome but also in the first of their wider roles, as metropolitan, is thus already to raise the whole question of the evolving relationship between the papacy and the college of cardinals in the early modern era. That the institutional powers of the college with respect to the pope had been seriously reduced by the end of the sixteenth century is widely agreed. But it is also generally accepted that this was the result of a relatively long process, not of sudden changes in the immediately post-Tridentine years, and that the reorganization by Sixtus V of the college and the Curia, 1586–88, was the culminating confirmation of this process, not a new departure. The sense of grievance which at the end of the sixteenth century Cardinal Paleotti clearly felt about the cardinals' reduced powers in the real governing of the Church was therefore understandable but perhaps lacked a full perspective. His own hopes, at elevation to the dignity immediately after the conclusion of the Tridentine Council, had obviously been heightened, possibly to an unrealistic degree, while his experiences as bishop and archbishop of Bologna had disillusioned him. He was also frustrated in his ambition to publish a memoir of the Council based on his formative experience of its work, because of Roman concern to present the Conciliar decrees as definitive and beyond discussion.[4]

By comparison with Paleotti's treatise on the role of cardinals, the brief composition on the office of cardinal by Agostino Valier seems to mark a calm acceptance of reality, as he had experienced it by the beginning of the seventeenth century. In conjunction with Cardinal Valier's other writings of the same period, it points to the influence which a zealous cardinal might still exercise individually, not least if a resident diocesan bishop, over and above advice given directly to the pope. Valier's exemplary model in all this was explicitly Charles Borromeo of Milan but he himself was a conscientious bishop of Verona in the post-Conciliar period. Specific functions which cardinals still performed, above all the election of a new pope, were also the subject of semi-public memoranda, such as that on this question by Cardinal Federico Borromeo.[5]

The vacancies of the papal office, before and during each conclave remained the moment when at least nominally the collective authority of the college of cardinals was once again demonstrated. But while the Dean of the Sacred College presided over the conclave, with the other 'heads of orders', the senior Cardinal Priest and senior Cardinal Deacon, the interim administration of the Roman Church, carefully confined in scope, was the responsibility of the Cardinal Camerlengo; and the frequent signs of popular disorder during these interregna did not do much to enhance the college's authority. Theoretical dignity and political reality were obviously distinct in any case. The usually accepted legal immunities of a cardinal were breached by Catholic secular rulers in exceptional circumstances. The arrest in the early seventeenth century of Cardinals Klesl and Lerma by the Austrian and Spanish Habsburgs respectively amply demonstrated this.

Papal negotiation for their release was complemented by Urban VIII's decision to grant to cardinals the title of 'Eminence' in place of 'Most Illustrious'. But elsewhere in Europe a few great prelates were confident of their institutional eminence, whether personally cardinals or not: the three electoral archbishops of the Empire, obviously, and, in their own minds at least, the prince-archbishops of Salzburg; also the Polish primate, who as Interrex claimed the honours due to a fellow sovereign from the elected kings of Poland. By contrast, even those cardinals resident in Rome met less frequently in collective

4 P. Prodi, *Il Cardinale Gabriele Paleotti (1522–1597)* (2 vols, Rome 1959–67), I, 10 f., II, 389 ff.; F.C.M.: A.S.V., Segreteria di Stato: Nunziatura in Venezia: filza 266, fo. 116: 13 May 1575; G. Paleotti, *De Consultationibus sacri Consistorij Commentarius*, Editio altera, quae est in Germania prima (Ingolstadt 1594).
5 *Vita B. Caroli Borromei Item Opuscula Duo, Episcopus, et Cardinalis Ab Augustino [Valerio] Card. Veronae Conscripta, et Nunc Omnia Denuo Edita* (Verona 1602); cf. Federico Borromeo, *De Prudentia in creando Pontifice Maximo*: B.A.V.: MS Barberiniani Latini 1251.

encounter with the pope. The frequency of Consistories declined precisely from the last two decades of the sixteenth century. In the first half of the seventeenth century this declined further, to an average of two meetings a month, with subsequent reduction during the rest of this period. Formal business, especially the filling of sees and benefices, occupied much of these meetings anyway. From Clement VIII onwards, some popes rather relied on consulting cardinals individually, while consultation with a restricted circle, who might not even be mainly cardinals, proved unfortunate in the case of Benedict XIII.

In this period even the effective authority of a Cardinal Protector was shown to be questionable, once extraordinary affairs were at issue. The notorious outburst against Urban VIII in 1632 by Cardinal Borgia had indirectly very wide repercussions, affecting even, for example, the fate of Galileo. But in institutional terms the episode can certainly be seen as confirming papal dominance of a Consistory, in that the challenge to the Spanish Cardinal Protector to speak only as and when requested, in his role as cardinal, and desist from unrequested ultimatums pronounced as royal representative was decisive in the immediate context. It is important, however, to recall the potential obligations owed to Catholic rulers by cardinals other than Cardinal Protectors themselves. While the financial problems of the Spanish Crown meant that cardinals who were subjects or servants of the Catholic monarch, other than the Protector himself, could not necessarily be assured of a dependable income if resident at Rome, the resources of the monarchy were at times expended on patronage to a wide range of prelates. Even cardinals who were not immediately or obviously dependants of Spain might be for a while in receipt of a Spanish pension. This was true of archbishops of Bologna, in papal territory, both in Paleotti's case and in that of Ludovisi, despite the latter's less than harmonious relations with Spain as pope subsequently.[6]

This in its way reflected the changing position of cardinals in relation to the papacy, in that the direct diplomatic relationship between popes and Catholic rulers in the post-Tridentine period was a chief reason for the diversion, most of the time, of business other than the more formal aspect of clerical preferments from Consistories to the network of nuncios, papal nephews and popes. On the other hand, cardinals other than papal nephews also contributed to the visible exaltation of the papal office during this period, as was only natural in the long reaction to Protestant attack on Petrine authority. Papal primacy might have been formally defined by the Council of Ferrara-Florence in the mid-fifteenth century, but after the Reformation challenge conspicuous celebration of this was still valuable. Thus the completion of the basic structure of the new St Peter's allowed a commission of responsible cardinals, already in the pontificate of Urban VIII, to plan an altar for the terminal apse of the basilica, beyond the central papal altar, which would celebrate the papal

---

6 L. von Pastor, *The History of the Popes, from the Close of the Middle Ages* (Engl. trans., 40 vols, London 1891–1953), XXVII, p. 48.

primacy. Revision of the plan removed features which were personal to the piety of Urban himself, but even in an early design by Bernini those subsequently omitted features were combined already with the definitive association of the *cathedra* of St Peter and the supportive witness of Fathers of the Church, though not yet the presiding illumination of the Holy Spirit.

Cardinals' backgrounds

The background experience of those whom the popes chose as cardinal in this period was naturally varied, reflecting the various roles of the popes themselves. It is not surprising that some cardinals, especially those from Italy and those particularly from the papal states and Rome, had served in administrative roles, such as the office of Treasurer, or in temporal government, whether under Legates governing parts of the papal territories or under the Governor of Rome itself. Others had previously assisted the Cardinal Vicar of Rome, and throughout the period some had been resident bishops of dioceses, alongside the many whose chief career had been in papal diplomatic service. The functions performed traditionally by cardinals similarly continued to include not only the Rome Vicariate, exercising the pope's local jurisdiction, but also the office of Penitentiary, at the head of the entire system in the Church by which the papal Power of the Keys was dispensed in the internal forum. The external forum, the vast judicial and administrative structure of the Church, continued to imply the importance, among other offices, of the lucrative Vice-Chancellorship. Yet this position must be distinguished from the personal position of Cardinal Nephew. They often acquired it, but the office did not automatically revert to a new cardinal at the election of a new pope.

The location of an important Roman church, that of San Lorenzo in Damaso, within the walls of the Vice-Chancellor's habitual and by this time official palace, gave an opportunity for some pastoral supervision to even the most magnificent prelate. The post-Conciliar transformation of Cardinal Farnese, in which he received ordination as a priest and consecration as a bishop, was associated with his Vice-Chancellorial intervention to improve pastoral provision in that church. Such action thus complemented the work of wealthy as well as less wealthy cardinals to restore or rebuild Titular churches in Rome, establish episcopal residences in the Suburbicarian Sees or repair the fabric of abbeys of which they had commendatory charge. From Farnese's patronage the abbeys of Grottaferrata and Farfa thus benefited, and also the cathedral of Monreale, as well as the interior of the church of San Lorenzo. But Farnese also provides a conspicuous example of another contribution to church life in Rome which a munificent cardinal could make. His famous patronage of the new Roman church of the Jesuits, *Il Gesù*, is a reminder that Cardinal Protectors of religious orders could benefit old and new churches of the regulars, in Rome as well as outside the city and diocese. Cardinals who were themselves regulars or became popes could also embellish regulars' churches, as the Dominican Orsini did at S. Maria sopra Minerva and S. Clemente in Rome.

The post-Tridentine college of cardinals might no longer be a turbulent baronage but it remained essentially aristocratic in spirit, even if as an aristocracy more thoroughly of office than of birth. The reduction in normal times of the Consistory to routine business certainly enhanced papal supremacy over the cardinals. Meetings of the Holy Office, the first of the new tribunals of the sixteenth century which were inserted into the Curial organization, might regularly be chaired by the pope in person, though this revived form of the Roman Inquisition was otherwise run by cardinals. Cardinals too headed the Congregation of the Council, created after the conclusion of the assembly at Trent and the papal confirmation of the Tridentine decrees. In the decisions of such distinct tribunals, select cardinals could thus have some influence over the affairs of the Church, including affairs in Rome itself, in the Roman province and the papal states, as well as more universally. It was thus logical for Sixtus V to specify that within the service nobility which the cardinals could now be seen to resemble, at least in part, there should be a minimum number who were qualified theologians. Since cardinals were to help popes examine candidates for bishoprics, with some rigour under Clement VIII for instance, it was also apt that the examiners should share some of the competence they were testing in the examined.

Cardinals' income

The effective authority and influence of cardinals also of course turned on their financial position. This observation is generally valid for the Western European society of the early modern period, and not only for egregious cases such as Richelieu and Mazarin. Calculation of income is difficult in less conspicuous cases, not least because of the variety of currencies of account and the fluctuation of exchange rates, quite apart from alterations in the cost of living throughout this period. The chief difficulty, however, derives from the multiplicity of sources where income might be recorded: even major sources, such as the annual French pension of 1,000 scudi reported in 1767 as being received by the Cardinal Governor of Rome, did not represent more than one item in the disparate revenues of a prelate. More certain, arguably, is the importance of disposable patronage in maintaining the authority of cardinals. Even leading figures, such as Cardinal Quiroga in the late sixteenth century, required papal permission to make a will, and, as in that case, the papacy could impose conditions which limited the free disposal by testamentary bequest of a cardinal's resources.[7] Important while cardinals who were diocesan bishops were still alive was a papal indult allowing them to fill within their see benefices of less than a certain value which would otherwise fall to papal provision.

During their lifetime cardinals could also patronize their officials and servants at the moment of relinquishing benefices or disposing of the income of sees they held. Four of Cardinal Morone's household in 1571 benefited in this

7 Biblioteca Nacional, Madrid: MS 13044, fos 128r ff.

way when he reserved 300 ducats as a pension on the revenues of the see of Modena. The lengthy will made in 1587 by Cardinal Savelli produced legal challenge from relatives whose expectations had been disappointed, but in this case one of the ultimate beneficiaries was the papacy itself, when in 1604 Clement VIII acquired Castel Gandolfo among former Savelli properties purchased then. The assessment of the income of cardinals ordered by Pius V in 1571 showed that the Tridentine opposition to the holding of sees in full plurality (retaining concurrent administration of a see being a different matter) was by then being observed. This was true of Italian cardinals at any rate, for political interests and defence of Catholic succession in Imperial territories meant that German bishoprics were still held in effective plurality, well beyond the sixteenth century.

Monastic foundations remained a more reliable source of income. In 1571 Cardinal Farnese derived 5,000 scudi annually from just one of his many *commendams*, that at Tre Fontane, and at the same time a *commendam* near Gubbio was valued at the same annual sum, *scudi d'oro in oro*.[8] From all sources, the total estate of Cardinal Savelli was estimated at his death to produce 40,000 scudi annually. In 1571 Cardinal Farnese declared a total income of nearly 77,000 scudi. By 1587 he estimated it to be worth 120,000 gold ducats annually, while of this income the cardinal's necessary annual expenditure was reckoned to require 40,000 ducats from sources regarded as non-patrimonial and more obviously ecclesiastical.

By the first decade of the seventeenth century the status of a cardinal resident at Rome, even without the spectacular patronage exhibited by a Farnese, was thought to necessitate a supporting annual net income of 8,000 écus or 24,000 livres calculated in French money. Yet profitable positions for Curial cardinals were not of course lacking. The opportunities, in the process by which provisions were made in Consistory, for a succession of cardinals who were Chamberlains of the college of cardinals should not be overlooked, for this office must be distinguished from that of Cardinal Camerlengo.[9] Curial office, however, was obviously not a monopoly of cardinals. The relative restraint which began to be observed by at least some cardinals after the Council of Trent, in the accumulation of benefices and profitable offices, introduced the problem of 'poor' cardinals. To maintain the collective dignity of the college of cardinals, pensions for such as were not otherwise able to support a minimally suitable household were thought necessary by some popes, both soon after the Council and at the end of the sixteenth century already.

Both Cardinal Protectors and other cardinals, whether subjects of a given ruler or merely acknowledging a relative dependence stemming from support for promotion or family association for example, could be well placed to benefit from the ruler's further patronage. The role of Cardinal Protectors in handling the filling of sees and other benefices within a state, particularly those

8 B. McClung Hallman, *Italian Cardinals, Reform, and the Church as Property* (Berkeley, CA 1985).
9 A.G.S.: Patronato Eclesiastico, Leg. 147: 1594–95.

to which a ruler possessed a formal right of nomination, presented an obvious opportunity for subsidiary advantages, such as the 'pensions' levied on new appointments to sees and substantial benefices and reserved for the enjoyment of some other person. While these pensions, when arranged at the request of a nominating ruler, were not always reserved for a clerical beneficiary, even under so conspicuously devout a ruler as Philip II, cardinals were certainly among ecclesiastics who benefited from such levies. This type of income complemented that from other ecclesiastical positions or institutions which lay in the effective gift of a ruler. In Spanish-ruled Sicily of the late-sixteenth and seventeenth centuries, for example, the revenues of monastic houses to which the Crown could nominate commendatory abbots substantially benefited cardinals, particularly those seen as acting in the Spanish interest at Rome. The monarchy could similarly nominate a cardinal as archbishop at the cathedral priory of Monreale, a see with relatively limited duties even if a few prelates sought to provide proper pastoral care there.

Pensions for the support of cardinals and other prelates imposed on sees and benefices at each vacancy were not a device employed only by Catholic secular rulers, however. The post-Tridentine papacy itself continued this practice and thus helped to maintain the dignity of cardinals, but also some indirect influence, by means of patronage, on their loyalty. Commendatory abbacies of wealthy Italian monastic houses were also granted to cardinals, especially the Cardinal Nephews of popes. The accumulation of revenue from these sources supported the position and in turn the potential patronage of important papal nephews, above all Cardinal Scipio Borghese in the first part of the seventeenth century. Such a system was not without difficulties of its own for the transfer of revenue on a large scale to Rome from an abbey situated outside the papal states, in Venetian territory for example, could provoke resistance from the secular power concerned. A related concern was less often visible with pensions imposed on other Italian sees and benefices outside papal territory since tolerance of the diversion of such income to Rome could be seen as a means to obtaining favour and influence with the pope's nephew or other cardinal.

The comprehensive financial benefits bestowed on many Cardinal Nephews by some but not all popes during this period deserve further consideration, in discussion of the complex nature of the Cardinal Nephew's role. But in reviewing the relations of popes and cardinals including papal nephews, it is important to note that even the most conspicuous concentration of revenues could include a truly ecclesiastical dimension, as well as obviously family advancement and artistic celebration of this. Exhaustive analysis of the compound office and revenues enjoyed by Scipio Borghese, a singular example even when compared with the shared riches of the Barberini nephews has shown that in some of the many cases where a *commendam* or effective control of a religious institution was enjoyed, the Cardinal Nephews intervened in the internal affairs of the house to restore regular observance or to replace incorrigible inmates with other ecclesiastics who would better perform their duties or serve local needs.[10] That the more reformed orders, with a greater commitment to poverty might also better serve the interests of the commendator is true. But other cardinals of the post-Tridentine era, whose zealous devotion to ecclesiastical duty and personal austerity is more immediately evident, also used their commendatory control of decayed institutions, especially in central and Southern Italy, to install more observant religious or provide better pastoral care in the area.

The authority of cardinals could also of course be deployed in ways which were less clearly of benefit to episcopal reform. It has been aptly noted in the case of Perugia that the Cardinal Protector of a religious order was well placed to promote that order's interests at Rome, even in the face of the priorities of episcopal reformers. This observation is indeed more generally valid. But papal approval of a cardinal's succession to the role of an order's Protector could lead to positive results as far as internal reform of the order was concerned. In the post-Tridentine era the Trinitarians were thus reformed, with the involvement of Federico Borromeo as Cardinal Protector. The most dramatic case in the immediately post-Conciliar decades was the papal suppression of the order of the Humiliati by virtue of Charles Borromeo's experience that they were incorrigible. For it is important to remember that papal policy was in any case not necessarily bound by the wishes of Cardinal Protectors.

The papacy in the seventeenth century determined, after investigation begun formally by Innocent X, on the suppression of some religious houses and even orders. More notoriously, the eventual eighteenth-century papal suppression of the Society of Jesus concerned an institution which had long been prominent and influential, and the Jesuits since the sixteenth century had not lacked powerful protection from cardinals, even if they chose to discontinue the role of a Protector, to signify the Society's immediate dependence on the pope. The formal position of Cardinal Protector of an order was thus distinct from the role of cardinals who were themselves members of an order. Those Oratorians at the end of the sixteenth century and beginning of the seventeenth who were most determined to preserve their identity as secular priests were anxious that the role of the two members of their institution who were made cardinals, Tarugi and Baronius, should not be regarded as that of Cardinal Protector. In the convoluted evolution of the Oratory it was vital, from this point of view, to resist any suggestion of assimilation to the position of a religious order. This concern was thus parallel to the insistence that if the intervention of another cardinal did occur, it should be that of the Cardinal Vicar of the Rome diocese, not of cardinals charged with the supervision of regulars' affairs.

Nor more generally was the formal position of Cardinal Protector of a particular interest the only means by which that interest was promoted among the cardinals. When at the end of the sixteenth century the exiled English

10 V. Reinhardt, *Kardinal Scipione Borghese (1605–1633). Vermögen, Finanzen und sozialer Aufstieg eines Papstnepoten* (Tübingen 1984).

Catholic, Cardinal Allen died, there was hopeful speculation, even if destined to be disappointed, among other Catholic Recusants that the pope would create a native successor to the 'Cardinal of the English', distinct from any Italian Protector. Not that papal choice of Protectors was confined to Italians of course. In 1596 the pope appointed as Vice-Protector of England the Spanish Jesuit, Cardinal Toledo, a choice which in the political circumstances of the time could hardly fail to complicate the disturbed affairs of the English Recusants and the English Colleges abroad. By the early sixteenth century the English monarchs, like the French monarch and the Emperor, had established the practice of choosing their own Cardinal Protector at Rome. But the Reformation obviously disturbed such arrangements. In the case of England, the unfortunate Cardinal Campeggio, who failed to satisfy Henry VIII's needs, was the last Cardinal Protector chosen in this way by the Crown, despite the subsequent Marian restoration, and whatever the later role of the exiled Stuarts.

While the Emperor might continue to make his own choice of Cardinal Protector, the Protectorate of an area substantially lost to Catholicism, such as England, became a matter for papal determination. By 1621, for example, Cardinal Ludovisi was Protector of England, as Morone had been earlier, after Pole's death. The Protectorate of the English College in Rome, newly established in 1579, was explicitly entrusted to Morone by the terms of the papal Bull of Foundation, with extensive powers in the administration of the seminary, the regulation of its statutes and admission of students.[11] The subsequent succession in the Protectorate of this institution exemplifies the scope of papal choice. Cardinal Buoncompagni, nephew of Gregory XIII, succeeded Morone and was in turn succeeded by Cardinal Caetani. During his long Protectorate, some other eminent Italians, including future popes, acted as Vice-Protector: Cardinals Aldobrandini, Sega and Borghese.

The Protectorate of England, with its extensive powers, was confirmed by Clement VIII to Caetani and then given to Cardinal Farnese, who was followed by Francesco Barberini, nephew of Urban VIII, with another Italian, Cardinal Millini as Vice-Protector. Only in the last decades of the seventeenth century was a native English Protector appointed, the Dominican Cardinal Howard, after which an Italian succession resumed to the end of the eighteenth century. But Howard had been made Cardinal Protector of England and Scotland by the exceptional intervention of the monarch of Protestant kingdoms, Charles II, before the consolidation of the office of Protectors by Innocent XII in 1694. It should also be remembered that the institution of Cardinal Protectors did not preclude direct papal intervention in affairs normally entrusted to them. An example is again supplied by the English College in Rome, which received a personal Apostolic Visitation in 1701 as the prelude to specially commissioned investigations by a cardinal of renewed troubles at the College, during a period when the formal Protectorate was vacant. But in

---

11 M.E. Williams, *The Venerable English College, Rome: a History 1579–1979* (London 1979).

1773, when the Jesuits were finally suppressed, the immediate direction of the College was taken over by Cardinal Corsini as Protector.

The institution of Cardinal Protectors did not, however, consistently enhance papal authority. Cardinals, whether Protectors or not, who in the early modern period displayed the arms of a secular ruler on their Roman palaces, were giving public notice of their allegiances. Diplomatic claims to privileges within the city of Rome, when representatives of foreign powers claimed extensive zones immune from ordinary police measures, are best considered in relation to the temporal government of the papacy. But the secular and the ecclesiastical could not always be easily separated. The attempt of the Portuguese in the mid-seventeenth century to recover their independence from Spanish rule involved, of necessity, an attempt to establish distinct representation at Rome. In the face of Spanish pressure the pope insisted that he could not refuse audience to the Portuguese bishop who had come to Rome at this juncture: any bishop must have reasonable access *ad limina apostolorum*. But in an effort to avoid painful complications with Spain, elaborate precautions were taken to try to prevent any encounter between the bishop and the Cardinal Dean of the Sacred College, which might be taken as signifying diplomatic recognition of the prelate as a royal envoy.

THE SUBURBICARIAN SEES

Among the Suburbicarian Sees held by the Cardinal Bishops, that of Ostia could be claimed by the most senior of the cardinals, as Dean of the Sacred College, for whom a palace at Velletri, for use when resident in the see, had been built by Cardinal Farnese. The advanced age of such senior prelates implied a usually short episcopate, and a consequent lack of pastoral continuity. Over thirty-five Cardinal Bishops of Ostia succeeded each other between 1564 and the end of the eighteenth century. Because of internal promotion among Cardinal Bishops, the second see in seniority, that of Porto, attached to the Sub-Deanship of the Sacred College, saw an even more rapid turnover, with nearly sixty bishops in the equivalent period. But, partly because of the possibility of a prelate retaining another see while a Suburbicarian Bishop, this did not exclude figures of pastoral importance. While Cardinal Ottoboni was elected pope, as Alexander VIII, when Cardinal Bishop of Porto, Orsini latterly held Porto as well as Benevento before combining the latter with the see of Rome as Benedict XIII. The succession at Sabina showed a rate of turn-over nearer that of Porto than that of Ostia, and included figures of the international importance of Granvelle and Joyeuse, a reminder that through seniority non-Italian cardinals might come to occupy these sees near Rome, in contrast to the Italian monopoly of the see of Rome throughout this period.

The distinction between seniority and age among cardinals, however, made possible the relatively prolonged episcopate of Cardinal Albani at Sabina, between 1730 and 1743, during which his pastoral activity included the holding of a synod in 1736. The Cardinal Bishops of Palestrina between 1564 and the end of the eighteenth century numbered over forty; the number at Frascati in the same period was nearer fifty. But among the latter was not only Orsini, already archbishop of Benevento, before his translation to Porto, but also Corsini at the time of his election to the papacy as Clement XII. During the post-Tridentine era Frascati was provided with a new cathedral, and at the end of the eighteenth century the Cardinal Bishop was the zealous Henry Stuart, Duke of York. At Albano the succession featured nearer fifty than forty bishops between 1564 and the end of the eighteenth century, but despite this relatively rapid turn-over, one cardinal found time to erect a seminary in 1628. At vacancies in this see the senior Cardinal Priest among the members of the Sacred College could accept promotion or decline the option. But in certain circumstances a senior Cardinal Deacon of the Roman Church could rapidly advance into the ranks of the Cardinal Bishops.

At intervals during the seventeenth century there were papal interventions, at promotions to the Suburbicarian Sees, designed to secure closer pastoral supervision: for Frascati in 1668, in 1671 with reference to Albano, Porto and Palestrina, to Sabina in 1677, and in 1680 in relation to Ostia for instance. Between 1726 and 1734 Cardinal Pignatelli exceptionally remained Bishop of Porto as Dean of the Sacred College by papal permission. The papal recall to pastoral obligations was renewed with reference to Albano in 1731 and 1763; and in relation to Ostia in 1738, where an exceptional variation in the Decanal promotion was again made in 1763 for health reasons. Indeed, this recall became a standard formula in the eighteenth-century promotions to the Suburbicarian Sees. Depending on the accidents of longevity and seniority by years of membership of the Sacred College, the filling of these sees could thus be determined during a given pontificate by the creations of cardinals made long before by previous popes. But it is also important to remember that cardinals were among the most influential prelates in the implementation of post-Tridentine reform, in dioceses which were not Suburbicarian Sees and which were not necessarily within the Roman province. The example of Bologna under Paleotti and later under Lambertini has already been noted, as has the outstanding position of Milan under Cardinals Charles and Federico Borromeo: influences distinct from that of Rome which will be considered again in due course, in this chapter and the next respectively.

The care of Gabriele Paleotti for the Suburbicarian Sees of Albano and Sabina had equally extended to holding a diocesan synod in each and at Sabina erecting a seminary. The administration of that diocese was reordered and ancient buildings repaired; while at one restored church the reformed Franciscan Observants were for a while established. Paleotti also concerned himself with the quality of preachers and confessors in the diocese, as was noted by his Vicar General, who himself represented a link with the Roman Oratory and with Cardinal Baronius in particular. Paleotti's further appointment of an episcopal vicegerent for effective visitation of the diocese, in addition to his personal visitation of Magliano, the episcopal seat at this time, anticipated a similar arrangement made subsequently for the see by Cardinal Scipio Borghese.

Paleotti's diocesan regulations moreover were not isolated, as decrees were also issued by his predecessors and successors at Sabina.

In seventeenth-century instances of popes recalling pastoral obligations at the promotion of cardinals to Suburbicarian Sees reference is also found to a preliminary duty of reporting to the Cardinal Vicar of Rome on the state of the diocese. In this way a beginning was suggested of some involvement, at least *de facto*, of the Rome Vicariate in the affairs of these sees: a prelude to much later modern developments. At the Roman provincial council of 1725 the participating cardinals included the bishops of Porto, Sabina and Palestrina, and although the Cardinal Bishops of Frascati and Albano were only represented by proctor, these two prelates were resident in their dioceses of Naples and Bologna respectively. Naples too should be counted among those dioceses where bishops who were cardinals set a truly eminent example of implementing reform: among such Neapolitan archbishops were Cardinals Gesualdo and Acquaviva, in the period from the end of the Tridentine Council to the archiepiscopate of Pignatelli. Similarly, a specific result of the 1725 Roman council was the apostolic commission to the archbishop of Ancona, Cardinal Bussi, to hold a visitation at Loreto, where the ordinary authority of the diocesan seemed incapable of repressing clerical disorder, but where the papacy had a special responsibility for the image of the Church presented there to pious pilgrims at the celebrated Marian shrine.

BENEVENTO, BOLOGNA AND OTHER DIOCESES

The papacy more generally had a particular responsibility for the dioceses of the Roman province other than the Suburbicarian Sees – the Immediately Subject sees – and those situated in the papal states or forming papal enclaves. The impact of papal policy on these has been seen as negative by some historians. So the results of their immediate dependence, in various ways, on the papacy must be carefully considered. The emphasis on preaching which Benedict XIII had maintained at Benevento before his election to the papacy was sustained in his actions as metropolitan of the Roman province, as has been seen; while his diocesan synods before he became pope reached the remarkable number of thirty-eight. Benedict's personal devotion to Benevento itself was the more important because at an earlier date, between 1635 and 1642, the see of this papal enclave had remained vacant for six years.

After Cardinal Savelli, who held the archbishopric at the time of the Council of Trent's conclusion, a majority of the archbishops were also cardinals between 1607 and 1796, including all but two in the eighteenth century. This implied that they had other interests and duties beyond the purely diocesan, which was certainly true of Savelli. The retention of Benevento by Benedict XIII had a less satisfactory aspect also, in that he made Cardinal Coscia his coadjutor there, with right of succession and even with the right to the archiepiscopal pallium. Although his succession took place on Benedict's death, his own disgrace led to a swift loss of the see, to which a vicar apostolic had in the interim been appointed. The two archbishops of the later eighteenth century, who were not cardinals however, were both in residence in their see at the time of their death.

After the Council of Trent the bishop of a major see in papal territory, Paleotti of Bologna, established a reputation for his zealous attempts to implement Conciliar reform. For a while the hopes of episcopal reformers elsewhere were focused on Bologna as well as on the Milan of Charles Borromeo. But papal territory in fact proved less fruitful ground for post-Tridentine reform, as the experiences of Cardinal Paleotti revealed. Despite the elevation of the see to an archbishopric in 1582, Paleotti's eventual departure for Rome, where he spent his last years in Curia, as a Suburbicarian Cardinal Bishop, marked considerable personal frustration, not least over obstacles presented by aspects of temporal papal government. Nevertheless, his coadjutor at Bologna, Alfonso Paleotti, on his own succession, attempted to maintain something of the Tridentine reform spirit in the archbishopric.

The cardinals who subsequently held the see in the seventeenth and eighteenth centuries included, in the first half of the seventeenth, the papal nephews Borghese and Ludovisi. Between these two, however, as has been noted, Alessandro Ludovisi, before his election as pope in 1621, represented a revival of pastoral concern. In the eighteenth century, as has equally been observed, Cardinal Lambertini, before his own election as Benedict XIV, maintained the same tradition as had the future Gregory XV. His retention for a while of Bologna, after his election, was arguably less ambiguous in its results than those in the case of Benedict XIII at Benevento. At Bologna, indeed, Paleotti achieved some partially successful intervention in the disordered affairs of the Spanish College there, both as archiepiscopal Visitor *ex officio*, and as specially commissioned Apostolic Visitor, whereas Spanish sensitivity and the natural independence of the college authorities tended rather to resist intervention by Cardinal Legates governing the city.[12]

This pattern may be compared with that in an Immediately Subject see, within both the Roman province and the papal states. The bishops of Perugia, from the conclusion of the Council of Trent to the end of the eighteenth century, were in the majority of cases not cardinals. It has been argued that the obstacles to Tridentine reform presented by aspects of papal temporal government were very much experienced by the post-Conciliar bishops of Perugia. But it should initially be recalled that bishops intent on implementing Tridentine reform in Italy encountered difficulties not only under papal temporal rule, as at Bologna, but in other states including Piedmont, the Venetian Republic, Tuscany, Lucca, under Spanish rule in Naples, Sicily and Sardinia, and famously in the Milanese case of the Borromeo archbishops in Spanish-ruled Lombardy. Analysis of the work of the bishops of Perugia between the end of the Council of Trent and the middle decades of the

---

12 D. De Lario, *Sobre los orígenes del burócrata moderno. El Colegio de San Clemente de Bolonia durante la impermeabilización habsburguesa (1568–1659)* (Bologna 1980); cf. Prodi, *Paleotti*, I–II.

seventeenth century has itself revealed real achievements, despite difficulties.[13] Pastoral visitation was carried out, a seminary established, nuns' convents enclosed, the presence of the Jesuits encouraged. Further to this, charitable provision was enlarged, churches restored, educational opportunity increased, and other religious orders brought to Perugia or supported there.

Diocesan synods complemented new initiatives in the care of the sick and of prisoners, while the lengthy process by which the Oratorian priestly way of life was established at Perugia was part of a long and complicated history affecting such institutions in many parts of Italy and their ambiguous relations with the Roman Oratory. The diocesan synods between 1564 and 1632 numbered at least ten, and diocesan administration was reordered on lines favoured by post-Tridentine reforming bishops elsewhere. The direct intervention of papal authority by means of an Apostolic Visitation in 1571 moreover reinforced local episcopal action to impose strict enclosure on female convents in the face of typical lay resistance and the complicity of male regulars. Papal intervention was in this case indubitably supporting pastoral rather than temporal interests, despite the fact that papal temporal government was certainly not unmindful of the mid-sixteenth-century revolt in Perugia. Nor was the intervention represented by an Apostolic Visitation in the post-Conciliar Church peculiar to dioceses in the papal states, as will be seen. This positive outcome in the case of the female convents should thus be set against the papal decision, after long post-Conciliar disputes, to allow the three chief confraternities of Perugia immunity from episcopal control. Here the sensitivity of papal government to lay interests, in the context of Perugia's troubled past, was doubtless uppermost.

This consideration is thus distinct from the alleged failure of the papacy to give adequate support to the bishops of Perugia in those pastoral responsibilities which brought them into conflict with the Cassinese monks of the wealthy Benedictine abbey there. The power of the older monastic orders to defend their privileges and exemptions after Trent was again not a phenomenon peculiar to the papal states. The analysis of conditions at Perugia indeed shows that the Cassinese there made their own pastoral and charitable provision, even before surrendering the bulk of their parochial responsibilities in the mid-seventeenth century. The papal ruling of the later sixteenth century that the abbey should be made to contribute to the costs of the university presumably helped the bishops of Perugia to establish their control of that foundation, evident by 1625. Specifically Tridentine forms of devotion there came to include conspicuous celebration of the cult of Charles Borromeo after his early seventeenth-century canonization. Given the saint's own dramatic but ultimately triumphant confrontations with secular authority in pursuit of his rigorous reforms at Milan, it would seem appropriate that his cult should be so spectacularly received at Perugia where, after all, the diocesans had not

13 C.F. Black, 'Perugia and Papal Absolutism in the Sixteenth Century', *English Historical Review*, XCVI (1981), 509–39; C.F. Black, 'Perugia and Post-Tridentine Church Reform', *Journal of Ecclesiastical History*, XXXV (1984), 429–51.

encountered systematic obstruction from the papal governors, who were often themselves bishops.

Where an ecclesiastic as governor in the decades immediately after Trent insisted that temporal jurisdiction extended to criminal clerics, it might easily be agreed that the letter of Tridentine provision was being questioned; but the clerical status of such a governor makes that distinction a much less telling one. This type of governmental preoccupation is hardly surprising in the light of a riot at Perugia in 1586, less than half a century after the revolt there. Similarly, the 1572 reform of the Perugian *Monti di Pietà* was admittedly not the work of the diocesan, but was made by the Apostolic Visitor, not by the governor. In this case the Tridentine ideal of pastoral regulation of charitable institutions, which bishops elsewhere sought to secure in the face of lay resistance, was clearly not being defeated by the priorities of temporal government. Such complementary action is indeed typified by the career of a clerical governor, Francesco Bossio, who subsequently became one of the city's post-Tridentine bishops, working in the spirit of both Paleotti of Bologna and Charles Borromeo. This can be compared with the work in an Immediately Subject diocese of the Roman province of one of the most outstanding Vicars General of Borromean Milan, Antonio Seneca, who subsequently as bishop of Anagni published his synodal decrees in 1613.[14]

At Ferrara, after its late sixteenth-century annexation by the papacy, the see was occupied by cardinals from 1611 onwards. In the mid-eighteenth century two diocesans, who both died in residence, were not cardinals, but this was after the elevation of the see to an archbishopric in 1735. Their successor, Cardinal Crescenzi, also died in residence in 1768, but the see then remained vacant until 1773, when Cardinal Giraud succeeded. This was not the first extended period *sede vacante* after the establishment of papal government at Ferrara. Between 1691 and 1696 the governing Legate, Cardinal Imperiali, was responsible for the administration of the see.

AVIGNON

In the papal enclave within French territory, Avignon and the comtat Venaissin, expulsion of heretics was the first aim of Roman policy in the decades after the Council of Trent, but by the end of the sixteenth century this essentially Legatine responsibility was being complemented by more positive pastoral provision. Clement VIII, at the start of his pontificate, chose a priest of an institution favoured by the new pope, the Roman Oratory, as bishop of Cavaillon. This appointment of Bordini was followed by an important succession at the archbishopric of Avignon itself, while Bordini was also to serve subsequently as Vice-Legate there. Later in the same year, 1592, Clement indicated to another Oratorian, Francesco Maria Tarugi, his intention of making

---

14 *Istoria della Città e S. Basilica Cattedrale d'Anagni . . . descritta da Alessandro de Magistris* (Rome 1749), pp. 123 ff.

him archbishop of Avignon. From the start, Tarugi, though reluctant to accept, saw the unavoidable appointment as an opportunity of introducing Roman and specifically Oratorian standards at Avignon and hence into France. His suite, which he took to Avignon in 1593, was formed from members and associates of the Oratory, while his solemn entry into his see was immediately followed by the Forty Hours' Devotion. Equally immediate was his imposition of reform on priests, friars and nuns there. After consultation with Bordini, he examined the confessors of the diocese, announced a diocesan synod and began a pastoral visitation of Avignon and its diocese.[15]

While Tarugi's household was run on the exemplary lines of other zealous bishops of the pre- and post-Tridentine era, he set up a group of secular priests to live and work on the model of the Roman Oratory. In pursuit of the Oratorian ideal of correct and impressive liturgical ceremony, he was able to make use of a Master of Ceremonies borrowed from Milan through the intervention of a friend of the Oratory, Cardinal Federico Borromeo. This exceptional loan from a diocese which under Charles Borromeo and subsequently guarded its ablest officials and priests jealously thus brought to French-speaking territory the severe standards of Milanese post-Tridentine reform as well. Even authorities at Milan itself wondered if the rigour of Clerici might not be counter-productive, in fostering local opposition to the new archbishop of Avignon. After his return to Lombardy, however, he became head of the Oblates of St Ambrose, to which he belonged, the elite congregation of diocesan priests founded by Charles Borromeo vowed to absolute obedience to the archbishops of Milan, rather as the inner cadre of the Society of Jesus was specially vowed to the service of the pope.

At Avignon by then attention was already being given to instruction of confessors, preaching and catechizing, sacred music and charitable relief. A seminary had to be virtually refounded, while the cathedral canons, as in so many cases after the Council of Trent, at first resisted reform of their chapter. As elsewhere too in the post-Conciliar Church, including Siena where Tarugi was later to be archbishop, the nuns initially found lay support for their refusal of strict enclosure.[16] But those at Avignon were reduced to conformity, with the help of Jesuits in support of the Oratorian archbishop. Clerical non-conformity was successfully repressed by the diocesan synod and this was followed by the summoning of a provincial council. Tarugi's work was thus influential in the subsequent diffusion of the Oratorian ideal in France, just as the post-Tridentine Church at Avignon more generally became a centre for the extension of restored Catholicism in the Southern parts of France particularly affected by the wars of religion and the spread of Protestantism. The female educational initiative of the Ursulines also spread from there. Tarugi, the future cardinal, managed with care the potentially difficult relationship

15 A. Cistellini, *San Filippo Neri, L'Oratorio e la Congregazione Oratoriana, Storia e Spiritualità* (3 vols, Brescia 1989).
16 C. Marcora, 'La corrispondenza del Card. Francesco Maria Tarugi col Card. Federico Borromeo', *Memorie storiche della Diocesi di Milano*, XI (1964), 124 ff.: p. 167.

with representatives of papal temporal government in the enclave, such as the Vice-Legate, Archbishop Genebrando.

Tarugi's synodal decrees, which another diocesan of the province, the bishop of Carpentras, was to take to Rome for papal confirmation, were published at Rome in 1597, the year of the Oratorian cardinal's translation to the archbishopric of Siena. Bordini, as Vice-Legate, cared for Avignon before succeeding Tarugi as archbishop there. Between 1593 and 1597 the Legation of Avignon had been in the hands of Cardinal Acquaviva, subsequently a zealous archbishop of Naples. His independence in the face of Spanish policy was already clear from his involvement as Legate in the negotiations leading to the reconciliation of Henri of Navarre. The final decision of Clement VIII in favour of this policy, despite Spanish protest, had been influenced by Oratorian advice, so that the episcopate of Tarugi at Avignon, with its importance for the beginnings of Catholic restoration in the surrounding French realm, formed in the end part of a coherent Counter-Reformation.

The tradition of Tarugi was not forgotten at Avignon itself. The future Cardinal Fieschi, archbishop between 1690 and 1705, made a new seminary foundation under Sulpician direction, and his successor Archbishop Gontieri held a provincial council in 1725. In this respect the tradition went back before Tarugi indeed, for despite the obvious difficulties of the Church in French-speaking territory in the later sixteenth century, the post-Conciliar archbishop, the Servite Capitone, had followed the Tridentine pattern by holding diocesan synods from 1566 and a provincial council in 1574. Although one seventeenth-century archbishop was for long absent in papal diplomatic service, some of his eighteenth-century successors died in residence. A pastoral tradition thus continued despite the vulnerability of Avignon to occupation by royal authority during conflicts between popes and the French monarchy during this period.[17]

NON-ROMANS

At Rome itself not all ecclesiastics of course were necessarily Italian, let alone native Romans. So even within the city the popes had oversight of many who were not simply subject to them in a purely diocesan context. The religious life of Rome reflected this too, as when precisely civic honours were paid each year to the memory of Philip Neri, effective founder of the Oratory, but a Roman by adoption rather than birth. The canonization of Neri in 1622 by Gregory XV, after anguished delay and Jesuit jealousy, followed that of S. Francesca Romana by Paul V in 1608. The popular enthusiasm in immediately pre-Revolutionary Rome for the foreign ascetic Benedict Labre represented him at his death as a saint of the city. But he arguably represented in fact that lay propensity to the eremitic life which was so marked in the Roman province from the later seventeenth century and even noted by Paleotti at

---

17 M. Venard, *Réforme protestante, réforme catholique dans la province d'Avignon au XVIe siècle* (Paris 1993).

Sabina at the end of the sixteenth, and which strikingly required regulation at the provincial council of 1725.[18]

Lay religious practice in Rome, as has already been seen, was not in any case confined to the strictly parochial. Nevertheless one of the achievements of Cardinal Savelli as Vicar of the Rome diocese immediately after the Tridentine Council had been the rationalization of the parochial structure between 1566 and 1569. To reflect a decreased lay population, the 130 parishes were reduced in number, but further modifications continued. For example, the Roman Oratorians relinquished the parish for a while attached to their new church in the early seventeenth century, after a relatively brief tenure. As the city population changed, the eighty-one parishes of 1695 were increased to eighty-six by 1715 but returned to eighty-two from 1766.

But if many of Rome's churches were not parochial, equally, not all secular clerics in the city, let alone regulars, were in stable parochial posts. Indeed, by the later eighteenth century many of the secular clergy who supported themselves precariously from minor benefices and Mass stipends in the city were not native Romans either, but clerics from the impoverished Southern and central territories of Calabria, Puglia and the Abruzzi. For it should be recalled that many clerics ordained in the kingdom of Naples were unable to penetrate the closed and self-perpetuating corporations of clergy which so strongly continued to characterize the post-Tridentine Church there, the *chiese ricettizie*. This feature of the secular clergy in Rome, however, reinforced the fact, already reflected in the decrees of the provincial council of 1725, that many had not studied for any length of time, if at all, in seminary. The presence of the Seminario Romano as an institution of the Rome diocese did not affect this outcome.[19]

There were indeed signs that in Rome itself the decrees of the provincial council and other efforts by Benedict XIII to improve clerical standards had not entirely had the desired effect among the seculars. The Vicariate noted the incompetence and carelessness of many priests there in 1766. But the Cardinal Vicar was still exhorting the clergy to improve their conduct, both in specifically ecclesiastical functions and in daily life, in 1775. On the other hand, apologists for the secular clergy countered that the superfluity of regulars in Rome precluded seculars from finding proper support, for example in established posts at institutes of learning and clerical education. It was even alleged, perhaps less convincingly, that regulars had come to exclude seculars in staffing the dicasteries of the Roman Curia; though regulars obviously continued to be conspicuous as Lenten and other special preachers in the Rome diocese. If, then, there was one ecclesiastic to every fifteen or so persons in Rome before

18 G. Paleotti, 'Ordini da osservarsi per quelli, che in abito di Eremita averanno la licenza di stare nella Diocesi di Sabina, fatti per commissione dello stesso Cardinale Vescovo l'Anno 1594', in *Constitutiones Synodales Sabinae Dioecesis editae ab Hannibale Cardinale S. Clementis Episcopo Sabinorum . . . 1736* (Urbino 1737), pp. 87 ff.
19 V. De Vitiis, 'Chiese ricettizie e organizzazione ecclesiastica nel Regno delle Due Sicilie dal Concordato del 1818 all' Unità', in *Per la storia sociale e religiosa del Mezzogiorno d'Italia*, II, ed. G. Galasso and C. Russo (Naples 1982), pp. 349–481.

1740, that figure cannot of itself reveal much about pastoral provision for the laity.

In response to this presence in the city of clerics who were not natives of the diocese, including those who were nevertheless from the Roman province, the papacy made a gradual extension during this period of opportunities for clerical education in the city, quite apart from the special seminaries training priests for specific areas elsewhere, such as the English College, the Greek College, the German College and eventually the Propaganda Fide College. The foundation by Clement VIII of the Collegio Clementino in 1596 provided secondary education for young noblemen, many of whom, though not all, became clerics. It was entrusted not to the Jesuits, about whom Clement was always somewhat reserved, but to the Somaschi, a sixteenth-century New Order which in the Tridentine period was for a while at least in charge of a number of seminaries. Its boarders eventually came from a wide range of European territories, including some under Protestant domination. The Collegio Nazareno was under the direction of another New Order, the Piarists, founded with a specifically educational purpose. This foundation, the achievement of the bishop of Cesena, Cardinal Tonti, from the 1620s provided boys with a gentlemanly education, even if they were not destined to become clerics, and survived a reputation for Jansenist sympathies among the staff in the eighteenth century. The Ecclesiastical Academy established in 1704 was, by contrast, a truly papal foundation, intended by Clement XI to train a clerical elite, drawn from those of noble birth both from the papal states and from further afield. The restricted numbers ensured that the products of this pontifical institute formed a fast-stream of entrants to ecclesiastical office.

Given the attractions of such establishments, the intervention of Alexander VII to revive the failing life of the University of Rome, the Sapienza, was all the more necessary by the mid-seventeenth century. The building which housed the lecture-rooms and church of St Ivo came to shelter not only the library he established and a printing press, but also an anatomy theatre, even if this was not of the same fame as that at papal-ruled Bologna. The pope's provision of a botanical garden also allowed comparison to be made with the Venetian Republic's University of Padua, noted for its medical and botanical study. Such positive intervention did not prevent renewed decline, though, and the relative eminence which was restored to legal studies and retained by medicine was secured by further papal action, in the pontificates of Innocent XII and Clement XI. Benedict XIV had exercised a positive influence on higher education and scholarship at Bologna, and attempted as pope to reorganize the Roman Sapienza. New professorial provisions were made, especially after Benedict was able to entrust supervision of the institution to a cardinal more amenable than Cardinal Albani, from 1747. The decayed botanical garden was restored, but student numbers remained distinctly small until a further reform on the eve of Revolution, in 1788. The only increase immediately before that had, by an irony, been an effect of the interruption of Jesuit teaching at the Collegio Romano.

After the suppression of the Jesuits, in Rome as elsewhere, it was not only the English College which, of necessity, required new staff. Difficulties in finding enough adequate substitutes meant that the Seminario Romano found itself integrated with the Collegio Romano under a single commission of cardinals. Other colleges and seminaries in the city which had been run by the Jesuits also had to be given new staff, who were supposedly to come from the secular clergy. Since this proved difficult it is necessary to consider the clerical population of Rome, by that date, a little further. The ecclesiastics among the Roman population included not only bishops and secular and regular clergy, but also, from a legal point of view, lay brothers, nuns and seminarians. On this definition the proportion of the total population represented by ecclesiastics remained relatively constant from the last years of the seventeenth century to the 1760s.

Between 1770 and 1790, however, the proportion shrank a little, to just over 5 per cent. The ratio of regular to secular clergy also remained fairly stable from the late seventeenth century to 1775, peaking at over one and a half to one between 1761 and 1765. But between 1776 and 1785 the ratio was reversed, at under one to one. This represented the growth of the secular clergy in Rome, from a figure below 3,000 before 1774 to above that level between then and 1788. Since the total proportion of ecclesiastics declined from that same era, however, this would seem to suggest an absolute and not just relative decline among other ecclesiastics present in the city, including possibly the regular clergy, for previous momentary increases in the secular clergy's presence in Rome can be related to the influx of pilgrims in Jubilee years.

Nuns, including both choir-nuns and lay sisters, provided up to 2,000 of the city's ecclesiastical population before 1771. Thereafter a decline, though not consistent, towards 1,500 was evident. Yet the percentage of nuns among the specifically female population of Rome remained relatively constant until 1765, with only a very gradual decline from a high point at the end of the seventeenth century. Only between 1766 and 1790 did the percentage drop from below 2.5 to only just over 2 per cent. So an absolute decline in the presence of regular clergy and lay brothers at Rome in the pre-Revolutionary decades again seems impossible to exclude. Above all, the effects in the city of the suppression of the Jesuits must be taken into account, not least in the disruption of the seminaries previously directed by the Society of Jesus.

POPES AND RELIGIOUS ORDERS

The Jesuits were not of course the only order to be affected by the evolution of papal policy during this period. In Rome itself the various religious houses already numbered about 103 by 1630. A new addition, for example, had been made under Pius V, with the formation of the Roman Charterhouse from one part of the remains of the Baths of Diocletian, adjacent to the tomb of Pius IV in the Church of S. Maria degli Angeli, which that pope had engaged

Michelangelo to construct out of the main section. Outside the city, however, and by the later eighteenth century, the papacy was effectively an impotent onlooker as Catholic secular authorities in French- and German-speaking Europe dissolved religious houses of orders deemed to lack a justifying purpose or viability, following local suppression of the Society of Jesus itself. Where such dissolution met with at least implicit episcopal tolerance this could be seen as symptomatic of uneasy relations between bishops and regulars which had continued ever since the Council of Trent. The Conciliar decrees had extended episcopal supervision to the pastoral work of regulars, above all preaching and the hearing of confessions. But bishops had not always been able to realize this restored authority, in the face of regulars' defence of their independence. For that reason, consideration of the popes' role beyond the Rome diocese must also extend to their general relations with the religious orders.

Papal policy was indeed crucial. In principle the papacy supported the Tridentine provisions, for it was only in the missions beyond Europe that the pre-Tridentine privileges which exempted the mendicants from episcopal supervision of even directly pastoral work were eventually restored, overriding the Conciliar decrees, for instance. But in specific cases within Europe, nevertheless, papal support for episcopal authority against regulars was not always secure. By contrast, the post-Tridentine popes did defend the distinctive features of Basilian religious life against Spanish governmental criticism. The royal design to impose the uniformity of the Latin rite on the Basilian monasteries of Sicily was resisted at Rome, where the antiquity of the Basilians' Greek liturgy was appreciated as a symbol of papal claims to universal jurisdiction, a matter of particular importance in the light of relations in Polish and Venetian territory with Christians who were not of the Latin rite. Papal intervention indeed secured the reorganization of the Basilians in Southern Italy.[20]

Roman policy after the Council of Trent tended to encourage older orders to greater centralization in their internal affairs, reproducing a feature of the New Orders of sixteenth-century foundation, most of which, and not only to a singular extent the Jesuits, were organized in this way. The majority of the Oratorians in Italy, on the other hand, proved exceptionally resistant to such a model, precisely because of their determination to remain a movement of secular priests. But the papacy after the Council had more generally to defend the principle of international organization in the religious orders against Spanish attempts to set up distinct Iberian provinces under local superiors. That policy was aimed not only at the Jesuits, whose constitutional difficulties at the end of the sixteenth and the beginning of the seventeenth centuries turned largely, though far from wholly, on the hostility encountered by the Society from influential interests in the Spanish Church, Inquisition and royal government. Such hostility eventually declined, from the succession of Philip IV

20 A.G.S.: Secretaría Provincial: Sicilia: Varios: Libros 776, fos 1[bis]r ff.; 779, fos 26v f.: 1586–1627; cf. A.S.V. Spagna, XXXIII, 85r ff., 103r ff.; XXXV, 362r–v: 15 Nov. 1586–3 Mar. 1590.

onwards, but a similar danger of enforced reorganization on a peninsular basis had for a while faced the Cistercians also, and even the Carthusians. The distinction of the Charterhouses remaining elsewhere in Catholic Europe ensured continued papal approval, and the eremitic element in religious life itself, as opposed to that of individual lay hermits, was reflected in other orders too, in Italy the Camaldoli for instance. The eremitic revival of the later medieval Church was not confined to Italy, however, as the Hieronymites in the Iberian peninsula demonstrated.

Benedictine monasticism had also experienced a partial redirection, again starting before the Council of Trent, with the formation in some parts of Western Christendom of congregations linking certain houses, achieving a new degree of common organization. This tendency within Benedictinism was prominent in the Iberian realms but was also encouraged in Italy by papal support for the centralized structure of the Cassinese congregation. That support was maintained in the post-Tridentine Church despite the suspicion aroused for a while in the sixteenth century by some theologians of the congregation.[21] The papacy's approval was also sought by the English Benedictines in exile for their claim to an independent role in the mission work in Protestant England itself. Within the Cistercian movement, on the other hand, and specifically the reformed element, a new initiative to achieve extreme austerity won Roman approbation after the founding of La Trappe.

Attempted reform among the various groups of canons regular in the Western Church continued after the Council of Trent, but still with rather varied results. The replacement of a few remaining Spanish cathedral chapters of canons regular by supposedly more satisfactory secular canons was a royal plan which for once did not seem to encounter papal opposition. But whatever the merits of the pastoral activity of Premonstratensian canons, in parts of German-speaking Europe for example, the papacy could not regard all canons regular with equal favour. The selective dissolutions pursued by popes of the seventeenth century thus came to include canons of the body associated with S. Giorgio in Alga, in the Venetian lagoon. The more successful reform imposed on the Trinitarians has already been noted in this chapter, though this degree of success was not achieved among the French Trinitarians.

In the Italian states, however, the post-Tridentine popes faced a peculiar problem posed by the criminal behaviour of individual Knights of St John. The privileges of the Knights, as a military order, were strenuously defended by the popes, who relied on these regulars for the continued defence of Malta against Islam, throughout the period from the loss of Cyprus in the later sixteenth century to the fall of Crete in the later seventeenth and beyond. The Knights' exemption from secular justice but immunity also from local ecclesiastical tribunals placed responsibility for their criminal activity and its punishment directly on Rome. In the Iberian kingdoms the complaints against military

---

21 B. Collett, *Italian Benedictine Scholars and the Reformation. The Congregation of Santa Giustina of Padua* (Oxford 1985).

orders, the powerful peninsular orders even more than the Knights of St John, came rather from diocesan bishops. These felt that papal defence of the orders' privileges left large numbers of parishes, controlled by the orders, beyond effective episcopal supervision.[22]

The substantial maintenance of the privileges of the religious orders, after the Council of Trent, was then a policy which benefited not only the Jesuits, for all their conspicuous claim to a specially close association with the papacy. In many ways it was the mendicants who still collectively demonstrated this papal favour most obviously, not least because of their continued involvement in pastoral work as well as other activities. The Dominicans remained influential as theologians, not least at Rome itself, which was one reason why papal favour towards the Jesuits could never be entirely assured. Although this influence in one specific area was gradually eroded, as the popes from the late sixteenth century onwards cautiously, gradually, but in the end consistently gave their support to the contested Marian doctrine of the Immaculate Conception, against Dominican conservatism, the Order of Preachers secured one undoubted success after the Council of Trent. This was the papal elevation of Aquinas to the status of Doctor of the Church, by which in 1567 Pius V virtually assimilated Thomist authority to the authority of the Fathers of the Church.

The criticism by Dominicans as well as other mendicants of the innovatory missionary practices of the Jesuits in the Far East also contributed to the cumulative papal condemnations of much of this experimental method, which undermined the Society's efforts in China decades before its suppression in Europe. Franciscan rivalry with the Jesuits in the overseas missions, in Japan and the Far East even more than in America, also had some effect on this aspect of papal policy. But the attempts of post-Tridentine popes to regulate the division of labour between Jesuits and mendicants in the Far East proved largely ineffective, for political and logistic reasons. The Franciscan missionaries in America, on the other hand, achieved some substantial success in preserving papal support in their rivalry, not least financial, with the secular clergy and the bishops there. While the two main strands of Franciscan life, the Conventual and the Observant, continued in the post-Conciliar Church, the papacy gave encouragement to movements of further reform, the varieties of reformed observants which developed in Italy and Spain for example.

The most austere offshoot, the Capuchins, for some time suffered opposition from the Franciscan authorities themselves, and were not helped by their momentary association with heresy in sixteenth-century Italy. But papal protection was eventually extended to the Capuchins, by the early seventeenth century, and their effective independence was thereby established. The truly mendicant nature of the Capuchin life had been preserved by the Tridentine decree excepting them from the general permission given to religious orders

22 B.A.V. MS Ferrajoli 61, fo. 68r; A.S.V.: Segreteria di Stato: Lettere di Principi, vol. 48, fo. 246r; cf. vol. 53, fo. 7r–v: 1590–94.

to acquire property. But where religious houses, of whatever order, relied so wholly on popular alms, a problem of competition for limited resources could result. The post-Conciliar papacy agreed to a rule by which truly mendicant foundations could not be created within a certain distance of each other.

The Augustinians had developed their own internal reform movement before the Council of Trent, affecting houses which became linked together in various parts of Europe and sought papal protection. Their friaries in the post-Tridentine Church led an essentially conventual not an eremitic existence. The passionate disputes over reform which affected the Carmelites, primarily in Spain, led to some uncertainty in papal response. The post-Tridentine popes were not swift in their support for reform among the Spanish friars, because of the confused evolution of the movement, but in the end the Strict Observance was approved, alongside the existing branch of the order. The Servites survived the decided papal anger engendered by the Venetian dissident, Paolo Sarpi, which continued beyond the friar's most influential moment, as advisor to and apologist for the Venetian Republic during the Interdict imposed by Paul V. State protection prevented papal punishment of Sarpi, however, and the papacy was in no position to stop his critical history of the Council of Trent being published in Protestant England. The Servite was thus indirectly responsible for the eventual papal decision to authorize an orthodox history of the Council, entrusted to a Jesuit scholar. The scientific interests of some of the French members of the order of Minims in the seventeenth century did not create such problems, by contrast.[23]

The continued development during this period of New Orders, of sixteenth-century or later foundation, was also ultimately dependent on papal approval. The persistent critics of the Society of Jesus, especially in late sixteenth-century Spain, raised a large issue, of importance to orders other than just the Jesuits. The allegation, chiefly by mendicants, that the Society lacked the essential characteristics of a regular order, and hence any claim to the privileges of one, challenged implicitly the freedom to develop new forms of the religious life. But the sixteenth-century papacy had already given clear approval to the concept, radically innovative at the time, of clerks regular, distinct from either canons regular and monks on the one hand, or mendicants on the other. Thus the Theatines continued after the Council of Trent to form a clerical elite which supplied a number of zealous bishops, devoted to the implementation of the Conciliar reforms. This in itself positively affected the papal choice of bishops, at least for sees where no secular ruler enjoyed a right of nomination. The influence of the Theatines was demonstrated by the persistence in post-Conciliar Italy and Spain of the use of the name in a generic as well as a specific sense. Zealous prelates, conscientious secular clerics, Jesuits and associates of the Roman Oratory were all at times given this epithet.

23 P. Sarpi, *Historia del Concilio Tridentino* (London 1619); S. Pallavicino, *Istoria del Concilio di Trento* (2 vols, Rome 1656–57); cf. P.J.S. Whitmore, *The Order of Minims in Seventeenth-century France* (The Hague 1967).

The Somaschi and Barnabites might not achieve this wider recognition but papal approval ensured their continued existence and geographical extension. Since the fundamental criticism of the whole concept of clerks regular was thus doomed to failure, the opponents of the Society of Jesus concentrated on more distinctive features of the Jesuits' constitution and activity. While it has already been noted that not all popes between the end of the Council of Trent and the suppression of the Society were wholeheartedly favourable to the Jesuits, it is important to recall that, on the other hand, the peculiar relationship between the Society and the papacy was not simply a figment of Jesuit imagination. The Society's theologians at the Council of Trent had conspicuously defended papal authority in all its plenitude. The influence of the Jesuit Cardinal Bellarmine in the consolidation of Catholic doctrine after the Council, by means of his catechetical and controversial works, by far outweighed the momentary disfavour aroused by his moderate statement on the extent of papal temporal authority. Jesuit theologians remained central to internal Catholic debate after Trent, at Rome itself as well as at Louvain or in Spain, and Jansenist opposition from the seventeenth century ensured, by an irony, that this continued to be the case until the suppression of the Society.

The constitutional problems which faced the Society at the end of the sixteenth century and beginning of the seventeenth were not caused entirely by external critics, but also partly by internal dissidence, not least in Spain. The original constitution of the Society, with its characteristic highly centralized authority, ensured an international quality which was the antithesis of Iberian inclination towards peninsular organization of religious orders. But though papal confirmation of the original constitutional arrangements had not been without delay or difficulty in the sixteenth century, it was sufficient to allow the rapid expansion, numerically and geographically, which was already evident by the end of the century. This swift enlargement inevitably placed new strains on such a highly centralized body, and the impatience of Clement VIII, for instance, reflected a desire to see necessary constitutional revision efficiently completed, not an opposition to change. The pontificates of Clement and of Paul V proved, however, that the close and conspicuous association of the Society with the papacy could prove of doubtful benefit to the Jesuits. After a period of expulsion from much of the French kingdom, the Jesuits were subsequently excluded from Venetian territory until later in the seventeenth century, following Paul's imposition of an Interdict on the Republic.

This response to Jesuit defence of papal authority and the Society's influence in educated circles of Venetian society was thus markedly different from the Republic's reactions in the case of certain other religious, including Theatines and some friars. For these were largely readmitted to Venetian territory after the lifting of the Interdict, despite their own part in supporting the Interdict against Republican orders for its non-observance. This was a warning that the position of the Jesuits in Catholic Europe and overseas was singular and liable to remain so. The pontificate of Clement VIII after all was also marked by his attempts, however inconclusively, to assess the claims of Catholic theologians who attacked Jesuit teaching on essential Catholic doctrine, despite the supposedly definitive clarification at Trent of questions such as that of Grace. The effect, on balance, of these controversies, at least in constitutional rather than doctrinal terms, was nevertheless to consolidate the links between the Society and the papacy. A disavowal of the Society would obviously have been unlikely after the Venetian challenge to papal power. Papal agreement to the revised structure of the Society was obtained, from 1608, and so in Spain itself critics of the Jesuits had to modify their more fundamental objections to the Society's presence, lest they be seen to challenge papal authority directly.

Defence of the religious orders was in any case a natural policy of the Tridentine papacy, since Reformation criticism had attacked the entire concept of the religious life as well as the institution of the papacy, and not just the human failings in either. This defensive tendency was if anything fortified by the fact that at Trent the more vociferous demands that certain practical applications of papal authority be limited had come from bishops, some of whom also harboured ambitious, if in the end unavailing, plans for a radical reduction of the regulars' privileges and exemptions from episcopal jurisdiction. Yet the papal source of such privileges had in one sense been safeguarded by the Council itself, by virtue of its explicit concluding reaffirmations of papal authority. The bishops had in practice been most successful at Trent in extending episcopal supervision over female regulars, rather than in relation to male monastics, mendicants or canons regular. For even before the Tridentine reforms there was a crucial distinction in Catholic Christendom between some female convents which were immediately dependent on male regulars, usually of the same order, and others which were under the direct supervision of the local bishop. The papal response in the post-Tridentine Church to questions about female religious reflected this important difference.

The immediately post-Conciliar popes began one essential policy which applied to both types of female convent, however. This was the aim of imposing strict Tridentine enclosure on female houses, irrespective of original rule or order. Subsidiary elements of the policy were designed to secure this end, including the ideal of testing the personal vocation of girls seeking entry to the conventual life. The chief difficulty in all this was the entrenched social attitude to female convents found in Catholic Europe. Parents sought to preserve their ability to determine a daughter's future, especially as rising expectations of the size of marriage dowries among propertied families in Western Europe reduced the likelihood of making a suitable marriage for more than one daughter. The parents at such levels of society also wished to control the traditionally more manageable entry-dowries paid when a girl entered a convent as a choir-sister. While the relatives of such girls were anxious to conserve convents as the proper location in which conspicuous chastity and hence family honour were demonstrated, the concept of honour involved opposition to public changes such as the imposition of strict enclosure. Social access for girls' relations was defended, and enforced enclosure was challenged on the grounds that it defamed the nuns' past behaviour and hence their families too.

The success of this consistent papal policy was thus only partial. A degree of stricter enclosure was in most parts of Catholic Europe gradually extended to female convents, from the later sixteenth century onwards, especially as an older generation of nuns passed away and the popes refused to allow unenclosed communities to recruit. It was the relative success of the papacy on this front which produced the clash with more innovative forms of female religious life, as with the Ursulines and the activity of Mary Ward, where a desire for a less enclosed existence in the pursuit of female education was obstructed for a while by the male hierarchy of the Church. Even so, the papacy's success on this front was not complete, since in Spain for instance the groups of females living a communal life, like that of tertiaries, but avoiding solemn profession or formal enclosure, known there as *beatas*, survived despite papal and episcopal disapproval. But even such incomplete success must be balanced against a long-term failure in the other strand of hierarchical policy. The ideal of reducing female convents to purely voluntary communities, by testing personal vocation as opposed to parental decision, proved in the long run almost impossible to achieve. The priorities of lay society might here be said to have defeated the consistent ambitions of the popes.

A further qualification of papal policy reflected the distinction already noted between female convents subject to male regular superiors and those houses directly under episcopal oversight. The post-Conciliar popes generally, if not universally, favoured the transfer, where opportunity arose, of female convents from the first to the second category. But since such opportunity was commonly engendered by allegations of scandalous behaviour, the male regulars were usually swift to defend their own conduct and preserve their orders' repute. The objection to relinquishing control to the local bishop was often supported by parental refusal to countenance the transfer, precisely because it would reflect badly on the nuns' behaviour and tarnish family reputation. There were other practical difficulties encountered by the popes in pursuing such transfers of responsibility, and not all female convents, by any means, were taken into direct episcopal care. But one other tendency in the post-Tridentine Church, to which the papacy consented, further enhanced episcopal authority over the affairs of female religious. Many of the male New Orders refused to allow their membership to be involved in institutional direction of female regulars, so that new female orders, from the later sixteenth century onwards, however much inspired by and imitative of male New Orders, were often from the start under episcopal supervision.

The immediately post-Tridentine popes gave some support to bishops intent on fulfilling their duty, explicitly imposed by the Conciliar decrees, to supervise and audit charitable foundations and pious bequests. While secular authority might resist this, in defence of lay control of essentially lay funding, frequently such dispute necessarily raised the question of episcopal control of lay confraternities; especially if already in existence before the Council of Trent, as opposed to those of subsequent creation, some of which were under episcopal direction from the start. Some, too, of the pre-existing confraternities were under the guidance of religious orders, while among the New Orders, the Jesuits were prominent in establishing sodalities under the Society's aegis, often based on their educational establishments and usually drawing membership from upper- and middle-class males.[24] In the peculiar conditions of Recusant England, the lay sodalities more widely fostered by Jesuits confirmed both the importance of the regulars' mission work and the proprietary basis of household churches, in the face of the uncertain authority of the Archpriest or Vicars Apostolic at the head of the secular clergy. In the long term the papacy could be seen more generally as relatively content to allow continued regular direction of many lay confraternities, whatever bishops' objections or reservations.

It might be said that during the two and a quarter centuries of the post-Tridentine era the papacy acknowledged a continuing and substantial independence in the devotional life and organization of the lay confraternities of Catholic Europe. This was arguably as clear as the sustained dominance of lay priorities with regard to female convents. The heroic determination of some bishops, especially of the earlier post-Conciliar generation, to impose episcopal authority on either type of institution did not lead to any overwhelming success in reality; and this was despite the efforts not only of the Borromeo archbishops of Milan, for example, but of others too, including for instance archbishops of Seville. In the latter city, as also at Granada, it was not even certain how far the popes would support the archbishops in their attempts to supervise and reorganize charitable foundations. On the other hand, while in Portugal the archbishops of Evora might lament that papal encouragement of Jesuit education had been maintained even when this was at the expense of a diocesan seminary's survival, a few Spanish bishops still looked to the papacy to protect the jurisdiction of diocesans against the dominance of the Inquisition in its Spanish form. Their hopes here were destined to be only ambiguously realized.[25]

But the support given by a specific lay confraternity to the Roman Inquisition, in many Italian states, was certainly encouraged by the papacy, which eventually extended the spiritual benefits enjoyed by this confraternity to the distinct network of lay familiars of the Inquisition in Spain. In the case of such a confraternity in Venetian territory, papal protection was indeed necessary after the conclusion of the early seventeenth-century Interdict, as the Republic sought to remove it from regulars' direction and subject it to greater oversight by lay magistrates.[26] The spiritual benefits which attracted membership of many confraternities prominently included indulgences, despite the caution

24 L. Châtellier, *The Europe of the Devout. The Catholic Reformation and the Formation of a New Society* (Cambridge 1989).
25 Archivio Segreto Vaticano: Archivio della S. Congregazione del S. Concilio: Relatio, Visita ad limina, 311, Evora: 1592–1630; cf. St Patrick's College, Maynooth, Ireland: Russell Library: Salamanca Papers: Santiago de Compostela: Irish College: Various Documents, for Evora, 1613–17.
26 A.S. Ven.: Senato: Dispacci di Rettori: Brescia: 1614.

enjoined by the Council of Trent over their grant, in the face of Protestant criticism. The popes of this period continued to grant indulgences in many situations, but were anxious that precisely Roman authority should predominate in this. In Jubilee years, indulgences normally available at places other than Rome were generally suspended. It was only by occasional privilege that in Jubilees the faithful might gain the same indulgences available at Rome while performing the set devotions in some specially favoured episcopal city elsewhere. The association at other times of local confraternities with Roman archconfraternities, involving some share of spiritual benefits, more clearly suited papal policy than episcopal control of lay devotion.

The regulars, in the supervision of confraternities under their control, could also still attract lay membership by the grant of indulgences, which were renewed under relatively stricter control by the post-Tridentine papacy, after the recognized abuses in this area of the later Middle Ages and Renaissance. Papal agreement to the one major indulgence which was, in effect, still sold, in Spain and increasingly in other Spanish territories, represented a compromise with the Spanish monarchy on the use of ecclesiastical revenue in the Counter-Reformation. But this Crusade indulgence, while benefiting some Spanish Inquisitors, canons and regulars as well as the Crown and the papacy, certainly undermined important aspects of episcopal authority. On the other hand, the popes usually supported the efforts of bishops in Catholic Europe who were encouraging new confraternities to specialize in charitable care of different classes of social and medical need, repress blasphemy and violent feud, or catechize. The gradual spread, initially in the Italian states but subsequently more widely, of lay sodalities involved in the systematic provision of catechizing for both boys and girls was a major achievement of the 'long Counter-Reformation' which drew on a combination of lay initiative, episcopal direction, regulars' encouragement and papal approval. This by far outweighed the resistance of the state-controlled confraternities, the *Scuole Grandi* at Venice to ecclesiastical supervision for example.

Regulars, from both old and new orders, were also involved in the spread of new forms of popular devotion during this period, but the ultimate responsibility of the papacy was again in evidence. Some forms of devotion, like the Stations of the Cross, aroused little problem. But the papacy's reserve, for long towards active promotion of the cult of the Sacred Heart of Jesus, was not based solely on concern about the opposition demonstrated by some of the critics of the Jesuits. On the other hand, in parts of central and Southern Italy, where confraternity life was often more limited, at any rate in the sense of confining any charitable provision to members and their dependants as opposed to turning outwards to meet wider social need, the internal missions of the Passionists and Redemptorists reinforced popular piety and owed at least something to papal encouragement. Confraternity activity, of a more than simply pious nature, ultimately involved questions of funding and hence of control. Clement VIII was still intent on the Tridentine ideal of ecclesiastical

supervision at the beginning of the seventeenth century. But where confraternities received renewed papal permission to solicit alms, even if under more
stringent conditions, this did not necessarily suit episcopal attempts to prohibit unlicensed begging. The Tridentine reassertion of episcopal authority
did not fundamentally alter the close relationship more generally between the
papacy and the religious orders in fact.

CHAPTER 4

Primatial leadership and Italian problems

In the immediately post-Tridentine period, at least, the papacy managed to extend an effectively primatial authority over the states of mainland Italy. This has been acknowledged by the expert on the early modern papacy, Paolo Prodi, in his work published in Italian. Other Italian scholars have more recently noted that one aspect of this *de facto* authority, the activity of the Holy Office, remained important at least until the end of the seventeenth century.[1] The Roman Inquisition was not, however, the sole manifestation of this effective primacy within the peninsula, nor even at all times and in all places the most influential. The other ways by which the post-Tridentine popes established a special degree of control over the dioceses of mainland Italy can be examined to assess how long and how well this was maintained in the centuries before the French Revolution.

The political evolution of the peninsula during this period obviously affected the papacy's ability to conserve such distinctive leadership of the Church in the Italian states, beyond the confines of the papal states themselves. While the late sixteenth century saw the further consolidation of Spanish power within the peninsula, the papacy was nevertheless able to find some support by a working alliance with the restored Medici in Tuscany. The abnormal breach with Venice in the early seventeenth century should not be allowed to obscure papal success in negotiation over the management of ecclesiastical affairs with other Italian states. The Spanish government itself recognized the close relationship between the Church in Lombardy and Rome, in the later sixteenth and early seventeenth centuries; quite apart from the papacy's nominal over-lordship in the kingdom of Naples. The revival of Franco-Habsburg confrontation in the peninsula, most obviously in Northern Italy, posed problems for the papacy in the first half of the seventeenth century. But the popes of that period were not willing to surrender the potential enlargement of Roman independence within a Spanish-dominated peninsula achieved at the end of the

---

1 G. Romeo, *Inquisitori, esorcisti e streghe nell'Italia della Controriforma* (Florence 1990).

sixteenth century by Clement VIII in his recognition of Henri Bourbon as Catholic king of France.

This is indicated by his successors' attempts to exclude warfare as well as heresy from Northern Italy, however unsuccessfully in the case of the former. Such independent defence of peninsular interests was in one sense more difficult still, after the European upheavals of the mid-century. The demonstrable military and diplomatic weakness of the papacy, evident to all by 1648, left the popes highly vulnerable to the impact of Bourbon power, as the arrogant policies of Louis XIV from the start of his personal rule revealed. In one sense this was certainly a decline from Rome's evident ability, even after the Council of Trent, to intervene, for example, in the troubled internal politics of the Genoan Republic and encourage the restoration of stability there and hence more widely in the peninsula.[2] But a moral authority in the second half of the seventeenth century could still be exercised in Italian affairs, as the conspicuously pastoral popes of that period sought to show, and as has been noted with reference to the Holy Office.

An arguably more important watershed came at the end of the century, as the Italian peninsula again became a theatre of European rivalry, in the Spanish Succession War. The eventual triumph of the Austrian Habsburgs in Lombardy and Southern Italy redefined but did not remove, from Rome's perspective, the peninsular problem of Habsburg dominance. But the later replacement of the Habsburgs by the Bourbons in Southern Italy was to cause even more tension between the papacy and the various Bourbon Courts of Catholic Europe. Failure to prevent the political rearrangement of the peninsula or obstruct armies whose movements brought suffering to the native population of the Italian states is thus not the best test of papal leadership during this period. It could be argued that early modern conditions meant that European politics were inherently unstable, with dynastic attempts to alter ill-defined frontiers more a continual norm than an abnormality. What, however, distinguished mainland Italy during these centuries was an ecclesiastical rather than a political coherence.

For despite the obvious persistence of local traditions and state involvement, not only in Venetian territory but also in other and smaller peninsular states, the post-Tridentine papacy arguably extended over the mainland dioceses an unusually effective degree of supervision. The imposition of Roman authority made possible the relative success of some Tridentine reforms, certainly more swiftly than elsewhere in Catholic Europe, even if this degree of centralization also obstructed or distorted other changes planned at Trent. This determining control of Tridentine Church life, as far as mainland Italy is concerned, was largely but not solely the result of post-Conciliar reorganization of the Roman Curia. But other mechanisms, away from Rome itself, were also involved in the establishment of this effectively primatial authority. The fact that such devices proved relatively effective on the mainland but

2 F.C.M.: Segreteria di Stato: Nunziatura in Venezia: filza 266, fo. 78: 19 Mar. 1575.

were obstructed off-shore, as in Sicily and Sardinia, underlines the sense in which the post-Tridentine popes acted as primates of an Italian Church defined in geographic as opposed to political terms. Such primatial leadership was thus a further dimension of papal activity between the Council of Trent's conclusion and the French Revolution, affecting the Church in the peninsula beyond the boundaries of the Rome diocese or the confines of the papal states.

The Council of Trent had itself provided that papal authority should confirm, interpret and ensure implementation of the Conciliar decrees. This was over and above the Conciliar decision to remit to the papacy certain incomplete but potentially highly influential areas of reform, including publication of a catechism and revision of liturgical texts. The establishment at Rome, after the conclusion of the Council, of the Curial Congregation of the Council thus marked the new programme of centralized direction, which was subsequently enhanced by the reorganization of the Curia and the creation of other Congregations with specific responsibilities, all headed by cardinals. But, as already suggested, such initiatives were not confined to the Roman Curia itself. A two-way process of control was established additionally during the post-Conciliar decades, systematized by Sixtus V between 1585 and 1588.

Diocesan bishops were required to pay *ad limina* visits to Rome at stated intervals to report on the condition of their sees, a duty which was supposed to be fulfilled in person. Despite some conflict on occasion over this, with the Republic of Venice for example, the papacy was relatively well placed to insist on this regular contact and report for mainland Italian dioceses. Indeed, popes of the late sixteenth and early seventeenth centuries were sometimes still finding it difficult to impose diocesan residence on bishops preferring to live in Rome. For dioceses beyond the peninsula the papacy had much greater difficulty in enforcing *ad limina* visits, especially by bishops in person rather than by proctor, despite differentiated intervals for places further away. Such known difficulty was exploited by the Spanish government with regard to Sicilian or Sardinian dioceses, denying the papal claim that these were under the same obligations as mainland sees, despite being transmarine; and the Venetian Republic adopted the same challenge in respect of its Dalmatian dioceses.[3]

The relative success of such a regular and visible mark of subjection to Petrine authority also implied that uniform implementation of Tridentine reform might more nearly be achieved in the Italian mainland dioceses. The distinction between peninsular Italy and places further away, even Sicily and Sardinia, was also evident in two related matters. By the end of the sixteenth and beginning of the seventeenth centuries, in the pontificates of Clement VIII and Paul V, the papacy was insisting that candidates for Italian mainland

3 A.G.S.: Estado: Roma: Legs 937, fos 24 f.: 14 Nov. 1580; 972: 13 Sept. 1600; Secretaría Provincial: Sicilia: Varios: Leg. 1510: Discurso [*c.* 1633]; cf. A.S.V.: Segreteria di Stato: Venezia [hereafter A.S.V. Venezia], XXXV, 126v f.: 28 Oct. 1600.

bishoprics present themselves in Rome for personal examination of their suitability according to the Tridentine criteria for educational, moral and other qualification. Since this obviously affected the larger issue of episcopal appointments, it is not surprising that on occasion conflict arose over such examination, as over candidates for the Patriarchate of Venice for instance. But again, the more evident distinction proved to be between the Italian mainland bishoprics on the one hand and transalpine or transmarine dioceses on the other.

Thus the Spanish government was again able to assert its effectively free choice of nominees for Sicilian or Sardinian sees, just as for those in Spain itself. For, in the second related issue, the post-Tridentine popes found it impossible to intrude their own interim administrators, as Apostolic Vicars, into Sicilian sees, for example, when dispute over royal nomination left a bishopric vacant or when a bishop, for absence or some other reason, left his diocese in the island conspicuously unsupervised. That the popes, into the seventeenth century, attempted to employ such Vicars in Sicilian sees, is nevertheless a reminder of a device which could, in more favourable circumstances, be used as an additional way of imposing Roman direction on local Church affairs.[4] Once again the failure of a papal policy attempted off-shore rather emphasizes the coherence of the mainland Italian Church under enhanced papal authority. But the limitation of that authority was not readily conceded, as Clement VIII showed in attempting to standardize the range of cases reserved for episcopal (as opposed to priestly) absolution, not only for the mainland bishoprics but also those in the adjacent islands, Malta and Corsica included, and in Dalmatia.

Such reinvigorated papal action after the Council of Trent involved, as previously noted, a two-way process of control. Soon after the conclusion of the Council the papal nephew, Cardinal Borromeo, determined to make his entry, as archbishop and not just as administrator, to the see of Milan. It is striking that for this initial progress from Rome to Northern Italy he was invested with the extensive powers of papal Legate. He was subsequently employed, beyond the confines of the ecclesiastical province over which he presided as metropolitan, as another representative of papal authority in an immediate and active sense. For many of the reform decrees of the Council had empowered diocesan bishops to act as delegates of the Holy See, in the hope of outflanking those such as canons and regulars whose privileges and exemptions, commonly granted at Rome, had often impeded the exercise of episcopal jurisdiction. But the post-Conciliar popes introduced a new form of precisely papal supervision of dioceses and their bishops, while the Tridentine decrees had effectively reduced any ordinary metropolitical rights of visitation.

4 A.S.V. Venezia, XXXV, 27v ff.: 29 Jan. 1600 onwards; XXXVIII, 13r ff.: 7 July 1607 onwards; A.G.S.: Secretaría Provincial: Sicilia: Varios, Leg. 1510: 1577–1633, especially 1585–87, 1602–4, and particularly 12 Mar. 1604; Biblioteca Nazionale Marciana, Venice [hereafter B.N.M.]: MSS italiani, classe VII, n. 1553.

In this way Charles Borromeo was given extensive powers as Apostolic Visitor, to visit certain sees within the Venetian Republic. His vigorous activity at Bergamo, for example, helped to bring the Church there, situated on Republican territory but within the Milanese ecclesiastical province, into greater conformity with that version of Tridentine standards which he was intent on imposing not only in the diocese of Milan itself but throughout the province of which he was metropolitan archbishop. But Apostolic Visitation was not just a means by which Borromean uniformity could be imposed in areas beyond Spanish-ruled Lombardy, for Borromeo's own diocese, including foundations claiming exemption, in turn received an Apostolic Visitor, astutely appointed in the person of a Venetian subject, Bishop Ragazzoni, who visited ecclesiastical and charitable institutions which even Borromeo, as diocesan, had not visited. Borromeo was also authorized by Rome to visit Swiss valleys lying north of Milan and supervise the consolidation of Catholicism in that outwork of Catholic Italy, as well as being sent to reinforce inquisitorial authority in post-Conciliar Mantua.[5]

The importance of such post-Conciliar developments was not lost on contemporaries. The Venetian Republic proved very sensitive to Borromeo's Apostolic Visitation, and as far as the city of Venice itself was concerned, secured a specially confined visitation conducted by trusted prelates, including the nuncio himself, but not Borromeo. But Venetian prelates could also be trusted by Rome, and it was by agreement between Rome and Venice that a future cardinal such as Valier, bishop of Verona, could hold an Apostolic Visitation in Istrian or Dalmatian dioceses of the Republic. More problematic, as already indicated, could be the appointment of bishops. Here again the Venetian Republic showed a particular sensitivity, not least because the Patriarchate of Venice was the only see to which it had a full and clear right of nomination.

After the loss of Cyprus there still remained, for another century, the Cretan archbishopric of Candia, but the complicated mechanism for filling that see allowed the Republic the right to short-list candidates rather than to nominate absolutely. Yet papal appointments to the dioceses of the Republic otherwise proved readily acceptable for the most part, and in fact an informal process of co-operation and understanding brought to Venetian sees bishops who usually enjoyed the confidence of both Rome and Venice: members of the ruling patrician families to the most important sees of the Venetian mainland most commonly, and provincial nobles or 'citizens' of Venice itself to dioceses in the Mediterranean empire, for example. The preoccupation of the Republic with episcopal appointments in the immediately post-Conciliar period was nevertheless not unreasonable. It was correctly observed that the papacy was trying to recover greater control of such patronage within the Italian states. Mantua was forced to surrender the nomination of the city's bishop to

---

5 *Gli Atti della Visita Apostolica di S. Carlo Borromeo a Bergamo (1575)*, vols Ii–IIiii, ed. A.G. Roncalli et al. (Florence 1936–57); S. Pagano, *Il processo di Endimio Calandra e l'Inquisizione a Mantova nel 1567–8* (Vatican City 1991).

Rome, the duke in effect being compensated by the liturgical privileges which he desired for his splendid palatine chapel.[6]

Co-operation between the post-Conciliar popes and the Medici ensured that the grand-dukes retained an effective patronage in the appointment of Tuscan bishops, while Rome recovered financial resources related to the filling of bishoprics. In Spanish-ruled Lombardy only one bishopric lay in governmental patronage, all the rest being filled by the papacy directly, even if with some care to ensure that those chosen would prove acceptable to the Spanish Crown and receive the formal grant of their temporalities. The Spanish monarch could nominate to only some of the bishoprics in the kingdom of Naples, unlike the case of Sicily or Sardinia. The others, including the archbishopric of Naples itself, were at the direct disposal of the papacy. The popes indeed retained control of episcopal appointments in much of mainland Italy, though ducal nomination of Savoyard bishops was successfully extended *de facto* to Piedmontese sees. Ultimately, the wishes of secular rulers could not be ignored because the exclusion of a bishop by secular authority, as for a while at Lucca, was not desirable from a pastoral point of view.

State interests could also be involved where the post-Tridentine papacy redrew the boundaries of dioceses or ecclesiastical provinces, even if Venice was satisfied by the post-Conciliar creation of Crema as an independent bishopric. Such pastoral rearrangement could thus be more difficult than in the case of the elevation of Bologna to an archbishopric, detached from the metropolitan authority of Ravenna, where the power of Rome within the papal states was capable of overriding local sentiment. Elsewhere, even prelates well connected at the papal Court might not see their wishes fulfilled. Charles Borromeo, as archbishop of Milan, was frustrated in his desire to have the diocese of Como, to the North, brought within his ecclesiastical province. Despite his concern that the bishops of Como were not always to be relied on to govern the diocese according to the severe standards of Milan itself, the see remained, in this period, part of the ancient ecclesiastical province of Aquileia, which stretched across Northern Italy.[7]

The potential power of the papacy to make such changes in the relations between Italian dioceses and provinces nevertheless emphasized once again the effectively primatial role performed in the peninsula. After the Council of Trent, this dimension of papal control over the Church in mainland Italy was also evident in the revision at Rome of the decrees of diocesan synods and provincial councils. Such review was not just a formality, especially in the

6 A.S.V. Venezia, XXXII, 445r ff., 533r ff., 696r ff.; XXXIII, 248v ff.: 27 July 1602–24 Apr. 1604; XXXVIII, 167v f., 269r ff.: 17 Nov. 1607–23 Feb. 1608; A.S. Ven.: Secreta Archivi Propri Roma, 17, fos 59r ff., 71r ff.: 11 Aug., 8 Sept. 1565; 18: 9, 16 Mar. 1566–2 Aug. 1567, especially 8 Feb. 1567; Collegio: Relazioni: Busta 62, fos 137r ff.: 1581; cf. Busta 81: Relatione, 1639.
7 A.S.V. Spagna, XXXII, 111r–v, 138r ff.; XXXIII, 149r: 23 Apr.–21 Dec. 1586; XXXIV, 527r ff.: 10 Oct. 1588; A.G.S.: Secretaría Provincial: Napoles: Visitas y Diversos: Libros 39, fos 21r ff.; 44, fos 101r ff.; 110, fos 240 ff.; A.S. Ven.: Secreta Archivi Propri Roma, 17, fos 61v ff., 63v f., 65v ff., 68v ff., 71r ff.: 18 Aug.–8 Sept. 1565; 18: 24 Nov. 1565–28 Dec. 1566, 25 Jan., cf. 19 Apr. 1567.

latter case. Charles Borromeo's exemplary series of provincial councils and diocesan synods at Milan, throughout the two decades of his archiepiscopate, set a standard of regularity, implementing the Council's own prescription, which other pastors were urged to emulate. For all that, Borromeo found on at least one occasion that confirmation of his decrees was delayed at Rome, as the Curia took note of local opposition to his reforms.

Yet such local implementation of Tridentine reform by Italian mainland bishops could on occasion be supported by yet another aspect of papal authority in the peninsula. The evolution of permanent nunciatures affected Italian Courts just as much as those of Catholic rulers elsewhere in Europe. Nuncios resided not only at Venice and Turin, for instance, but also in the kingdom of Naples, governed by a Spanish viceroy. Here again the geographic limits of effective Italian primacy were demonstrated, since the Spanish Crown's claims to exercise a Legatine power in Sicily, by virtue of the *Monarchia Sicula*, excluded a papal nuncio. In the crucial period following the Council of Trent, in the last decades of the sixteenth and the first two decades of the seventeenth centuries, when the foundations for implementing the reform decrees in Italy were being set, it would be misleading to regard the resident nuncios as merely diplomatic representatives of the pope's political power.

During that immediately post-Conciliar period the nuncios were commonly, in the peninsula as elsewhere, bishops of Italian sees themselves, seconded for a tour of diplomatic duty, and often having personal experience of the realities of diocesan reform. From their own knowledge of the difficulties in implementing the Conciliar decrees, they could provide encouragement to local bishops and sympathetic representation at Rome of the diocesans' needs. While this did not necessarily preclude all occasions of friction between diocesan bishops and the nuncios as representatives of Roman interests, in the kingdom of Naples for instance, practical co-operation could occur, as in Venetian territory. Where bishops found themselves less able to take the initiative, a nuncio might be able to pursue local reform by co-operating with the secular authority, as in the case of the Medici in Tuscany.

The most important permanent nunciatures outside Italy, as in France and Spain, were obviously affected by the change from the 1620s in the nature of papal diplomatic representation, though in France, where the role of the nuncio was severely limited in any case, Franco-Italian dynastic and family interests had arguably influenced the work of the nunciature from the early post-Tridentine era itself onwards. Indeed, the move away from diocesan bishops on secondment to career diplomats pursuing an essentially Curial course of advancement was itself a response to the political problems created for the papacy by the conflicts within Catholic as well as non-Catholic Europe, with the escalation of the Thirty Years' War. But even if the introduction of Curialists as professional diplomats gradually affected all nunciatures, those within Italy were still able to give some attention to the more pastoral questions raised by diocesan bishops. At Venice, for example, the necessary volume of political reporting after the outbreak of the Thirty Years' War did not exclude attention to the needs of the diocesan bishops within the Republic's territories.

Some nuncios held local responsibility for clearly non-political or non-diplomatic business. The nuncio at Naples sometimes acted as the delegate of the Holy Office, while the nuncio at Venice was an ordinary member of the Inquisition tribunal there. By the seventeenth century the papal representative in Malta came to act as Apostolic Delegate and Inquisitor, despite the Spanish objection that Malta's ecclesiastical dependence made it subject to the *Monarchia Sicula*. Indeed, in Sicily, as in Sardinia, it was the Spanish Inquisition which operated, with resident inquisitors appointed and sent from mainland Spain. The jurisdiction of the Roman Inquisition, and by extension the authority of the Roman Index of prohibited literature, were thus excluded from the islands. In the Spanish-ruled kingdom of Naples, by contrast, a peculiar and com-plicated arrangement allowed the Holy Office to delegate cases for local invest-igation and hearing, the nuncio or local prelates or a combination of these acting on different occasions. This unexpected procedure, which characterized the period of Spanish rule in the kingdom at least, was the result of popular resistance to any introduction of the distinct Spanish Inquisition.

Such successful resistance essentially made room for the intervention of the Holy Office; and in Spanish-ruled Lombardy it was in the long-term inter-ests of the papacy as well as of the local bishops and native population that the Inquisition had not been subjected to Spanish direction, at a time when Lombardy was only newly subject to specifically Spanish as opposed to Imperial rule. Instead, a tribunal of the Roman Inquisition sat in Milan, essentially such as those which existed elsewhere in mainland Italy. The degree of supervision of such tribunals which the Venetian Republic insisted on, both by the pres-ence of state magistrates at the meetings of the tribunal in Venice itself and by parallel procedures in the tribunals of the Republic's mainland territories, obviously affected, but certainly did not bring to a halt, the workings of the Inquisition there. Even the notorious breach between the papacy and the Republic, in the Venetian Interdict of 1606–7, resulted in the exclusion for some decades of the Jesuits from Venetian territory, but not the permanent breakdown of inquisitorial activity. The friars who headed the local tribunals by Roman appointment in the Venetian mainland territories, and the lay confraternities associated with support for the Inquisition, might find them-selves under further constraint after the Interdict, but their existence was not itself in question. Only in the small Republic of Lucca was the exercise of Roman Inquisitorial jurisdiction more seriously challenged, and even here, by the last decades of the sixteenth century, republican authority itself was active in demonstrating the defence of orthodoxy.

Thus, the presence of the Roman Inquisition as one expression of papal primacy in Italian ecclesiastical affairs again confirmed the geographic area in which this could be effective. Even allowing for the peculiar arrangements in Naples, peninsular Italy was characterized by tribunals or the *ad hoc* equivalent which recognized the authority of the Holy Office in Rome and received orders and direction from there. By this measurement, a frontier could be detected which clearly included Piedmont or the Venetian mainland territories within Catholic Italy, leaving beyond it not only Savoy but also the equally 'Gallican' Val d'Aosta (in which there was some resistance to the Bull *In Coena Domini*), and the truly marginal areas to the north and east in the case of the Swiss lands or the territories of the Austrian archdukes. It excluded too, in this respect at least, the prince-bishopric of Trent itself. Even so, local book-censorship there helped to maintain a frontier against heresy. Only as the eighteenth century progressed did this relatively clear distinction break down, in Lombardy under Austrian Habsburg rule for example. But recognition of the jurisdiction of the Holy Office, headed not only by cardinals alone but by the pope in person, was not necessarily proof of effective papal power more generally. Nevertheless, in the later sixteenth and early seventeenth centuries at any rate, important suspects demanded by the Holy Office for investigation in Rome itself were commonly handed over, after whatever diplomatic manoeuvres, by the Catholic states of mainland Italy, Venice included.

Of less certain practical effect was the Roman Index of prohibited literature, the authority of which was equally recognized by these states. For even Venetian sensitivity to Roman intervention in the economically important printing and book-publishing trades at Venice had, as its most permanent effect, a doubling of censorship, as the Republic introduced more complicated measures of state licensing in addition to the control exercised by the Inquisition. The Roman interest in the publishing trade at Venice had in any case a peculiar dimension, in that the drive to control liturgical texts above all was not simply a measure of protectionism in favour of Roman printers. It also indicated the aim of imposing post-Conciliar liturgical uniformity. The real effects of Index restrictions on literary culture elsewhere in the peninsula are more difficult to determine with absolute certainty, even after the relative moderation of the revised Index issued in 1596 by Clement VIII.[8]

The Roman Index, whatever its origins as a simply prohibitive list, in fact evolved, like the Spanish Index, as both a prohibitive and expurgatory document. Thus, earlier vernacular texts of Italian literature could in fact continue to circulate after expurgation of anti-clerical passages for example. But the importance attached by the papacy to the Index as well as to the Holy Office should not be doubted. The decision to delegate the censorship responsibilities of the Roman Inquisition to a distinct Curial tribunal, the Congregation of the Index, was a mark of the importance accorded to this area of business, not a downgrading. It was after all in the name of the Congregation of the Index that Cardinal Bellarmine handed down the directive which was supposed to govern the terms in which Galileo might in future treat the cosmological hypotheses.

This delegation of one important area of inquisitorial issues marked, moreover, a crucial evolution of papal administration on a wider scale still. The

---

8 P.F. Grendler, *The Roman Inquisition and the Venetian Press, 1540–1605* (Princeton, NJ 1977).

revived and revised Roman Inquisition predated the Tridentine Council and the creation, after its conclusion, of the Curial Congregation of the Council. The Holy Office, as already indicated, had an assured pre-eminence in papal administration, not least by virtue of the pope's own presidency, for all the day-to-day management of business by the presiding cardinals. Yet in another sense the post-Conciliar reorganization of the Roman Curia and creation of a whole set of specialized Congregations put into perspective the role of the Holy Office as but one, even if the most eminent, of the agencies by which papal authority, especially over the Church in mainland Italy, was exercised. Just as the workings of the Congregation of the Index derived from the responsibilities of the Inquisition, so the original Congregation of the Council was to become flanked by other Congregations with special areas of competence, as well as the more or less reformed branches of the pre-Conciliar Curia. The potentially unlimited range of the Congregation of the Council was thereby refined, but Roman centralization was nevertheless confirmed, not diminished.

THE ROMAN CURIA

The crucial step in this process of centralization was taken by Sixtus V in 1587–88, who instituted fifteen Congregations, headed by cardinals, in which the Holy Office and the Congregation of the Council were included. In the inherent delegation of specialized functions, one Congregation, for example, was to deal with the large sphere of business involving bishops, and in due course the relations between bishops and regulars became its chief focus. This was not the end of the evolutionary reordering of business between the Curial Congregations, it is important to note. Some further Congregations were to evolve out of originally *ad hoc* commissions of cardinals. Thus, for instance, the seventeenth-century Congregation created by Gregory XV in 1622 to supervise missionary work overseas, the Propaganda Fide, emerged from a pre-history of commissions, set up to deal with the affairs of non-Catholic areas and relations with non-Catholics.

It has been argued that the balance of business for which the various Congregations had responsibility, which from the start included such questions as the completion and administration of the basilica of St Peter and the government of the papal states themselves, indicated the supremacy of the papacy's temporal interests over more properly ecclesiastical or indeed religious priorities. But the centrality of the Holy Office, not least in the pontificates of the second half of the seventeenth century, as already indicated, might immediately suggest otherwise. Furthermore, it is not clear that the subsequent evolution of the original set of Congregations created by Sixtus V demonstrates the point either. The striking innovation of the Propaganda Congregation, as an expression of the supreme pontiff's universal concerns, arguably had a greater impact on the global development of Catholicism, before the French Revolution, than did bodies charged with financial or administrative oversight of the papal states, however expansive their activity.

On the other hand, the impact of the system of Congregations on the Consistory was perhaps clearer. Where business was transacted within a Congregation, under its presiding cardinals, the general importance of the Consistory was obviously in some measure reduced. Indeed, it has sometimes been suggested that the post-Conciliar Consistory became a formality, largely confined to the routine procedures for filling major benefices. But while it can be agreed that by the end of the sixteenth century some cardinals felt their role, individually or collectively, was being eclipsed, as Paleotti apparently did, the complex and evolutionary nature of the transformation should be noted. In the first place, the Consistory on occasion remained the scene of the most dramatic confrontation between the pope and some at least of the assembled cardinals. The verbal attack by Cardinal Borgia on Urban VIII, which marked the climax of the pope's difficulties with the Spanish monarchy, is a reminder that the seventeenth-century Consistory was not inevitably a matter of formulaic routine.

Moreover, to the degree that the real transaction of Church business did move out of Consistory, this was not simply an effect of the system of Congregations. As important, arguably, was the enhancement of the Cardinal Nephew and eventual formalization of the Cardinal Secretary of State as roles which filtered and controlled the flow of business receiving the pope's attention. Such intermediary control was itself advanced by the turn of political events in the seventeenth century. The vast problems presented to the papacy by conflict between the European Catholic powers, particularly from the outbreak of the Thirty Years' War onwards, ensured that an increasing amount of business was directed from the nunciatures to the Secretariate of State and only thence to the pope; and equally of course in reverse.

If it is argued that confusion of personal or family interests with what later historians would seek to distinguish as properly state concerns was characteristic of many early modern European governments, this might merely seem to reinforce the suggestion that the post-Tridentine papacy, and the Roman Curia in its name, subordinated truly ecclesiastical aims to the priorities of temporal administration. But first, this picture can be questioned for the papal states themselves, as has already been seen. Secondly, the pattern is surely different in any case for the other states of mainland Italy. Bishops of peninsular Italy, outside the papal states, were obviously aware of the Congregation of the Council, and various other essentially ecclesiastical Congregations such as that of bishops and regulars, the Sacred Rites Congregation, with regard to both liturgical and canonization questions, and perhaps only on occasion the Holy Office or Congregation of the Index. Their dealings with Rome might also at times be conducted via the nunciature, and hence via the Secretariate of State, especially in Venetian and Neapolitan territory, for example, but even there not invariably so.

Moreover, it is vital in considering the new Congregations not to overlook the continuing dominance at Rome of the older, pre-Conciliar organs of the

Roman Curia, not all of them wholly or even much reformed in their operations. While the Penitentiary was reordered by the post-Tridentine papacy, the importance of the Chancery and the Datary remained unquestioned in financial and administrative business, including the filling of benefices. The tribunals of the Rota and the Signaturae equally retained an undoubted influence on the affairs of the Church throughout mainland Italy, quite apart from those of the rest of Catholic Europe. Yet these organs and tribunals, with which peninsular bishops had regular contact, can hardly be described as agencies of a new or expanded dominance by the papacy's temporal administration.

CARDINAL NEPHEWS

As far as an effective primatial authority exercised by the post-Tridentine papacy over the Church in the states of mainland Italy is concerned, then, the creation of the Congregations at the Roman Curia is one important way in which this was imposed, though not the only vehicle of this reassertion. Peninsular bishops had to take account not only of new Congregations but also of Cardinal Nephews, or later Cardinal Secretaries of State, and it is necessary to consider the role of these too. Some early modern rulers, not all of them Catholic, found it necessary or seemingly desirable by the first half of the seventeenth century to consolidate or even formalize not only control of physical access to themselves but, above all, superintendence of the engulfing tide of government business by means of a chief secretary or chief minister, often, but unhelpfully, known in English historiography as a favourite. It might be argued that, once again, the procedures of the papal Court had evolved in a precocious way, allowing for the difference that an hereditary monarch might best trust someone he had elevated from an unrelated position outside his own dynasty, while an elected pope might initially at least regard a relative who owed his elevation to that election as the most trustworthy personal assistant. The potential drawbacks of elevating a nephew to the position of virtual first minister were to manifest themselves too, however.

It is sometimes suggested, for instance, that the undoubted ability of Clement VIII, at the end of the sixteenth and in the first years of the seventeenth century, was to a degree at least undermined by the counter-productive competition between the two young relatives whom he elevated to the college of cardinals. It is certainly even more arguable that in the subsequent pontificate the dominant financial interests of Paul V's nephew, Cardinal Scipio Borghese, complicated papal policy unduly, as for example in the already strained relations with the Venetian Republic. Much has also been made recently of the distorting effects exerted on the administration of Urban VIII by the interests of the Barberini nephews, especially of the two elevated to cardinal status. The patrimonial aggrandizement of the Barberini has been seen as some sort of unholy climax to Baroque Nepotism, but in terms of bureaucratic evolution it might also be suggested that the pontificate of Innocent X deserves consideration.

Not the least bizarre aspect of this pontificate, which it has already been proposed here ran against many of the long-term characteristics of the post-Tridentine papacy, was what might be called the search for a suitable Cardinal Nephew. The attempt to preserve a familial link in the right-hand assistantship to the papacy produced the ultimate resort of adoption, signifying a system on the verge of collapse. But the pope's adopted nephew proved so obviously unsuitable that even this artificial familial connection had to be ignominiously abandoned. The gradual enforcement on the papacy of a more bureaucratic choice, a Cardinal Secretary of State who was not necessarily a relation, was already foreshadowed even among the immediately post-Conciliar pontificates, by use on occasion of a chief minister who was not Cardinal Nephew. The process was further enhanced by those popes of the later seventeenth century who adopted a conspicuously anti-nepotistic stance.

But this should not be reduced by anachronistic judgement to a contrast between abusive self-interest and public disinterestedness. Some of the early Cardinal Nephews, viewed as Secretaries of State *avant la lettre*, were of courage as well as ability. Cardinal Ludovisi, under Gregory XV, is a clear example. Nor is it apparent that more routine business, passing through Nephews' administration, was either necessarily neglected or commonly mismanaged even under Borghese or the Barberini, let alone under Clement VIII's Aldobrandini nephews. To Cardinal Nephews, after all, as later to Cardinal Secretaries of State, attached able Curialists, assisting these papal ministers; and the advent of Secretaries of State did not preclude papal elevation of nephews to cardinal status, nor in some pontificates control of all important business by a nephew to the exclusion of the Secretary.

MILAN

In relation to papal authority as a primatial force in mainland Italy, the figure of Charles Borromeo, papal nephew during the closing stages of the Council of Trent and in the immediately following period, has already been noted. But it must also be remarked that for the duration of his Milanese archiepiscopate, until his death in 1584, he represented a momentary but important variation on the theme of Rome as head of the peninsular Church. After his uncle's death he resided mainly in Milan, though retaining considerable influence at Rome under subsequent pontificates, as contemporaries were aware. The former city thus became the immediate object of attention focused on the implementation of the Conciliar decrees, which he had latterly influenced, while still at Rome, by his correspondence with the presiding Legates at Trent. His ability to secure continued papal support for his archiepiscopal example in implementing them ensured Roman commitment to the Tridentine programme, which would not therefore be dismissed as the purely personal project of the late Pius IV and his nephew.

Even after his own death and in the interval before his canonization in 1610 the papacy was willing to acknowledge the importance of the Milanese example in this. That should be balanced against over-large deductions occasionally drawn by modern historians from Roman insistence that the standard image of the canonized archbishop show him in cardinal's dress, as a member of the Roman entourage of the papacy. Contemporary Italians, learned or less educated, knew perfectly well that the Cardinal of S. Prassede, the Cardinal Archpriest of S. Maria Maggiore, was the saintly archbishop of Milan, to be invoked against the plague, when epidemic struck Northern and central Italy again in 1630–31 for instance. The pastoral archiepiscopate of Charles Borromeo was integral to his role as an additional, and above all Italian, saint to be addressed in such need. While Charles lived, on the other hand, there was a sense in which the moral, as opposed to formal, leadership of the Church in Italy temporarily rested at Milan; nor was the papacy at the time unwilling to employ this 'alternative' leadership, as not only the initial Legatine authority but also the subsequent tours as Apostolic Visitor make clear.

That contemporary Milanese reference to the Borromean city as 'another Rome' was not just a parochial delusion of grandeur can be shown in a slightly wider context too. The example of the Ambrosian Church did not detract from Rome's revived authority because although singular, it was not for a while unique. In the decades after the conclusion of the Council well-informed Italian opinion placed hope on another centre of ecclesiastical reform, which was also expected to demonstrate in exemplary fashion how to implement the Tridentine decrees. This was Paleotti's Bologna, enjoying the supposed advantage of being situated in the papal states, not under the sometimes difficult regime of a Spanish Governor in Lombardy. Despite the formal favour eventually shown to the Bolognese Church, under a pastor who had had first-hand experience of the Council as well as of the Curia, by its elevation to archbishopric, Paleotti's difficulties, precisely under papal temporal government, caused the attention paid to his work to fade, at least relatively and by comparison with the sustained interest in Milanese activities.

But the momentary influence of these 'alternative' centres of moral leadership in the immediately post-Conciliar Italian Church can be seen in the production of an English Catholic exile, Gregory Martin, better known for his work on the vernacular Bible for the English Catholics. His 'Roma Sancta' naturally described the glories of papal Rome under the post-Conciliar papacy, its churches, convents, confraternities and charities. But, reflecting late sixteenth-century expectation, it devoted subordinate passages of praise to Paleotti's Bologna and above all Borromean Milan.[9] More lastingly, the cult of the canonized Charles, not confined only to the popular classes in Italy or indeed elsewhere, was accompanied by the circulation among Italian bishops, as well

9 Gregory Martin, *Roma Sancta*, 1st edn from the MS by G.B. Parks (Rome 1969), chap. 34: pp. 246 ff.

as those further away, of the published monuments of Borromean reform, the *Acta* of the Milanese Church.

Borromeo's position with regard to Roman authority in the post-Conciliar Church should not be misunderstood, however. Despite his firm defence of the ancient Ambrosian Rite within the city and diocese of Milan, he was elsewhere unsympathetic to local liturgical idiosyncrasy. Outside the area of Ambrosian usage he was clear that uniform adoption of the Roman Rite should be imposed. Thus one of the most striking features of the post-Tridentine papacy's assertion of an effective primacy over the Church in mainland Italy was the gradual but decisive imposition of liturgical uniformity. This is not to overlook either the Ambrosian Rite on the one hand, or the distinct question of Greek-rite communities in the peninsula, some of which were subject to 'Latinization' at the very end of the sixteenth century, on the other.

The Council of Trent's bequest to the papacy of unfinished business in the revision of liturgical texts had important and lasting consequences for drawing the Church in the mainland Italian states into a new degree of liturgical uniformity. The revised Roman Missal published by Pius V was gradually imposed, as was the revised Roman Breviary, on the dioceses and secular clergy of the peninsula. Local variations in the calendar, to reflect approved local cults were still found, and for a while liturgical peculiarities survived in some places, above all in Venice. The proprietary chapels of rulers could also retain exceptional usages, as famously the doge's chapel of St Mark's, distinct from the then cathedral of Venice, or the duke of Mantua's palatine basilica. But the printing of missals or breviaries for Italian use which did not essentially conform to Roman usage was eventually eradicated (with the necessary exceptions of the Ambrosian Rite and certain religious orders always allowed). Serious challenge to the devotional effects of this peninsular uniformity came rather in the eighteenth century, with the attempt of secular authorities in some Italian states to moderate popular piety, not least by intervention to reduce the number of major holydays.

Under Clement VIII, the Pontificale, together with the Caeremoniale, also introduced a new degree of uniformity into the ceremonies presided over by Italian bishops. The Roman Rituale issued under Paul V, for the administration of the sacraments, equally set a new standard of uniform practice, but perhaps took longer to have an effect throughout the peninsula. After all, the decisive factor here was the energy with which diocesan bishops enforced the possession by parish priests of an up-to-date version of the Rituale, whether printed in Rome or published in a more local centre. Nevertheless, even allowing for subsequent revision of the Roman Breviary by Urban VIII, and modifications by later popes, the clear trend in the dioceses of mainland Italy and among the secular clergy of its states was towards liturgical and devotional uniformity. In the long run this in some measure affected popular piety as well, with all allowance made for local feasts and traditions.

The relative coherence in official worship at any rate established in mainland Italy during the long period from the Council of Trent's conclusion to the eve of the French Revolution may be measured by comparing the undoubted survival of liturgical variety in the post-Tridentine Church elsewhere. This could be detected not only in many French sees, not necessarily under bishops of Jansenist sympathy, with their characteristic tolerance of the vernacular during parts of the liturgy, but also for example in dioceses of German-speaking Catholic Europe. To complement revision of the Roman Breviary, the Roman Martyrology was also revised, achievements of the pontificates of Pius V and Gregory XIII. Such success contrasted with the more troubled history of revision at Rome of the Vulgate text of the Bible, unlike the post-Conciliar papacy's increasingly firm grasp of canonization procedure and hence of saints' cults. The need for Clement VIII to reissue a corrected version of the imperfect edition made by Sixtus V did not escape critical Protestant notice, but the papacy had at least fulfilled another of the Tridentine Council's implicit mandates, alongside a programme of producing new Roman editions of Patristic texts.

It was an explicit legacy from the Council to the papacy, however, which arguably had the greatest impact on the people of the Italian peninsula. By using materials first gathered by a working group at the Council, the post-Conciliar papacy, with Borromeo's approval, was able to issue the Roman Catechism as a standard of the doctrinal orthodoxy clarified at Trent. This partly drew on texts, including one which had already been the object of censure, the vernacular catechism of the unfortunate Spanish primate, Carranza, whom the post-Conciliar papacy at least finally managed to bring to Rome from Spanish Inquisitorial detention. But it is important to note that the Roman Catechism issued by Pius V was a Latin document directed specifically to parish priests, and not arranged in dialogue form. On the basis of this text, however, it was possible in time to publish Italian translations, and above all to construct other approved catechisms, more readily arranged for teaching and memorizing. Of these, the most influential in Italy were probably those drawn up by the Jesuit Cardinal Bellarmine.

The spread of 'Sunday Schools', the Schools of Christian Doctrine which met both on Sundays and on major feast days, gradually brought the Catholic catechism to the peninsular population in a newly systematic way, admittedly over a long period. But the systematic reordering of such originally lay initiatives originated once again not in Rome but further north in Italy. It was the supreme organizer of ecclesiastical life, Borromeo, who chiefly systematized the Schools, as far as their original, North Italian form was concerned at any rate. The origins of similar initiatives elsewhere in the peninsula too should not be forgotten. But for the post-Tridentine spread of the institution in mainland Italy the moral leadership of an 'alternative' centre, found at Milan for two vital decades after the Council, is once again crucial.[10]

10 P. Rodríguez and R. Lanzetti, *El Catecismo Romano: Fuentes e Historia del Texto y de la Redacción* (Pamplona 1982); P. Rodríguez and R. Lanzetti, *El Manuscrito Original del Catecismo Romano* (Pamplona 1985), especially pp. 102–4; *San Carlo Borromeo. Catholic Reform and Ecclesiastical Politics in the Second Half of the Sixteenth Century*, ed. J.M. Headley and J.B. Tomaro (Washington, DC 1988).

ITALIAN CONDITIONS AND FOREIGN PRESSURES

Papal prompting and encouragement of Italian bishops to create diocesan seminaries, as specified at Trent, produced relative but distinct success, which once again distinguished mainland Italy from other parts of Catholic Europe. The results of this papal influence were certainly not absolute. Impoverished, usually smaller dioceses, especially in Southern Italy, were not always able to conform. Recent scholarship has also drawn attention to the fact that not all the institutions on which, by the end of the seventeenth century, Italian bishops relied for the training of their diocesan clergy were Tridentine seminaries according to the pristine Conciliar specification, but seminary-colleges, in which paying pupils not necessarily destined for the priesthood were educated alongside the future clergy. Nevertheless, the relative success of the programme to create diocesan seminaries of some recognizable sort was evident from an early post-Conciliar date in mainland Italy, certainly in the North and the centre, and also in places in the South.

This can be seen most clearly by comparison with other areas of Catholic Europe: not only France, where the spread of diocesan seminaries was delayed by almost a century, but also Spain, for all its conspicuous Catholicism, where many dioceses lacked a proper seminary, often until the suppression of the Jesuits in the eighteenth century. In mainland Italy, the creation of a diocesan seminary did not necessarily replace other, parallel institutions for the education of some clerics. In Southern Italy, the effective papal primacy which may be detected in other areas of peninsular Church life certainly failed to bring serious change to the essentially patrimonial foundation of the *chiese ricettizie*, at which local clerics were co-opted to share in the revenues. Another peculiarity surviving in Calabria were the impoverished *chierici* (or *diaconi*) *selvaggi*, parish clerks or sacristans, often married, who nevertheless claimed full legal immunity.[11] Elsewhere in post-Conciliar Italy papal support was often necessary for episcopal reordering of parochial boundaries, to meet changed social need, in order to override local opposition or state intervention, whether in the North or in Naples for example.[12]

Despite Venetian sensitivity on such an issue, the distinctive conditions of religious life in the Republic are best seen as an exception against which to assess the norm of papal involvement in the direction of the Italian Church. The Republic successfully protected the major confraternities in the city of Venice, the *Scuole Grandi* from Apostolic Visitatorial inspection, just as it did the female convents of the city and lagoon, which were collectively and individually under the supervision of lay magistrates of the ruling patriciate. Other magistrates, similarly, not only controlled the existence of the Jewish

11 A.G.S.: Secretaría Provincial: Napoles: Visitas y Diversos: Libros 54, 95; A.S.V. Venezia, VII, 17 ff., 36v ff.: Sept.–Oct. 1569.
12 A.S.V. Venezia, XXXVIII, 61r ff., 154v, 155r ff., 183r ff., 231v f., 281r–v, 288r ff., 304r–v, 330v ff.: 11 Aug. 1607–19 Apr. 1608; A.S. Ven.: Secreta Archivi Propri Roma, 18: 5 Apr. 1567; Capi del Consiglio dei Dieci: Lettere di Ambasciatori: Roma: 26, nos 10, 102, 104, 109, 110; fos 200r ff.: 18 Sept. 1574–4 Oct. 1578; B.N.M.: MSS italiani, classe VII, n. 1556, fos 113r ff.

communities in Venice but also policed popular blasphemy, and by an extension the matrimonial disputes of at least the lower orders of the city itself. Yet
even if such magisterial interventions were arguably increasing in the last
decades of the sixteenth century, Venice did not provide an immediate paradigm for secular authorities' involvement in religious and moral affairs throughout the other peninsular states. Partial parallels developed at Naples, but only
later in Piedmont.

In the immediately post-Conciliar decades, the Medici proved remarkably
sensitive to papal authority in the matter of Church property. A proposal
debated at the Florentine Court to restrict the continued growth of ecclesiastical mortmain was abandoned, in recognition that the state could not limit
giving to the Church, whatever the social and economic consequences of
further alienation of secular property. Here the papacy benefited from its
working alliance with the restored Medici, whose sovereign territory at that
time was flanked by enclaves housing Spanish garrisons and naval bases. Such
a presence both guaranteed the restored regime and yet acted for the Medici
and the papacy as another reminder of Spain's power in the peninsula. Venetian
alarm at the papal annexation of Ferrara at the end of the sixteenth century
was chiefly triggered by fear of Spanish and Habsburg encirclement of the
Republic being tightened.

The question of government restriction on ecclesiastical mortmain was
dangerously topical by the early seventeenth century. Republics like Lucca
or Genoa, with finite cultivable land within their territory, were tempted to
impose such limitation, or to reduce clerical immunities. Papal power might
still be sufficient to resist these attempts in smaller republics, but the extensive
territory of the Venetian Republic raised a larger problem. More was at stake,
but the risks in confrontation were greater. The Interdict of 1606–7 saw the
papacy essentially defeated over Republican limitation of new alienations to
the Church, as over the related control by the state of new conventual foundations. This was in addition to papal failure to reverse the Republican tradition
of ignoring clerical immunity where charges of serious crimes were involved.

In Piedmont the papacy was, in the course of time, faced with a more
gradual erosion of influence. The state came to exercise its own effective
censorship by the later seventeenth and into the eighteenth century; and this
eventually became true of control of education, including higher education,
too. Of course, such state supervision included the guarding of Catholic
orthodoxy, for quite apart from the occasional 'irredentist' plans of the dukes
to attack the Calvinist citadel of Geneva, the seventeenth century also saw
ducal campaigns against the remaining enclaves of Waldensians who had survived in certain valleys. In this case the state drive for confessional conformity, sometimes described as a facet of absolutism, lay behind the attempt to
realign the religious and geographic frontiers of the peninsula, rather than any
papal leadership. Yet Piedmontese respect for Roman authority was still distinct from the more Gallican traditions affecting the Church in the dukes'
territories in Savoy, despite the eventual project, by the 1740s, for a royal

Chaplaincy General, of archiepiscopal status, which would enhance independence from the local episcopal hierarchy.[13]

On the other hand, what arguably made Italian states, not least Venice and Piedmont, increasingly alert in relation to papal authority, from the late sixteenth to the later eighteenth century, was the renewed vigour of the Roman Curia, not just in the new Congregations but in the older departments and tribunals. Roman involvement in benefice appointments throughout the peninsula was after all constant, and litigation over such appointments naturally tended to concentrate at the Roman Curia. This clearly lay behind much of the Venetian Republic's apprehensiveness in the early seventeenth century, and indeed beyond that, for instance. In some mainland states tension over this was arguably less, perhaps because of a tradition which reserved certain places on Roman tribunals for lawyers from a given state. This appeared true of Lombardy in the later sixteenth and early seventeenth centuries, but governmental confidence in its own control of the temporalities of benefices was perhaps greater too.

The Venetian Republic, after the Interdict of 1606–7, escalated campaigns to improve state control of admission to the temporalities of benefices in its mainland territories. But the Spanish regime in Lombardy inherited an arrangement made with the papacy itself that allowed joint Roman and state oversight of the administration of vacant benefices' revenues and admission of new appointments to the temporalities. This procedure was not without its problems, particularly for bishops in Lombardy, but the working agreement between Rome and the secular government of the duchy persisted. In the kingdom of Naples, on the other hand, more trouble was caused, in the immediately post-Conciliar period at any rate, by papal demands for payments from the estates of deceased bishops and special levies occasionally imposed on the clergy as a whole. Such financial dispute complicated the functions of the nuncios at the viceregal Court, especially at a time of wider conflict in the kingdom over attempts to recover alienated Church land and revenue.[14]

Benefice cases were not, however, the only business to come before the Roman tribunals, even though papal indults to cardinals to appoint to benefices of a certain limited value which would otherwise have been in papal gift represented another way in which the Roman Curia was constantly involved in the disposition of benefices in the mainland states. This was in addition to the retention of commendatory positions of a compatible nature, often the titular headship of religious houses, by cardinals resident in Curia rather than

13 *Nunziature di Venezia*, VIII–X, ed. A. Stella (Rome 1963–77); XI, ed. A. Buffardi (Rome 1972); M. Grosso and M.F. Mellano, *La controriforma nella arcidiocesi di Torino (1558–1610)* (3 vols, Vatican City 1957); A. Erba, *La Chiesa Sabauda tra Cinque e Seicento. Ortodossia tridentina, Gallicanesimo savoiardo e assolutismo ducale (1580–1630)* (Rome 1979).
14 A.S.V. Venezia, XLII, 471v f.: 30 June 1612; A.S. Ven.: Collegio: Relazioni di Rettori: Brescia, busta 37: 1628; Senato: Dispacci di Rettori: Brescia: 29 June, 2 July 1613; B.A.V. MS Ottoboni Latini 2361: Mediolanens. Economatus; A.D. Wright, 'Relations between Church and State: Catholic Developments in Spanish-ruled Italy of the Counter-Reformation', *History of European Ideas*, IX, 4 (1988), 385–403.

in the area where the institutions were situated. The exemptions enjoyed by cardinals in their benefices, as well as certain religious orders, disturbed the financial arrangements agreed between the papacy and the Venetian Republic, by which the state benefited from levies on the clergy of its territories that were designed to support the confrontation with the Islamic power of the Ottomans. After the Interdict of 1606–7, however, it was only the Jesuits, as a whole order, who were long excluded from Republican territory. While some other individuals, who had been among the relatively few ecclesiastics to resist government pressure and give wholehearted support to the papal position during that incident, were prevented from returning, there was no retention of a wholesale ban on Theatines or Capuchins for example.

The laity of the mainland states were also on occasion involved in recourse to the Roman tribunals. The clarification of the conditions defining for the future a valid sacramental marriage had been made by the Council of Trent and the relevant decrees, as the Council specifically required, had been published in the localities. Since this legislation was not retrospective, there remained, for a generation or so after the Council, inevitable cases that were complicated by the old confusions as to whether or not a binding and valid marriage had been effected. Dispensations for irregularities still, in certain circumstances, had to be sought at Rome itself. This lasting involvement of the Roman tribunals in both clerical and lay affairs throughout the peninsula was what perhaps chiefly stimulated the growth, by the eighteenth century, of a more hostile attitude among governments of many of the mainland states.

The Bourbon tradition, exported not only to Naples during that century but also to smaller states like Parma-Piacenza, was even less reluctant to resist aspects of Roman authority than the Spanish Habsburgs had been. What is conventionally described as absolutism, involving a determination to exercise greater state control over ecclesiastical affairs while still maintaining doctrinal orthodoxy, was clearly making an impact in the peninsular states from 1700. However, as has previously been suggested, this was not the copying of a more 'absolute' priority given to temporal administration in the papal states, since, on the contrary, the papacy was anxious not to give precedents to secular rulers for the overriding of ecclesiastical immunities. The mainland states of the eighteenth century might be less respectful of certain manifestations of Roman authority, involving for example the Holy Office or the Index, but the political context, within the peninsula as much as without, had obviously changed since the late sixteenth century, when the papacy had still operated a galley fleet of sufficient importance to be the subject of serious naval co-ordination with the galley fleets of Naples, Sicily and Malta, in the confrontation with Turkish Islam.

By the second half of the seventeenth century already, the papacy was largely an impotent spectator as the Venetian Republic struggled to resist Turkish conquest of Crete, admittedly with more sympathetic support from Catholic France than the papacy could subsequently secure for the Imperial Habsburg interest in besieged Vienna. The ability of papal diplomats and prelates managed, though, to obtain the readmission of the Jesuits to Venetian territory, as the Republic accepted every source of financial relief in the war. The consequences of the Cretan War, then, seemed to include a papal triumph, despite Venetian loss of the Republic's most important remaining island possession. The Society of Jesus, associated in a public and special way with papal authority, was once more operative throughout the Italian peninsula. Yet before the French Revolution the papacy was forced to accept the suppression of the Jesuits in various mainland states and finally to agree to the suppression of the Society as a whole.

The precisely political campaign against the Jesuits did not originate in Italy but, in different ways in different areas, such as France and Portugal, beyond the peninsula. The relations between the various Bourbon Courts of Europe meant, however, that once Spain or France had adopted the demand for the suppression of the Society, it was virtually impossible to resist its application to Naples or Parma. The acceptance of the demand by the Austrian Habsburgs obviously affected Lombardy, and also Tuscany, where the earlier end of the Medicean line had eventually resulted in a Habsburg succession. The final agreement to suppression of the whole Society, even in the papal states and Rome itself, could not fail to represent a major blow to the authority of the papacy, since the special link between the inner elite of the Society's membership and the popes was a matter of such notoriety, forming indeed one of the allegations against the Jesuits, as supposedly dangerous to the preservation of any state. Such essentially political accusations against them went back, even in Catholic Europe, to the sixteenth century itself, and were involved in the long exclusion from Venetian territory on which the Republic insisted after the early seventeenth-century Interdict.

But in fact the papacy had also had to deal, from the later sixteenth century onwards, with a more ecclesiastical strain of Catholic anti-Jesuit sentiment, in Italy as well as in Spain or France, for example, involving not least rival religious orders, such as the Dominicans. While theological controversy was a large part of such rivalry, educational influence was another area of tension, in this case between Jesuits and existing educational authorities. The state university at Padua, within the Venetian Republic, was the scene of such tension even before the Interdict; for the problem was not confined to other parts of Catholic Europe such as Spain, France or the Southern Netherlands. By the eighteenth century, in Italy, the occasional unease of diocesan bishops about the activities of regulars was becoming, among some at least, a more specific reserve precisely towards the Jesuits. Being a numerous, influential and supposedly wealthy order, the Society seemed to attract a focused resentment, as a symbol of the papal favour to regulars which seemed to undermine the proper authority of diocesan bishops.

The ostensible defence of bishops' interests had already been adopted by the Venetian Republic in the seventeenth century, as a polemical tactic in disputes with Rome; though Republican treatment of some bishops in its territories, even those of patrician stock, revealed the more Erastian nature of its policy towards all ecclesiastical jurisdiction. The eighteenth-century states of the peninsula were also alert to the advantage of insisting on the rights of diocesan bishops, who were, however, more immediately amenable to government pressure than were Roman tribunals or a Society subject to its Roman general headquarters. For the campaign against the Jesuits, in the Italian states, should be seen as part of a wider move, attempting to bring ecclesiastical business back to diocesan tribunals, for settlement within the frontiers of the state. The climax of this development, by the time of the Revolution, was the Synod of Pistoia of 1786, by means of which the bishop, Ricci, hoped to encourage the Tuscan episcopate to adopt self-determining policies, inspired by the Jansenist schismatics of Utrecht, which would have implied not just a reassertion of episcopal jurisdiction but a local doctrinal self-sufficiency too. Subsequent caution among the Tuscan bishops and hesitation by the Grand-Duke Leopold, before his departure to replace the deceased Emperor Joseph II, clearly limited the impact of the programme, however.

The degree of popular reaction which was triggered by such semi-separatist policies shed interesting light on the evolution of Italian piety over the previous two centuries. By the end of the sixteenth century there was evident Roman approval of the enhanced status accorded to a material focus of peninsular devotion, the Holy House of Loreto in the papal Marches. This Marian shrine was, by the end of the century, a place of pilgrimage for prelates and princes, foreign as well as Italian, and not just the populace. To suggest that Marian devotion exclusively characterized the piety receiving papal approbation would be to overlook some important qualifications, however. The eighteenth-century critics of the Jesuits, not least in Italy, suggested that the Society fostered an unbalanced lay piety, but the devotion chiefly complained of was not Marian but Christological, the cult of the Sacred Heart of Jesus.

By then, the Italian critics, in their calls for a well-moderated devotion, were thus opposing a Christological cult, though one they regarded as distorted or unbalanced. Yet whether or not openly sympathetic to Jansenist opponents of the Jesuits beyond Italy, in the Netherlands or France, such critics could not easily reproach the papacy over this, since for much of the eighteenth century the popes maintained a cautious reserve towards the cult of the Sacred Heart. What the papacy had not been able to do, even in Italy let alone Spain or France, was to settle other matters which had yet more important pastoral implications. These concerned the appropriate frequency of lay communion, and, related to that, the ease with which confessors might or should give absolution. Such practical questions again raised the issue of papal authority because of penitential restrictions which still retained certain sins as reserved cases, for which absolution had to be sought from higher authority, ultimately at Rome.

By the eighteenth century, indeed, the Church in the Italian states was no longer susceptible to Roman direction alone, but was now also receptive to developments taking place within Catholic society beyond the peninsula. Whereas Borromean Milan housed a special seminary, the Swiss seminary (to export well-trained priests for the marginal areas in which St Charles extended the frontiers of firmly established Catholicism, to the linguistic boundary and beyond), the influences affecting the Italian Church by the eighteenth century were in part extraneous.[15] The papacy might deplore but could not prevent the interest shown at the University of Padua in the schismatic Catholics of the Netherlands, those of the Jansenizing party who had developed from the early eighteenth century as the Church of Utrecht, a name which recalled the last non-Italian pope at that date and his hopes of ecclesiastical reform. But it is also important to remember that the popes during the long period between the conclusion of the Tridentine Council and the suppression of the Society had not all shown enthusiasm for the Jesuits. Theologians of the Society had famously defended papal prerogatives at Trent, thereby initiating a long-lasting suspicion of Jesuit attitudes among some bishops. But while popes were certainly to be found, like Gregory XIII and Gregory XV, who showed appreciation of the Jesuits' efforts, others were more reserved, as has already been noted of Clement VIII. Nevertheless, for some critics in eighteenth-century Italy, the suppression of the Jesuits represented a long-delayed re-dressing of the balance between papal and episcopal authority which had only precariously and rather ambiguously been settled at Trent, after long debate and manoeuvre.

The enforced suppression also represented the final outcome of a long contest over the authority of the pope and the power of the states within the peninsula: a contest which might even be seen as having a longer pre-history still, stretching back well before the creation of the Society in the sixteenth century and eventual papal confirmation of its constitution. Some immediately post-Tridentine popes had indeed tried to impose on the Society changes in its nature and organization which would have removed features distinguishing it from other and earlier orders. Even after these demands had been reversed or had lapsed, following the deaths of Pius V and Sixtus V, continued conflict within the Society itself, both over its educational directives and more generally over its whole purpose and structure, exasperated Clement VIII. Subsequent popes were not always confident that the Jesuit Generals were able to maintain adequate control of the Society's expanding membership. Clement certainly resisted pressure for the canonization of Ignatius Loyola, who was finally canonized by Gregory XV, but in company with other Iberian saints and also Philip Neri, regarded as the founder of the Roman Oratory.

By the eighteenth century, however, the campaign for the suppression of the Jesuits was intimately connected, in Italy as well as elsewhere in Catholic Europe, with a parallel demand that the papacy abandon the post-Tridentine form of the Bull *In Coena Domini*. This Bull was intended for annual publication, on Maundy Thursday in formal terms, and its wording was revised after the Council, reaching a definitive version from 1627. In it, canonic penalties

---

15 A.D. Wright, 'Le Milanais Borroméen et l'Italie du Nord au temps de la Contre-Réforme', in *Foi, Fidelité, Amitié en Europe à la période moderne. Mélanges offerts à Robert Sauzet*, ed. B. Maillard (2 vols, Tours 1995), II, pp. 451–6.

were pronounced on those who infringed ecclesiastical liberties, and these immunities were expansively defined. In the later sixteenth century Catholic governments already complained about it and, outside Italy, even in Catholic Spain for example, impeded its publication, at least in a vernacular translation readily understood by laity. The papacy attempted in such cases to ensure that confessors made known its terms to their penitents, but the struggle over the Bull was still unresolved by the time of the Spanish Succession crisis. The Bourbon Courts of eighteenth-century Italy renewed the demand for the abandonment of the Bull.

Thus even while stalemate over the Bull continued, the campaign against the Jesuits represented the pursuit of state triumph over the papacy, since the Society was deemed to be the champion of papal prerogatives. Even the interim victory of enforcing the dissolution of the Society within a particular Italian state could be seen as the defeat of Roman pretensions. The total suppression which followed, of course, removed not just in Italy but in Catholic Europe more widely, as well as overseas, an agency capable of spreading a specifically Roman influence. But the eighteenth-century popes were in any case increasingly having to react to policies set by secular rulers, even in the Italian peninsula. The ecclesiastical boundaries of what might be considered the Italian Church, that part of the Western Church which responded in an immediate way to the papal exercise of an effectively primatial leadership, were themselves altered.

From the later sixteenth century onwards there had been continuous difficulties in the north-east of the peninsula, over the territories of the Patriarch of Aquileia. The patriarchal territories represented a border zone, overlapping the possessions of the Venetian Republic and, in the other direction, the lands of the Habsburg archdukes. The popes immediately after the Council of Trent had encouraged the entrenchment of Catholicism on this dangerously open frontier, first by challenging the personal orthodoxy of one patriarch and attempting to ensure a less ambiguous succession in the see, but then more positively by encouraging the implementation of Tridentine reform there. In this programme jurisdictional dispute with the Venetian Republic could not be avoided. This was so even when, in the face of Habsburg pressure, the affairs of the patriarchate were not treated at Rome as part of those of the Church in German lands, for ultimately more serious was Austrian occupation of parts of the patriarchate.

By the eighteenth century previous working arrangements, by which the patriarch used Udine rather than Aquileia itself as his seat, and employed in the zone of Austrian occupation a Vicar General acceptable to the secular authorities, were being challenged. The papacy was hampered in meeting this challenge by the traditional reluctance of the Venetian Republic to allow the patriarch much independence, and Austrian pressure finally secured the dismemberment of the ancient patriarchate and revision of the ecclesiastical provincial boundaries in that area. Although the pope was able to ensure an immediate improvement of episcopal supervision in the Austrian zone, the geographical and religious frontier of Catholic Italy had been revised, whatever Rome's interests. By the 1780s the prince-bishops of Trent also felt increasingly oppressed by revived Austrian intervention, to the point of offering, though unsuccessfully, to surrender their principality, largely but not wholly coterminous with the diocese. Here post-Conciliar reform had gradually spread from Trent itself, to distinguish most of the see, Italian or Ladin in speech, as part of the Italian Church, in clear contrast to conditions in the most northern parts, which were German in language and within Tyrolean secular jurisdiction.[16]

Even by the mid-seventeenth century, in fact, the papacy's response to Italian problems was visibly affected by pressures from outside the peninsula, exerted above all by the competing powers of Catholic Europe, Habsburg and Bourbon. Yet papal determination to maintain an authority in religious terms which could no longer be successfully exercised in more political ways was equally evident. The papacy was still exercising an effectively primatial leadership in Italian religious practice, but the protection of the peninsula as a holy land of unblemished orthodoxy had been endangered repeatedly, by the threat of alien invasion. The reluctant attempts of the papacy in the early stages of the Thirty Years' War to garrison the Valtelline were interrupted by the ignominy of French invasion directed by a cardinal, Richelieu.

But these attempts to create a *cordon sanitaire* on the frontier of peninsular Italy were not just directed against the competing powers of Catholic Europe beyond the Alps, Habsburg and Bourbon. The feared reality, as events were to prove, was that the overspill of warfare into peninsular Italy would bring troop movements which might spread contagion. In the campaigns over the Mantuan Succession, the immediate contagion proved physical, as epidemic in North and central Italy followed a food shortage between 1628 and 1631. The papacy had feared lest German troops spread the contagion of heresy too. The protection of the saints was undoubted, but evil had also to be positively resisted.

In this context the exceptional intervention of Gregory XV to order a watch against witchcraft can best be understood. His caution, only seemingly at odds with the concerns of other popes throughout this period, was calculated with an eye to the Alpine frontier of Italy which he was trying to fortify by spiritual means while planning to police it by a military presence. The revival of the association between heresy and witchcraft derived from these moments of crisis in the mid-1620s. Urban VIII, who still felt the pressures placed on the papacy by the continuing and increasing conflict between the Catholic powers of Europe, was highly sensitive to allegations that astrological forces were being manipulated against him, and this politically related sensitivity was not to help Galileo. Though the immediately post-Tridentine papacy had

16 *Il Trentino nel Settecento fra Sacro Romano Impero e antichi stati italiani*, ed. C. Mozzarelli and G. Olmi, especially M. Meriggi, 'Il principato vescovile e il "farsi stato" dell'Impero', pp. 677–91 (Bologna 1985); cf. C. Nubola, *Conoscere per governare. La diocesi di Trento nella visita pastorale di Ludovico Madruzzo (1579–1581)* (Bologna 1993).

repeated condemnation of judicial astrology, a new emphasis on condemning abortion had then given way to papal concern to eradicate solicitation of penitents in confession.[17]

GALILEO

Precisely as military and political weakness became more of a constraint, it became all the more necessary to demonstrate an independent authority in the preservation of doctrinal orthodoxy. The often misunderstood treatment of Galileo's case by Urban VIII in fact exposes this situation with striking clarity. Older Italian scholarship already accepted that, before his final trial in Rome, Galileo had encountered appreciation of his work and publications among archetypes of Counter-Reformation propriety in Italy, such as Federico Borromeo, archbishop of Milan from 1595 to 1631. More recent research by Italian scholars has equally shown the range and variety of the intellectual circles in which Galileo had moved in the Venetian Republic, while employed at the University of Padua, including friends and supporters of the Jesuits as well as associates of the anti-papal dissident, Paolo Sarpi. It is also well known that the prior history of Galileo's relations with the cultivated Urban was happy enough. Indeed, it is just because the pope's sudden disapprobation seems so puzzling, in this context, that bold new analyses are still occasionally advanced.

The best publicized recent explanation, that offered by Pietro Redondi, argued for a secret cause of Galileo's condemnation, intentionally concealed beneath the ostensible and public grounds. According to this thesis, Galileo was condemned as a potential heretic, for threatening, by an atomic theory of matter, the Catholic doctrine of the eucharistic Real Presence, which the Council of Trent had in the end decided should most 'aptly' be described by the traditional philosophic formula of transubstantiation.[18] A more useful starting-point in analysis of the case is, however, Urban's relations with the Jesuits. Whatever the Society's effect on his own education and the development of his poetic and literary tastes, the high-water mark of Jesuit influence on papal policy had arguably already passed with Urban's election to the papal throne. In the preceding brief but singularly important pontificate, Gregory XV and his nephew, Cardinal Ludovisi, showed great favour to the Society, in its work both in Europe and in the overseas missions. But the pontificate had also been marked by tension between the papacy and the Habsburg powers, particularly the Spanish monarchy.

---

17 Archivio Segreto Vaticano: Archivio della S. Congregazione del S. Concilio: Visita ad limina, 315, Elvas: 1591; 370A, Granada (I): 1596; 785A, Tarragona (I): 1598, 1601; Archivio della Curia Arcivescovile, Milan: Archivio Spirituale: Carteggio Ufficiale, vol. 127: Q. 10, no. 27: Sixtus V, 1588; cf. Prohibitio Iudiciariae Astrologiae . . . 1585.

18 A. Favaro, 'Federigo Borromeo e Galileo Galilei', *Miscellanea Ceriani* (Milan 1910), pp. 307 ff.; G. Cozzi, *Paolo Sarpi tra Venezia e l'Europa* (Turin 1979), especially 'Galileo Galilei, Paolo Sarpi e la società veneziana', pp. 135–234; P. Redondi, *Galileo: Heretic* (Harmondsworth 1989).

Such tension of course persisted in Urban's pontificate, amid the difficulties created for papal policy by the Thirty Years' War and its extension into the Italian peninsula. As already noted, even before that extension brought the full impact of food shortage and epidemic, fear of such terrors had induced Gregory himself to issue a warning against witchcraft, alerting the Italian faithful to the dangers inherent in diabolic manipulation of nature. In the first years of Urban VIII, who proved so sensitive to any suggestion of astrological speculation during his pontificate, Cardinal Ludovisi maintained his presence at the papal Court, and by 1632 he was still Vice-Chancellor of the Roman Church, occupying the influential and lucrative position at the head of the Chancery. But in 1631–32 Spanish criticism of Urban's supposedly Francophile policies reached a climax, loudly voiced by Cardinal Borgia as spokesman for the monarchy at Rome. In a famous episode, Borgia made an intemperate verbal attack on the pope, at a Consistory in 1632, which he nearly succeeded in disrupting, despite the fierce reaction of the pope's Capuchin brother, the elder Cardinal Antonio Barberini. Less well-known, though pointed out long ago by von Pastor, is the support which Ludovisi was regarded as giving Borgia in this outburst. While for reasons of diplomatic necessity Urban delayed his retribution against Borgia and the Spanish cardinals who supported him, he had no such hesitation with regard to the Italian Ludovisi.

The cardinal was ordered to leave the papal Court and take up residence in his archiepiscopal see of Bologna. Borgia urged Ludovisi not to obey, promising Spanish defence, but Ludovisi in fact complied, leaving the Cancelleria after visiting his favoured Jesuits at their main Roman house, at *Il Gesù*, and hearing Mass there. By March 1632, then, the Jesuits were dramatically associated with the disgrace of an influential cardinal, a patron of the Society both as Cardinal Nephew under Gregory and subsequently. Ludovisi's death in November of the same year does not remove the importance of Urban's extreme exasperation by this date with those who seemed to be associated with his critics and opponents. Plans for the canonization of Francis Borgia, Jesuit and ancestor of Cardinal Borgia, were interrupted. The wide repercussions of the episode are also demonstrated by the fate of a much less famous figure than Galileo.

The unfortunate bearer of the order that Ludovisi should retire to his archbishopric, Cecchini, found himself to have lost the favour of both the pope and the cardinal simultaneously. Galileo's own associates had included Federico Cesi, and both men had been involved in the direction of the scientific Accademia Lincea at Rome. Both Cesi and the Accademia, furthermore, were intimately linked with German scholars and scientists, some of whom had ambitions to redirect papal policy towards a more pro-Habsburg line, while the Jesuits had become increasingly cautious already about any cosmic studies which might be seen at odds with Gregory's opposition to magic. Yet Urban was naturally sensitive to accusations that his allegedly pro-French policy suggested tolerance of French alliance with Protestant heretics; and his own election had involved some doubt about the revised conclave procedure designed by Ludovisi to reduce Spanish pressure. After 1630 and the death of Cesi, the role of the Accademia became dangerously exposed, its position vulnerable. Ciampoli, a member of the Accademia, was also ordered to leave Rome, partly on account of his support for Galileo, but also because of his alleged connections with Cardinal Borgia and the Spanish critics of papal policy. On Cesi's death, the Cardinal Nephew, Francesco Barberini, had already refused the invitation to succeed him as head of the Accademia.

Such considerations, of patronage and policy, are as important to remember as the precise nature of Cardinal Bellarmine's role in defining the boundaries within which, after 1616, Galileo was expected to confine his own expositions. The personal certificate of May 1616, which declared that Galileo had not been subjected to any formal abjuration or penance, in respect of his earlier involvement with Inquisitorial authority, referred precisely to the authority not of the Holy Office, but of the Sacred Congregation of the Index, by this date a distinct body. Bellarmine's experience of seeing his own work momentarily included in the Index of Sixtus V reflected that pope's view that the full extent of papal power in all things, spiritual and temporal, had not been adequately defended and expounded in the cardinal's writings. But rulings of the Congregation were thus not any less serious or binding than decisions of the Holy Office, even if, in this case, the terms of the ruling may possibly reflect a Jesuit as opposed to Dominican approach. Bellarmine might himself no longer be alive after 1621, but between 1616 and 1624 Roman attacks on Copernicanism, as articulated by Ingoli, had provoked Galileo to reply. In any case, the official record of the certificate of May 1616 for Galileo states clearly and precisely that the Copernican cosmic 'doctrine', as 'contrary to Scripture', 'cannot be defended nor held', and that this is so according to a declaration issued by the Sacred Congregation of the Index, and that Galileo has been informed of it. The defence of ecclesiastical and above all papal authority was indeed at the heart of Galileo's final trial and sentence.

Bellarmine's certificate for Galileo further specified that the Sacred Congregation of the Index had issued precisely a declaration of the Holy Father. The pope who reigned in 1630, Urban VIII, felt himself under attack from critics of his policies, who thereby challenged his authority. There had long been criticism in Spain of certain aspects of the patronage and financial systems of the Roman Curia. These were held to harm the proper rights and interests of Spanish clerics. Yet royal and Roman patronage and financial interests were inextricably linked, whether in Spain itself, or in Naples or distinctly in Sicily.

The reign of Philip II had nevertheless seen a series of moments, during diplomatic crises, when Roman involvement in the operation of the Church in Spain had been the subject of criticism. Such attacks continued beyond Philip's death, from the end of the sixteenth century, following papal recognition of an independent Catholic and Bourbon monarchy in France, and on into the seventeenth century. After further episodes of particular tension during the reign of Philip III, the financial difficulties of the monarchy and exasperation with the apparently Francophile policy of Urban VIII produced a new challenge, precisely in 1630. In that year Olivares put to use a review by the royal Council of Castile of the often criticized operation of the nuncio's tribunal in Spain, which had both judicial and financial functions. On the consequent advice of the Council of State, Philip IV was persuaded in 1631 to summon a *junta*, the type of special commission much favoured at this period within Spanish government, to consider what Spanish terminology traditionally called 'the abuses of Rome' and the nunciature.

The *junta* finally produced an inconclusive report in 1632; but the implicit threat to papal financial interests and above all authority in the Church was not yet removed. In 1633 two royal counsellors were ordered by the king to present to the pope a summary of the grievances noted by the *junta* and demand redress for the monarchy. The tone of the representation went far beyond the cautious and respectful terms of the original *junta* report. It did not produce immediate results; but this prolonged challenge to papal authority and financial independence had threatening implications for the papacy's choice of policy in war-torn Europe.[19] Even before the later seventeenth-century pontificates of men closely associated with the Holy Office, it was arguably already crucial in 1630–33, in the face of the challenge to Urban's authority, to reassert that which neither financial circumstance nor military fortune nor diplomatic pressure could undermine.

The doctrinal authority of the papacy was ultimately what the Habsburgs had always claimed to be defending. What was essentially at stake in Galileo's case, as Redondi himself has conceded in places, was doctrinal authority itself, rather than any one specific doctrine. The Holy Office passed judgement for Galileo's infraction of that authority, as previously expressed by the alternative organ of the Congregation of the Index. To the extent that Habsburg accusations had momentarily been outmanoeuvred, it is perhaps less surprising that the signature of Cardinal Borgia, though one of the cardinals of the Holy Office, was lacking from the final sentence on Galileo in 1633, even if the independent Spanish Index conspicuously refrained from following Roman condemnation. Redondi's own analysis admits that a denunciation from a now uncertain source clearly forced consideration of Galileo's position at the highest level, in the circumstances of his publication of the cosmological *Dialogue*, for it was this publication, not the *Assayer*, which in chronological terms triggered the process against him.

Indeed, the unusual device of an initial, limited commission of investigation on Galileo, preceding the eventual formal process by the Holy Office, indicates other aspects of the event, possibly reflecting an initial hope that his publication might serve to defend Rome's prior condemnation of Copernicanism. Precisely because the Holy Office, distinct from other Curial Congregations, had traditionally been under the immediate supervision of the pope, its procedures, though normally unvarying, were by definition susceptible to

19 C. Hermann, *L'église d'Espagne sous le Patronage Royal (1476–1834)* (Madrid 1988).

alteration by personal papal intervention. Such involvement demonstrated papal authority, in the person of Urban VIII, in a way in which no turbulent scenes in Consistory could entirely undermine. The procedures of the Holy Office were evidently not capable of independent direction by even an experienced member like Cardinal Borgia. Rather, the initial papal commission to specially appointed theologians to investigate whether a charge lay against Galileo proved a telling precedent for the extraordinary commission of the 1650s set up by papal authority for preliminary consideration of the charges against Jansenist doctrine.

Ever since the end of the Council of Trent and its explicit confirmation that the papacy was invested with the sole interpretative and declaratory authority in all questions concerning the Conciliar decrees, there had been occasions when popes felt impelled to demonstrate and exercise that authority; and to do so not only via the regular procedures of the Roman Congregations, above all the Holy Office, but in more personal and extraordinary ways. Clement VIII, who had equally faced Habsburg resentment of his recognition of an independent, Bourbon, Catholic France, also attempted to deal by special methods with the crisis over the doctrine of Grace, 'De Auxiliis', which made so public the conflicts between Jesuit and other theologians, above all the Dominicans. The Society of Jesus was not at its most influential during that pontificate, nor was it in 1630–33, during the pontificate of Urban VIII, it may be argued. The disgrace of Cardinal Ludovisi hardly enhanced the Society's position in papal Rome. If Father Grassi, as architect of the great church at the Jesuits' Collegio Romano which was patronized by Ludovisi, was also sent away from Rome, that is hardly surprising. The crisis, at this same moment, in the affairs of the Accademia Lincea, for reasons equally connected with the challenge to Urban's authority in the conduct of papal policy, left associates like Galileo newly vulnerable if charges against them arose.

The timing of the presumed denunciation, after publication not of the *Assayer* but of the cosmological *Dialogue*, reveals the nature of the problem that Galileo, in these circumstances, presented for Urban. A pope facing such a challenge to his position could not at this point refuse to react to accusations of contempt for doctrinal authority. Galileo's offence was indeed to have demonstrated disobedience to a clear, previous Roman ruling on a precise area of contested doctrinal interpretation. Urban was defending papal authority in allowing the case to pass from the special commission to the formal process by the Holy Office. It could indeed be argued that the early eighteenth-century decision of Clement XI to publish the Constitution *Unigenitus*, despite all the conflict which was to ensue, was a demonstration of that doctrinal authority which Habsburg pressure had long demanded be exercised in the distinct issue of the Immaculate Conception. But Clement's pronouncement on questions largely disputed in France reasserted the remaining doctrinal authority of the papacy precisely when political pressures, not least in the Italian peninsula itself, over the Spanish Succession, seemed to be reducing papal power to an absolute minimum.

The degree to which the popes were in personal control of the Holy Office had been demonstrated in a striking way immediately after the Council of Trent, though in an episode known to very few contemporaries. Whatever his success in bringing to a safe conclusion, not least from Rome's point of view, the endangered and disputed proceedings of the Council, Cardinal Morone had a problematic past, in that, like Cardinal Pole, he had been the object of formal investigation by the revived Roman Inquisition, a result of the obsessive suspicion of Paul IV. Despite his subsequent release from imprisonment and public rehabilitation, followed by his triumph as presiding Legate at the Council, the dossier on Morone still existed at Rome. What few contemporaries knew was that even after the successful conclusion of the Council, a secret order was given for the dossier to be reopened and reviewed. In the event no action was taken against Morone himself, who survived into an honoured old age. Indeed, he was even chosen by the pope to exercise his diplomatic gifts as papal mediator in settling the political disputes within the Republic of Genoa, which were threatening the stability of the peninsula. But the episode, however little known at the time, remains instructive.

In the immediately post-Conciliar epoch the Roman Inquisition was, in more public fashion, being used to eradicate from the mainland states any remaining vestiges of mid-century heterodoxy, as judged at least by the newly clarified standards of Tridentine faith. The success of this campaign was undoubted, even if the sensitivity of secular rulers about the image of their Catholic states had to be considered, a matter of importance not only in the Venetian Republic but in the duchy of Mantua for example. The papacy, after the end of the sixteenth century, had less clear success in its insistence that the Tridentine profession of faith be sworn by graduands at peninsular universities, even if non-Italians, at least as far as German students at Padua were concerned.[20] The execution in Rome itself of Giordano Bruno in 1600 was therefore a watershed, though not, as so often assumed, because it began any new rejection of science. Bruno was exceptional in that he had returned to Italy from an existence outside the peninsula, but his execution for heresy nevertheless marked an end to the immediately post-Conciliar decades of *épuration* of Italian society, rather than the beginnings of a new climate of supposed hostility to 'science'.

The disenchanted bishop from Venetian Dalmatia, Marc'Antonio de Dominis, who subsequently reversed his flight to England and returned to Rome a disillusioned ex-Anglican, died in prison in 1624, of natural causes,

---

20 A.S.V. Venezia, XLII (D), XLII (G), *passim*: 1616–18; A.S. Ven.: Collegio: Relazioni di Rettori: Padova, busta 43: 1586, 1611, 1616; Capi del Consiglio dei Dieci: Lettere di Rettori: Padova, busta 83, nos 119, 120, 122; 84, nos 38, 58, 59, 60, 61, 116; 88, no. 1: 1571–82, 1620; Lettere di Ambasciatori: Roma, 26, no. 62: 1575; Secreta Archivi Propri Roma, 18: 22 Oct., 10 Nov. 1565; 26 Jan. 1566; 22 Mar. 1567; Riformatori dello Studio di Padova, filza 64: 17 July 1599; B.N.M.: MSS italiani, classe VII, n. 1553; n. 1556, fos 108r–v, 109v ff.; ed. M. Firpo and D. Marcatto, *Il processo inquisitoriale del cardinal Giovanni Morone*, vols 1–6 (Rome 1981–95); cf. M. Firpo, *Nel labirinto del mondo. Lorenzo Davidico tra santi, eretici, inquisitori* (Florence 1992); ed. D. Marcatto, *Il processo inquisitoriale di Lorenzo Davidico (1555–1560)* (Florence 1992).

before Inquisitorial judgement was executed on his remains. But from the early seventeenth century, the Roman Inquisition, via its tribunals in the Italian mainland states, was arguably more conscious of popular 'superstition' or even 'magic' than of heresy as requiring detection and sanction. This is not to say, however, that there was anything remotely resembling a 'witch-hunt' or 'witch-craze'. On the contrary, in peninsular Italy, as opposed to the Alpine frontier which chiefly alarmed Gregory XV, the Roman Inquisition, with its local tribunals, showed a marked lack of systematic concern about alleged witches. As has recently been well demonstrated with regard to the Venetian tribunal, the caution enshrined in the most authoritative manuals used by inquisitors operating under the direction of the Roman Holy Office effectively limited the escalation of cases concerning superstition or magic into accusations of diabolic witchcraft. Where casual superstition or even ill-educated abuse of sacramentals was not automatically identified with formal heresy, the dangers of a full-scale witch-craze were dramatically decreased.[21] It was thus no accident that peninsular Italy, as opposed to its Alpine margins, was characterized by a relatively small number of capital executions of 'witches'.

Unlike Bruno, Campanella, the protagonist of the Calabrian revolt against Spanish rule, was not executed but imprisoned from 1600, by eventual agreement between the papacy and the Spanish government. The suspicion of heresy was present, but the act of rebellion was certain.[22] Disorder in the Italian peninsula was increasingly evident from about 1590 in many areas, affected by economic recession and a related surge in violent feud and vendetta. The papal states, as well as the kingdom of Naples, were also suffering a conspicuous problem of banditry in the last decades of the sixteenth century. Yet precisely in those post-Conciliar decades the papacy was strenuously insisting, in dealings with the governments of other mainland states, on the preservation of sanctuary, the immunity of ecclesiastical property in which even criminals might seek shelter.

Conflict over this issue persisted, not only in the Venetian Republic, and with some states the papacy came to an agreement as to the precise operation of sanctuary, especially in relation to the most serious crimes. But the creation in the 1620s of a Curial Congregation, that of Immunities, registered the continued papal determination to preserve the essence of ecclesiastical liberty. This has indeed been acknowledged to represent an important limit or interruption, in the papal states themselves, in any supposed trend towards the dominance of temporal government interests over properly ecclesiastical priorities. This was so despite the fact that even after the Council of Trent, in Italy as elsewhere, the religious orders, and not only the secular clergy, continued to include disorderly or criminal elements. At Venice dispute over such regulars centred on the claims of the nuncio's tribunal to competence in their cases.

21 R. Martin, *Witchcraft and the Inquisition in Venice 1550–1650* (Oxford 1989).
22 A.G.S.: Estado: Napoles: Legs 1095, fo. 285; 1096, fos 105, 106, 111, 119, 123, 125, 178, 180; 1097, fos 2, 20, 24, 33 f.; cf. T. Campanella, *Supplizio*, ed. L. Firpo (Rome 1985).

EXTERNAL INFLUENCE AND ITALIAN TRANSFORMATION

Yet secular governments within Italy, just as beyond, had their own ways of influencing Roman policy, even if indirectly. The cardinals who at Rome served the interests of a particular state or dynasty, whether or not in the formal office of Cardinal Protector, often received subsidies, either in the form of gifts, or by presentation to a compatible benefice, or by allocation of a pension drawn on the revenues of a benefice within the state in question. Venetian cardinals and other prelates, admittedly, were confined by Republican vigilance as to the benefits they might receive, even directly from the papacy. In this the Republic showed its increased sensitivity about the extent to which the adult males of patrician families were involved in ecclesiastical affairs. By the time of the Interdict, and beyond, the Venetian state was enlarging the definition of 'papalist', as applied even to patrician laymen, to those whose degree of family or individual connection with the Church debarred them from voting on specific issues or indeed carrying out certain functions as magistrates.

But other cardinals could and certainly did accept subsidy from secular rulers, even an independent-minded figure like Paleotti for example. In this context it is perhaps worth noting that whatever the routine nature of most Consistory business, the collective interests of the college of cardinals could still be quite effectively pursued, and not only in the special circumstances of a conclave. In the promotion of benefice business in Consistory a ruler might need to consider the interests not only of the Dean, the senior Cardinal Priest and senior Cardinal Deacon, but also, in addition to the Cardinal Camerlengo himself, of the cardinal who as Camerlengo of the college supervised the collection of the Curial dues payable for Consistorial provisions. Yet cardinals who were not resident either in Curia or in the peninsula could on occasion have a major influence on Italian developments which affected papal policy. Richelieu's role in disrupting papal plans to police the Valtelline has been noted. French encouragement of native unrest, pursued by the Italian-born Cardinal Mazarin, contributed to the eventual revolt of 1647 against Spanish rule at Naples, whose uncertain course left Innocent X in a state of indecision.

It was at Naples that a crucial transformation of sentiment in at least educated Italian society had arguably become evident from the end of the seventeenth century already. In what were to prove the final decades of Spanish, though not Habsburg, rule at Naples, the long-standing anti-Curialism among lawyers and intellectuals, consolidated from the end of the Council of Trent onwards, reached an important new articulation. The trial from the end of the 1680s of Neapolitan intellectuals accused of 'atheism' aroused a specific attack on the functioning of the Holy Office's authority within the city and kingdom. The more than jurisdictional implications of the conflict were noted by the writer Valletta, while Gravina added a specifically anti-Jesuit note. These prepared the way for the even greater fame which was to be achieved by Vico and Giannone.

Thus out of the conservative regalist challenge to Tridentine change, which had characterized Neapolitan legal tradition since the Council, there emerged a much broader and more profound criticism of papal authority, at least as represented by the Holy Office on the one hand, and the Jesuits on the other. At Naples itself part of this tradition was continued into the Bourbon regime, in that the royal Chaplain General appointed by the Austrian Habsburgs was retained in office at the change of dynasty in 1734. From the period of Spanish rule this appointment was of great influence, since the viceregal government insisted that the Chaplain General was to review all Roman orders or provisions affecting the kingdom, and that these should not receive the viceregal confirmation necessary for their application without the Chaplain's prior approval. Papal hesitation over fully recognizing the Bourbon succession at Naples provoked a further intensification of anti-Curial sentiment, which, despite a concordat signed in 1741, produced the abolition of the Holy Office's authority there as early as 1746.

The dissolution of some religious houses during the 1760s and 1770s was enforced in Bourbon Naples and Sicily. Following the suppression of the Jesuits in Portugal and France, the Society was expelled by 1767 not only from Spain but also from Naples; and in 1768 even the Knights of Malta expelled the Jesuits from their island. Papal suzerainty over Naples itself was finally rejected, following threats made earlier under the influence of Tanucci, when in 1788 the traditional symbol of recognition, the annual tribute of the *chinea*, was refused. The long papal resistance to the secular claim of legatine authority in Sicily, the *Monarchia Sicula*, was finally abandoned by Benedict XIII, and by 1741 the papacy was forced to agree concordats regulating Church appointments in the interests of the state for Sardinia as well as Naples. By the end of the Ancien Régime the Inquisition had also been abolished in Bourbon Sicily. Even in the early eighteenth century, as Piedmont exchanged possession of Sicily for that of Sardinia, it was already less clear that the previous contrast between the Church in mainland Italy and conditions in the two islands remained.

Jurisdictional confrontation had occurred in Savoy-Piedmont as early as the 1720s, with an attack on Jesuit involvement in higher education. In 1727 Benedict XIII felt compelled to sign a concordat with the ruler of Piedmont that was very favourable to the interests of the house of Savoy, elevated since 1713 to royal status. Though Clement XII tried to challenge the terms of this concordat in 1731, political realism caused him not to provoke the Italian governments further, when Cardinal Alberoni's quixotic attempt to incorporate the Republic of San Marino in the papal states proved a fiasco. The Venetian Republic systematized more restrictive policies towards the Church within its territories from 1766.

The European dynastic struggles and rearrangements of the mid-eighteenth century saw the loss of papal suzerainty over Parma and Piacenza from 1731, even before Clement XII and Benedict XIV proved unable to prevent papal territory itself being invaded by Spanish and Austrian armies in the wars of

1733–35 and 1741–48. In the Bourbon duchy of Parma, the limitation of mortmain in 1764, anticipated by the Genoese Republic in 1762, was followed by abolition of the local tribunal of the Inquisition in 1769. As the Bourbon Court of Parma pursued the expulsion of the Jesuits, Clement XIII tried to prolong resistance in 1768 by threatening the excommunication of the duke and his ministers. But the co-operation of the Bourbon Courts meant that Clement XIV then faced not only French occupation of Avignon, but also Neapolitan occupation of Benevento. It was thus the conclusion of a long struggle when, in 1768–69, the governments of Venice and Lombardy, as well as Parma, Naples and Spain, suppressed in their states the Bull *In Coena Domini*, in response to the papal confrontation then with Parma and, by extension, with the other Bourbon Courts. On this major issue it was once again Clement XIV who yielded, formalizing in 1774 the tacit abandonment of the Bull from 1770.

Under the regime initially succeeding the Medici in the eighteenth-century grand-duchy of Tuscany, that of Francis of Lorraine, there were selective monastic dissolutions, and ecclesiastical involvement in censorship was reduced in 1743. The Regency Council, on behalf of Francis, also introduced the limitation of mortmain in 1751. Under the Habsburg succession there, Leopold imposed new restrictions on the Church from 1766, including the dissolution of religious houses deemed to be of no social benefit. In 1782 the Inquisition in Tuscany was suppressed, and in 1786 the nuncio's traditional jurisdiction was rejected, confining the nunciature to the bare role of diplomatic representation. Yet even in 1787 the meeting of the bishops of Tuscany proved to lack enthusiasm for the anti-Roman positions adopted by the Synod of Pistoia.

The insistence that Roman rulings needed the confirmation of secular authority for their local validity, found in Spanish-ruled Sicily and Sardinia, was adopted in Austrian-ruled Lombardy in 1762, while censorship there was removed from inquisitorial control in 1768. Restrictions on regulars were already imposed in Lombardy before the death of Maria Theresa, and the Austrian government there created in 1765 a *giunta* to supervise clerical affairs, restricting the judicial immunities of the Church, before the curtailment and then suppression of the Inquisition. From 1786 the ecclesiastical courts in Lombardy were themselves suppressed, as part of a major reconstruction of the state. Jansenist teaching, favoured in Lombardy during the government of Maria Theresa and Joseph II, was further encouraged by state-inspired reform of the University of Pavia. The jurisdictionalism of Joseph could be preached to future clergy once the imperial programme for replacing diocesan seminaries with regional General Seminaries under state control had been applied in Lombardy as well as elsewhere in his territories. From Pavia the ideas of Tamburini were exported to Habsburg-ruled Tuscany, at the Synod of Pistoia, while Joseph ordered the removal from Rome to Pavia of the German College, originally founded by the papacy to train a clerical elite for Germany and Hungary.

The papal visit to Vienna of 1782 and Joseph's visit to Rome in 1783, though followed by a concordat in 1784, did not represent a true resolution of jurisdictional dispute. Throughout the Italian states in the eighteenth century there were some genuine sympathizers with Jansenism, often among scholarly clerics who shared in anti-Jesuit sentiment. A more positively doctrinal attachment to Jansenism was perhaps found in the Republic of Genoa, before the developments in Tuscany of the 1780s. Such Jansenism should be distinguished from the rigorism, earlier in the century, of the Dominican Concina or subsequently, in more moderate form, of Alphonsus Liguori. The eighteenth-century revolts in Corsica against Genoese rule, of eventual benefit to France, removed that island from any papal oversight of the Italian Church, even before the Revolution.

On the eve of the Revolution, then, the effective primatial control of the Italian Church previously exercised by the post-Tridentine papacy might be seen to be collapsing. The decline of such leadership had nevertheless been gradual and extended over a long period. Of the many pressures from the peninsular governments experienced by Clement XIV, that for the reduction of major holydays was easy enough to accept, since a precedent had been set by Urban VIII in 1642, and Benedict XIII had removed for some feasts the requirement of abstention from manual labour. The independent duchy of Modena remained a haven for Jesuits and a base for their self-defence against critics almost until the final suppression of the Society. But the papacy's own attempts to defend ecclesiastical rights had not otherwise aroused such exemplary policy.

PAPAL RESILIENCE

Jurisdictional challenge

Such gradual change should also not be predated. For all the momentary polemics over papal authority at the time of the Venetian Interdict of 1606–7, including the republication of earlier Gallican treatises, the cautious conduct of Venice after that unintended outcome of perennial diplomatic manoeuvring did not fulfil the exaggerated hopes of Protestants outside Italy. Whatever Paolo Sarpi's private disillusionment, the Republic had clearly never intended as more than a bargaining counter its contrived 'leak' that it might in future seek consecration of its bishops not from prelates in communion with Rome but from the schismatic patriarch of Constantinople, who in any case was under the control of the Turkish enemy of Venice.[23] The anti-papal adjustments made by Marc'Antonio De Dominis during his Anglican exile to the text of Sarpi's polemical *History of the Council of Trent* were part of the tradition of Protestant polemics against Rome. In Italy itself the extension of an effectively primatial authority, at least in the mainland states, begun with such

23 A.S. Ven.: Inquisitori di Stato: Lettere agli Ambasciatori a Roma, busta 165, nos 9 f.: 31 Dec. 1594, 7 Jan. 1595.

vigour by the immediately post-Tridentine popes, could certainly be seen to have survived for at least a century.

Canonizations

But a more profound Roman influence, within Italy and also beyond, could be seen to have had an even more enduring effect. During the seventeenth century the papacy had developed another mechanism, of a more truly underground nature, for bringing an aura of Rome to the rest of Catholic Christendom. Among the remarkable features of ecclesiastical and cultural life in late sixteenth- and early seventeenth-century Rome was the beginning of a more systematic exploration of the catacombs. An enthusiasm for the remains of supposed saints found under the city grew steadily, and what were believed to be martyrs' relics were exported to churches outside Rome, under a system of nominal authentication by the Roman authorities, newly regulated from 1672. Whole skeletons were translated to churches in Italy and beyond, and were eventually exposed for veneration under Austrian or Bavarian altars and even further afield.

By contrast with this successful inflation of saintly honours, the post-Conciliar papacy also demonstrated an increasingly firm authority in taking control of saints' cults. The procedures for canonization, after initial dispositions by Clement VIII and others, were defined by Urban VIII in the mid-seventeenth century, and were thereafter maintained, despite review, in the next century by Benedict XIV. The crucial aspect of this regulation of saints' cults was the insistence on a formal, Roman judicial process to establish sanctity. Under Urban VIII the most crucial business of the Congregation of Rites relating to canonizations could only be transacted in the presence of the pope himself, but this emphasis on the importance of the matter was balanced by a restriction in the number of meetings. Diocesan investigations to establish a *prima facie* case for Roman consideration were still involved, but again only under Roman supervision. Any unauthorized cult attributed locally to figures of veneration would automatically create an impediment to consideration of a case. The papacy could still sit in judgement on the deceased, in other words, while the involvement of the Sacred Rites Congregation in these procedures was a reminder of the related aim to introduce liturgical uniformity.

The result of these developments was perhaps clearer than that of attempts by post-Tridentine popes, again particularly Clement VIII and Urban VIII, to insist on the Conciliar provision for ecclesiastical control of lay confraternities. The immediately post-Conciliar popes did almost nothing to alter the long silence of the sixteenth century in the matter of declaring new official saints. The eventual canonization of Charles Borromeo in 1610 certainly gave the Italian peninsula a new saint, and one created within a quarter-century of his death, an interval subsequently considered too brief in papal legislation for future canonizations. The canonization of the born Florentine and adopted Roman, Philip Neri, was accompanied, as already noted, by a group of Iberian elevations to the altar, including the long-delayed canonization of Loyola; and these simultaneous canonizations followed that of a truly Roman saint, Francesca Romana. Thereafter the pace of canonizations did not advance more than steadily, and even after the clarification of the interim stage of beatification, for candidates for canonization, some processes remained halted at just such preliminary or intermediate points. Nevertheless the beatifications and canonizations of the seventeenth and eighteenth centuries, as determined at Rome, provided new saints from and for Italy, though not to the total exclusion of others; and in this way too the papacy retained a real influence on peninsular piety.

The organization of religious orders

Another important influence on lay piety in the peninsula also remained outside the sphere of episcopal direction but not beyond the impact of Roman authority. The organization of religious orders in mainland Italy was obviously independent of the diocesan structure. But the intimate link between the papacy and the regulars of the older orders as well as of new, Counter-Reformation creations again ensured Roman leadership in this aspect of Italian Church life, overriding by a kind of direct primacy the network of dioceses and metropolitan provinces. However, this connection between Rome and the Italian regulars should not be reduced to some crudely anti-episcopal coalition. The papal suppressions or forced amalgamations of smaller orders or impossibly small religious houses, in seventeenth- and eighteenth-century Italy, continued after the investigation of the peninsular regulars commissioned by Innocent X. But the later sixteenth-century suppression of the Humiliati in part vindicated the status of Charles Borromeo as archbishop, as well as Cardinal Protector and Apostolic Visitor.[24]

In this sense, for all the obviously wider and more dramatic implications for papal authority itself, the eighteenth-century papal compliance first in the suppression of the Jesuits in various Italian states and then in dissolving the Society of Jesus entirely was not an isolated or unprecedented act. From the later sixteenth century onwards most religious orders represented among the peninsular regulars received papal attention, not always welcome, as with the general dispositions for all regulars made by Clement VIII. Among the orders of friars in the peninsula, for example, the Conventual Franciscans had not found the interventions of Sixtus V particularly favourable. The Roman convent of the Minims, on the other hand, was not disturbed in the distinguished scientific experiments there which derived from the order's French houses, despite the order's founder having originated in the ecstatic world of Southern Italy. Other New Orders of Counter-Reformation origin were certainly made aware of papal authority, as when the Ministers of the Sick received Roman

24 *L'Inchiesta di Innocenzo X sui Regolari in Italia*, ed. G. Galasso: I, *I Teatini*, ed. M. Campanelli (Rome 1987).

determination of the contested boundary between their physical care of the ill and wider pastoral provision. Other new hospitaller institutions also found their precise canonic status altered by fluctuations in papal policy.

Papal approval, not always immediately forthcoming or uninterrupted, was necessary for New Orders devoted to educational purposes to establish themselves in Rome, let alone elsewhere in the peninsula. The Society of Jesus established itself in Borromean Milan only with some difficulty and eventually under unusual episcopal specifications. The sense of Milan as 'another Rome' could only be enhanced by the creation of a special diocesan force of priests, bound by a particular vow not to the pope, as in the case of the inner elite of the Jesuits, but to the archbishop of the day. However, Roman intervention in the affairs of the Oblates of St Ambrose was not absent in the period immediately following Charles Borromeo's death.[25]

At Naples, alongside vigorous archiepiscopal reform akin to that of the Borromeo archbishops of Milan, the Jesuits were well established. The Oratorians also opened a famous house there, ultimately distinct from the Roman Oratory and its different traditions. Elsewhere in the peninsula though a network of Oratorian houses was gradually extended which tended to look to Rome, thus bringing to provincial Italy another link with the papal city. The specifically Jesuit colleges in the peninsula also of course represented a Roman connection for laity as well as future clerics, though bishops were far from certain to employ Jesuits for the direction of diocesan seminaries, as they were gradually set up in mainland Italy. But the eventual existence of a Curial Congregation precisely entitled 'Of bishops and regulars' is not just indicative of the perpetual potential for tension between diocesan bishops and religious orders.

The episcopate and the regulars in Italy were intimately bound together because the papacy often chose to appoint regulars, most often mendicants, to bishoprics. This was particularly true, in the post-Conciliar Church, of the often impoverished, frequently small dioceses of the southern half of the peninsula. By contrast, some of the new institutions of Counter-Reformation creation resisted preferment to such positions, unless their members were positively ordered by the pope to accept. This was admittedly not the case with the aristocratic Theatines, whose *raison d'être* was to set an example to the diocesan clergy of Italy. But the resistance to papal preferment was not merely yet another idiosyncrasy of the Oratorians, who were secular priests and not regulars in any case. It was the norm in the Society of Jesus, despite the period when Bellarmine was ordered away from papal Rome, to give archiepiscopal attention to Capua.

What papal confirmation of the New Orders and other new institutes in the post-Tridentine Church brought to Italian religious life, then, was yet further

25 A.S.V.: Archivium Arcis (Armaria Inferiora): no. 6118 [fo. 2r]; Biblioteca Ambrosiana, Milan: MSS G. 141 inferior, fo. 127: 12 Jan. 1588; G. 145 inferior, fos 41r, 252r: 26 July, 9 Aug. 1589; G. 260 inferior, fos 139r, 207v: 25 Mar., 28 Oct. 1594; cf. F. Rurale, *I Gesuiti a Milano. Religione e politica nel secondo Cinquecento* (Rome 1992); Archivio della Curia Arcivescovile, Milan: Archivio Spirituale: Carteggio Ufficiale: vol. 1, no. 1, Q. 1 [fos 6r–7v]: 11 Feb. 1586.

variety in the ecclesiastical ministrations also available to the laity. To the diocesan and parochial structure, the existing network of rural and urban monasteries and friaries, the priories of canons regular and the houses of sixteenth-century congregations like the Somaschi and Barnabites, were added male nursing and teaching orders as well as the expansion throughout the peninsula of the Jesuits. The interior missions in mainland Italy were for a while associated particularly with the Jesuits, but both in the sixteenth century and beyond Capuchins were also conspicuous in this role, as well as in special ministry during epidemics; quite apart from the involvement of a few from either order in delicate diplomacy between the papacy and other Catholic powers. By the eighteenth century the Passionists and Redemptorists were employed in interior missions, especially in central and Southern Italy. Despite jurisdictional conflicts and associated internal tensions affecting the missioner orders in eighteenth-century Naples, their work again represented a specific link between papal Rome and provincial Italy.

Female convents

Italian society, as well as the religious orders, was again affected by papal policy towards female convents, from the conclusion of the Council of Trent onwards. The immediately post-Conciliar popes set a lasting pattern, by insisting on strict enclosure for female houses, with a consequent reduction in the ease of family access. Houses resisting strict enclosure or internal reform were to be put under new superiors introduced from other convents, and incorrigible bodies of nuns even dispersed among other institutions or forced to amalgamate with the more reformed. Lay and state resistance to this clear programme, which post-Conciliar popes and mainland bishops co-operated to pursue, was vigorous, whether in the Venetian Republic or Naples, for instance, or even in Medicean Siena or Borromean Milan. Yet in the matter of enclosure itself, the papacy evidently established a relative triumph in due course.

In mainland Italy, as opposed to Spain for example, female tertiaries were in the end forced to choose between enclosure, characteristic of professed nuns, or a clearly lay existence. This also of course limited the originally bold plans for the enlargement of female education envisaged by the Ursulines, at least in Northern Italy (though the limitation was perhaps less absolute in papal Bologna).[26] It also notoriously thwarted much of what the English Catholic, Mary Ward, had hoped to achieve in the sphere of female education. But where Roman exercise of effective primatial leadership of the Italian Church met its limitations was rather in other aspects of the originally severe programme for female convents. In the long term lay resistance in the peninsula circumvented the insistence on strict abandonment of private property among

26 L. Ciammitti, 'Una santa di meno. Storia di Angela Mellini, cucitrice bolognese (1667–17..)', *Quaderni storici*, XLI (1979), 603–43.

choir-nuns, and defeated the efforts of both popes and bishops to ensure that only individual personal vocation and not family inheritance restrictions dictated the composition of female convents.

The canonic penalties against those forcing or inducing girls into conventual life involuntarily did not achieve their aim, any more than did the device of episcopal examination of a girl's private intentions, to be made only when she had some experience of secular society, at an interval from any schooling in the convent. All this suggests that lay support and co-operation, or their absence, partly influenced the papacy's ability to play an effectively primatial role in the peninsula.[27] The female convents of the peninsula, for all the severity of papal pronouncement and supervision by the male hierarchy of diocesan bishops or male regulars, remained in reality more a special estate within lay society rather than a perfectly controlled sector of the institutional Church. Families who entered their daughters as choir-nuns, paying or crediting an entry dowry, naturally expected to retain some degree of control of these institutions. The local boards of nobles who managed conventual property in parts of Italy were made more rather than less important as the papacy insisted that female superiors take office triennially and no longer perpetually.

The demands of peninsular rulers and states

The post-Conciliar popes also, however, had to respond to the demands of peninsular rulers and states for the redrawing of the boundaries between provinces of given orders to meet political sensitivities. Indeed, the papacy's attempted direction of Italian conventual life, male or female, ultimately encountered a more fundamental obstacle, before the outbreak of the French Revolution. One long-term result of the Spanish Succession War of the early eighteenth century, as it affected Lombardy, where Austrian Habsburg replaced Spanish Habsburg rule, was the impact of the Josephine monastic dissolutions. The papacy was unable to prevent entirely the pursuit by Joseph II of his inherited programme of suppressing those orders and houses which, by his standards, served no justifying social purpose. Indeed, by the later eighteenth century, in Italy as well as elsewhere in Catholic Europe, there was some suggestion of episcopal impatience with the religious orders and their papal favours, even after the sacrifice, to more specifically anti-Jesuit sentiment, of the Society and its inner elite's particular link to the papacy.

This was a distant echo of sixteenth-century episcopal antagonism to the extent and variety of regulars' privileges and exemptions, still evident in only partly submerged form during the closing stages of the Council of Trent. Yet in Catholic Europe, Italy included, the papacy had with a relative constancy, at least compared with policy towards the mendicants in overseas mission fields, maintained the Tridentine settlement, by which the precisely pastoral work of the regulars should be subject to the control of diocesan bishops. In

27 Archivio Storico Civico, Milan: Collezione Gride: no. 17: 1626.

the daily life of the Church, after all, it was chiefly in the regulars', usually the friars', work as preachers and confessors that episcopal frustration might be aroused most easily, unless over funerals and burials. But preaching and hearing confessions were not the only channels through which regulars in Italy contacted and influenced the laity. The peninsular laity remained attached to their local confraternities, despite Tridentine enhancement of the place of the parish church in the religious life of the faithful and post-Conciliar episcopal insistence on the fulfilment of precisely parochial duties. Here again the papacy after the Council can be seen as employing, additionally, a sort of direct primacy in relation to the mainland population.

Confraternities

A degree of peninsular uniformity was also pursued by Rome in the matter of confraternities. This was a policy of attraction, not enforced subordination, however. The terms of papal privileges for the Roman archconfraternities allowed them to extend their own members' benefits, most importantly indulgences, to members of Italian confraternities elsewhere who sought formal, collective aggregation. This promoted some concept of Roman centrality in Italian religious life not just for dioceses beyond the confines of the papal states but more generally among the peninsular population, even where the regime was 'foreign' in the sense of non-native, as in Lombardy under Spanish rule, before the later attack of Joseph II on the confraternities. A partial parallel to this were the privileges granted from Rome to the Confraternities of St Peter Martyr, existing in various parts of Italy to support the tribunals of the Holy Office. But while the attraction of the indulgences granted to these was not in dispute, the claim of their members in some Italian states to carry otherwise prohibited arms raised possibly counter-productive conflict with secular authorities, such as that again in Spanish Lombardy, quite apart from the ever-vigilant concern of the Venetian Republic.[28]

By 1600 the papacy was already successful in attracting to Rome, especially for Jubilees, the stream of Italian as well as foreign pilgrims who sought to obtain the indulgences on offer in the apostolic city. The Italian pilgrims were often in organized groups, most often based on local confraternity membership, for here again formal association with a Roman archconfraternity could provide welcome material benefits to pilgrims in an overcrowded city, while on the road to Rome other local confraternities sharing a similar association might be expected to offer travel assistance. While many special indulgences normally obtainable elsewhere in Catholic Europe were usually suspended in Jubilees, a demonstration of Roman favour could grace an Italian city, when the local population was exceptionally allowed to gain the Roman indulgences by visiting specified churches in their own native city. The papacy's outreach

28 A.G.S.: Estado: Milan: Legs 1272, fos 138r ff., 139r ff.; 1273, fos 63r ff.: 4 July, 22 Sept. 1593; A.S. Ven.: Senato: Dispacci di Rettori: Brescia: 30 Sept., 29 Oct. 1614.

to the Italian population, even into the eighteenth century, by means of the network of confraternities throughout at least the north and centre of the peninsula should not be underestimated. But what Italian pilgrims in the pre-Revolutionary era chiefly came to visit, it must be stressed, was still the Petrine and Apostolic shrines, the saintly relics and the churches, not yet the person of the Holy Father, valuable though his blessing undoubtedly was when bestowed on crowds at the great ceremonies or on a select stream of individuals.

The unsought mantle of Revolutionary martyrdom had not yet settled on the bishop of Rome; but for all that the Ancien Régime papacy was still the source of the most generous indulgences, the more so given the Conciliar concern to limit those granted by lesser prelates. Italian diocesan bishops after the Council were evidently still frustrated at times by the claim of some confraternities to grant to members indulgences whose authenticity was doubtful. This frustration was more acute in the case of those lay confraternities directed or even erected by regulars, whether older orders like the Dominicans or New Orders like the Jesuits. Here the sense of a link between papacy and regulars which bypassed the proper exercise of the Ordinary's authority did recur. It is hardly surprising in this context if in Borromean Milan an attempt was made to organize local confraternities under a diocesan superstructure, rather than encouraging aggregation to the Roman archconfraternities.

But in any case this was not the limit to papal influence on the Italian population via confraternities and related foundations. The peninsula, at least in the North and centre, was richly endowed with charitable institutions, whether managed by confraternities or otherwise in lay administration. Because such charitable foundations were in a very immediate sense supported by lay alms, whether permanent bequests or occasional gifts, the mainland states were always anxious to reserve the freedom of lay management from clerical direction. Tridentine provision for episcopal audit was certainly explicit, but as difficult to establish as supervision of lay confraternities. The papacy, on the other hand, was able to intervene in one type of innovative charity beyond doubt. By the end of the sixteenth century the institutions which acted as Christian loan-banks based on the mechanisms of the pawn-broker's, known as *Monti di Pietà*, were quite widely spread in Northern and central Italy.

Essential to their functioning, particularly in times of recession such as affected parts of Italy from the last decade of the century, was the accumulation of capital out of which loans were made. To encourage deposits which renewed the capital there was the Catholic doctrine by which charitable giving, even if institutionalized and not casual, repaid an eternal dividend to the donor's soul. But bad debts and administrative costs, quite apart from misappropriation of funds, diminished capital to a dangerous degree, necessitating an additional incentive to depositors in the form of earthly and monetary interest. This required more careful justification than the demand for a low charge to be paid on the loan itself by the borrower, where technical considerations allowed the loan to be slightly less than the valuation of the item pawned. The papacy was an indisputable source of arbitration, and it is striking that local *Monti*, even in the Republic where Venice so fiercely and absolutely guarded such charitable institutions from the slightest clerical intervention, ensured that their administrators sought papal permission before moving the low interest rate on deposits, even if altering it by only half a per cent. This degree of papal influence on social provision in mainland Italy is in decided contrast to more sweeping assertions of authority over mercantile practice, especially the conditions of interest taking, which cannot be seen to have had much practical impact in the peninsula. The attempt of immediately post-Conciliar popes to limit the peninsular presence of non-Italians or circumscribe the movement of Italian traders, especially on the northern borders of the peninsula, to and from non-Catholic areas was similarly devoid of lasting effect.

Some of the immediately post-Tridentine popes also sought to place restrictions on Jewish communities in the peninsula, beyond the confines of the papal states. But the regulation of the Jewish communities in Venetian territory remained solidly a preserve of the Venetian Republic. The Inquisition in Venice could only consider cases where a suspect could be shown to have Judaized, in the precise sense of apostatizing after Christian baptism. The duke of Piedmont encountered papal opposition in the later sixteenth century when proposing to allow the presence of Marranos, those of Iberian origin who were the usual suspects when accusations of Judaizing arose. Until the last decades of the sixteenth century Lombardy remained anomalous among Spanish-ruled territories, but the Spanish government then decided to extend to that duchy the expulsion of Jewish communities, though a few families in fact remained beyond that point. Papal views on the admission of Jews to Tuscany were, however, essentially irrelevant as the Medici determined to develop Livorno as a freeport.[29]

A gradual decline, then, in the papacy's primatial leadership of the peninsular Church could be detected during the pre-Revolutionary century, from the 1680s to the 1780s. This was above all connected with the succession of non-Italian powers other than the Spanish Habsburgs in the government of Italian states, specifically the Austrian Habsburgs and the Bourbons. Yet on a purely ecclesiastical front the relative success of the campaign to implement the Tridentine reforms in mainland Italy, slowly pursued for over two centuries, owed much to this dimension of papal office. The eighteenth-century studies of Muratori on the ecclesiastical and other antiquities of Italy partly reflected the influence in the peninsula of foreign, above all French, scholarship from the end of the previous century onwards. Nevertheless, the extent to which an 'Italian Church' with the papacy at its head had come into being was already indicated by the first edition (1643–62) of Ughelli's monumental *Italia Sacra*.

---

29 A.G.S.: Secretaría Provincial: Milan: Consultas, Legs 1795, 1796: 1590–92; Varios, Leg. 2042: 1688; B. Pullan, *The Jews of Europe and the Inquisition of Venice, 1550–1670* (Oxford 1983); B. Pullan, *Rich and Poor in Renaissance Venice* (Oxford 1971), pp. 429 ff.

CHAPTER 5

Patriarchal authority in Western Europe and political obstacles

Effective limitations to the authority of the papacy over Western Christendom between the end of the Council of Trent and the outbreak of the French Revolution did not turn simply on questions of title. In this period the ancient incorporation of a patriarchal dimension in the composite authority of the papacy was still represented by the title of the major basilicas of Rome, associated with specifically papal ceremonies: the patriarchal basilicas. That this did not imply, any more than in much earlier centuries, that the pope was but one patriarch among others was obvious. In the most solemn papal Masses repetition in Greek of elements of the Latin liturgy, the Epistle and Gospel, was an immediate reminder that the patriarchal headship of Western Christendom was combined with claims to a more universal jurisdiction. But the patriarchal dimension is still worth distinct consideration, precisely because the popes after the Council of Trent did not confine their concern for the Christian Church to Western Europe, even though within Western Christendom their failure to recover control of areas turned Protestant was being consolidated. The post-Conciliar popes indeed renewed their efforts to maintain relations with Eastern-rite Churches in communion with Rome, or bring them into communion, with varying degrees of success over longer or shorter periods.

RITES AND PATRIARCHATES

Partial or temporary successes could be found among the most ancient of the Churches of the East, such as the addition of a second branch of the so-called Nestorian Church recognizing Roman authority, following an initial reunion before the end of the Council of Trent. This second Uniate Church, based in Southern Iraq, was a seventeenth-century complement to the original Uniates of Kurdistan.[1] It was nevertheless not surprising, given logistic and political difficulties of contact, that both branches abandoned recognition of Rome

1 The term 'Uniate' (alternatively 'Uniat') is not usually favoured by the Churches often so described. Its use here is simply intended to reflect commonly received and therefore recognizable historiographic convention.

146

during the eighteenth century. Yet, in partial compensation, in 1741 the Coptic prelate in Jerusalem led his part of the originally Monophysite Churches into Uniate status, a move prepared under Clement XII, after the negotiations of Clement VIII with the patriarchate of Alexandria. Similarly, among those Churches, the Tridentine and post-Conciliar Jesuit missions to Ethiopia, intended to bring the Church there into communion with Rome, proved an heroic but unquestionable failure; a result not altered by the quixotic plan by Benedict XIV in 1741 to engage the Knights of Malta to support a proposed new Franciscan mission. But among the so-called Jacobite Christians of Syria, an archbishop of Aleppo, subsequently elected patriarch in 1782, established a Uniate Church ultimately based in Lebanon. This resurrected a more short-lived Uniate programme, originally pursued by a Syrian patriarch of Antioch, between 1662 and 1701.

In the same way, despite the existence in seventeenth-century Persia of a Uniate tradition among Armenian Christians, an attempt by an Armenian bishop from 1712 to establish a Uniate Church was itself a failure, but led to the consolidation at Venice of the famous Armenian Catholic monastery of San Lazzaro. This in turn partly stimulated the local creation of an Armenian-rite Catholic patriarchate for Cilicia, recognized by Benedict XIV in 1742 – a parallel to Roman recognition of an Armenian Uniate Church in Poland by the end of the seventeenth century. The so-called St Thomas Christians of India, during the period in question here, moved from their original link with the Nestorians to a partial association with the originally Monophysite Copts and the Syrian Jacobites. But that transition, and the related divisions among the Malabar Christians were precisely a response to the problems emerging from their contacts with Western European Christians newly arriving in India. Although assertions of Roman authority were very much involved in this, even if only partially successful, the context and subsequent problems were provided by the Portuguese presence and claims to local ecclesiastical jurisdiction, by virtue of the papal grant of the *padroado*. For that reason discussion of Roman relations with the St Thomas Christians is better postponed to subsequent consideration of the papacy's universal role in missionfields beyond Europe (see Chapter 6).

The Greek liturgy of the Basilians in post-Tridentine Italy, on the other hand, has already been mentioned. More generally, throughout the period considered here, Greek-rite communities survived in Southern Italy and Sicily, despite some pressure from local post-Conciliar bishops to adopt the Latin rite. Oversight of the Greek rite in such communities was extended from the Roman Curia, however, in the same immediately post-Conciliar decades, despite the complication that married clergy were legitimately found among them, by virtue of Greek canon law; and Clement VIII appointed a Greek-rite bishop to reside in Rome and provide priestly ordinations.[2] Recognition of Roman authority in such a context could at times prove problematic, as in the

2 A.G.S.: Secretaría Provincial: Napoles: Visitas y Diversos: Libros 95, 105.

case of the possibly schismatic prelates allowed by the Republic to head the Venetian Greek community both in the late sixteenth century and again in the eighteenth century. But in the earlier of these cases this was essentially part of the manoeuvres which also led the Republic at that time to allow a diplomatic 'leak' supposedly suggesting that Venice would abandon obedience to Rome and instead maintain an episcopal succession by consecrations under the authority of the schismatic patriarch of Constantinople.

The declining Greek communities in Sicily and Southern Italy were in the course of time reinforced by Albanian refugees from Turkish rule, most of whom were of the Eastern rather than the Latin rite. Those of the Eastern rite who did not initially recognize Roman authority did so after arrival in Italy. Thus by 1742 Benedict XIV was able to authorize a canon law code for them, following the educational provisions made for them in Southern Italy by Clement XII. Beyond that date, for a while longer, an Eastern-rite community survived in Albanian Epirus until 1765, and it had recognized Roman authority since the mid-seventeenth century. In the early part of that century there had been some local limited interest in Uniate status among Serbian refugees from Turkish rule, but given the political conflicts still involving the piratical Uskoks operating under Habsburg protection at the head of the Adriatic, the circumstances were not favourable, and there was some reaction against the Uniate tradition from the late seventeenth century. Under a subsequent Habsburg regime, that of Maria Theresa, some Ruthenians moved south into the Balkans, and Pius VI regularized the status of the Uniates in greater Croatia, after difficulties from the late sixteenth century onwards, only partly resolved by the mid-seventeenth century, over vernacular liturgical usage among those in communion with Rome there.[3]

While the Venetian Mediterranean empire lasted, particularly in the major island of Crete, the papacy was able to pursue a policy assuming the continuity of the reunion achieved with the Greek Church at the mid-fifteenth-century Council of Florence, as far as Republican territory was concerned. Greek rejection of the Council from 1484 onwards was thus treated as if concerning only those Greeks under Turkish rule, by the time of the post-Tridentine pontificates. The degree to which this involved a legal fiction is not at issue here, because despite momentary difficulties over the supervision of its Greek subjects the Republic was anxious for its own reasons not to challenge this assumption explicitly. Thus, the use of directly Apostolic authority to reorder the chaotic ecclesiastical affairs of Crete, rather than that of the Latin-rite bishops there who were subjects of Venice, might provoke conflict, and the jurisdiction of the Roman Inquisition over Greek Christians within Republican territories might be resisted. But Venetian magistrates at first welcomed Jesuit enterprise in Crete and only subsequently did the Republic

---

3 A.S.V. Venezia, XXXVIII, 167v f., 269r ff.: 17 Nov. 1607, 23 Feb. 1608; F.C.M.: A.S.V.: Segreteria di Stato: Nunziatura in Venezia: 265, fos 188, 200: 1574; A.D. Wright, 'The Venetian Mediterranean Empire after the Council of Trent', in *The Church and Sovereignty: Studies in Church History, Subsidia IX in Honour of M.J. Wilks*, ed. D. Wood (Oxford 1991), pp. 467–77.

exclude Greeks of its dominions from study at the Greek College in Rome, largely because of the association of the Society of Jesus with this seminary to train Greek-rite priests who recognized Roman authority, founded in 1576 by Gregory XIII. Seventeenth-century Venetian objection to any intervention by the Roman Congregation De Propaganda Fide in the affairs of its Greek subjects suggested a natural political sensitivity, as the Republic's defence of its Mediterranean empire became more difficult and the influence of France and other European powers at Constantinople increased.

The centrality in papal policy of the Council of Florence and the nominal reunion of East and West was also shown by the committee of cardinals and scholars who after Trent published the surviving Greek *Acta* of that earlier Council. At the end of the sixteenth century some cardinals were also much involved in maintaining Rome's relations with the Maronites, especially after the foundation in 1585 of a Maronite College in Rome and a papally inspired synod in 1596. Papal interest in the internal affairs of these Eastern-rite Christians subsequently encouraged the seventeenth-century publication at Rome of their liturgical books and in 1736 a reordering of their whole Church hierarchy, which was subsequently revised and approved at Rome. This latter followed the 1724 schism within the Eastern-rite patriarchate of Antioch. (Such patriarchates must be distinguished from those titular patriarchates, as for example of Antioch or Alexandria or Jerusalem, which the papacy during these centuries awarded to honour Latin-rite prelates of Western Christendom.)[4] This division consolidated a Uniate or Catholic Church of the Melkites, separated from other Melkites, and looking to French and Roman patronage against Ottoman and Greek Orthodox control, following earlier, tentative moves ever since 1587 by individual prelates of the patriarchate. The possibility thus remained of Eastern-rite Churches re-entering communion with Rome after the Council of Florence and after the Council of Trent, as was also shown by the Rumanians of Transylvania by 1700.

Reaction among Eastern-rite Christians in Transylvania to seventeenth-century political pressure in favour of Protestantism and a momentary apparent sympathy for Protestantism in the patriarchate of Constantinople led to the synod of Alba Julia in 1698 at which union with Rome was accepted. The Rumanian Uniates persevered in the eighteenth century, with encouragement from popes such as Clement XI and Innocent XIII as well as from the Habsburgs. Their adoption of a vernacular liturgy, thus in a Romance language, was a distinguishing feature setting them consciously apart from the Old Church Slavonic of the Orthodox of Moldavia and Bulgaria. Less easy for the papacy to regulate were the affairs of certain Eastern-rite Christians of sub-Carpathian Ruthenia. A fear of Protestant pressure once again caused priests and laity to proclaim a union with Rome in 1646, but their acquisition of an episcopal succession from a Rumanian episcopate which had not yet perfected its own attachment to communion with Rome naturally perplexed the papacy,

4 A.S. Ven.: Secreta Archivi Propri Roma, 18: 3 Nov. 1565, 16 Mar. 1566, 14 Feb. 1567.

which fully recognized their pro-Roman union of Uzhorod only in 1655. Further papal regulation of these Christians' affairs was provided at Habsburg request in 1771, and again, with rather more divisive results, in 1787.

Arguably the greatest achievement of the papacy in its relations with Eastern-rite Christians during the post-Tridentine period, however, was the so-called Ruthenian union of 1596. This undoubted triumph of Clement VIII, drawing on his diplomatic expertise, saw a union decided on by the metropolitan of Kiev and other bishops in 1594, which was accepted at Rome in 1595 and ratified in 1596 by the synod of Brest-Litovsk. Although in the Eastern Ukraine Cossack disaffection caused a reversion to Orthodox and pro-Russian allegiance from 1620, the union was maintained in the Western Ukraine under Polish rule, until the first of the eighteenth-century partitions of Poland raised political prospects which were to prove disastrous for the Uniates after the second and third partitions. Prior to that, Eastern-rite Christians in Lithuanian Vilnius also became attached to the Uniate position from the beginning of the eighteenth century. The post-Tridentine papacy thus valued the universality symbolized by the Uniates. Under Urban VIII a Roman edition of the composite liturgical book for the Greek rite, the *Euchologion*, was prepared and eventually published at Paris in 1645, and a further edition appeared in 1756.

BOHEMIA

In the Bohemian lands Roman obedience was also officially restored from 1621 onwards, in the case of the former Utraquists. Until the Habsburg victory at the so-called Battle of the White Mountain, these had in fact survived as a major religious movement, whatever the increasing uncertainties of Habsburg policy, particularly under the Emperor Rudolph II. Indeed the papal concession, after the Council of Trent, for lay communion in two kinds in specific areas, as in parts of German-speaking Europe, seemed superficially to underline the degree of ambiguity which had previously surrounded Utraquist–Roman relations. But while the Utraquists might claim to have preserved valid priestly orders, which Rome ought to recognize, and while their liturgy remained in many respects perfectly traditional, their defining demands on adult and child communion raised questions which were, as both the Council of Trent and the papacy had noted, doctrinal and not merely disciplinary. Moreover, the question of ecclesiastical and particularly papal authority, thus raised long before the Council of Trent by the evolution of the Utraquists, had proved virtually impossible to resolve by peaceful agreement, given the complication of the issue by their monopolization of Church endowments in Bohemia and exclusion of ecclesiastical superiors recognized by Rome. Eradication of the Utraquist position and re-imposition of obedience to Rome therefore necessarily awaited the turn of military and political events in Bohemia in and after the 1620s. While thereafter internal, Catholic dispute about the use of ecclesiastical resources in Bohemia remained, any potential loss of mainstream Utraquism to Protestantism had been prevented.

150

Liturgical uniformity

The popes in the post-Tridentine Church were, then, not simply exercising an agreed patriarchal leadership of all those Western Christians who had not adopted Protestantism. However, even in the exercise of headship over non-Protestants of Western Christendom the popes of this period were not absolutely imposing a Roman uniformity. This has already been noted with reference to the Ambrosian Rite in Milan and a parallel in the post-Conciliar Church could be added for the Rite of Braga, preserved in that cathedral city and primatial see of Portugal.[5] These examples of non-Roman usage preserved after the Council of Trent are of much more significance than liturgical peculiarities surviving in the same period elsewhere, as within the patriarchate of Venice at the ducal basilica of St Mark or at Mantua in the palatine basilica of the dukes, important though these were for the innovative splendours in Church music associated with Monteverdi. More challenging to the exercise of papal authority in the post-Tridentine Western Church were the signs of attachment to local liturgical traditions in French- and German-speaking territory during the seventeenth and eighteenth centuries. Even where no Jansenist doctrinal dissidence was intended, liturgical use of the vernacular came on occasion to be involved. This was at odds with the implicit Tridentine assertion of the liturgical necessity of Latin, although the Conciliar decrees had not explicitly imposed Latin for all Christian worship.

UTRECHT

Jansenism, however, raised many more problems than simply the regulation of liturgy, and not least the question of hierarchic authority itself. Nowhere was this finally clearer than in the Northern Netherlands, where the papacy of the post-Tridentine centuries eventually failed to preserve the unity of non-Protestant Christians. The schism of the Church of Utrecht was thus the one major and unambiguous failure of the post-Conciliar papacy to maintain the communion with Rome of all Catholics of the Western rite. The difficulties of a formally clandestine Catholic community in the Dutch Republic, as Calvinistic Protestantism officially established its dominance there, shared with those of the British Catholics under penal proscription at least one important characteristic: that of abnormal and indeed uncertain hierarchic supervision. In the Dutch case these problems were faced by the Vicars Apostolic who tried to lead the Church in the Republic after the latter's incorporation of the see of Utrecht, following its elevation in 1560 to an archbishopric as part of the attempt of Philip II to reorder and defend the Catholic Church throughout the Netherlands. Their position again included at least one aspect similar to the English situation: the difficult relations of such leaders with the religious

---

5 A.S.V.: Archivio della S. Congregazione del S. Concilio: Visita ad limina, 141 Braga: 1594–1625.

orders as opposed to the secular clergy, and specifically (in both cases) with the Jesuits.

The conflict over these relations provided an opportunity for the spread of Jansenist influence from areas outside the Republic, including the contacts between Saint-Cyran and the Vicar Apostolic Rovenius. The French insistence in this context on episcopal as opposed to papal rights thus came to strike a sympathetic chord among secular clergy in the Republic, even before the anti-Jansenist policies of Louis XIV in France itself caused an influx of Jansenists and their sympathizers into the Netherlands, reinvigorating the Netherlandish roots of Jansenism. From 1697 Roman accusations of Jansenism were concentrated on the Vicar, Codde, who was formally censured in 1702. The prolonged crisis from 1713 over the papal Constitution *Unigenitus*, against Jansenism, led to French Jansenist complicity in the design to restore, in the face of Roman opposition, a local episcopal jurisdiction of Utrecht; and thus from 1724 an apostolic succession was constituted which separated the Church of Utrecht from the Roman communion. Despite continued contacts at times between Rome and Utrecht during the eighteenth century, this schism was not ended.

Indeed, after the failure of negotiations in mid-century, the archbishop of Utrecht convened a synod of supporters and sympathizers in 1763, even though respect was paid at this to a primacy of the Holy See. Rome nevertheless condemned the proceedings of the synod in 1765, which did not prevent the summoning of another synod the next year. That the political and ecclesiastical influence of the French was crucial in this result is clear, even though Codde was not the first Vicar Apostolic in the Dutch Republic to be suspect at Rome for pro-Jansenist tendencies. Nevertheless, before him, the Vicar Neercassel had appeared for a while to establish more harmonious relations both with some of the religious orders and with the papal internuncio at Brussels; and this might even seem to promise Roman sympathy with the desire of the leading secular clergy, still organized as chapters at Utrecht and Haarlem, for a recognized local episcopal jurisdiction. Jansenists who had been excluded from the University of Louvain in the Southern Netherlands were also important, however, in providing arguments in support of the chapters, between 1719 and 1722, as they pursued an independent episcopal succession.

Dutch Republican policy was equally able to capitalize on the schism, preventing Roman loyalists obtaining a Vicar Apostolic who might block a continuation of the schism in 1725. Instead, with continuing French complicity, the Church of Utrecht maintained its schismatic succession of archbishops, until in 1742 the see of Haarlem was restored and in 1745 a bishop was provided for Deventer, within the same schismatic context, thus ensuring a purely local mechanism for continuing an episcopate. Yet from 1741 the Church of Utrecht renewed an approach to Rome, initially through Cardinal Passionei as intermediary, encouraged by the accession of Benedict XIV. Secret negotiations in 1744–45 were unsuccessful, but were revived in 1747–48 by other participants, though equally without success. In 1770 French Jansenist capitalizing on the anti-papal schism of the Church of Utrecht was still apparent, though now from the politically Jansenist position of the *parlementaires*. By 1786–88, on the eve of Revolution, the catholicity of the Church of Utrecht was again being reasserted, in response to Italian criticism, following the failure of new approaches to Rome under Clement XIII and Clement XIV.

CONDITIONS IN THE EUROPEAN STATES

The seeming impotence of the papacy in the face of the one formally schismatic outcome of the prolonged Jansenist crisis in the Western Church needs to be put in a wider context. Outside the Italian peninsula and its adjacent islands, the popes did not in fact exercise the same formal powers throughout the rest of non-Protestant Western Christendom. Or rather, though they claimed a uniform authority, they could not use the same mechanisms to assert this authority in all areas. That much was the result of fifteenth- and sixteenth-century policies pursued by the papacy with regard to different European states and their rulers. The jurisdiction of the Roman Inquisition, as reorganized in the mid-sixteenth century, was in particular ineffective beyond the frontiers of the Italian peninsula for most practical purposes. In Spain, ever since the era of the Catholic Monarchs at the end of the fifteenth century, a virtually independent Inquisition operated, whatever the delegation of papal authority to each royally nominated Inquisitor General in turn. Indeed, the post-Tridentine continuation of the case concerning the primate of Spain, Archbishop Carranza, showed beyond any doubt the absolute determination of the Spanish monarchy to preserve that effective autonomy.

This also meant a practical independence in the evolution of the Spanish Index, which naturally differed from editions of the Roman Index in treatment of works critical on the one hand of certain royal powers or policies or, on the other, of specifics within the exercise of papal authority. This pattern spread progressively to the Spanish overseas dominions too. A similar state of affairs characterized Portugal (and subsequently also Goa, and to a degree Portuguese Brazil, outside Europe). Indeed, the combination of an Inquisitor General's powers with a more avowedly papal delegation of legatine authority had been exercised by Cardinal Henry, sometime primate and subsequently the last king of independent Portugal before the Spanish succession in 1580. This provided a useful precedent for the Spanish control of Portugal by the Habsburg archducal viceroy in the immediate sequel to the succession of Philip II, when Cardinal Albert took the position of Inquisitor General in addition to the legatine authority, initially agreed to by Rome and subsequently extended for exercise in Albert's absence by a vice-legate. In the Netherlands, in the decades after the Council of Trent, the Spanish attempt to impose effective inquisitorial jurisdiction aroused not only the fierce attack of local authority intent on defending provincial and civic liberties, but also papal complaint that, whatever the theory, the Inquisition in the Netherlands proved unamenable to

Roman supervision.[6] In the Southern Netherlands, which eventually retained Catholicism and returned to Habsburg control, the most crucial role in the censorship of books and ideas, from the end of the Council of Trent onwards, came to be exercised by the theologians of the University of Louvain, with their own bitter internal divisions.

In the kingdom of France the royal courts never recognized the jurisdiction of the Roman Holy Office as reconstituted in the mid-sixteenth century. The one local Inquisition which survived for a while into the period considered here, based in Toulouse, was essentially a Dominican vestige of the old, medieval Inquisition. Effective censorship in Bourbon France was conducted in the name of the monarchy, and the prolonged crisis over Jansenism, within France itself, demonstrated the difficulty of co-ordinating royal and papal condemnation of books and ideas, not least when Jansenists were defended at different times by elements in the Gallican episcopate or Paris theological faculty or by members of the Paris *parlement*. The issues on which representations made by the papal nuncios in Bourbon France would be officially accepted, let alone heeded, could thus easily be limited. The award of legatine authority to Cardinal Albert in the initial phase of Habsburg rule in Portugal similarly meant that the nuncio at the Spanish Court could not readily raise Roman concerns on behalf of the Church in Portuguese territory.

For the Spanish kingdoms themselves the nuncio nevertheless possessed a tribunal with potentially extensive powers, which could in certain circumstances be exercised in benefice as well as matrimonial cases for example. Yet the very extent, at least potentially, of these powers made Spanish reaction to their existence uncertain. In some respects the tribunal represented for Spaniards a welcome alternative to the more costly transaction of categories of business at Rome itself. But dispute over benefices and finance, not least, aroused Spanish hostility to the tribunal, and its alleged 'abuses' were used in anti-Roman argument during the pontificate of Urban VIII, and indeed over a longer period, until another crisis in eighteenth-century Bourbon Spain.

Such practical limitations on the exercise of Roman authority in much of Western Catholic Christendom were thus very different from the Italian conditions in which, for instance, by 1600 a comprehensive investigation of the conventual libraries of the peninsula could be completed. Nor was this contrast much altered by virtue of the Apostolic Press, the Vatican printing-house organized by the post-Tridentine papacy, which was in any case not exactly identical with officially approved or privileged publishing in post-Conciliar Rome.

Finance

The aspect of Roman authority which could more often provoke attention elsewhere in Western Europe was that of finance. Just as in the kingdom of

6 A.S.V. Spagna, CCCXX, 151r ff.; CCCXXII, 148r: 1594–95; A.S. Ven.: Secreta Archivi Propri Roma, 17, fos 71r ff.: 8 Sept. 1565; 18: 20, 27 July, 24 Aug., 5, 19 Oct. 1566, 5 Apr. 1567.

Naples, so for a while in Spain the papacy maintained, separately from the nuncio, an Apostolic Collector, to claim the revenues, from the estate of deceased bishops for example, which all too often became an object of contest with other officials representing the claims of the Crown. Abandonment of this division of duties did not necessarily resolve such conflict, for while the Apostolic Collectors lacked the degree of diplomatic privilege nominally accorded to the nuncio, the latter in practice often found his own jurisdiction obstructed, by the inhibition or even arrest of his tribunal's officials by royal agents, such as the royal council in Castile. In Portugal under Habsburg rule a related problem arose. While the presence of an Apostolic Collector might in principle enable the papacy to be more truly represented than by a viceregal legate or his deputy, the use of local sub-collectors drawn from the lowest ranks of clerics or even schoolmasters did nothing to enhance respect for the papacy. In the crisis which led to the native challenge to Habsburg rule and the eventual recovery of Portuguese independence, the Apostolic Collector did play, almost by accident, a crucial role. But this did not lead to easy relations between Rome and the newly independent Portuguese monarchy.[7]

Spain and its Kingdoms

From the immediately post-Conciliar years onwards, the effective exercise of papal power within the Hispanic kingdoms was challenged in a number of ways. In Castile the royal council claimed the right to inspect papal bulls before approving their publication, and *de facto* a similar control of other papal communications and Roman benefice provisions was maintained. A similar pattern in other parts of the peninsula was created by the intervention of the royal courts and chanceries, and by royal orders sent directly to viceroys and other parts of the royal administration, such as the Council of Aragon.[8] Such procedures were not simply a matter of jurisdictional punctilio; they had very real implications for the papacy's ability to direct the Western Church beyond the confines of Italy. The decision of Philip II, at the end of the Council of Trent, to accompany his public acceptance of the Conciliar decrees with secret instructions to his viceroys and governors throughout his Spanish and Italian territories that none of the decrees which infringed royal authority and privileges were to be implemented, was crucial.

It was followed, for example, by an order to the Spanish bishops that the erection of diocesan seminaries, for which the post-Tridentine popes repeatedly pressed them, should await the agreement of a common plan within

7 A.S.V.: Archivio della S. Congregazione del S. Concilio: Visita ad limina, 141, Braga: 1594 [1624?].
8 Archivo de la Corona de Aragon: Consejo de Aragon: Legs 594, 607, 651, 686; Archivo del Reino de Valencia: Clero: Jesuitas: Leg. 86; Cancilleria Real: Cortes por Estamentos: Libros 524, 525; cf. Archivo de la Real Chancillería, Valladolid: R. Ejecutorias, Sección Antigua, Leg. 1102 (Expediente 71).

Spain for resolving the financial and other difficulties associated with such creations. Some bishops managed to institute a diocesan seminary despite the continued absence of such a plan, but many did not, which was one reason why many Spanish dioceses lacked a seminary until the later eighteenth century. The demand of the post-Tridentine popes that Spanish bishops, as well as those elsewhere in Catholic Europe, should make their periodic *ad limina* reports to Rome in person met with very effective obstruction, on most occasions, from Philip II or his viceroys acting on his explicit instructions. Yet the post-Conciliar papal rules on such visits were not totally unrealistic, allowing a slightly longer interval between visits for bishops in places like France and Spain than for those within Italy, an intermediate interval for those in areas of Europe further away from Rome, and the longest intervals for the visits which bishops in the overseas territories were, in theory, obliged to pay. The papacy, after the Council of Trent, had very often to be content with *ad limina* reports presented by the proctors of bishops even within Europe; nor were such reports presented from every see at each required occasion.[9]

After the conclusion of the Council of Trent, Philip II insisted that the initial provincial councils in the Spanish realms could only assemble in the presence of a royal representative and could only discuss a limited and approved agenda. His objection to that part of the Tridentine programme which implied provincial discussion of the necessary qualities of those in future chosen to be bishops typified his defence of the Crown's existing privileges, in this case the right of nomination to episcopal sees. But his refusal to allow provincial councils subsequently to meet without adequate royal supervision produced Roman refusal to grant unambiguous and public approval to the proceedings of such councils as did thereafter assemble. Metropolitan archbishops who sought Roman confirmation of the decrees of provincial councils in order to combat local resistance, as in the Iberian peninsula in the post-Conciliar decades, might also find that papal approval could be long delayed.[10] For obvious and related reasons the post-Tridentine popes were even more guarded in the matter of sees which claimed not only metropolitan but primatial status. Within the Iberian peninsula the competing claims of Toledo, Braga, and at times Compostela, were treated with a judicious reserve by Rome.[11]

The post-Tridentine popes certainly experienced difficulties with Philip II of Spain, as with the desire to see the Spanish primate remitted by the Spanish Inquisition to Rome itself, only eventually achieved after the 1565 legatine mission to Spain of Cardinal Buoncompagni, subsequently Pope Gregory XIII. The greater intransigence of Sixtus V led to further confrontations despite

---

9 A.G.S.: Patronato Real: Leg. 22; Secretaría Provincial: Napoles: Visitas y Diversos: Libro 102; A.S.V. Spagna, XLIII, 262v ff., 383v ff.: 6 Nov. 1593, 14 Aug. 1594.
10 A.S.V. Spagna, XXX, 419r ff.; XXXI, 19r ff.; XXXIV, 404r ff.: 1584–85, 1588; A.G.S.: Patronato Real: Leg. 22; Estado: Negociación de Roma: Leg. 968: 1596–97; Biblioteca Nacional, Madrid: MSS 13019; 13044; 6148, fos 32r ff.
11 Biblioteca Nacional, Madrid: MSS 13044, fos 1r ff., 163r ff.; 6148, fos 85r ff.

Spanish hopes of his favour towards the monarchy. By the mid-seventeenth century it was clear that, in Spain itself, the campaigns of immediately post-Conciliar popes against bull-fighting had achieved no serious success. The relations between the Spanish Crown and the immediately post-Tridentine popes did not turn simply on this or any other issue in isolation, however. The papacy found itself engaging in prolonged and not particularly success-ful negotiations about the affairs of the Church throughout the monarchy's Iberian and Italian possessions and indeed in the Spanish overseas empire. The questions at stake in Spain itself also concerned ecclesiastical finance, and the Church's financial support for the Crown. The latter relied on the periodic papal renewal, and indeed enlargement, of the concessions by which origin-ally or essentially ecclesiastical revenue was supplied for the monarch's struggle both against Islam and against heresy in Western Christendom itself.

A 'crusade' indulgence was still issued effectively in return for cash pay-ment in Spain itself and increasingly in other Spanish territories. From the Spanish clergy the Crown received royal tithes and a Subsidy. From 1567 the *excusado* tax on parochial wealth was also granted, and from the 1590s onwards further clerical contributions were progressively imposed. From the returns on the 'crusade' indulgence the papacy withdrew a quota, the 'Fabric Fund', dedicated to the completion of St Peter's and later also the repair of the Lateran basilica. Financial questions were also involved, for instance, when the king wished to see Cardinal Albert succeed, in the late sixteenth century, to the revenues of the primatial see of Toledo, as coadjutor or subsequently as archbishop. When the Spanish claim to the Portuguese succession was realized from 1580, the papacy was similarly confronted with more complex problems than simply the polite avoidance by the Spanish monarchy of papal proposals to arbitrate. Spanish concern about the supposed unreliability of some Domin-icans and Jesuits in Portugal was accompanied by demands for the confiscated revenues of the pretender Dom Antonio as Prior of Crato.[12]

As the reign of Philip II grew visibly towards its end, papal frustration at the apparently fruitless negotiations conducted periodically with the Crown grew greater. One frustrated nuncio caused offence by comparing the obstruc-tion of papal wishes with the activities of heretics in divided France or even in England. The sense that the Habsburg monarchs did not respect the proper rights of the Church was still made explicit in papal complaints to Philip III. From the end of that monarch's reign, the outbreak of the Thirty Years' War introduced further strains, not least as the Crown's financial needs became even more acute. The military achievements of the Cardinal Infante, Ferdinand, in the war were supported from the revenues of Toledo, as well as Portuguese revenue from Crato and Tomar, by papal agreement. But the legacy of Philip II was still defended by royal councillors, by means of refusing concessions to some long-standing papal demands.

12 A.G.S.: Estado: Portugal: Leg. 410; Patronato Eclesiastico: Leg. 147.

Philip II had intervened in ecclesiastical detail, as over the dress of Spanish bishops in 1588, or their titles of honorific address, but the royal council in Castile after his death continued the policy of insisting that the decrees of diocesan synods could only be published after conciliar review and licensing. On the other hand, the Roman Curia after the Council of Trent continued to pursue its own traditional interests, only partly moderated by Conciliar decrees and post-Conciliar papal reforms. This was evident in the disputes over the nomination to Spanish benefices of non-Spaniards, or rather of non-Castilians, non-Aragonese or non-Valencians, for example, in the case of the different kingdoms. The objection to alien enjoyment of beneficed income was naturally fundamental, irrespective of post-Conciliar papal insistence on the priority of residence in benefices with cure of souls, as opposed to simple benefices. Roman Curial interests also reduced the chances of agreed reform of the problematic proprietary control of benefices in impoverished parts of north-eastern Spain, despite, again, general papal encouragement of Tridentine competition for parochial benefices.[13]

Such complications in turn reduced the chances of Roman success in opposing the Spanish tradition of appeal by ecclesiastics to the royal council against the discipline of their superiors. Yet the papacy allowed the effects of the sale of the 'crusade' indulgence to weaken episcopal authority in Spain and gave scant support to the few quixotic bishops who attempted to revive their own vestigial jurisdiction against heresy in the face of the all-powerful Spanish Inquisition. Papal campaigns against clerical solicitation in confession similarly led to acquiescence in Inquisitorial action in Spain, even where bishops demanded greater involvement in the disciplining of their clergy. Philip II had gained papal agreement to the setting up of new dioceses in southern Spain designed to improve ecclesiastical organization in areas of Morisco population. But the confused policy adopted within Spain to the Moriscos saw the Roman response following an equally uncertain line, until the royal decision to expel them in the early seventeenth century.

Local tensions and rivalries within the Spanish kingdoms complicated papal reactions to demands that new saintly patrons or co-patrons be approved for the realm or places within it. The claims of local churches, commonly supported by reference to the power of saints or relics, could extend to demanding that a cult not approved by Rome be nevertheless allowed. Episcopal authority at this local level remained weak, despite the strengthening by Clement VIII of bishops' powers over confraternities and charitable foundations. Some bishops in post-Tridentine Portugal were able to publish the Bull *In Coena Domini* in its revised, post-Conciliar form even in the vernacular, but few Spanish bishops succeeded in publishing this defence of the Church's liberties, especially in the vernacular.

---

13 A.S.V. Spagna, XXXIV, 220r ff.; XXXV, 26r: 1588; XL, 584r ff., 628r ff.: 1594; Archivio della S. Congregazione del S. Concilio: Visita ad limina, 167A, Calahorra (I): 1598, 1603, 1616, 1624, 1629; 805A, Toledo (I): 1630; Biblioteca Nacional, Madrid: MS 6148, fos 172r ff.

Portugal

After 1640 the tensions over unfilled bishoprics which accompanied the recovery of Portuguese independence, while the papacy still suffered intense pressure from Spain to refuse recognition of the native regime, cast a long shadow over subsequent relations between the popes and the Portuguese Crown, with regard to the Church not only in Portugal itself but also in the overseas empire. By the eighteenth century the continuing need to attempt a better relationship with the Crown suggested to the papacy, as in its treatment of other Catholic rulers in Europe by that period, the virtue of conceding ceremonial privileges. To prevent a serious breach with the Portuguese Crown it proved necessary, in long negotiations, to allow extraordinary privileges to the see of Lisbon, where the monarchy's demands eventually meant combining a major prelacy with the ancient archbishopric, so as to form a patriarchate, and extended to claiming that each patriarch be elevated to the college of cardinals. To the patriarchs of Lisbon the papacy was constrained to grant unique rights to use elements of vesture and ceremony, short of the tiara itself (except in an armorial context), which suggested a papal grandeur. Yet such concessions did not prevent the Portuguese attack on the Society of Jesus in the Crown's territories. The Lisbon patriarchate might be described as titular, in the sense not of a see devoid of real pastoral duties as being *in partibus infidelium* of course, but of an archbishopric which was not the head of a distinct Church or Rite such as those of the Uniates. In that respect the parallel was with the sees of Venice and Aquileia, where the title of patriarch was already in use before the Council of Trent, long before in the latter's case, despite the dismemberment which was to overtake it in the eighteenth century. Portuguese claims for the archbishop of Goa to be entitled primate of the East were more nearly akin to Spanish conjunction of a nominal or titular patriarchate of the Indies with the reality of royal supervision of the Church in Spain's overseas empire: a matter better included in later discussion of such areas.

Beyond the Iberian peninsula

Within Catholic Europe the effective obstacles to uncontested papal supervision of local Churches also occurred in areas of Spanish Habsburg rule outside the Iberian peninsula itself. This was true in both Besançon and Cambrai, for example, before their acquisition by Bourbon France. In the Southern Netherlands the resolution of the long conflicts, not confined to Louvain, between Jansenists and their opponents was made more difficult by the sensitivity of the secular government to the issue of any papal documents not given prior state approval, even before the Austrian Habsburg regime succeeded the Spanish there. The post-Tridentine popes reacted with increasing caution to such 'nationalism' in the conduct of Catholic states and their rulers. Whereas the immediately post-Conciliar popes looked for regular fulfilment of the Council's programme for provincial councils, to be assembled at intervals by each metropolitan archbishop in Western Christendom, later popes were often happier to encourage diocesan bishops to perform their part of the original plan, by holding frequent, even if not annual, diocesan synods.

Local independence and Roman loyalty

Within the Holy Roman Empire the seniority of Mainz among the Electoral Archbishoprics had to be accorded tactful treatment, which became increasingly difficult in the eighteenth century. The question of primatial status within Lorraine also arose. In the southern parts of the Empire the Prince-Archbishops of Salzburg interpreted the primatial status confirmed to them earlier in the sixteenth century as enabling them to supervise the filling of the suffragan sees within their ecclesiastical province without necessarily making prior reference to Rome. Such a claim the papacy did its best to ignore, but in the eighteenth century found a judicious way of reasserting Roman supremacy by insisting that Passau be, and despite Salzburg protests remain, detached from the province. Yet even such manoeuvring was obviously of less importance, ultimately, than any threat to the nominal unity of non-Protestant Western Christendom created by more defiantly 'national' programmes.

Within seventeenth-century France the relations of metropolitan archbishops with the other diocesans of their ecclesiastical province proved increasingly problematic, as tensions over both Gallicanism and Jansenism grew. But while the ancient claim of a see to primatial status might be effectively ignored, any rumour, even if only part of diplomatic bluff, that Richelieu would favour a plan to create a quasi-independent patriarchate of the Gauls, as the real head of the Church in Bourbon France, had to be treated with great delicacy.

Within Catholic Europe the papacy could make some use for its own advantage of titular and ceremonial privileges. Favoured or deserving prelates could be rewarded with titles of dignity, as a Domestic Prelate for example, which gave a precedence among the Assistants at the Papal Throne at ceremonies in the papal chapel. Such essentially Court honours were thus a way of attracting the loyalty of prelates from various parts of Catholic Europe, not necessarily confined to those normally resident in Rome. These awards were parallel to those made on occasion to Catholic rulers or their consorts, the Sword and Hat, the Golden Rose, or the blessed Swaddling Clothes, distinguished from the more routine grant of a waxen *Agnus Dei*, blessed by the pope, or of personal dispensations and indulgences. But an inflation of such honours, especially by the eighteenth century, ultimately devalued their worth as bargaining weapons, by contrast with the continued necessity for archbishops to receive their pallium from Rome. By the eighteenth century rulers of states such as Portugal or Poland were demanding with increasing stridency that papal nuncios to their Courts should be created cardinals, as of right, before or after the end of their tour of duty, to match the elevations increasingly expected of nuncios at the major Habsburg and Bourbon Courts. Manoeuvring on such issues in the end, however, did little to affect the course of major disputes, as over the exclusion of the Jesuits or the suppression of other religious orders or houses.

Even in the seventeenth century, by contrast, the papal need for Sicilian grain to relieve Rome in years of particular shortage still affected negotiations with Spain over questions of ecclesiastical rights, as for example in 1621–22. At that moment, at the start of the pontificate of Gregory XV, papal diplomacy, exercised not least by the Capuchin envoy Giacinto da Casale, was also necessarily devoted to gaining the release of two cardinals detained by the Habsburgs. Full liberty in Rome was restored to Cardinal Klesl, originally in custody in the Tyrol, in 1623. The Spanish detention of Cardinal Lerma was part of a political change, affecting Lerma because of his previous activity as royal favourite under the deceased Philip III. Spain was also trying to obstruct the pope's proposed reform of the procedure in papal conclaves, in defence of the Crown's means of bringing pressure to bear on the choice of the cardinals.

France

The problems which the post-Tridentine papacy faced in France were inherent in the succession of the Bourbons to the throne. Despite promises made at the time of his reconversion to Catholicism and subsequent reconciliation allowed by the papacy, Henri IV did not secure official reception of the Tridentine decrees within the kingdom. Later unilateral adoption of the decrees by the French Church did not remove the obstacle to their application presented by the continued non-recognition by the royal courts. In many senses this was a greater problem for Catholic restoration in Bourbon France than the famous concession of specific privileges to the Huguenot minority by the Edict of Nantes after Henri's succession. It added to the papacy's difficulty in advancing the claim, specified at Trent at the Council's conclusion, that it was the sole source of arbitration and authoritative interpretation of the decrees in the post-Conciliar Church.

The theological faculty of the University of Paris continued, as in pre-Tridentine times, to assert a competence to adjudicate on theological issues, and on occasion the Paris *parlement* was willing to pronounce on essentially doctrinal disputes. Both features enormously complicated the policy which the papacy attempted to pursue in response to Jansenism. The resurgence, from the late sixteenth century, of explicit Gallican assertions of a range of 'liberties' and an effective degree of autonomy in the management of Church affairs in France was not least a reaction to the extended support of the immediately post-Conciliar popes for the ultra-Catholic opposition of the League to the claims of Henri of Navarre. As such opposition came to be seen increasingly as 'unpatriotic' by the more moderate Catholic *politiques*, in the face of clearer Spanish ambitions to control the French succession, papal delay in recognizing Henri enhanced resentment, especially after the involvement in the French struggle of a papal military contingent, sent in 1591 by Gregory

XIV. Moreover, in the confused circumstances of continued competition over the French succession, papal legates rather than just nuncios, in the first half of the 1590s, and even initially after 1595 and papal recognition of Henri IV, had tried to bring some better order to the anarchic state of the French Church, as to episcopal appointments, but their attempts to deploy direct papal authority on an enlarged scale also encountered Gallican antagonism.

The brave decision of Clement VIII to reverse papal policy and allow the king formal reconciliation to the Roman Church could not destroy such accumulated feeling, even though the opinions of the Gallican episcopate came to be tempered by internal challenge from the Richerist campaign for the rights of priests in relation to bishops. Such inherent difficulties can now be seen to help explain the genuine favour with which Richelieu, when first a bishop, was initially regarded at Rome, as he provided a still fairly uncommon example of a diocesan attempting to implement within the limits of one see something of the Tridentine programme. Before his eventual and far from swiftly sure achievement of power within royal government, a partially positive example of Catholic restoration and reform pursued on a wider French stage by the deployment of both papal authority and royal support had been provided by Cardinal Rochefoucauld. Even by the use of delegated papal authority, with regard to the religious orders for example, the results achieved were limited though real, however. Gallican theory continued, in any case, to stipulate supposed limitations to the exercise of papal jurisdiction.[14]

The ancient association of St Paul with the see of Rome, in addition to that of St Peter, allowed Gallicans to emphasize at times the foundation of the Roman Church upon both of these apostles. This challenged the papal tradition which argued for a unique, divinely bestowed plenitude of power in the Petrine office, in contrast with other patriarchal sees of undoubtedly apostolic honour and origin. But by 1647 the Holy Office had censured a clearly Jansenist equation of Petrine and Pauline authority. Post-Tridentine Spanish bishops were happier to allow that the Roman see enjoyed the special inspiration of the Holy Spirit. But though the Council had not enunciated any formula of a personal papal infallibility, the post-Conciliar popes throughout this period could not always prevent debate surfacing on the indefectibility of the Petrine office.

The Tridentine decrees had in no way altered the existing royal rights of nomination to bishoprics, in France just as much as Spain. In France, on the other hand, the refusal of the secular courts to recognize the Tridentine decrees affected the Catholic laity and not just the clergy, as for example in bishops' attempts to discipline insubordinate priests. For the Tridentine decree on marriage, requiring, on its own terms, prior local publication of the conditions which would in future govern valid Catholic marriage before these took

---

14 J. Bergin, *Cardinal de La Rochefoucauld. Leadership and Reform in the French Church* (New Haven, CT 1987); J. Bergin, *Cardinal Richelieu. Power and the Pursuit of Wealth* (London–New Haven, CT 1985); J. Bergin *The Rise of Richelieu* (New Haven, CT–London 1991); *Acta Nuntiaturae Gallicae*, vols 1 ff. (Rome 1961 onwards), ed. J. Lestocquoy et al.

effect in any area, was thus also difficult to enforce. The cumulative effect of French legal rulings on marriage by the seventeenth century might be to produce a set of conditions very similar to those in the Tridentine decree. But this secular regulation of marriage also demanded parental consent in certain circumstances, directly at odds with the Conciliar decision, and incidentally contradicting the theological reasons for the Council's final verdict after long debate. The post-Tridentine papacy was no more able to alter this outcome than to ensure uniform observance of the Conciliar regulation of marriage within Catholic society in the states of the Empire. In Spain, as in the Italian states, by contrast, the popes were more successful in supporting bishops who were gradually enforcing, in the face of social attachment to older patterns of betrothal and marriage, the Tridentine conditions and procedures; and imposing the related Conciliar limitation of the number of godparents allowed a child at baptism. In clandestine Catholic communities, such as those in the British Isles, application of the Tridentine marriage regulations was obviously impossible in any case.

It could not be said that the papacy had been much able to influence the Valois, or Catherine de' Medici in particular, towards policies which might in the long term best safeguard French Catholicism. That Gregory XIII celebrated at Rome news of the Massacre of St Bartholomew under the impression that what had occurred was the timely prevention of a Huguenot *coup d'état* is now widely accepted. But that obviously did not affect the use made of this response by contemporary Protestant propaganda. Partly as a result, moreover, in the 1580s papal envoys to the Imperial Diet were not entirely able to prevent the adoption of policies which seemed, from a Roman perspective, alarmingly concessionary to Protestantism. Indeed, the Habsburg response to what the immediately post-Tridentine popes attempted could prove reluctant or ungrateful.

The Habsburg lands

In the Netherlands a pre-Tridentine tradition in some places that the laity might receive unconsecrated wine after communion in one kind may presumably have influenced the earlier optimism of Charles V that to concede lay communion in two kinds might halt defections to Lutheranism in the Germanic lands. The Council of Trent in the end confined its own discussion to the theory of the matter, stating that no absolute obstacle to the concession existed. After the Council had remitted the practical decision on the question to the papacy, papal authority and a concessionary permission were inextricably linked. This was as one influential prelate at the Council, the archbishop of Braga, had argued it must explicitly be, lest the Protestants claim that their case for an absolute right to communion in two kinds had been acknowledged. The papal grant of the chalice to the laity in central and Southern German lands did not seem to affect the religious loyalties of the people, in the event, and the concession for carefully confined use in the duchy of Bavaria had been withdrawn before the end of the sixteenth century. The fears expressed by Philip II at the conclusion of the Council that the papacy might also allow clerical marriage in the German lands proved in the end superfluous.[15]

In the post-Conciliar decades, defence of the Catholic faith seemed threatened by the apparently tolerant policies adopted towards the Lutherans by the Emperor Maximilian. Subsequently, Clement VIII also felt it necessary to give his attention to Christian confrontation with Islam in Hungary. His encouragement of a Hungarian campaign was part of a long-term papal policy. For a long history of calls for such campaigns, made in specifically Conciliar contexts, had culminated in the wording of the summons of the Tridentine Council, stressing the need for Christian unity against Islam. The post-Conciliar popes continued to pursue this aim, despite the constant obstacles posed by Franco-Spanish rivalry and other divisions within even non-Protestant Western Christendom.

In the case of the Hungarian campaign, however, the Spanish Crown failed to respond positively, whatever the projected benefit to Habsburg fortunes in Hungary itself. Papal collection of funds from the clergy in Spain or the Neapolitan kingdom was resented or opposed, just as later, when the papacy attempted a clerical levy in support of the Catholic forces in the early stages of the Thirty Years' War. In the latter case, this was despite Spanish encouragement of the pursuit of a larger war, beyond Bohemia, essentially because of Spain's own strategic interests, which were at odds with a papal caution which still momentarily reflected the earlier opposition of Cardinal Klesl as a Habsburg counsellor to an aggressive Imperial policy. Dispute between the Emperor and the papacy over control of formerly ecclesiastical possessions recovered from Protestant hands marked the progress of the war. The eventual collapse of the policy epitomized by the Edict of Restitution was, from the Roman viewpoint, hardly offset by the virtual settlement of the long-standing Hussite problem in Bohemia.

Poland

The post-Conciliar papacy was certainly able to exert an influence in Poland from the later sixteenth century onwards. Despite the political uncertainty introduced by the creation of an elective monarchy, and related problems like the rivalry of the Protestant branch of the Vasa dynasty in Sweden, able nuncios were increasingly to exert a personal influence on the Polish kings and, more generally, on the aristocracy, not least by their encouragement of an Italian culture, in music and drama as well as the visual arts, which proved welcome. The dignity of the Polish primate required courtesy in the nuncios,

15 A.G.S.: Patronato Real: Leg. 22 [22/6; 22/26].

but a promising start to Conciliar reform under episcopal leadership had been suggested by Cardinal Hosius, who had been one of the presiding Legates at Trent. The nuncios were able to encourage the popular mission of Franciscans as well as the elite education provided by the Jesuits. The alliance between the papacy and the Polish monarchy in some senses reached its highest point, during the period under consideration, when in 1683 King John responded to the appeals of the pope for Christian aid to the Emperor as the Turks besieged Vienna for what proved to be the last time. This contrasted with the lack of positive response from Louis XIV, though Catholic France did respond rather more when its traditional Venetian ally faced the loss of Crete to the Islamic forces of the Turks.

Scandinavia

By contrast, 1689 marked the end of an episode which was the cause of initial papal triumph and subsequently some embarrassment, with the death in Rome of the Swedish Queen Christina. Her abdication of the Swedish throne in 1654 was not immediately followed by public declaration of a change of religion; nor were any allowed, during her Roman years, to treat her as other than a queen. Indeed the diplomacy, in all senses, required for her eventual reception into the Catholic Church was still marked, despite an extended prior history of secret contacts with representatives of Catholicism. Papal sensitivity was shown at its best when the erudite convert, Holstenius, of North German origin, was sent to the Habsburg Court at Innsbruck. There this papal librarian, rather than a prelate of nominally greater rank, received Christina's abjuration of Protestantism in 1655.

For Holstenius this was in many ways the high point of a career in which he had managed, from a slow and laborious start, to survive the end of the pontificate in which he had risen in Barberini service, gradually entering the service of Chigi, who succeeded Innocent X as pope. On behalf of both the Barberini and Chigi, the former papal envoy in Germany and at the Westphalia peace negotiations, he had fostered contacts with potential converts, as well as cultivating wide cultural and literary relations. After Christina's arrival in Rome he was able to watch over her library as well as that of the Barberini and the Vatican Library. Yet the official reception of the queen at Rome, celebrated as a public triumph, was followed by years of perplexity, caused both by her independence of mind and behaviour among those who frequented her Court, and by her occasional political manoeuvres, pursuing an interest in the Swedish throne once again or in the Polish Crown, for example. The immediately post-Conciliar papacy had for a while pursued negotiations aimed at reuniting Scandinavian Christendom, above all Sweden, to Rome. But by the end of the sixteenth century it was sufficiently clear that such attempts would not succeed, partly because of the question of returning confiscated Church property.

The Nunciatures

The crucial role which a nunciature could play had been demonstrated positively in Poland, but by the eighteenth century the issue of permanent papal
representation was proving a source of conflict within the German Catholic
lands. The Electoral Archbishops, at the head of the prince-bishops, prince-
abbots and other bishops of the relevant territories, regarded the nunciature
based at Cologne as the papacy's proper representation among them. The
Vienna nunciature was not disputed, since it supposedly represented the
papacy at the Court of the Emperor and with respect to the family lands of
Austrian and related territories. But to add another nunciature at the Court of
one ruler within the Empire, even one of the conspicuous Catholic piety
displayed by the dukes of Bavaria since the Tridentine era itself, would be
regarded as unacceptable by the Electoral Archbishops. Such a proposal,
affecting the German Catholic lands, confirmed the eighteenth-century growth
of Febronianism, which effectively made claims for a semi-independence in
local management of ecclesiastical affairs not unlike the Gallican assertions put
forward by elements in the French Church.

In any case, it could be noted, the papal policy, from the seventeenth
century, of maintaining a nunciature at the Court of the Catholic Netherlands
did not in the end prove an obstacle to the imposition of an unwelcome
reorganization of the Church there by Joseph II, in the last stages of the pre-
Revolutionary regime. But then the long existence of a nunciature at Vienna
itself did not prove sufficient to deter the Emperor from his programme
of reform in his other possessions. Even earlier public events suggested the
impotence of Roman representation, as with the failure to prevent those terms
of the Peace of Westphalia, at the end of the Thirty Years' War, which called
forth papal condemnation, equally ineffectual, over recognition of Calvinist
as well as Lutheran rulers' religious authority within Imperial territories. But
in Catholic territories the systematization of papal representation by means of
nuncios did not mean that more fully empowered Legates were no longer
appointed in the post-Tridentine Church. On the contrary, their use was continued for special missions to rulers, whether in Spain or France for instance,
and most commonly where an issue of great political importance arose, such
as an Imperial Diet.

Outside Catholic territory nuncios obviously could not reside, but the
Roman Congregation of the Propaganda extended its oversight not only to
non-European missions, but also to Catholic communities in marginal areas,
such as the British Isles. Within Catholic territories nuncios in the seventeenth
and eighteenth centuries also found themselves playing a further, secondary
role. In the absence of permanent representatives of individual Italian states at
many Courts outside the peninsula, and the natural restrictions on the representations of a Venetian ambassador, for example, on behalf of Italians who
were not subjects of the Republic, the nuncios sometimes found themselves
playing something of a 'national' role. They might act in quite small and

secular affairs as the nearest equivalent to an 'Italian' consul, to assist artists, craftsmen, traders or soldiers, for instance, from many parts of the peninsula. Such humanitarian and quasi-consular service was something which papal diplomacy could still provide.

The papacy's close involvement in the European affairs of the Knights of Malta also remained logical, since this truly international religious order possessed properties in, and derived revenues from, many parts of non-Protestant Western Christendom. Within the Order of St John periodic disagreement between elements of the international aristocratic membership, commonly involving Grand Masters and their critics, aroused the intervention of rival Catholic rulers. But these episodes also provided opportunities for popes or their delegates to intervene in the interest of restoring harmony. Pius V resumed a traditional ideal in papal diplomacy, the formation of a Christian front against the forces of Islam. Prolonged negotiations allowed the brief union of fleets responsible for the victory of 1571 at Lepanto, even though this proved of greater benefit to morale than to lasting defence of Christian territory.

Doctrinal dispute

In relations with secular rulers the popes of the post-Tridentine centuries faced pressures which at times extended beyond the political to the doctrinal sphere. The growing fervour in Spain for the specific Marian doctrine of the Immaculate Conception ensured that a doctrine on which the Council had refrained from binding positive dogmatic assertion would not cease to be a matter for debate, as between Dominicans on the one hand and those who favoured a positive declaration on the other. By the seventeenth century the Spanish monarchy responded to local enthusiasm by urging the merits of a positive pronouncement by the papacy. The Austrian Habsburgs supported this in due course. Universities and members of religious orders added their voice by involvement in public vows to defend the doctrine. But the doctrinal conservatism of the post-Conciliar papacy remained constant throughout this period, in the sense of resisting pressure for a definitive positive statement, as opposed to some liturgical concession.

Similarly, the popes faced pressure over the cult of specific saints, as Rome found in the initial post-Conciliar revision of liturgical texts, whether the Martyrology or Breviary for instance. Here patriotic objection to any suggestion of doubt about the historicity of St James's physical presence in Spain, as otherwise about the orthodoxy of St Ildefonso, much venerated there, focused resentment on Cardinal Baronius and even more on Cardinal Bellarmine as supposedly responsible for such historical and liturgical revisionism. The unachieved plans of Benedict XIV to reform the Roman Breviary were intended not least to counter liturgical peculiarities in places, such as some French dioceses, where local usage was informed by a sense of polemical confrontation with claims made over the centuries for papal authority. But the papacy also remained, in its public stance at least, conservative on questions of social morality such as the use of interest in financial transactions, as was demonstrated even by Benedict XIV himself in his ruling on such use in 1745.

Clandestine Catholic communities

At the furthest extreme from Catholic Spain, clandestine Catholic communities such as those in the British Isles, also presented the papacy with peculiar problems. The greatest problem facing the popes in this respect was the supervision of ecclesiastical life and the mechanisms for the delegation of authority. Irish bishops might still be appointed from Rome, even though they had normally no access to cathedral or ancient revenues of course. But that was not the case for Scotland, any more than for England and Wales, in the post-Tridentine Church. The tensions inherent in any proscribed group were arguably enhanced by an inevitable competition for resources to support priestly ministry, which in local terms could only be provided by the laity and, commonly, more easily for resident than itinerant clergy.

But not all the clergy working in England at the end of Elizabeth's reign were seculars, for quite apart from the beginnings of the presence of some regulars too, there were above all the Jesuits. Thus a crucial dispute, which the late Elizabethan and early Stuart regimes were able to exploit, came to concern the direction of the regulars, especially the Jesuits, within England. External agents charged from time to time with supervision of the affairs of the English Catholics, such as the nuncio in Brussels or the nuncio in Paris, were not in practice much better placed to intervene in local conflicts than was the nuncio at the Spanish Court when urged by the post-Conciliar popes to encourage royal support of the British colleges in the Iberian peninsula and the Netherlands.[16] The theory quixotically sustained by some of the secular clerics within England, that, in the enforced absence of a legitimate episcopal hierarchy, they had inherited authority as a supposed capitular body of clergy, understandably met with a negative response at Rome. But in any case this contention faced the obvious difficulty that settled capitular revenue was decidedly lacking.

The appeal of elements within the secular clergy for a local episcopate with full jurisdiction was aroused not least by the desire to see the regulars brought within a single system of control. But in the early seventeenth century, despite some French support, such a plan still engendered fierce resistance from Jesuits and their supporters, who were intent on defending their independent operations within England. When the papacy moved a fraction closer to meeting the demand, by allowing supposedly greater powers to precursors of the Vicars Apostolic in England, dispute between their supporters and opponents was only increased. Appeals and counter-appeals to Rome had already proved essentially inconclusive, because of the supposedly excessive favour shown to

16 A.S.V. Spagna, CCCXX, 125v: 1594; CCCXXII, 166r: 1595.

the Jesuits by the Archpriest who was nominally in charge of the English Catholics, and were in any case complicated by the political manoeuvring of France and Spain in the background of the conflict. The experiment of a supposedly fuller episcopal jurisdiction for a Catholic leader in England had hardly been a success, even before the disruption of the Civil War and Interregnum affected the Catholic community.

During the reign of James I the dispute over the Archpriest had been further complicated by the question of an oath of allegiance to the Crown, stemming from an intentionally divisive government suggestion at the end of Elizabeth's reign. Such an oath was condemned by Paul V in 1606 and again in 1607, but the Archpriest Blackwell finally took the oath the following year, as the culmination of a policy of seeking an accommodation with the Crown adopted by many of the seculars and their supporters, in the face of opposition from most of the Jesuit and pro-Jesuit party. Further negotiations over any form of an oath which might avoid condemnation from Rome continued under Charles I, but without fruit. In this respect, no more was permanently achieved for the relaxation of penal laws against the Catholics than during the negotiations over a possible Spanish marriage for Charles, in the last stages of James's reign, when the popes remained very cautious over any English promises of better conditions for the Catholic community. Nor in the event was the papacy able to reap much benefit for the English Catholics from the French marriage which Charles entered into with the daughter of Henri IV. Initial help to King Charles in his difficulties with the Scots and then with the English parliamentarians was nevertheless forthcoming from some English Catholics, but the pope, despite eventual appeals from Queen Henrietta Maria, was unpersuaded that the king's cause and that of Catholicism in Britain were synonymous.

The evolution of the Catholic communities in the British Isles suggested the continued practical limitations on the ability of the post-Tridentine papacy to direct their life and activity. In England, for example, regular clergy continued to reinforce the ministry of the secular priests, but could prove unamenable to control even by their own superiors. Thus the Benedictines who entered England for pastoral ministry were sometimes unresponsive to the commands reaching them from their mother-house in Paris. Regulars themselves occasionally acquired delegated Roman authority when they became one of the Vicars Apostolic administering the districts into which England was divided. However, they then found that their origins gave them no necessary advantage over regular clergy who persisted in regarding themselves as exempt from this chain of command, responsive, in theory at least, only to their own superiors, even if these were of necessity based outside England. The division of Scotland into a similar, though smaller number of districts did not guarantee perfect harmony among the Vicars Apostolic, since each held, on equal terms, an individual, delegated authority.

Nevertheless, in Scotland able Vicars Apostolic succeeded, whatever the feelings of the Catholic community, in making public the community's detachment from the Stuart cause, after the débâcle of 1745, before in fact the Protestant Episcopalian community's leaders had established an equivalent abandonment of a compromising association. This was obviously still more persuasive after the succession of Cardinal Henry to the nominal Stuart title, no longer unambiguously recognized by the papacy in any case, since with greater realism he in practice largely concentrated on his ecclesiastical duties in and around Rome. Before his succession, however, the Stuart pretenders continued to assert a right to nominate not only Cardinal Protectors of their claimed kingdoms but also ecclesiastical leaders sent to administer the Church in the British Isles. The survival of canonic bishoprics in Ireland, whatever the loss of possessions and resources to support diocesan titles, offered an obvious opportunity to intervene in such appointments. This preservation of a diocesan structure, as it appeared, was nevertheless grounded in a reality where regular clergy were a crucial part of the pastoral ministry and were not necessarily amenable to episcopal direction.

In a reverse-image of the assistance provided to Spanish diocesans by auxiliaries who were sometimes Irish friars promoted to become bishops *in partibus*, a Spanish friar was even at one moment appointed to an Irish bishopric. This indeed reflected the presence of Irish Catholic exiles in the Spanish armies engaged in continental European campaigns. But in Ireland the occasional more direct interventions of Roman authority arguably produced no better results for the Catholic community than in England or Scotland. Papal envoys sent to Ireland during Elizabeth's reign or in the crisis of Charles I's rule, or to England in the reign of James II were not favoured with much success in advancing a united Catholic interest. Indeed, between these latter episodes the Catholic archbishop of Armagh was put on trial in Protestant England and martyred there in 1681.

Foreign seminaries at Rome

In the long term, papal initiative was more productive in another way. This involved the post-Conciliar organization at Rome of special seminaries to train priests for an area where a network of diocesan seminaries was not simply delayed but obviously impossible. This was essentially a papal programme, despite initial help given on an individual basis to British clerics, for example, by Tridentine prelates such as Borromeo and Paleotti. It was also largely, though not exclusively, a Roman affair, despite institutions elsewhere, such as that at Linz for Scandinavian clerics. The obvious exceptions to this pattern were the English and Scots and Irish Colleges, mainly in Iberian territories (Spain itself, Portugal, the Netherlands), which to a greater or a lesser degree were supported by the Crown; with eventual parallels in France too.

But at Rome, in addition to the Greek College, there was the English College, reorganized by the papacy precisely as a seminary and entrusted, after difficulties and disputes not unknown in the other British Colleges abroad, nor without parallel in other Jesuit-run establishments, to the direction of the

Society of Jesus. In the case of the English College at Rome the initial discords, at any rate, were not unconnected with tension between English and Welsh. But there was never a Welsh College in Rome, though there were eventually Irish and Scots Colleges. Of great importance was the German College, organized by the Tridentine papacy, which attracted over the centuries a large number of clerics, usually of good birth, who eventually enjoyed episcopal or prelatical status in the territories of the Empire, the Austrian Habsburg lands or the areas of Hungary retained or recovered for Christian rule. Consolidation of Roman influence in this way was of clear importance.

A WINDOW OF OPPORTUNITY

As has now been seen, the post-Tridentine papacy was not able to exercise a uniform authority over all the Catholics in every part of Western Christendom. Political considerations could never be entirely neglected. When, for example, Clement VIII was contemplating reversing his predecessors' policy towards Henri of Navarre, and allowing his reconciliation, Venetian and, less openly, Medicean diplomacy sought to counter the known Spanish pressure on the pope to desist. Nevertheless, in this case, the final Roman decision to reverse papal policy was substantially independent. Clement's perspicacity equally enabled him to keep his distance from the revived project of the duke of Savoy to subdue Calvinist Geneva, which would certainly have upset the French.

Paul V, by contrast, failed to receive the total and public support from the Catholic Courts of Europe for which he looked during the Interdict imposed on Venice. Despite Venetian fears and a degree of ostentatious manoeuvring by Spain, the chief desire of the Spanish monarchy at the time was to defend the interests of Catholic states generally from unacceptable forms of papal intervention.[17] Bourbon France successfully intervened between the pope and Venice. The essence of the papacy's difficulty in making its authority effective outside Italy was thus clearly demonstrated before the 1620s, not only with reference to France. A window of opportunity for a more independent exercise of papal authority had lasted a bare quarter-century, from the reconciliation of Henri IV and the subsequent contribution of Clement VIII to the Peace of Vervins, in 1598, which substantially ended Franco-Spanish hostilities, to the early 1620s.

The tenuous peace between the two major Catholic powers in Europe provided a brief interlude during which the papacy was no longer dangerously dependent on the Habsburgs and above all Spain, without the counterweight of an officially and ostensibly Catholic France. But though open hostilities between the major Catholic powers did not resume fully until 1635, the looming crisis over the Valtelline and the related question of the Mantuan Succession

---

17 A.S.V. Spagna, CCCXX, 80r ff.: 1593; CCCXXII, 35r: 1595; A.G.S.: Estado: Negociación de Roma: Leg. 986: 1607.

obviously revealed the new difficulty which the papacy would face from the pontificate of Gregory XV onwards. The double pressure from the rival Catholic powers of France and Spain affected the policies which Urban VIII and his successors attempted to pursue, above all in trying to settle the emerging Jansenist question. Although this doctrinal controversy began in the Southern Netherlands, under Spanish rule, it also evolved in France as a dispute over pastoral practice, and came to involve both anti-Jesuit campaigns and a challenge to papal authority itself. The efforts of Gregory and Urban to prevent the conflict between Bourbon and Habsburg were not only unavailing, therefore, but proved incapable of prolonging the moment when the papal authority necessary to resolve such a controversy might be deployed with relative freedom from political constraints.

FRANCE AND JANSENISM

Spanish resentment of the pursuit of such independence, whether by Clement, Gregory or Urban, was clear enough, as has already been seen. A corresponding Gallican resentment of the prolonged papal support for opposition to the Bourbon succession in France, prior to Clement's courageous decision, has also been noted. Such Gallican sentiment seriously hampered the papacy's ability to determine the Jansenist controversy swiftly and definitively. The royal lawyers were determined that the legitimacy of the Bourbon succession to the French throne should not be thought to rest on papal recognition or rehabilitation of Henri of Navarre. Their sensitivity over theories of a papal deposing or legitimizing power was made all the more acute by the dangerous attempt on the life of Henri IV, after his succession, at a time when there was still uncertainty over a legitimate male heir. When his eventual assassination led to his son Louis inheriting the throne as a minor, in the unstable circumstances of the regency, such sensitivity increased still further.

Lawyers intent on defending the continuity of independent French monarchy also recalled the Valois conflicts with aspects of papal policy after the Council of Trent. Both the Crown and the Paris *parlement*, before the end of the Valois line, had proved unwilling to grant official recognition in France to the Conciliar decrees, or allow publication of the revised Bull *In Coena Domini*. While much of the conflict had turned on questions of ecclesiastical finance and appointments, as well as of foreign policy, there was at that stage a dangerously unexamined assumption, on the French if not the Roman side, that the disciplinary rather than the doctrinal decrees were the immediate problem. This was to provide an unpromising background when an originally doctrinal issue arose, in the form of Jansenism, which the papacy could hardly ignore. Moreover, the Bourbon regime remained more insecure than retrospective historical acclaim has, until recently, allowed.

The image successfully projected by Louis XIV, after the mid-century revolts known as the Frondes which challenged his precarious authority as another long-awaited male heir succeeding as a minor under another female regency, was quite distinct from the reality of financial and social disorders during much of his reign. Accordingly, even when the king eventually sought papal intervention to attempt the resolution of the Jansenist controversy, he was so intent that this should only be on his own terms, that it arguably produced a distortion of the intended effect. The failure to achieve an immediate disposal of the problem was obvious to Louis himself, and it was striking that in the end he abandoned his initial insistence that the four Gallican Articles passed by the French clerical assembly of 1682 be official teaching for the future clergy, including their revived Conciliarism and inherent rejection of a papal plenitude of authority in doctrinal pronouncement. Yet what the papacy itself had sought was rather to avoid a ruling which positively accepted or imposed an exclusive Augustinianism in Catholic doctrine, as demanded by the Jansenists. Its own aim was to defend the Tridentine solution which had left certain issues without such a definitively exclusive interpretation, even though the Conciliar decrees had not been officially received in the French kingdom.

Throughout the post-Tridentine period, indeed, Roman authority was scrupulous in assessing contested doctrinal assertions by Catholic authors. As recent scholarship has shown, a precise register of categories of error was deployed when disputed statements were examined by Roman authority. What all these fine gradations implied, however, was acceptance of current Roman evaluation as authoritative, not in the sense of being demonstrably scholarly, but in the Tridentine sense of definitive and binding pronouncement. The Jansenist attempt to argue from the historic weight of textual evidence, in this case Augustinian and other patristic exegesis, was inherently unamenable to such adjudication. Roman refusal to acknowledge a unique authority in Augustine's treatment of divine grace, as asserted by Jansenism, had the incidental advantage of not seeming, by an implied exclusion of the doctrine of the Greek Fathers, to substantiate accusations from Constantinople or Moscow that the ancient faith was subverted by papal power.

But it has been persuasively argued that in this difficult task the papacy was led by French pressure to make one seriously miscalculated move, in pursuit of a magisterial settlement of the Jansenist crisis. The turning-point was arguably the response of Alexander VII to French governmental impatience with Jansenist attempts to claim that propositions already censured by papal authority were not in fact to be found in Jansen's posthumous publication, the *Augustinus* of 1640. The further papal Bull of 1656, *Ad Sacram*, determined a question of fact, demanding obedience to the ruling that the censured propositions were indeed derived from the text. But the use of papal authority to insist on disputed facts relating to a recent publication was arguably fatal, as it returned debate from the realm of timeless Roman definition, categorizing specific propositions in a negative manner but leaving ample room for orthodox belief, to the issue of papal inerrancy in the reading of a given text and assertion of a contemporary finding. Not all French Catholics, by any means, were willing to defend the latter.

The initial attempt at intervention in the Jansenist controversy, by the Bull *In Eminenti*, issued in 1643 towards the end of the pontificate of Urban VIII, was of little effect in France, not least because of the politically disturbed circumstances in which the regency of Anne of Austria began. The determination of Mazarin, by the early 1650s, to oppose Jansenism encouraged the renewed attempt of Innocent X, by the Bull *Cum Occasione* of 1653, but this still demonstrated a traditional care in the precise categorization of error, even if a subsequent papal Brief seemed to venture rather more into the area of contested fact. This Bull proved to be of more immediate value against Jansenists in the Southern Netherlands than had *In Eminenti*. However, a further intervention by Alexander VII himself, by the Bull *Regiminis Apostolici* of 1665, failed to settle the extended controversy stimulated in France by his own earlier bull, over the possible and necessary modes of deference and assent involved in the signing of an anti-Jansenist formulary. Superficially, however, it seemed that the consequent prolongation of damaging dispute over papal authority had been interrupted by the calculated flexibility of Clement IX, from 1668, over the signing of a formulary.

Only the belated realization of Louis XIV that essential dissidence in fact remained reintroduced Roman authority centrally and directly, when Clement XI responded to repeated royal demands for a new bull, supposedly to outlaw duplicity. But dissident reaction to the Bull *Vineam Domini* of 1705 represented no improvement, and indeed included the project of appeal to a future general council of the Church. The fatal issue of papal authority in questions of fact was thus revived and the pope's belated agreement to royal requests for yet another bull, which emerged in 1713 as the Constitution *Unigenitus*, relaunched the whole controversy over papal authority, both in France particularly and in the Church more generally. In the Constitution the attempt was made to bring condemnation of Jansenist dissidence up to date by condemning 101 propositions attributed to Quesnel. Those were condemned by the deployment of traditionally distinct categories of error, but these qualifications were not attached to specific propositions. That the propositions were properly attributed in a purely textual sense was not now at issue, but rather whether they did not include direct quotations from patristic sources beyond reproach.

The problem of context thus re-emerged, and in that sense at least the boundaries of papal authority were once again open to challenge. The French governmental interventions in an originally doctrinal controversy had thus brought papal authority into question for the remainder of the eighteenth century, not just in France and the Netherlands, but throughout non-Protestant Western Christendom. That the papacy from the 1620s was hampered in its freedom of action by Franco-Habsburg rivalry, and all the more so after open conflict between the major Catholic powers resumed in 1635, has already been noted. It is equally obvious that the popes could not ignore the power of France after the Peace of Westphalia in 1648, the Peace of the Pyrenees which ended the war with Spain to French advantage in 1659, and the beginning of the personal rule of Louis XIV from 1661. The papacy was given apparent opportunities to make its authority effective in France after all, but on terms and in circumstances which proved overwhelmingly counter-productive, not only there, but more widely.

THE WIDER CONTEXT

It therefore remains important to examine further the process by which this situation came about and its long-term consequences. The treatment of the papacy by Louis XIV during his reign was logical from a Gallican viewpoint, even if ironic, given the crucial role of Clement VIII in consolidating the first Bourbon monarch's claim on the loyalties of all French Catholics and exclud-ing Spanish hopes of gaining control of the French succession. Clement's contribution to the peace of 1598 between France and Spain had been better acknowledged by the support he received from Henri IV in the annexation of Ferrara, and the subsequent French involvement in pursuing a resolution of the Interdict imposed on Venice in 1606–7 by Paul V. The initial plans for papal policing of the Valtelline made by Gregory XV had a short-term success at least in postponing open war between France and Spain as well as the overspill of the Thirty Years' War into peninsular Italy. In this context Gregory nevertheless continued a papal subsidy to the Emperor, engaged in the early stages of the War, as being in the wider interest of the Catholic cause. Yet Spanish subsidy was necessary for the projected papal garrison in the Valtelline.

The pope's attempt to delineate the frontier between Catholicism and Pro-testantism, as also in his ban on heretics residing in the Italian peninsula, was based on an optimistic view of the state of Catholic fortunes in the struggle north of the Alps. This concern for clear delineation was also evident in the withdrawal at this time of any remaining papal concession of lay communion in two kinds in German areas. But the consolidation of Catholicism was pursued in other ways in papal policy towards France. Although relations with the French Crown were complicated by the Valtelline question and the revival of confrontation between the Crown and the Huguenot community within France, the pope urged the need for internal reform of the Church in the kingdom. While legal recognition of the Tridentine decrees was still lack-ing, the disorders in French Catholicism, remaining after the long wars of the sixteenth century, were perpetuated by the ability of ecclesiastics to appeal against their superiors to the secular courts and royal council.

In response to this unsatisfactory situation the pope agreed to a reorganiza-tion of the diocesan structure, to allow Paris the status of an archbishopric at the head of its own metropolitan province, while delegating powers to Cardinal Rochefoucauld, intended to allow him to begin a reform of the older religious orders, of pre-Tridentine origin, within France. However, in the Catholic areas of the Empire and adjacent territories under Habsburg rule the Thirty Years' War disrupted attempts to pursue Tridentine reform, despite the papacy's ability after the Council itself to secure the reception of the decrees by members of the German Catholic leadership. Papal difficulties in subsidizing the Imperial cause in the War were directly financial, as well as deriving from the unease caused by resurgent Imperial power among even Catholic princes of the Empire. This was the context of papal urging that the Emperor should order the restoration of ecclesiastical property to the Church in areas recovered from Protestant control. The pope was also confronted by the related difficulties involved in the restoration of Catholicism in reconquered Bohemia, such as the tension between Jesuits and episcopal authority there.

Payments received by the papacy on the occasion of the canonization of four Spanish saints, including Loyola, Francis Xavier and Teresa of Avila, as well as of Philip Neri, were also diverted to support not only the Emperor but the Catholic cause more generally in the War in Germany. Yet by this stage of the War, Spain was already in serious financial difficulty itself, so that the payment in full of the fees necessary at any individual's canonization was a matter of considerable sensitivity at the Spanish Court. The welcome educational involvement of the Jesuits in Bohemian and German areas of Catholic reconquest raised the further problem of how recovered Church property should be used, whether in support of such new ventures or in restoration of older religious orders, for example. This tension within the Catholic camp was indeed to remain. It did not prove as easy to resolve as the papal acquisition of the Palatine Library, after Catholic occupation of the Palatinate, which Bavaria was happy to facilitate, in pursuit of papal support for transfer of the Electoral title to the duke.

That Urban VIII, caught between the conflicting pressures of France and the Habsburgs, was regarded in Spain as pro-French and thus complacent in relation to French Protestant alliance has already been seen. Yet the failure to gain compensating support from France was evident from the French expulsion, at Richelieu's orders, of the papal garrison from the Valtelline. The pope was able to secure some religious rights for the Catholic population of the territory, but was unable to prevent the Mantuan Succession crisis bringing warfare and devastation to Italy after all. Urban's larger aim of maintaining papal independence while pursuing the long-term advantage of Catholicism can arguably be seen in his initial opposition to French subsidy for the Protestant Swedes' campaign in the Thirty Years' War, and his attempt to improve the conditions of the English Catholics by sending to the royal Court resident envoys to Queen Henrietta Maria. But his exercise of papal authority was more successful in a limited sphere, the codification of procedures for what would subsequently be classified as beatification, under Roman control, as a preliminary to canonization.

Urban continued to have to address religious issues within a political context which he could not ultimately control. The pastoral and not merely speculative theological problems raised by French Jansenism were evident when Arnauld published in 1643 his arguments tending against frequent lay communion, a matter of contention in subsequent pontificates as well. That Urban had inherited considerable problems was indeed obvious from the lack of substantial results achieved by the Legatine embassy to France of the pope's chief nephew, Cardinal Francesco Barberini. Cardinal Richelieu remained un-yielding in opposing a papal garrison in the Valtelline. The Legation arguably provoked Richelieu by encouraging the ultra-Catholic French who criticized his seemingly pro-Protestant foreign policy, despite his internal confrontation with the Huguenots. This friction certainly diminished the hopes of some Gallican prelates that the English Catholics might be accorded a full episcopal leadership, in the face of Roman resistance.

A similar Legation to Spain was effectively aborted by Richelieu's ability to make an independent agreement with Spain over the Valtelline, though his own adoption of this reflected the momentary success of the Queen Mother and Bérulle in urging a more pan-Catholic, less anti-Habsburg policy. A rare interlude of Catholic unity thus seemed to safeguard the Valtelline Catholics, preserve Italy from war for the time being, and even temporarily defer to papal authority by the interim reconstitution of a papal garrison. But such a positive interlude was indeed brief as well as rare. The internal, ultra-Catholic critics of Cardinal Richelieu did not secure much advantage for English Cath-olics from the French Catholic marriage of Charles I of England, which the cardinal had secured on the final collapse of the Spanish marriage negotiations. Their opposition to Richelieu's encouragement of Transylvanian resistance to the Emperor had also not removed the long-running Imperial problem of retaining Catholic control of those lands of the Hungarian Crown not under Islamic occupation.

The respite from the threat of war in the Italian peninsula ended as the impending conflict over the Mantuan Succession loomed, at a time when Spain's relations with Urban were already deteriorating, to the point of an interdict imposed on the Spanish church of S. Giacomo in Rome. The defeat of the Huguenots in France left them still in possession of their religious as opposed to other liberties, as well as freeing the French monarchy to confront the Habsburgs. But it was in the papal diplomatic negotiations to try to resolve the Mantuan Succession crisis in Northern Italy that the Barberini protégé who was subsequently to emerge as Richelieu's political successor established his credentials, the future Italian cardinal who would be known by a French form of his name, as Mazarin. Initially, however, his work in secur-ing peace in Northern Italy was threatened by the short-lived nature of the French co-operation promised by the Capuchin diplomat, Père Joseph, when the latter's agreement was disavowed by Richelieu, quite apart from papal dis-satisfaction with the terms of the peace. Urban was also facing the Emperor's attempts at independent control of Church appointments in all the ecclesiast-ical territories due to be returned to Catholic possession by the terms of the Edict of Restitution, even before the counter-productive effects of that measure for the Catholic campaigns of the Thirty Years' War became fully evident.

Despite Habsburg criticism of his allegedly French sympathies, Urban still made financial concessions to both the Emperor and the Bavarian interest in the divided Catholic front in Germany. Even the subsidy to Bavaria was argued to prove papal favour to France, however, in the escalation of Habsburg complaints which reached a climax in the notorious outburst of Cardinal Borgia. While Urban's condemnation of the cardinal's behaviour involved a general defence of papal control of business in Consistory, it also reflected the pope's sense that Habsburg pressure on the papacy was indeed intolerable and necessitated the pursuit of understanding with other Catholic powers as some sort of protection. Yet Richelieu was capable of threatening a French schism if Urban were to succumb to Spanish pressure and excommunicate him or the king, as the prospect of France's direct entry into war against the Habsburgs grew. Nevertheless, far from simply resisting demands from either side that the papacy join a formal alliance, the pope was still hoping in 1633 to find a way of uniting the Catholic powers of Europe in a coalition against the Turks as well as against the Protestant forces led by Sweden.

The only eventual fruit of this, however, was the plan subsequently adopted in the negotiations to end the Thirty Years' War, of one set of discussions bringing together the Catholic powers and a separate set involving the Protestants. But meanwhile the immediate papal aim of peace between the Catholic powers was still actively pursued by diplomatic means from the mid-1630s, despite the threatening violence between French and Spanish retinues in Rome itself as France directly entered the European war. The 1635 Peace of Prague within the Imperial sphere of operations, which in one sense represented the effective failure of the Edict of Restitution, did at least, in practice, mean the consolidation of Catholicism in existing Catholic territories, including the Emperor's hereditary lands, despite papal complaints. In such circumstances, as indeed generally from the end of the Council of Trent onwards, the fact that some cardinals in Rome were in receipt of either Spanish or French pensions was another complicating factor. It was symptomatic of the impact on Roman life of the conflict within Catholic Europe that the two Cardinal Nephews of Urban and the wife of his lay nephew, the Prefect of Rome, had at this time to host separate performances for the French, the Spanish, and native high society in Rome of the religious music drama, 'The Life of St Theodora' by Rospigliosi, the future Pope Clement IX.

The team of extraordinary nuncios sent to the Catholic powers in the second half of the 1630s to urge peace was, in formal terms, headed by the special Legate based in Cologne, but little was achieved, for all this diplomatic effort. In Bohemian, Transylvanian and Hungarian areas recovered for Catholic control the papal envoys could do more, by passing on directives of the Roman Congregation De Propaganda Fide for the real consolidation of Catholicism there. Mazarin, however, was already representing French interests to Rome rather than vice versa, by relaying Richelieu's encouragement to the Barberini nephews to think of France as a potential protector from the Habsburgs when the inevitable end of Urban's pontificate eventually came. By 1643–44, when negotiations for peace finally began at Münster involving Spanish, Imperial and French delegates, the opportunity for Chigi, as resident nuncio at Cologne, to display the diplomatic abilities of a future pope was the greater because the previous series of extraordinary nuncios and Legates had achieved virtually nothing. Urban's death indeed occurred just before the arrival of the future Alexander VII at the peace conference.

The future pope's concern for the suppression of Jansenism, as a destabilizing complication within a divided Catholic Europe, dated from this period. Richelieu's death did not, though, remove opportunities for France to disturb the peace negotiations, as Spanish rule was challenged in Catalonia, Portugal and Naples. This was despite the fact that Mazarin's direction of French affairs was to face its own internal challenges, following the deaths of Richelieu and Louis XIII. What was of concern to Rome in the momentary rise of *parlementaire* leadership against Mazarin's administration was that the Paris *parlement* had been prominent, under Richelieu, in attacks on the Jesuits within France. Moreover, such dispute had turned not least on the still vexed question of direct or indirect papal power in temporal affairs and in relation to secular rulers.

This Gallican conflict drew on tensions which, after the Council of Trent, had already embarrassed the relations of the Jesuit Bellarmine with the pope, in Italy itself, and given the dissident critic of the post-Conciliar papacy, Paolo Sarpi, opportunity to publicize his anti-Roman views. Such open dispute reflected the perspicacious warnings about assertions of papal authority expressed at the time of the Council by the saintly primate of Portugal, Batholomew de Martyribus, who had had such an influence directly on Charles Borromeo and, by that route, indirectly on a whole generation of post-Tridentine bishops in Catholic Europe. Richelieu had also attempted to limit the effective authority of nuncios in France by manipulation of Gallican sentiment in both the *parlement* and the Sorbonne, as well as among elements within the French episcopate and clergy, hoping to acquire an officially Legatine position in France himself. In such manoeuvres Richelieu had felt able on occasion to withdraw co-operation even from the Barberini, though in a dispute over the appointment of a Cardinal Protector of France Urban VIII showed his own diplomatic ability by leaving the position vacant and fulfilling in person one of the duties of a Protector, to bring forward in Consistory nominations to the kingdom's bishoprics. Under Mazarin, after the start of the regency which followed the death of Louis XIII, the royal Council of Conscience, which came to be involved in episcopal nominations, was for a while fortified by the presence of the truly conscientious Vincent de Paul.

This was some improvement on a previous situation where Richelieu had tried to prevent the nuncios acting as the conduit for reports to Rome on the suitability of episcopal nominees, a matter in which Urban had still tried to pursue Tridentine standards. Richelieu had indeed contributed to the gradual improvement in the quality of French episcopal nominees during the first half of the seventeenth century. But the visible supervision of the post-Conciliar Church by specifically papal authority was thus still contested in practice, just as in the more immediately post-Tridentine decades, when the nuncios in Spain had been urged from Rome to ensure that Spanish nominees for bishoprics made their profession of faith, as required from that epoch onwards, to them in person.[18] From Urban's pontificate, however, the Roman grant of faculties to diocesan bishops was reorganized, resulting in their being granted in future on a quinquennial basis. This therefore sustained the detailed administration which individual bishops could hope to establish in their dioceses, within the scope of the Conciliar decrees, under clear Roman authorization.

But while such papal action might hope to reduce previous friction between bishops and the Roman Curia, as over the filling of benefices, Urban's successors were still constrained in their general policies by political developments. The promotion of peace in Catholic Europe continued, but in the closing years of the Thirty Years' War the actions of Innocent X, originally intended to deal with the adverse effects of the papal nephews' accumulation of power under Urban, could not avoid political implications, when the Barberini fled to the French Court. The papacy thus became embroiled with Mazarin, as he faced essentially political opposition within France, while the Franco-Spanish conflict was perpetuated beyond the end of the war in Germany. Because Mazarin's opponents during the Frondes included Gondi, coadjutor to the archbishop of Paris and subsequently Cardinal de Retz, there was further conflict with Rome over French attempts to exclude the cardinal from succession to the archiepiscopal see. Thus although Mazarin supported the initial condemnation of Jansenism by Innocent in 1653, his long and originally political rivalry with Gondi enabled the latter to represent himself at times as the true defender of Roman authority against the Gallicanism of the French government.

After Mazarin's death, following the final achievement of Franco-Spanish peace in 1659, the necessary calm for independent treatment of the Jansenist question was still lacking. The beginning of personal rule by Louis XIV was marked by violent conflict in Rome itself over the diplomatic immunities claimed by the French ambassador. Such dispute also involved French occupation of the papal territories at Avignon, in a pattern which was to be repeated in subsequent Franco-papal conflicts. Despite such precarious relations with the king, there was momentary co-operation with the campaign of Alexander VII for an anti-Turkish alliance by 1664. But attacks on the alleged Jesuit defence of laxism, in spiritual direction, posed further difficulties for Rome in relation to French confrontation between the Society of Jesus and its opponents.

The attempts of the Society's leadership over a long period to remove any grounds for such accusation, and the relative favour of the anti-Jansenist pope towards the Jesuits, did not prevent Alexander VII's condemnation of certain laxist propositions in 1665 and 1666. Partly compensating for this was his encouragement of the Jesuit group known as the Bollandists, who were inaugurating a more truly historical approach to hagiography, in the face of criticism from other religious orders. As has been seen, Alexander did not in fact secure the Jansenists' submission over their assertion of a distinction between 'fact' and 'right'. By contrast, the superficial association of Clement IX with

18 A.S.V. Spagna, XXXIII, 134r–v: 1586.

peaceful settlement seemed momentarily confirmed by the state of relations between the Catholic powers of France and Spain and the eventual papal recognition of Portuguese independence, despite Spanish pressure. More specifically, the four French bishops who had refused to sign the formulary of Alexander VII were induced to submit, giving a brief appearance that the Jansenist conflict had been pacified.

Any real peace in the French Church was disturbed by the royal Gallicanism of Louis XIV, however, who in 1673 confronted Clement X with unilateral extension in geographical terms of the *régale*, by which the temporalities of French sees when vacant and new bishops' access to these were ultimately controlled by the Crown, even if, by this date, for the benefit of the new bishop. The partial counter-measures adopted in Rome itself by the papal nephew, Cardinal Altieri, were truly counter-productive, as the dispute over diplomatic immunities was thereby reopened. Royal policy also threatened to interrupt papal relations with religious orders and houses within France. Thus internal French conditions rather than international divisions in Catholic Europe were now preventing papal resolution of the Jansenist problem. Renewal of Franco-Habsburg conflict, however, implied French obstruction of papal plans for action against the Turks, which the pope was encouraging the Poles to undertake.

Relations between Louis XIV and the papacy deteriorated further under Innocent XI, whose election the king had no longer been able to prevent, despite diplomatic intervention at the time of the conclave. Escalation of the *régale* conflict, as the Crown maintained its claimed control of the spiritual *régale*, involving certain ecclesiastical appointments, below episcopal level, during episcopal vacancies, produced the Four Gallican Articles of 1682. Yet the austerity of an episcopal opponent of royal policy, Bishop Caulet of Pamiers, turned him in this case from a pro-Jansenist to a papalist. By contrast, the pope refused episcopal appointment to two royal nominees who had taken part in the clerical assembly which had voted for the Articles, while wider conflict over the filling of French bishoprics was also prolonged. The question of diplomatic immunities at Rome took an even more violent turn, leading to an interdict on the French church of S. Luigi in the city.

There was also a political dimension to the dispute over the succession in the Electoral Archbishopric of Cologne, whose territories were potentially of great strategic importance. The Bavarian candidate was supported by the Habsburgs, despite the tradition of Franco-Bavarian alliance earlier in the century, and Louis XIV opposed this with the claims of a rival candidate. Papal choice of the Bavarian prompted not just the occupation of Avignon, but also the detention of the papal nuncio and Louis's attempt to raise the Conciliarist threat once again. But papal policy in the Cologne dispute was not unaffected by disapproval of French refusal to co-operate in Imperial defence against the Turks. Relations with the pope in the sequel to the successful occupation of the English throne by William of Orange, following the flight of James II, deteriorated to the point where a Gallican schism was feared.

The Revocation of the Edict of Nantes also failed to improve the pope's opinion of Louis XIV, who had encouraged the episcopal leadership of the French Church to secure the adoption by the clerical assembly of 1682 of the Four Gallican Articles. The explicit Conciliarism contained in the Articles was a challenge which the papacy could not ignore, even though in subsequent manoeuvring the royal insistence that they be part of the syllabus of clerical education in France was eventually abandoned. By 1687, however, Innocent had been persuaded to condemn propositions attributed to a new movement which had attracted royal hostility, the Quietists. The condemnation not only supported royal opposition to the Quietists in France but also advantaged Bossuet as he subsequently developed his rivalry with Fénelon by attacking the latter's supposed Quietist sympathies. This was to a degree ironic, since Bossuet had been crucial in the clerical assembly of 1682, while Fénelon was to prove his more direct loyalty to papal authority not only by his anti-Jansenism but conspicuously by his public submission in 1699, following condemnation of propositions from his own writing as Quietist.

But the papacy was not distracted from its own natural priorities in all this. The condemnations of Alexander VIII were not confined to Jansenist propositions but extended to Gallican assertions, above all the Four Gallican Articles. Despite this he was able by 1690 to recover Avignon and the adjacent Venaissin from French occupation, for political isolation caused Louis to adopt a more accommodating policy during this pontificate, as did the prospect of new hostility towards France over the looming question of the Spanish Succession. The claimed asylum for criminal suspects at the French embassy in Rome was also abandoned.

As a Venetian, Alexander VIII was also anxious to assist Republican defence against the Turks, though by the late seventeenth century French policy, for commercial as well as diplomatic reasons, was clearly pro-Ottoman, even if that implied abandoning a traditional French favour towards Venice. But his insistence, like that of other popes of the late seventeenth and early eighteenth century, on the doctrinal authority of the Holy See was maintained despite the obvious political weakness of Rome. In 1690 the pope condemned attempts to distinguish between divine law and natural moral law. However, the consequences of 1682 still affected Franco-papal relations. Innocent XII insisted that even if other royal nominees were to be accepted for bishoprics, those involved in the assembly of 1682 could not be, without an adequate satisfaction for the honour of the Holy See. In the end the king agreed that the bishops particularly in question should send to Rome a formal expression of regret at any offence caused by the assembly, especially as far as the Articles affected papal authority.

But this relative rapprochement with France could not prevent a deterioration of papal relations with the Emperor, in the context of the impending Spanish Succession crisis. The Imperial proposal to create an additional Electorate, for the benefit of Protestant Hanover, obviously displeased Rome, and the Imperial ambassador in turn reopened the question of diplomatic immunities in the city. Such tensions influenced the pope's advice to the expiring ruler of Habsburg Spain, Charles II, to name the French claimant, the duke of Anjou, as his successor. Nevertheless Clement XI encountered the hostility of both main camps in the following Spanish Succession War. In the Peace of Utrecht which concluded the Succession struggle, Catholic interests were partially secured, as by the French acquisitions in the Rhineland, both in the initial treaty and in the subsequent variations introduced by consequent treaties.

But, at this moment, the papal Constitution *Unigenitus*, far from ending the Jansenist crisis in France and in Catholic Europe, enlarged it from 1713 onwards, even to the point of the revived appeal from papal judgement to a future General Council. Yet to this date the difficult papal relationship with the Bourbons had not been without benefit, including the eventual restoration of Catholicism in the dynasty's original Navarrese kingdom, in Béarn. It had nevertheless been striking that some of the more influential encouragement of Catholic restoration within France, after the disruptions of the sixteenth century, had to come from outside the borders of the kingdom, and not merely because of anti-Jesuit sentiment. This was true not only of papal Avignon, as a source of stimulus to Catholic recovery in Southern France, but also of Lorraine. In that state, adjacent to the kingdom, the Jesuit educational establishment at Pont-à-Mousson had been very influential.

The proximity of the Catholic Southern Netherlands proved decidedly more ambiguous in its effects. Despite the supposed settlement of the controversy over the views of Baius in 1570, confirmed in 1580, Jesuit and anti-Jesuit scholars at the University of Louvain persisted in perennial conflict. The understandable Jansenist criticism there of the direction of French foreign policy instigated by Richelieu, because of its division of Catholic interests and threat to Catholic areas like the Catholic Netherlands themselves, further complicated the papal response to problems within France. For the French Jansenists in one sense built on the Catholic reform programme of an earlier generation of ecclesiastics and devout laity, typified by Bérulle, both in appealing for the repristination of the Catholic Church within the kingdom, and in opposing foreign policy which directly undermined Catholic solidarity or involved open alliance with Protestants. From a Gallican perspective, the generations of Bérulle and Olier might seem 'ultramontane' in their respect for Rome, but the Jansenists, in their preoccupation with supposed purity of doctrine and sacramental discipline, came in the end to a fixed confrontation with papal authority.

Thus despite moments when individual pro-Jansenist prelates sought papal support for independent episcopal jurisdiction, against royal interference, the Jansenist movement as a whole evolved in increasingly obsessive opposition to the exercise of that authority. In his last years, Louis XIV gave firm support to *Unigenitus*, but continued French resistance was led by the archbishop of Paris, Cardinal de Noailles. Condemnation and excommunication of those who appealed against the Constitution to a General Council was published in 1718, but the cardinal did not submit until 1728. The elevation by Clement XI of St Anselm to the rank of Doctor of the Church was an intelligent response to the Jansenists' strident assertion of the unique authority of St Augustine, as emphasizing the range of Catholic orthodoxy. Innocent XIII refused the request of some French bishops for withdrawal of *Unigenitus*, despite his personal doubts as to whether the Constitution as issued had been opportune, and he deployed the authority of the Holy Office against their appeal.

Papal difficulties with the regency administration, after Louis's death, were only partly relieved by compliance with French demands that the statesman Dubois be made a cardinal. Benedict XIII faced a different problem, in any case, in the continued disputes over *Unigenitus*. As a Dominican his priority was to defend his order's teaching from tendentious use of it by opponents of the Constitution. It was in this context that the pope confirmed the Constitution in 1725, for all his supposed sympathy with the Jansenists. The submission of Noailles was only achieved after complicated manoeuvres. Cardinals de Rohan and de Bissy, together with Fleury, subsequently a cardinal too, denounced the supposedly Augustinian but allegedly Jansenist articles sent to Rome by the archbishop, optimistically seeking their approval. The bishop of Senez published his support for the articles and criticism of the popes from Clement XI onwards.

A provincial council under the archbishop of Embrun suspended the bishop of Senez, who received a royal order of exile, but the Paris *parlement* proclaimed its defence of him and its opposition to the Constitution. The political power of Cardinal Fleury enabled him to outmanoeuvre Noailles and a dozen other bishops who denounced the condemnation of the bishop of Senez, and allowed Rome to confirm the decision of the provincial council. Fleury also secured legal recognition of *Unigenitus*, enforced in France from 1730. Clement XII renewed the distinction between approval of Dominican theology and condemnation of Jansenist claims that this entailed rejection of the Constitution. He also condemned in 1734 the letters of two French bishops which publicized the purported miracles at the Parisian tomb of a Jansenist proclaimed by the so-called Convulsionaries. Fleury again intervened to overcome the objections of the Paris *parlement* to the proposed canonization of Vincent de Paul, as a supposed attack on Jansenism.

But the Paris *parlement* renewed its opposition by an attack on the archbishop of Paris for his orders that persistent opponents of the Constitution be denied the sacraments. In this case, as French Jansenism seemed increasingly *parlementaire* and political, the clerical assembly itself looked to Rome, and the papal response in 1756 reaffirmed the necessity of accepting the Constitution while moderating denial of the sacraments. Further political opportunity for the *parlementaires* to attack the Jesuits in France was found in an attempt on the life of the king and the involvement of the Society of Jesus in the failure of a commercial enterprise. Royal suppression of the Society in France, in 1764, followed papal refusal of an interim demand that the French Jesuits be placed under an autonomous Vicar General, in breach of the order's international nature. But the papal response of 1765, confirming the status and privileges of the Society, was not thought opportune by all at Rome. Indeed, the rapidly escalating confrontation between the pope and all the Bourbon Courts of Europe, which stimulated French occupation once again of Avignon and the Venaissin, demonstrated how broad the crisis over papal authority had become.

After the Peace of Utrecht the new Bourbon regime in Spain had become embroiled in its own disputes with the papacy. These initially concerned not only the allocation of Italian territories, in the peninsula and the islands, but also Roman refusal of the archbishopric of Seville to the Italian Cardinal Alberoni, who was the influential minister of the Spanish Crown. After the expulsion of the nuncio from Spain, Alberoni too found himself forced to seek shelter at Rome, following Spain's reconciliation with the Emperor in 1720. The later pliancy of Benedict XIV allowed both Spain and Portugal concessions over ecclesiastical nominations and restriction of ecclesiastical immunities, but he was not able to divert the threat to the Jesuits represented by the Hispano-Portuguese accord from 1750.

The expulsion of the Jesuits from the Bourbon states of Naples and Parma in 1767 followed the example of Spain itself. A partial concession, by which the pope associated an anti-Jesuit, Cardinal Negroni, with Cardinal Torregiani, a pro-Jesuit, in the Secretariate of State, did not prevent the continuation of the Bourbon attack on the Bull *In Coena Domini*, and the final demand in 1769 for the suppression of the Society. Concessions over the Bull and the elevation of the brother of Pombal, the Portuguese royal minister, to the college of cardinals did not deflect the Bourbon Courts. By 1772 Spain was accompanying renewal of the demand by a threat that otherwise all religious orders there would face suppression. The pope nevertheless dismissed the more positive offer of the return of Avignon (as well as Benevento in the Italian peninsula) if a suitable decision were made.

Clement X had helped the necessarily long process of restoring better relations between Rome and the Portuguese monarchy, once independence was regained, by an accommodating approach when the new regime faced its own internal crisis over a suitable succession to the Crown. Benedict XIV made a grant of titular honours in response to Portuguese demand, when in 1748 the king was awarded the epithet of 'Most Faithful', to match the 'Catholic' and 'Christian' titles of the Spanish and French Crowns. Indeed, the pontificate ended with agreement to Portuguese insistence that an Apostolic Visitor investigate the affairs of the Jesuits in the kingdom. The severe restrictions imposed on the Portuguese Jesuits by the Visitor were subsequently modified by Clement XIII, but intervention against them was then instituted by Pombal, on the pretext of their responsibility for the attempted assassination of the king. Papal response even sought Spanish mediation, but in vain, and exiled Jesuits from Portugal had to be provided for in the papal states.

After the papal suppression of the Jesuits in 1773 the General, Ricci, was incarcerated with other leading members of the Society, but the special tribunal which examined them passed no public sentence. The pope might thus feel that a major schism within Catholic Europe had been averted, but the damage to papal authority itself, so long associated with the Society, was obvious. The papacy was in any case unable to enforce the suppression in non-Catholic territory, specifically Russia and above all Prussia. The return of Avignon and occupied Italian possessions of the papacy could not provide much compensation.

The choice by Cardinal Braschi of the pontifical name Pius VI, recalling the independence of the post-Tridentine Pius V, was a more positive omen. A concordat with Portugal was achieved and Pombal was imprisoned by the monarch. The broader form of eighteenth-century Jansenism, not least as an anti-Jesuit campaign, had thus certainly affected Catholic Europe generally, and not just Bourbon Spain. Jansenist ideas had also spread from the Netherlands, where the Southern Netherlands were now under Austrian Habsburg rule, to other Austrian and Italian Habsburg possessions, which were increasingly linked in both cultural and political terms, as well as to the Bourbon states in Italy. This later Jansenism thus often seemed to approximate to a Catholic Erastianism, encouraging rulers and their ministers to make unilateral reorganization of Church structure and finance.

The suppression of the Jesuits had, however, eased the papacy's relations with the Swiss confederation. The Jesuit presence among the Swiss Catholics, as at Luzern, had existed alongside the presence of papal nuncios, ever since the post-Conciliar decades, and the latter had for a while exercised an almost episcopal oversight in the same city. But quite apart from the internal tensions between the Catholic and Protestant Swiss territories, and the marked Erastianism of the latter, external influences from surrounding states had affected the Catholic communities. As well as Gallicanism and Febronianism, Josephinism also finally had an impact. In some parts of Catholic Europe, indeed, local ecclesiastical traditions had never been successfully challenged by the post-Tridentine papacy.

The cathedral chapters of the Empire retained their power in the election of bishops, though in 1694 Innocent XII attempted to prohibit the practice of their imposing formal concordats on a bishop at his election. Yet arguably the gradual liberation of Imperial bishops from the force of such concordats had been aided chiefly by the political upheavals of the Thirty Years' War. But the problem of bishoprics which had oversight of territories lying partly without and partly within the Austrian Habsburg family lands remained until the reign of Joseph II. With the advent of the Austrian Succession crisis, Benedict XIV had already had to face the danger that ecclesiastical territories in the Empire, such as Salzburg, Passau, Freising or Eichstätt might be secularized. After papal recognition of the rights of Francis I, however, papal relations with the Empire improved for a while from 1746.

Clement XIV was aware that, in addition to the crisis over the Society of Jesus, the papacy faced a growing threat from Febronianism in German-speaking Catholic lands. The author of the literature which inspired the Febronian views of the Electoral Archbishops of the Empire, Hontheim, was forced to make a formal retraction of his opinions in 1778, but a further publication in 1781 under his pseudonym of Febronius suggested little alteration in fact. Yet Pius VI had the relative satisfaction of seeing that the Punctuation of Ems, in which the three Electoral Archbishops and the Prince-Archbishop of Salzburg joined in 1786, to demand practical restrictions on the exercise of Roman authority within the German Church, did not in the event meet with support from other bishops. Even that, on the other hand, did little to offset the effect of the Toleration Edict of 1781, by which in his family lands Joseph II removed the distinct, privileged position of Catholicism and formalized state control of the local publication of papal documents. Unilateral alterations in religious affairs introduced by Joseph in the Austrian lands concerned not only popular devotion, as in the restriction of pilgrimages, but also the crucial control of clerical education. With the replacement of local seminaries by so-called General Seminaries, an approved doctrine, not least with reference to Church and State, would be taught.

When papal protest and diplomatic representation proved ineffectual, papal recourse to Vienna in person was tried. But the pamphlet literature circulating before the pope's visit to Vienna now questioned the whole authority of the papacy. Josephinism certainly did not establish a schism, but, despite popular enthusiasm and official honour, the pope did not secure any serious concessions. Some marginal consolation was afforded the pope, after he left Vienna and crossed Imperial territory. During his return journey he was received at Augsburg in circumstances which could be represented as a Catholic triumph, even in an area of traditional religious division and ambiguity. Pius VI, returning in 1782, was received with honour in the city which had given its name to the official formula of Lutheran faith. Joseph's policies, as for example over monastic suppressions and enforced diocesan reorganization, nevertheless persisted.

At first sight a contrast with the areas firmly ruled by Bourbons and Habsburgs was suggested by the abnormal, elective monarchy of Poland, where even a pope who was in political terms relatively weak, like Benedict XIII, could exert his authority with some success. Despite the difficulties of the Spanish Succession struggle, Clement XI had tried to organize an alliance to defend the Venetian Republic against the Turks, reviving preoccupations of Clement X and also of Innocent XI, who in 1683 had provided help to Poland as well as to the Emperor, for the anti-Turkish struggle. Innocent had even hoped to create a grand alliance against the Turks, involving not only Poland but also Russia, the Hungarian Crown and Venice, as well as the Persians, thus reviving the idea of a double-fronted attack which had never entirely disappeared since the time of Philip II. The pope, however, complemented this by urging the internal strengthening of Catholicism, as for example by the reform of the Cistercians in Poland. Yet the eighteenth-century papacy lacked the authority to prevent the partitioning of Catholic Poland.

All the same, the skill of Benedict XIV in dealing with the European Catholic rulers still suggested what for a while could be achieved. His supplementary marriage regulations at last provided for those communities where the Tridentine norms could not apply. His systematic treatment of the procedures for canonization and control of saints' cults exemplified an able conjunction of the papacy's teaching office and the imposition of uniformity by papal authority. The independent exercise of that authority was also evident in his constitution of 1753, allowing some eventual relaxation of the Roman Index of prohibited literature, marked by the more tolerant approach of the 1758 revised Index to Copernican views in particular. Benedict also renewed the condemnation of duels by the Tridentine Church and post-Conciliar papacy.

His defence of the critical hagiography of the Bollandists was balanced by defence of the orthodoxy of Cardinal Noris against renewed posthumous accusations of a Jansenist Augustinianism and condemnation in the Spanish Index. Yet the imperative need to conserve papal authority, against Jansenist and other criticism, by conspicuous adherence to orthodoxy was also indicated by his inconclusive but traditionally restrictive response to the published views of Scipio Maffei on the legitimate use of interest in financial transactions. Jansenist and related critics of the papacy, by the eighteenth century, claimed a defining patristic authority for their self-proclaimed austerity of doctrine and discipline. But to the end of the Ancien Régime the popes attempted to provide a continuing and contemporary supervision of non-Protestant Western Christendom. It was the political obstacles encountered in Catholic Europe itself which increasingly limited their ability to exercise that patriarchal leadership in the West.

CHAPTER 6

The Supreme Pontiff

The ideal of Christian unity, not least as a common front against Islam, was still actively pursued by the popes of the post-Tridentine period. But from the Roman viewpoint this obviously implied recognition, by Christians of other rites, of papal supremacy. For a brief moment, starting in the late sixteenth century, a dazzling prospect of obtaining such recognition from Eastern-rite Christians in Russia itself, and not simply in the Polish dominions, seemed to open up. After the expulsion from Sweden of Jesuits in 1580, the ubiquitous member of the Society, Possevino, made his way to Muscovy, initially to mediate in the war between Poland and Ivan the Terrible, and with a view to fostering an anti-Islamic crusade against the Turks. The latter was not achieved, but for a while some hopes were retained of acquiring Russian obedience to Rome, not least in the light of Possevino's contribution to the ultimately successful union of the Greek-rite Christians in much of the Polish territories from 1596. The pretender who challenged the occupation of the Russian throne by Boris Godunov, the first of the 'false Dmitris', was awarded papal recognition in 1604, as he invaded Russia with Polish support.

THE ORTHODOX

The arrival of Jesuits, however, also alarmed the Orthodox, and the new regime, increasingly seen as alien, was overthrown by 1606. When a second 'false Dmitri' was eventually ousted, by a redirection of Polish involvement, the subsequent 'time of troubles' was ended only by the election of a Romanov, and his consolidation of power with the crucial support of the Moscow Patriarch. Following the earlier elevation of the Moscow metropolitan see to a patriarchate, national resistance to Polish intervention thus established a decidedly anti-Roman authority. This produced a consequent expulsion of the Jesuits from Russia in 1719, while Peter the Great, on his visit to Paris in 1717, had taken note of Jansenist and episcopalist opposition to the papal imposition of *Unigenitus*, before returning to Russia and suspending on a more permanent basis the vacant position of the Moscow patriarch itself. Such internal upheaval frustrated the tentative approaches to the Russian Church of the most anti-papal elements among the French Jansenists. It was nevertheless symptomatic that in 1727 the conversion to the Catholic faith of Princess Dolgorukaja involved her profession not to a papal representative, in any emulation of Christina of Sweden, but to the schismatic Jansenist archbishop of Utrecht.

A protest against the 1596 Union in Poland had been issued on behalf of the patriarch of Constantinople by a Greek Orthodox who was to remain much affected by his unsuccessful representations against this submission to Rome by the Polish-Lithuanian Eastern-rite Christians. A majority of them, however, had repudiated contact with a patriarchal authority based at the capital of the Turkish empire, which confronted the Poles on the Southern frontier of the kingdom. The devoutly Orthodox Loukaris had also been encouraged in his own anti-Roman sentiments by the Greek prelate allowed by the Venetian Republic to reside in Venice despite papal suspicion of his public ambiguity. But the evolution of Polish royal policy towards a clearer commitment to Catholicism had also provoked anti-Roman approaches from various Protestant sources to the Orthodox Church both within Poland and at Constantinople. In itself this had been merely counter-productive, as suggested by Gregory XIII's foundation of the Greek College in Rome and publication of the Greek *Acta* of the Council of Florence, both achieved by 1577, or the subsequent publication of a Greek edition of the decrees of the Council of Trent. Indeed, Loukaris himself had momentarily seemed more conciliatory towards Rome, as in his apparent approach to Paul V in 1608. But from 1612 Loukaris pursued his own contacts at Constantinople with Protestant diplomatic representatives, especially the English and Dutch. Such anti-Catholic contacts opposed the political and commercial interests in the area of the Emperor's envoys and, increasingly, the French. The first period of his patriarchate, from initial election in 1620, coincided with the growth of French support for the more active Catholic presence which came to be associated with the work of the Jesuits, Capuchins and the Congregation De Propaganda Fide, as the Venetian empire in the Mediterranean, complete with its own Greek-rite Christian population, gradually declined. This was the background to the patriarch's supposedly 'pro-Calvinist' manoeuvres against rivals who were willing to seek French or Imperial support by seeming more sympathetic to Rome or the Jesuits. Loukaris overcame repeated depositions and recovered his position as patriarch for four further periods of office, but was finally strangled by his opponents in 1638.

The Bulgarian Church under Ottoman rule equally produced its own understandable internal friction. But Catholic intelligence of such difficulties, which included even sectarian dissidence, was not the same as successful exploitation. No Uniate movement emerged, for indeed the Orthodox Churches under Turkish rule in Europe were obviously well placed to resist any approaches from Roman authority, whatever the restrictions imposed by that rule. It might even be argued that the relative success of the post-Tridentine papacy in fostering Uniate Churches encouraged the firm opposition of the Orthodox throughout this period to any assertion of papal supremacy. This picture did not seem substantially altered by the momentary recovery of Venetian power in part of the Greek lands at the beginning of the eighteenth century. Nor was it ever easy to persuade the Russian Orthodox state to join Catholic alliances against the Turks. The Georgian Church deposed its Catholicos in 1755 when it seemed he was responding favourably to proposals for Uniate status made by Capuchins and Theatines. Important sections of the Armenian Church, in the same century, resisted moves towards such status and maintained associations with Constantinople and subsequently Russia.

After the partition of Poland had begun, Russian pressure, including threats of forced conversion to Orthodoxy among the Catholic and Uniate population of the territory acquired by Russia, imposed papal recognition of an unsuitable episcopal leader whose pretensions accorded with government designs. Clement XIV and then Pius VI felt constrained to agree to the gradual enlargement of the prelate's authority, culminating in archiepiscopal jurisdiction which gave him in this territory an authority practically independent of Roman direction.

The failure of the Jesuit missions to Ethiopia had dashed hopes of confrontation with Islam on that front, but the attempt to reorientate the Ethiopian Church towards Roman obedience, detaching it from its traditional links with the ancient patriarchate of Alexandria, was naturally difficult in a country where the supreme secular authority had a virtually sacral status. Elsewhere in Africa, in the kingdom of Kongo, the lingering sense of a Catholic Christianity, among the nobility at least, was not something which the papacy seemed much able to exploit.

PROTESTANTISM

In Europe the obvious problem confronting any plan for Christian unity was the presence of Protestantism. The immediate post-Tridentine alarm of the papacy at the prospect of losing the Netherlands to Protestantism was understandable, but after papal urging of firm reaction to dissidence, there was soon Roman disquiet, even in the case of Pius V himself, over the virtual independence of the Inquisition under Spanish rule there and the likely consequences. The rapidly counter-productive effects in the Netherlands of Rome's agreement in 1561 to the Spanish plan for redrawing the diocesan boundaries and increasing the number of bishoprics there were, after all, evident. Even in the early seventeenth century, Roman reaction to the prospective expiry of the Twelve Years' Truce in the Netherlands still recognized the difficulty of securing easier conditions for Catholics in the Northern Netherlands, whether in restored peace or renewed war.

Conditions in the Holy Roman Empire after the Council of Trent necessitated continued papal intervention to protect Catholic interests and prevent interpretations of the Peace of Augsburg which might favour Protestant states. After the death of the experienced diplomat Cardinal Morone, it was particularly important to find papal envoys who could command respect and inspire confidence, in circumstances such as the meetings of the Imperial Diet, where lobbying between Catholic princes and Protestant leaders for influence on the Emperor was common. While positive encouragement of Catholic prelates in the Empire to adopt stricter ecclesiastical discipline was slow to produce visible results, negative pressure was necessary, especially on cathedral chapters, to prevent applications of the Peace which would allow the further establishment of Protestant rights in particular territories. Furthermore, the experience of Catholic rulers, such as the duke of Bavaria, suggested that the immediately post-Conciliar papal concession of lay communion in two kinds within German provinces of the Church had not in fact produced the results, in retaining or restoring lay attachment to Catholicism, which some secular and clerical leaders in the Empire had expected. The concession for persons other than the celebrant at Mass to communicate in two kinds, operating under strict conditions in any case, was indeed withdrawn in 1584, two decades after its original grant.

Pius V had, by 1570, defeated the post-Conciliar threat of virtual schism in the officially Catholic lands of the Empire represented by the programme for the 1566 Diet at Augsburg and the policies of Maximilian II, though the latter's seeming sympathy with Protestantism continued to cause papal concern. Gradually and eventually there were better signs of Catholic restoration in the Austrian and Bohemian, if less clearly in the Hungarian, possessions of the Habsburgs. In the seventeenth century, after the outbreak of the Thirty Years' War, this encouraged Paul V to provide subsidies for the Emperor Ferdinand II, continued by Gregory XV. Even then, optimism was still possible about the specific defeat of Calvinism, as the Elector of Saxony maintained the Lutheran opposition, traditional among his predecessors since the later sixteenth century, to its toleration within the Empire. However the unavailing condemnation by Innocent X of the terms of the Peace of Westphalia could not in fact prevent the extension to Calvinist as well as Lutheran princes within the Empire of the right to impose religious uniformity in their territories.

It was in this context that Gregory XV had revived an expectation, more cautiously contained during Paul's pontificate, that Imperial authority should exact the restoration of ecclesiastical property in all territories recovered from Protestant control. Nevertheless the danger of this arousing the jealousy of even Catholic rulers within the Empire, chiefly of course Bavaria, was already noted at Rome. The fees charged at the multiple canonization ceremony of 1622, which famously ended the long delays over the Jesuits' founder Loyola, as well as elevating both other Spanish saints and also the virtual founder of the Roman Oratory, Philip Neri, were therefore to be divided between the barely co-operative forces of the Emperor and the Catholic League itself. As the prospect of Catholic restoration in northern parts of the Empire momentarily appeared, the pope's concern was that recovered ecclesiastical property should be available to support not necessarily traditional religious houses, but the active education and mission work of the New Orders, above all the Jesuits; and this had a pastoral rationale, over and above the known partiality of Gregory and Cardinal Ludovisi for the Society of Jesus. The same pastoral rather than political priorities were, after all, evident in the cardinal's provision at Rome for Catholic education of young Irishmen, and indeed the cardinal's ecclesiastical patronage in the city more generally exemplified a tendency for Counter-Reformation prelates to redirect the revenues they controlled as commendatory heads of older orders' houses, in Italy at least, to the educational and social work of New Orders.

In some respects the prospects for Catholic co-ordination against Protestantism still seemed promising in the early stages of the pontificate of Urban VIII, as Danish intervention in the war in the Empire proved to be less successful than had at first been feared, and as the Catholic powers of France and Spain were momentarily aligned against Protestant England. The French stance against England certainly appealed, as Richelieu calculated, to the ultra-Catholic interest still important within France, and was supported by Bérulle and the Queen Mother with the encouragement of the papal nuncio. Urban, however, resisted Richelieu's attempts to compromise the papacy directly, confining the promise of help to the traditional line of Sixtus V, that Roman funding would be made available only in the event of a successful landing of forces in England. Particularly, as he was aware of French diplomatic approaches to the Protestant Dutch and financial assistance to Protestant Denmark. For all that Urban was pleased by the victory of the French king and Richelieu against the Huguenot citadel of La Rochelle, participating himself in the celebratory Te Deum at the French Church in Rome, S. Luigi dei Francesi, despite fears on a previous occasion of a hostile reaction by the English government causing new difficulties for the Catholic Recusants. But as the Emperor's administration adopted increasingly strenuous measures to restore Catholicism in Bohemia, a potential division emerged between the Roman view, represented by the nuncio, which accepted the need for a reorganization and enlargement of the episcopal hierarchy in the kingdom, and the views of the Emperor's ever more influential Jesuit confessor, Lamormaini.

The confessor predictably stressed the crucial co-operation of Imperial and dynastic authority with the work of the regular clergy, not least the Society of Jesus itself, typifying an alliance which was only to be reversed in the Habsburg lands, in favour of the secular clergy, finally under Joseph II. Despite this, sufficient progress had been made in the reconversion of Bohemia to ensure that enforced Catholicism was not permanently overturned by the Saxon invasion of 1631 or the final attack of the Swedish army in 1648. The release of Cardinal Klesl, via Roman custody and then residence, permitted his eventual return to Vienna in 1628, where, until his death in 1630, he once again promoted a policy of moderation. The results of this in Lower Austria at least proved satisfactory, as Lutherans were distinguished from crypto-Calvinists and leading nobles were persuaded back to Catholicism by the promise of Imperial honours and preferment. But even before 1629 and the counter-productive Edict of Restitution, heavily influenced by Lamormaini, rivalry between the Emperor and Bavaria already complicated the filling of prince-archbishoprics and coadjutorships recovered from Protestant occupation in the centre and north of the Empire.

By encouraging an alternative conjunction of the Catholic powers of Bavaria and France, Urban thus hoped to prevent either the alienation of the former or the outright alliance of the latter with Protestant powers, even if such a policy inevitably contributed to Habsburg accusations that the pope was undermining the Catholic front against Protestantism. In fact the pope was more influenced by the desire to prevent France intervening in Italy itself, against the interests of both the Emperor and Spain, in the widely anticipated dispute over the Mantuan Succession. Thus while Urban's nuncios in the Empire and at Vienna were less alert to the dangerous reaction likely to follow the Edict of Restitution, they were still aware that diplomacy could not suffice against Protestantism, and that Catholic prelates of the Empire who were active in internal ecclesiastical reform, like the prince-archbishop of Salzburg, must at all costs continue to be encouraged.[1] Since Urban also feared that conflict in Italy over the Mantuan Succession would in any case distract Spain and the Emperor from confrontation with Protestantism in the Empire and the Netherlands, he was willing for a peaceful solution to be attempted by Imperial adjudication. But such considerations were essentially overtaken by the ironic effects of Richelieu's triumph over the Huguenots within France, which gave him greater freedom for open confrontation with the Catholic Habsburgs elsewhere in Europe.

The pope obviously applauded royal defeat of the Huguenot revolt in Southern France, and the reduction of Denmark to an agreed peace with the Emperor, even though both in fact increased the chances of violent conflict spreading into the Italian peninsula over the Mantuan question. The Edict of Restitution in the Empire, however, caused papal protest against the assertion of an Imperial monopoly in the filling of recovered bishoprics and benefices and administration of regained properties, to the exclusion of the Catholic League, or existing Catholic diocesans where relevant, or indeed the pope himself, despite his agreement to Imperial dynastic control of the strategic sees of Magdeburg, Halberstadt and Bremen. The damage done by the Edict to the wider Catholic cause was immediately evident, as the Catholic League refused support to the Spanish against the Dutch, and Catholic France's underwriting of Sweden allowed the latter to land its Lutheran troops in Northern Germany. Furthermore, Richelieu's disavowal of the peace terms agreed by Père Joseph, for the settlement of the conflict in Northern Italy, prevented Imperial forces being disengaged and sent against the invading Swedes. The cardinal might point to his own assistance in arranging an armistice for Catholic Poland with its dynastic Protestant enemy, Sweden, in 1629. By the terms of the formal treaty between France itself and Sweden in 1631, indeed, the Swedes

1 R. Bireley, *Maximilian von Bayern, Adam Contzen S.J. und die Gegenreformation in Deutschland 1624–1635* (Göttingen 1975); R. Bireley, *Religion and Politics in the Age of the Counterreformation. Emperor Ferdinand II, William Lamormaini, S.J., and the Formation of Imperial Policy* (Chapel Hill, NC 1981).

were supposed to respect the neutrality of the Catholic League and maintain Catholicism in conquered territories.

The threat to German Catholicism, and especially to the gains made by Bavaria, despite French reassurances to the latter, was nevertheless obvious to the pope. This accounted for Bavaria's need of financial concessions from the papacy, irrespective of Imperial protest, and despite the annual deficits now recorded in the papal finances themselves. As Urban's relations with the Habsburgs, and particularly Spain, reached their dramatic and notorious nadir, Bavaria's need remained pressing, since, while the Emperor himself once again faced revolt in Transylvania, the death in battle of the Swedish king, in 1632, did not remove the threat to Bavaria. Thus the resumed advance of the Swedish army necessitated new financial concessions to both Bavaria and the Emperor by 1634, dashed papal hopes of reuniting Catholic powers against both Protestantism and Islam, and in fact brought nearer direct French entry into the war against the Habsburgs. The direction of France's policy was indeed indicated by its invasion of Catholic Lorraine, in the face of the pope's rejection of the plea that this was a suitable reaction to Swedish occupation of Alsace.

Far from agreeing to Catholic co-operation against Islam, France was also reviving a traditional policy of diplomatic approaches to the Turks, while both France and Spain were manoeuvring for control of the middle Rhine, in ways which treated the major archbishoprics there as no more than strategic principalities. In such circumstances Imperial resolution to maintain the Edict of Restitution in its fullest terms understandably wavered, despite opposition from Lamormaini as well as the pope, and naturally from Bavaria too. The Emperor was nevertheless forced to agree to the Peace of Prague, in 1635, which effectively conceded Lutheran demands for the Edict's application to be qualified, despite protest once again registered by the nuncio. While Imperial concession in due course won the long-sought election of Ferdinand's heir as king of the Romans, and thus acknowledged a Catholic heir *de facto* to the Imperial title, the papacy's further aim in defending Catholicism within the Empire was to ensure that English pressure for the return of the Palatinate to Protestant dynastic control was resisted. Swedish invasion of Bohemia in 1639 increased papal concern to establish supervision by the Roman Congregation De Propaganda Fide of educational and missionary work in Bohemian, Austrian and Hungarian territories.

As early as the Diet of Ratisbon in 1640, however, it was feared that formal peace in the Empire, though actively pursued by papal representatives, might allow major concessions to the Protestants, not least over former ecclesiastical property. It was thus an example of the collective or bureaucratic memory of the Roman Curia that the terms of the protest lodged by the papal envoy Commendone in 1566, against just such concessions, were copied to the nuncio at the Imperial Court. But it also suggested the limited achievements, within the Empire at least, of the papacy's long-standing defence of Catholicism's apparent interests. The advantage to be gained from the fact that the confessors of so many Catholic monarchs (other than those of Spain, until a later date) were Jesuits had proved to be less than Protestant adversaries might imagine too. This also suggests that even with the special agency of the Society of Jesus supposedly at papal disposal, the obstacles to Catholic unity against Protestantism before 1648, let alone thereafter, were insuperable.

The ineffective papal protest in 1648 against the terms of the Peace of Westphalia was accompanied by a ruling which released Catholics from any promises made in the pacification for the handing over of former ecclesiastical properties. But at the end of the century the opposition of Innocent XII could not stop the creation of a new Electoral dignity in the Empire for the ruler of Protestant Hanover, nor could Clement XI halt the Imperial recognition of the Protestant Elector of Brandenburg as king of Prussia. The papal protest in 1701 against the Elector's assumption of the royal title did nothing to help relations with Prussia, before the later absorption of a Catholic population in Silesia necessitated an accommodation between the papacy and the Protestant monarchy. Former Jesuits were indeed to continue to work in Silesia, after the suppression of the Society of Jesus, for some time. Only in the pontificate of Benedict XIV did Rome begin to suggest the possibility of conceding the royal title to the ruler of Prussia, which Pius VI began to allow in recognition of Prussian restraint in the *de facto* settlement of the complaints raised about aspects of Roman authority by the German prince-archbishops at Ems in 1786. Benedict secured in 1748 an accord on the position of the Silesian Catholics, but was not able to defend the organization of the Catholic Church in Prussian territory entirely from royal interference.

It was also not until Benedict's pontificate, in the 1740s, that an attempt was made to provide supplementary Roman regulations concerning marriages between Catholics and non-Catholics, which had remained a social phenomenon in Imperial territories, irrespective of the intentions of the Tridentine marriage decrees. But the ecclesiastical principalities of the Empire were themselves threatened with secularization, in 1743, in negotiations between the Emperor Charles VII and Frederick II of Prussia. The foundation of the German College in Rome had meant that over a long period from the later sixteenth century onwards much of the Catholic clerical elite who would hold office in Imperial and Hungarian territories had been educated in a papal institution, but such Roman influence was not sufficient to prevent the eighteenth-century growth of Febronian sentiment in the German lands. Benedict XIV was willing for the Index of prohibited literature to be administered in a less stringent manner, but after the degree of sympathy which he had shown to Enlightened thinkers and writers (though not to Freemasonry), Clement XIII felt the need between 1759 and 1766 to condemn further developments, such as the *Encyclopédie* and works by Helvétius and Rousseau.

The flexibility which Gregory XIII had shown the Swedish monarchy over secularized Church lands, in the interests of a possible restoration of Catholicism, remains well enough established. But the extent to which King John III ever in reality reconverted even to a personal Catholic faith is more doubtful in the light of recent research. Whatever the apparent inflexibility of the papacy on other issues at the time, Gregory's hopes for the reconciliation of the Scandinavian kingdoms to Catholicism had already proved illusory, between his death and the end of the sixteenth century, with the unilateral deposition of Sigismund from the Swedish throne in 1599 and the exclusion of Jesuits and Catholic priests, enforced by penal legislation in both the Swedish and Danish territories. It was thus logical that the papacy should encourage the setting up elsewhere of institutions to train Catholic clerics for eventual reinsertion into effectively missionary territory, and this was pursued in places in both Polish and Imperial lands. This tradition of encouraging on Catholic soil foundations for clerical training to benefit Catholic survival in Protestant territories was also continued in the case of a Scots College at Eichstätt.

By his creation of the Roman Congregation De Propaganda Fide, Gregory XV had instituted a body which could devote attention to non-Catholic as well as to non-Christian areas. For the latter, the Congregation certainly became influential, even if more immediately the bringing of the Ethiopian Church into communion with Rome, under Jesuit direction, proved only a temporary achievement. When Gregory established the Congregation, at Epiphany in 1622, he stressed that the popes' 'chief duty' (itself a specifically Tridentine echo) was the spreading of the faith. A supposedly secure income for the activities of the Congregation could only be assured from the Apostolic Chamber, in part by the diversion of funds previously intended for maintenance of Rome's cathedral, the Lateran basilica. For it was above all financial difficulties which under Paul V had impeded plans to establish a permanent Congregation of this sort, after an experimental beginning under Clement VIII.

Gregory's emphasis on a double task, the conversion of both non-Christians and heretics, did not diverge from the ideals of Clement's pontificate. In 1622 the pope also renewed Clement's attempt to ban the permanent residence of heretics in Italy itself, even if in Gregory's case this was part of his plan to prevent heretical contagion in the peninsula, given his perspicacious fears that the ostensibly religious war newly resumed in the German lands might spill across the Alps. However, an earlier model still was that of the paired Congregations created for a while from 1568, in the pontificate of Pius V, one of which was intended to work for overseas extension of the faith, but the other for restoration of the faith in areas affected by heresy.[2] Under Gregory, the nuncio in Poland, for instance, was able to use the improved relations with the Crown in urging bishops to encourage the religious orders (not only the Jesuits) working there for the reconversion to Catholicism of those who had adopted one of the many varieties of heresy. But the attempt at this time to reintroduce Jesuit and other regular clergy into Sweden and into Denmark and Norway met with a swift reassertion of the penal laws against Catholicism in the two Scandinavian kingdoms.

2 G. Piras, *La Congregazione e il Collegio di Propaganda Fide di J.B. Vives, G. Leonardi e M. de Funes* (Rome 1976).

Urban VIII found himself unable to deter Catholic France from alliance with Protestant Sweden during the later part of the Thirty Years' War, despite his supposed sympathy with France, denounced by the Habsburgs. Similarly, for Clement XI, facing the severe difficulties created within Catholic Europe itself by the War of Spanish Succession, it was less easy to assist Catholic Poland, confronting in Northern Europe both invasion by Protestant Sweden and uncertain relations with Orthodox Russia, despite crucial papal diplomatic interventions, on occasion, in the elections to the Polish throne ever since 1573 and 1588. At the end of the eighteenth century, the concession allowed to the Protestant king of Sweden, on his visits to the Rome of Pius VI, to enable Lutheran worship to take place, won some relaxation of the Swedish penal laws at last. Only as a result of persistent diplomacy was the papacy able to preserve the rights of Catholics in other territories which had changed hands immediately prior to the Peace of Utrecht, since by its original terms, in 1713, these rights had been largely excluded. But in the longer term papal diplomacy was unsuccessful in attempting to prevent the moves towards partition in Poland.

Papal policy with regard to the English Protestant regime had in one sense been set soon after the conclusion of the Council of Trent, when initial caution towards Elizabeth I was replaced by the excommunication pronounced by Pius V in 1570, theoretically releasing her Catholic subjects from their allegiance. Gregory XIII urged Philip II to take action against Elizabeth, but it was the Catholic leadership within France of the early 1580s, directed by the Guise, that first suggested a campaign against her, to be prepared by renewal of the excommunication. Papal urging that Philip abandon Spain's earlier reserve about such hostility towards Elizabethan England was in any case overtaken by the appeal of Sixtus V for a revival of the traditional 'crusade' against the Islamic forces in North Africa. Indeed, Sixtus increasingly suspected that Philip's ambitions with regard to England and the eventual succession, in whatever circumstances, to Elizabeth turned even more on dynastic than on religious considerations. The grudging promise of papal contribution to a Spanish enterprise against England, secured in 1586, involved only half the sum requested by Philip, and payment was dependent on a successful landing in England, which did not in fact materialize.

Though the execution of Mary Stuart in some ways resolved doubts about the pressing need for the defence of Catholicism in England to be attempted, it left the confusions in English Catholic circles over the rightful succession to the English throne increasingly evident. The sensitivity of this question could only be increased in turn by subsequent controversy over a legitimate Catholic succession in France, where Spain's interests were also ever clearer. It was obvious that both questions were equally linked to Spain's attempts to regain and retain control of the Netherlands. Amid the reflections on the failure of the Armada of 1588 the opportunity to suggest that the Spanish monarchy's infringements of ecclesiastical rights caused divine displeasure was not missed by the pope.[3] Philip II, however, still hoped to gain the right of nomination to bishoprics in a yet-to-be-conquered England, while urging on the papacy the claims of the Catholic League in France to receive subsidy.

But his appeal for a renewed attempt on England to be declared a crusade failed to secure papal agreement. The papacy was aware that the king was demanding subsidies from the Spanish bishops towards the projected replacement armadas which were still being planned. The periodic papal grants of ecclesiastical revenue raised within Spain itself were, however, intended to support first the traditional campaign against Islam, and only as a subordinate project attacks on Christian heresy. The papacy's own financial needs dictated the sale of alum from the papal states to Protestant England, despite Spanish obstruction. The death in 1590 of the native Catholic claimant to the French throne, the aged Cardinal Bourbon, could only undermine any Spanish and papal agreement on priorities, even before the conversion to Catholicism of Henri of Navarre in 1593.

King James of Scotland was also willing to hint at a possible conversion, in pursuit of his own claims to the succession in England and, hence, in Ireland too. James had in fact aroused little more than vague expectation at Rome, but he had helped secure the exclusion of an alternative, potential claim by Spain to the English throne. Such a claim, deriving originally from the marriage of Mary Tudor and Philip II, though controversially championed by the English Jesuit Parsons, would certainly not have fitted well with the inclinations of Clement VIII. Nevertheless, despite further profession of respect for the pre-eminent honour of the papacy, James made his perspective on papal jurisdiction clear enough by his suggestion that the pope should agree to summon a new, reforming General Council of the Church. This was, at the least, unrealistic, and obviously less likely to find an echo in Clement's Rome than the king's specifically anti-Jesuit views. However, already conspicuous was the royal challenge to any expressions of papal authority which could be construed as entering the temporal sphere, chiefly of course in relation to the excommunication or attempted deposition of monarchs.

Such concern was only made more urgent by the discovery of an apparent Catholic treason, the Gunpowder Plot, in 1605. As background to the question of an oath of allegiance to be taken by English Catholics, this was decidedly unpromising. Any oath which required explicit rejection of the pope's unfettered authority was obviously unacceptable, as was made clear by Paul V and Cardinal Bellarmine. The subsequent escalation of published polemics over papal authority was the result of James's literary ambitions. Whatever the co-operation of other scholars, the king was anxious that the polemical works should show his own authorship.

The *Apology* which first appeared in 1608 thus followed the Venetian Interdict, and, in response to Bellarmine, criticized supposed papal attack not only

---

3 A.S.V. Spagna, XXXIV, 65r ff.; XXXV, 47r ff., 64r ff., 447r–v: 1587–90.

on medieval rulers but also on Henry III of France and Elizabeth of England. Editions were published in Latin and French as well as English. While a revised version was being prepared, orders were also given for the editing of Barclay's *De Potestate Papae*, an absolute attack on any papal claims to temporal authority. But to the revised issue of his own work, James added a monumental preface, the *Premonition*. After a false start at the beginning of April, 1609, authorized editions appeared in May, not only at London in Latin, French and English, but also at Amsterdam in Latin and Leiden in Dutch. Catholic rulers other than Henri IV of France refused presentation copies, and when the Venetian Republic, after much manoeuvre and papal objection, accepted one, assurances were given that the work would receive no circulation at Venice.[4]

The anxieties of James were hardly reduced, however, by the assassination of Henri IV in 1610. The pontificate of Clement VIII had seen an end to Spanish involvement in Ireland, and Spain extended to James I as king of England the peaceful relationship which he had previously enjoyed as king of Scotland. But the problem remained of allowing the Catholic community in England itself an acceptable expression of their *de facto* loyalty to the Protestant monarchy in secular affairs, and papal authority was central to that. This was so even when it was made clear that the papacy had effectively suspended any requirement that English Catholics withdraw their obedience from the Protestant monarchs in matters other than religion. As the French clergy, encouraged by Cardinal du Perron, finally accepted the Tridentine decrees in 1615, following anti-papal resistance and assertion of Gallican rights at the Estates-General, James attacked this other cardinal in *A Remonstrance for the Right of Kings*, a publication which he had prepared with the assistance of a Huguenot polemicist. Latin, French and English editions once again appeared, and in Paris too.

But though this series of publications represented a high-water mark in the articulation of Protestant criticism of papal authority, it had in fact little effect on the evolution of papal office or of papal policy, despite the fact that Hobbes may have subsequently drawn on the attack made by Marc'Antonio De Dominis on both Baronius and above all Bellarmine for the latter's defence of papal authority. More long-lasting, on the other hand, was the effect of French controversy, renewed after the assassination of Henri IV, as a *parlementaire* attack on the supposed Jesuit defence of regicide advanced to a virtual rejection of any papal claims to temporal authority. The varieties of Gallicanism which were involved here did not, of course, necessarily support episcopal rights, as Cardinal Rochefoucauld recognized, in leading the French clergy to their acceptance of the Tridentine decrees in 1615. But though the internal divisions of Gallican opinion had already been further revealed, by the publication of Richer's views, asserting clerical as opposed to episcopal rights, the exercise of papal authority in France remained controversial. While the covert

4 A.S.V. Venezia, XXXVIII, 21r ff., 325v ff.: 1607–8; cf. A.G.S.: Estado: Negociación de Roma: Leg. 990: 1609.

200

anti-episcopalism as well as overt anti-papalism of the Venetian dissident Paolo Sarpi increasingly had a diminished practical effect in the Republic, after the Interdict of 1606–7, French sensitivity to papal authority and papal policy remained manifest.

In all such matters the received image of papal policy was arguably more potent than the reality, so that the 1572 massacre of French Protestants, that of St Bartholomew, was widely held by Protestants to be a horrid revelation of international Catholic conspiracy. But in England the penchant of James I for entering literary controversy on religious as well as political issues ensured that papal condemnation of an oath of allegiance remained a public question. That remained the case even though Charles I proved relatively more flexible than James I over the wording of an oath to be taken by the English Catholics; and this arguably contributed to the papacy's reluctance to allow the recreation of an episcopal hierarchy with ordinary jurisdiction over the Catholic community in England. From 1621, however, Gregory XV was able to use the tentative discussions of a Spanish match for the heir to the thrones of England and Scotland as an opportunity to pursue better conditions for British Catholics. For the aim of the English government was chiefly to modify Spain's treatment of James's son-in-law, Frederick, the Protestant Elector Palatine, after his brief interlude as king of the Bohemian rebels against the Habsburg Emperor. Prospects for concessions over the Catholic community in England seemed better than previously, when in different circumstances Paul V had refused to contemplate dispensation for an Anglo-Spanish marriage.

Despite diplomatic contact with the Prince of Wales via the nuncio in Spain, however, the treatment of Catholics in Scotland and Ireland was reported to be far from improved. After the punitive fiscal treatment of English Catholics following the defeat and execution of Charles I, the restoration of the monarchy in the person of Charles II raised some hopes of relaxation. But once again a Catholic marriage, in this case to Catherine of Braganza, from the royal house of Portugal as it recovered independence, did not in the event enable Rome to obtain much benefit for the English Catholics. While the Exclusion Crisis did not succeed in removing the king's brother from the succession on the grounds of his Catholicism, the so-called Popish Plot revived a more general persecution. The eventual succession of James II in 1685 proved the cause of even greater delusion, since the voicing of Roman alarm at the Catholic king's policies, for their potentially counter-productive effect within England, simply damaged relations, which were in any case complicated by the family interests of the queen, Mary of Modena. Anti-Catholic feeling in England was reactivated by the Revocation of the Edict of Nantes in 1685, when Louis XIV proclaimed the supposed conversion of the Huguenots to Catholicism.

The brevity of James's reign, as it turned out, meant the collapse of attempts to legalize Catholic practice and restore public Catholicism, following the king's flight in 1688; as well as an obvious check to James's hope of mediating between the pope and Louis XIV. Despite that, the initial difficulties faced by the Catholic communities in Britain following the succession of William and Mary in place of James II gradually gave way to an easing of conditions during the eighteenth century, until the anti-Catholic Gordon Riots of 1780. As the end of the Stuart line within Britain approached, Clement XI had failed to persuade Queen Anne to recognize the Catholic pretender, James Stuart, as her heir. Innocent XIII subsequently increased papal support for James, offering financial aid for an expedition to gain the British throne. But international diplomatic pressure had caused James to leave Avignon for Rome itself in 1717, where he remained until his death in 1766, with hardly an interruption. Although the papacy continued official recognition of the Stuarts in exile, to 1766 at least, the chances of restoring Catholicism in Britain by means of a Jacobite restoration were slim, as was indeed clear by the time of Charles Edward's residence in Rome itself. The dedication of Cardinal Henry, Duke of York, to his ecclesiastical duties subsequently allowed the tentative resumption of papal diplomatic relations with the Hanoverian regime.[5]

In the later sixteenth century, however, the fears of European Protestantism about the supposed intentions of the papacy remained acute, typified by the conviction that a meeting of the French Queen Catherine de' Medici with the duke of Alba and other leading Spaniards at Bayonne in 1565 was the occasion of a global anti-Protestant conspiracy. But the apparent increase in the power of Philip II, represented by the acquisition of Portugal in 1580, in fact enhanced papal caution over Spanish policy towards Protestant states, or divided states like war-torn France. In any case, a more immediate problem for the post-Tridentine papacy, anxious to avoid further schism and loss of Catholic obedience, was Valois nomination to French bishoprics of prelates who were suspected of heresy. The excommunication which Sixtus V had pronounced on Henri of Navarre, making him ineligible for the French throne as an apostate, was confirmed by Gregory XIV, despite initial signs that Henri might consider reconversion to Catholicism. Since Gregory had also contributed to the maintenance of the Catholic League, it was far from clear that papal policy would change after the succession of Clement VIII, even when Henri was received into the Church by leaders of the French episcopate.

Spanish pressure against a change of policy was counter-balanced by Venetian representations and information presented via Cardinal Alessandro de'Medici. The Tuscan ruling dynasty was to renew its relationship with France under Henri, the first Bourbon king, through his second marriage, though the Medici connection with the Valois had not helped to bring about legal recognition of the Tridentine decrees in France. Venetian and Tuscan interest lay in diminishing Spanish dominance over Catholic Europe in general and the Italian peninsula, the papacy included, in particular. The unilateral papal elevation of Cosimo de'Medici as *grand*-ducal ruler of Tuscany from 1569 had, however, seriously compromised Roman relations with the Emperor and with Spain for

5 A.S.V. Spagna, XXXIV, 569r ff.: 31 Oct. 1588; F.A. Gasquet, *Great Britain and the Holy See, 1792–1806* (Rome 1919).

some time. That Alessandro's pontificate (as Leo XI) in succession to Clement lasted only a month removed any possibility of this former Legate to France achieving what Clement had not managed to do, pursuing Henri's promise to bring about legal reception in the kingdom of the decrees of the Council of Trent.[6]

While in the British Isles the death of Elizabeth had allowed an Anglo-Spanish peace to be concluded by the new king from Scotland, training abroad for Catholic clerics who could then return to serve the Recusant communities remained a necessity. This was recognized by Clement's creation of a Scots College in Rome, as well as continued patronage of those colleges set up in Spanish territory, despite his resistance to any reassertion of Spanish dominance in the affairs of Catholic Europe. In the early decades of the seventeenth century the papacy was concerned about a prospective advance of specifically Calvinist Protestantism in Europe. But Calvinists were, if anything, even more alarmed at apparent signs of imminent Catholic repression. The confrontation between Paul V and the recalcitrant Venetian Republic, eventually adjusted with French mediation, caused concern to Protestant powers in Europe, including England. This was not because of any respect for papal sanctions, but rather because of fears that Spain was planning armed intervention in support of the pope, which the latter might have welcomed but on which Spanish policy was in fact far from decided.

The pastoral concern of Gregory XV to confront Calvinism whether in the Palatinate, the Netherlands or France was also interpreted in a political light. Thus his understandable alarm at the prospect of Huguenot insurrection in a still imperfectly stable though officially Catholic kingdom was represented as a desire to see Bourbon France prosper at the expense of the Habsburgs and of Spain in particular. The papal priority of keeping warfare out of Italy itself, in these circumstances, led to a momentary consideration of support for a diversionary attack on the Calvinist capital of Geneva by the duke of Savoy, a plan which the dukes raised at intervals but which more normally met with distinct Roman reserve. Nevertheless, as Louis XIII attempted to reassert his own authority in France after the political uncertainties following the assassination of Henri IV, Gregory insisted that force alone would not defeat French Calvinism; and that therefore better co-operation between Crown and papacy was necessary, if the long-delayed internal reform of the French Church, and especially of the religious orders, were to proceed. It was in this context that Cardinal Rochefoucauld was beginning to attempt reform of some of the French regulars, using, in effect, a combination of papal authority and royal authorization.

The recognition by the Peace of Westphalia of Calvinism, in addition to Lutheranism and Catholicism, within the territories of the Holy Roman Empire might therefore seem to indicate the failure of papal diplomacy. Yet it

---

6 A.S.V. Venezia, XXXI, 102r ff.: 5 July 1595; cf. M. Wolfe, *The Conversion of Henri IV. Politics, Power, and Religious Belief in Early Modern France* (Cambridge, MA 1993).

was precisely Imperial conditions which thereafter raised once more the question of potential reunion within Western Christendom. The highly personal and inevitably idiosyncratic initiatives of a few seventeenth-century individuals elsewhere, revealing French interest in the Anglican Church for example, were unlikely to produce substantial results. In the Netherlands, however, at the beginning of the century, the attractions to some of a Christian Neo-Stoicism, which seemed to rise above religious divisions, had at least paved the way for the international scholar Lipsius to return to Roman obedience after his temporary employment among Protestants. Similarly, in the first half of the eighteenth century, there were rather more sustained contacts between members of the Catholic Church in France and, less openly, of the Anglican hierarchy, but, given the Gallicanism of the French protagonists, Rome was unlikely to be impressed. The royalist prelate, Bossuet, had been more realistic in his famous correspondence with the Protestant philosopher Leibniz, following the start of the official campaign to enforce, by whatever means, the reconciliation of the Huguenot minority in France, when he insisted on the non-negotiable nature of the Tridentine decrees.

Within the Empire the potential fluidity of dynastic succession in different territories suggested other prospects. Some leading families were themselves divided in religion, as were the children of Frederick, the ill-fated Elector Palatine and sometime Calvinist king of Bohemia. In some areas Lutheran practice remained at least superficially conservative, as to the decor of churches (in conscious opposition to Calvinism), the splendour of church music and even a partial retention of the liturgical use of Latin, for instance. More striking than non-Catholics at Strasbourg for a while sharing the official status of members of the cathedral chapter were the alternations between Catholic and non-Catholic holders of the see of Osnabrück, which managed to leave in place a continuous Jesuit contribution to local education. Accordingly, a number of discussions about ecclesiastical reunion took place in the century and a half after 1648, prompted not least by the prospect of an individual's changing religion to secure the succession in one state or another. Although Catholic representatives were involved, like the Capuchin Magni, any Roman hopes of the recovery of Hanover for Catholicism, for example, were disappointed. This was despite the more prominent involvement in the 1680s and beyond of a Catholic prelate, Rojas y Spinola, who pursued a vision of religious reunion within the Empire.

The unusual degree of interest in this displayed by Clement X and Innocent XI was stimulated chiefly by their anxiety to encourage Christian unity against the Turks. The failure of the Turkish siege of Vienna in 1683, almost exactly a century before Pius VI felt forced to travel to the Vienna of Joseph II to defend the Catholic Church against the Emperor's own interventions, reduced the intensity of this anxiety. Thereafter, as the eighteenth century advanced, the desire of some German princes and prelates, whether Catholic or not, for religious reunion to strengthen the Empire was increasingly at odds with natural Roman distrust of such 'patriotism'. For it was associated with Febronian criticism of papal authority and of Roman Curial practice. Benedict XIV, it is true, reiterated in 1749 the long-standing ideal of Christian reunion; and Cardinal Quirini's scholarly knowledge of the sixteenth-century English exile and Marian restorer of Catholicism, Cardinal Pole, promised eirenic discussion. But figures of the pre-Tridentine and early Conciliar crisis of the sixteenth century, like Contarini and Pole, remained ambiguous for Catholic argumentation, the full range of their original opinions not necessarily being revealed in later publications.[7]

The continued schism of the Church of Utrecht provided a similarly ambiguous focus for debate. A Jansenist spokesman, Dupac de Bellegarde, attempted to act as a contact between the French and Dutch Jansenists on the one hand, and the Imperial Court and the German princely prelates on the other. But the essential anti-Romanism of his Jansenism, which might appeal to proto-Febronian feeling among the prelates critical of Rome and to a 'Josephinist' attitude at Vienna (which historians have stressed pre-dated the succession of Joseph himself as Emperor), was almost calculated to alienate the popes. Such sentiments occasioned caution even in an Electoral prince-archbishop who was otherwise anxious to see the schism in the neighbouring Utrecht province resolved, after all. Such prelatical reserve also countered a later reunion plan prompted by some Benedictines of Fulda, even without the inevitable disapprobation of the papacy. However, the continued absence of union between Catholics and Protestants was obviously not the only potential concern of the papacy; Western Europe was not of course synonymous with Western Christendom in any case.

JEWISH COMMUNITIES

The policy of the post-Tridentine papacy towards Jewish communities was in one sense typified by the positions adopted towards those in Rome, the papal states and other Italian states. In Rome, as at Ancona, the papacy, for its own financial benefit not least, allowed communities which practised Judaism, though under restrictive and disadvantageous conditions. Outside papal territory the Venetian government imposed its own strict conditions on Jewish communities in Venice itself, in Padua, or in Corfu and Crete. But papal concern, expressed in the case of Venice through the local Inquisition, was to prevent Judaizing, in the sense of the return to Jewish belief and practice of any who had once been baptized. Since this inevitably implied suspicion of those from families of Iberian origin, who were most likely to have received baptism, whether willingly or not, it was natural that the post-Tridentine papacy should attempt to dissuade the duke of Savoy from his plan to open his state to such persons. Elsewhere in Northern Italy, however, by the

7 M. Batllori, *Cultura e finanze: studi sulla storia dei Gesuiti* (Rome 1983), pp. 153–74; P. Simoncelli, *Il Caso Reginald Pole. Eresia e santità nelle polemiche religiose del Cinquecento* (Rome 1977), pp. 214–41; G. Fragnito, *Gasparo Contarini. Un magistrato veneziano al servizio della Cristianità* (Florence 1988).

beginning of the seventeenth century, the Spanish government had determined on the expulsion from Lombardy of the remaining Jewish families, and this was eventually carried out to a substantial degree.

The immediately post-Conciliar popes were in no way opposed to such a measure, and renewed papal restrictions on Jewish texts at this time illustrate a position adopted towards Jewish communities generally, throughout Catholic Christendom. By the eighteenth century the papacy would nevertheless approve a repudiation of the popular 'blood-libel', which had alleged systematic Jewish murder of Christian children. However, towards the end of that century some revival of anti-Jewish sentiment could be detected in Italy itself, despite the growth, for example, of a Jewish community in the Tuscan port of Livorno. Outside the peninsula the determination of policy was very much in the hands of Catholic secular governments, irrespective of papal attitudes. It is difficult, for instance, to see any precise evidence for the argument, though recently advanced with great articulacy, that supposed Counter-Reformation hostility to certain types of economic activity encouraged the growth of anti-semitism in pre-partition Poland.

For territories under papal temporal rule, however, Pius V had ordered the expulsion of all Jewish communities other than those of Rome and Ancona, in 1569. While the Comtat Venaissin was included in this order, the magistrates of the city of Avignon resisted it for reasons of financial interest. The pope at the same time renewed all restrictions on Jews imposed by previous popes since the time of Clement VII, removing their right to collect ancient debts from Christians and limiting their interest-taking and their rights against debtors generally. In 1578 Gregory XIII renewed the order for the expulsion of Jews from all papal territories, though once again the magistrates of the city of Avignon were opposed to this, just as they had seemed to ignore the edicts of Pius V against 'usurious' interest more generally. By 1580 the Jews of Avignon were succeeding in gaining papal permission to pursue their debtors, even, in certain cases, when otherwise prohibited by the bull of Pius V. In any case, the Cardinal de Bourbon, while Legate of Avignon, had exempted the Jews there from the effects of the bull. Gregory XIII eventually seemed to accept this situation, though it was he who at Rome, in 1584, reactivated the compulsory sermons designed to convert the involuntary audience of city Jews.

After a seemingly more relaxed atmosphere in the pontificate of Sixtus V, Clement VIII revived restrictive policies. His bull of 1593 ordered the expulsion of Jews from all papal territories, except for Rome, Ancona and Avignon, and a second bull ordered the destruction of Jewish books. The latter was reflected, for example, in decrees of the Avignon provincial council of 1594, which went further than those of the provincial council of 1574 which had insisted on the physical separation of Jews and Christians. Such responses were also encouraged through the tribunal of the Inquisition at Avignon, which by the end of the sixteenth century was clearly under the direction of the Roman Holy Office, rather than under indirect control via the governing Vice-Legates or the local bishops. The development of a *Monte di Pietà* in post-Tridentine Avignon, however, extended to that enclave the original Italian solution for providing a Christian source of credit; just as, in Italy itself, the government of the Tuscan state had developed such an institution at Florence, whatever the clerical doubts about the interest rates allowed there.[8]

Papal authority had allowed in 1564 the publication of a revised and expurgated version of what was in fact the Talmud, though the title was prohibited. But by 1592, anticipating the tone of Clement VIII's bull, the Cardinal Vicar, Rusticucci, renewed restrictions on the Roman Jewish community. Yet further north in the peninsula communities were expanding in the last decades of the sixteenth and first decade of the seventeenth century, at least in the territories of the duke of Savoy and in Mantua. In the states of the peninsula which contained communities, the Jewish population continued to grow, reaching perhaps 25,000 in 1637 and probably 30,000 by 1700. Among the policies pursued by Gregory XIII were his attempts in 1581 to reassert earlier prohibitions on Jewish doctors treating Christian patients and, with less effect, to extend Inquisitorial authority over alleged blasphemy by Jews.

The relatively more relaxed attitude introduced by Sixtus V, on the other hand, resulted in numerous Roman grants of licence for Jewish banks: 148 licences were granted to Jews in Rome, Ancona and the papal states, while between 1587 and 1609 more than 300 were granted for banks in Italian states other than the Venetian Republic. Indeed, in 1586 Sixtus had opened all trades to Jews, even where food-stuffs were involved, and permitted the hiring of Christian workers, though not domestic servants, by Jews. But the preceding restrictions of Pius V had had some effect beyond the papal states themselves. In 1567 the Republic of Genoa extended throughout its territory the expulsion of Jews already enforced in the capital. Between 1567 and 1571 the ducal authorities in Tuscany prohibited money-lending, cancelling existing contracts, imposed a yellow badge to be worn by Jews, and attempted to confine Jews in Tuscany to ghettos in Florence and Siena.

This took place in the context of the papal grant to the Tuscan ruler of the title of grand-duke, celebrated in 1569, which was the culmination in many ways of continued co-operation between Florence and Rome over ecclesiastical and other issues ever since the last stages of the Council of Trent. At Venice the publishing of Hebrew books remained possible, despite censorship and confiscations. The Republic's vote to expel the Jews in celebration of the Christian victory at Lepanto was swiftly reversed, while the papacy remained outraged rather by the Venetian peace treaty with the Turks, which did not recover Cyprus, but seemed to undermine the naval victory.[9] By contrast, Clement VIII's pontificate, despite restrictive policies towards Jews in other respects, saw a Jewish community confirmed at Ferrara, after its annexation to the papal states. At Rome itself the Jewish community was estimated in 1734

8 Archivio della Curia Arcivescovile, Milan: Archivio Spirituale: Carteggio Ufficiale: vol. 56, nos 8–9.
9 A.S. Ven.: Capi del Consiglio dei Dieci: Lettere di Ambasciatori: Roma: busta 25, nos 124 ff., 128 f., 164 f., 194, 195 ff., 205: 7 Oct. 1570–3 May 1573.

at just over 4,000 persons, excluding children under four years old, a figure very close to that reached by a census of the ghetto in 1656.

But the Roman community never recovered in economic terms from the papal prohibition of money-lending at interest in 1682. Debt accumulated in the eighteenth century, until the community formally declared its bankruptcy in 1755. Total private wealth within the community apparently shrank too, to less than a third of its original level, between 1701 and 1781. The issues involved in the baptism of the children of Jews (and other non-Christians) without parental consent were clarified by Benedict XIV, in such a way as to leave room for the Christian education of such children irrespective of parental wishes, while discouraging the forced baptism of either adults or children. But conversions to Catholic Christianity also of course included those from Islam.

ISLAM

The ideal of a united Christian confrontation with Islam was retained by the post-Tridentine papacy and actively pursued into the eighteenth century. The initial success of the immediately post-Conciliar papacy in stimulating the formation of a Catholic League against the Turks was the result of long and difficult negotiations, especially in the face of persistent suspicion between Spain and Venice as Mediterranean powers. The victory of Lepanto in 1571 was counter-balanced by the Venetian loss of Cyprus, and thereafter papal protests at recurrent Venetian truces with the Turks were usually ineffective, despite the threat to refuse permission for the Republic to levy the traditional *decime* on clergy in its dominions, nominally to support confrontation with the infidel. Papal criticism of aspects of Spanish policy equally touched on the periodic renewal of permission for the monarchy to raise ecclesiastical levies supposedly devoted to such campaigns. By the time of Clement VIII papal attention was concentrated on the Austrian Habsburgs and encouragement of campaigns in Hungary, such as the anti-Turkish war conducted from 1593–94 onwards. Financial support for such activity was nevertheless problematic, as even Spanish Habsburg co-operation, necessary for levies on clergy in Southern Italy for instance, proved difficult to obtain.

Papal efforts were more obviously successful in support of the defence of Malta against Turkish siege by the Knights of St John, but in the later seventeenth century the Venetian loss of Crete by 1669 represented the substantial failure to achieve adequate Catholic assistance to the Republic from other states. The problem of France's refusal to abandon its traditional and developing relations with the Turks, even in the face of the siege of Vienna in 1683, made it all the more crucial that the papacy was able to gain King John III Sobieski's intervention from Poland at that juncture. Thereafter the papacy faced the mixed results of Catholic reconquest, with some lasting success in the case of Austrian campaigns in Hungary and the Balkans by the early eighteenth century, but with no permanent result in the case of Venetian recovery for a while of Greek territory. More quietly consistent was papal support for a Franciscan presence in the Holy Land, under European protection. But otherwise the papacy's ability to defend the interests of Christian populations under Islamic rule was essentially confined to encouragement of Uniate Churches, alongside the work of religious orders devoted to the ransom of Christians from Islamic captivity. The reconciliation of Christian apostates, converted more or less willingly, usually while captive, once they had returned to non-Islamic society was an area of Inquisitorial activity, but the tribunals chiefly involved were those of the Spanish Inquisition, in Spain itself, the Balearics, Sicily and Sardinia.[10]

The Inquisition in Malta, which came to be under Roman direction, also dealt with such cases, but the island's security against the threat of Islam still had to be maintained even after the siege of 1565. The post-Tridentine papacy could only achieve, at best, momentary co-operation against Islam among Catholic states, the Protestant powers such as the Dutch and the English being more ready to establish working relations, for commercial benefit, with the Turks. The same was increasingly true in the seventeenth century of Catholic France, however, even if this provided some shield for the presence of Catholic ecclesiastics, such as Capuchins and sometimes Jesuits, at Constantinople. Papal priorities, on the other hand, involved expenditure not profit. The subsidies provided by Clement VIII to the Habsburgs in 1594–95 amounted to 600,000 scudi. Yet Clement appealed in vain for Spain and the Venetians to join a revived Holy League, like that of 1570, while hoping that the Swedish king, Sigismund III, would take up the struggle against the Turks in his other role as king of Poland.

By 1597 Clement was sending to the Hungarian front his own military force, under his nephew's command, and he repeated this in 1598, as well as subsidizing the efforts of the prince of Transylvania. Indeed, his nephew died during the renewed campaign of 1600. Attempts to secure Transylvanian independence from Habsburg hegemony could easily disrupt the Hungarian struggle, furthermore, as the papacy had already feared in the preceding decades. But in 1601 Clement was still hoping, as Philip II had done before, to encourage the Persians to open a second front against the Turks. After the long distractions of the Thirty Years' War, its closing stages coincided with the growing Turkish threat to Venetian-ruled Crete, which led Innocent X, after his election, to promise the Republic the possibility of levying troops in papal territory, something not always conceded in the past.

Indeed, after the pontificate of Urban VIII, whose choice of name harked back to the crusading era, something like the former Holy League appeared in 1645, when the Venetians' own defence of Crete was joined by five galleys sent by Innocent and galleys also from Tuscany, Spanish-ruled Naples and Malta. But French intrigue at Naples was soon to distract Spanish attention. By 1649–50 the pope was himself distracted, sending no galleys, because of his renewal of the war of Castro, in central Italy, so fruitlessly begun by

10 A.G.S.: Estado: Sicilia: Leg. 1163, fo. 173: Mar. 1609.

Urban VIII. In 1657 papal aid to the Venetians was again renewed, though the pope's nephew, commanding the squadron sent by Alexander VII, found it difficult to co-operate with the commander of the Maltese squadron which was also involved. The pope's own difficulties with France contributed to the refusal of Venetian requests for renewed French help in the Cretan War, despite French assistance to the Emperor in 1664.

The election of Clement IX in 1667 promised better relations with France. The new pope sent five galleys under his nephew as his own contribution. Thus after the conclusion of the Franco-Spanish hostilities of 1667–68, Louis XIV was prepared to revive the French assistance originally provided in 1660, after the Franco-Spanish Peace of the Pyrenees in 1659. Once again something like a Catholic League was formed, with the presence of galleys from Spanish-ruled Naples and Sicily, in addition to papal and Maltese squadrons, despite a repetition of the problematic relations between allied naval commanders. By 1669 papal efforts had obtained promises of co-operation in the struggle from both France and Spain, securing the French by recognizing the king's right to nominate to the bishopric of Tournai, a recent acquisition. Even so, the French contribution in 1668–69 had initially sailed under the flag of the Knights of Malta, in an attempt to avoid disrupting the traditional relations between France and the Turks. The French presence, however, did not prevent the surrender of Crete in 1669.

After papal failure to secure active French co-operation, as opposed to Polish relief, at the time of the siege of Vienna, Innocent XI had more success the following year, 1684, in confirming a Holy League to carry the war on against the Turks, in which the Emperor Leopold I, King John III Sobieski of Poland and the Venetian Doge were to co-operate. The pope himself also provided a military contingent, until the close of campaigning in 1687. Despite the extraordinary pressures which Clement XI faced during the Spanish Succession War, at the start of the eighteenth century, he tried to interest the Emperor Charles VI in helping the Venetians by an attack on the Turks in Hungary. When the pope himself finally established peaceful relations with the successful Philip V of Spain, in 1715, he also obtained a Spanish promise not to attack the Imperial possessions in Italy if the Emperor went to war with the Turks. Further concessions to the Emperor were necessary, in the form of permission for levies on Austrian ecclesiastical properties, parallel to Venetian privileges, and a Venetian promise to help guard Naples in the event of Bourbon attack. Only thus was an alliance in 1716 established between Charles and Venice to make war on the Turks.

An immediate victory by Prince Eugene allowed celebrations in Rome as well as Vienna. In order to capitalize on this, Clement made a new concession to the Emperor, who had received a subsidy of 400,000 florins in addition to the grant of 1716, allowing a further levy to be raised over five years on the clergy of Naples, Milan and Mantua. Venice too was given permission to impose a levy on the ecclesiastical possessions within the Republic for the two years 1716–17. Papal success seemed to go further, despite the unpromising precedents of the Spanish Succession struggle, when Philip V of Spain promised naval and military reinforcements, in return for papal permission for a royal levy on the Spanish clergy over five years. Portugal made an independent promise of assistance too.

But papal trust was once again misplaced, as the Spanish expedition of 1717 in fact occupied Sardinia, to the inevitable fury of the Emperor, dismay of the pope and embarrassment of the Venetians. Although the Spanish ambitions were in due course defeated by a European alliance, the Turks obviously gained a respite from this diversion, and the Emperor and Venice had also made peace with them. Thus from 1718 Imperial gains were consolidated but the balance of Venetian recovery and retreat was essentially negative. During the wars of 1768–74 and 1787–92 waged by Russia against the Turks, the Republic attempted to remain neutral, while its remaining Greek subjects demonstrated a solidarity with Orthodox Russia rather than with Catholic Venice. Joseph II and Kaunitz, the chief minister of Maria Theresa, in turn considered a plan to dismember the Venetian Republic, even if without pursuing the matter.

In the case of Poland, however, Clement X had encouraged defence against the Turks, and though the Protestant king of Sweden, Charles IX, refused assistance, Orthodox Russia eventually made its own alliance with the Poles. The pope and also Cardinal Odescalchi subsidised the army prepared by John Sobieski, prior to his election as king in 1674, but French moves against the Dutch once again proved a diversion from any united effort against the Turks. In the same way, despite the willingness of Innocent XI to send a papal representative to the peace negotiations at Nijmegen, in Protestant Dutch territory, Louis XIV accepted omission of any reference to papal representation in the ensuing pacification and unfavourable conditions for Catholics within Protestant areas. Innocent's hopes of a solid front against the Turks were further diminished by renewed tension between Russia and Poland, when Sobieski supported Hungarian revolt against the Emperor Leopold I, on the basis of promises from Louis XIV to deflect Turkish attack on Poland. Indeed, French pressure was working in Poland against papal encouragement of an anti-Turkish stance. The pope persisted in providing subsidies for the defence of Vienna as siege threatened, and kept the subsequent Holy League in being despite French attempts to detach Poland. The contrast was again evident, despite papal success in encouraging a renewed alliance between Poland and Russia, when Louis XIV ordered the bombardment of another maritime republic of Mediterranean Christendom, in 1684, in his attack on Genoa.

In 1688, once again it was the entry of France into European war that halted the Imperial campaign against the Turks, despite papal subsidies. Such aid diminished in any case after the election of Alexander VIII, because relations with the Emperor deteriorated, against a background of Venetian jealousy of Imperial military success. The pope's family finances, embarrassed by costly ennoblement in support of the Venetian war effort, stimulated his brief revival of conspicuous nepotism. Innocent XII had served as nuncio in Vienna as well as Poland, but as pope he saw relations with the Emperor again deteriorate. Polish policy was disrupted by the death of Sobieski in 1696, though from the elevation of the Elector of Saxony to the Polish throne the papacy was able to gain the eventual satisfaction of the new king's conversion to Catholicism. The papacy thus persevered in leadership of Christian Europe against Islam but with mixed success.

OVERSEAS MISSION

The effective limitations on papal ability to superintend the missionary extension of Catholic Christianity beyond Europe had already been established before the Counter-Reformation, indeed before the Reformation. At the Council of Trent no specific attention was given to the peculiar problems of the Church in overseas or non-Christian territories, and the role of the papacy remained essentially that determined by pre-Conciliar developments. The bull of Alexander VI of 1501 which conceded to the Castilian Crown tithe income from the Indies placed on the monarchy responsibility for the support of churches and clergy there. By a bull of 1508 the papacy awarded to the monarch the patronage of all the churches and the right of presentation to benefices there. In this respect the model for the papal privileges was the arrangement made after the conquest of the Islamic kingdom of Granada in Spain itself.

But what became the royal *patronato* exercised in control of the Church overseas was also based on two bulls issued by Alexander in 1493, one of which granted to the Castilian Crown sovereignty and jurisdiction over all islands and lands situated West of a notional meridian, and imposed the obligation of evangelizing the non-Christians of such territories; while the other accorded royal regulation of access and residence in these areas, which was understood to include the movements and presence of regular and secular clergy. The Spanish monarchy based on these foundations its further claim to order ecclesiastical communications from overseas to be maintained only with Spain, not directly with Rome, to exclude appeals from overseas to Rome, and to prevent unauthorized return to Europe by clerics sent abroad. The Spanish Crown did not acknowledge the jurisdiction of the Roman Congregation De Propaganda Fide, after this had been founded by Gregory XV, in any of its overseas territories. Thus, in this sphere of potential responsibility, the post-Tridentine popes were in fact limited by the actions of the pre-Tridentine papacy. This conditioned the development of ecclesiastical practice overseas.

For example, by the post-Conciliar era initial mendicant optimism in Mexico about the creation of a native clergy had given way to a hostility to such a notion shared by the mendicants and the Crown, and partly reflecting renewed concern in Spain itself about 'purity of blood' among the clergy and particularly the religious orders. The arguments of a Jesuit missionary with American experience, who managed despite royal policy to make direct contact with Rome, were in favour both of better pastoral provision for the imported negro population, and also of a native clergy, but in practice the papacy was impotent to alter Spanish opposition to the latter, which was maintained until a much later date. In questions which the popes wished to raise about the Church in the Spanish overseas empire representations to the king had to be made via the nuncio at the royal Court, and the monarch might or might not order a memorial to be passed to the Council of the Indies, which exercised royal jurisdiction in the overseas territories in all matters both temporal and ecclesiastical. The post-Conciliar papacy therefore suggested at times that nuncios or Vicars Apostolic should be admitted to the overseas empire. But though the Crown expressed momentary interest, if royal appointment of such a figure could be promised, this would obviously have limited the value to the papacy of any such envoy. Similarly, the Patriarchate of the Indies remained an essentially titular honour, held by prelates in Spain itself who acquired extensive jurisdiction over the chapel royal, and divorced from any real supervision of the Church overseas.

Royal control was underlined by the special oath of loyalty to the Crown introduced in 1629, after the creation of Propaganda Fide, further emphasizing the dependence of the overseas episcopate on the monarchy. The popes could not prevent the arrest of ecclesiastics by local secular authority overseas, not even of bishops, while overseas bishoprics often suffered long vacancies as nominations were made by the Crown, or nominees awaited permission to travel abroad, or waited in America for their episcopal ordination. Despite the occasional involvement of Spanish prelates in the affairs of the Council of the Indies, simony in ecclesiastical appointments handled by the Council was sometimes suspected.[11] The monarchy successfully controlled the finances of overseas dioceses, including the estate of deceased bishops and the revenue of vacant sees. It was not papal but royal policy which originally made possible the development of the famous, independent Jesuit Reductions in the interior of South America; just as Spanish, Portuguese and French expulsion of the Jesuits in the eighteenth century had an obviously traumatic impact on the overseas missions generally, before papal suppression of the Society.

Even the precocious ability of some metropolitan archbishoprics overseas to hold provincial councils, as ordered at Trent, at an impressively prompt date after the conclusion of the Tridentine Council itself, must not therefore be understood as a sign of papal influence. Provincial and diocesan, as well as eventually parochial boundaries were determined not at Rome but by the responsible royal council in Spain. The papacy intervened in this evolution chiefly to modify the relations of bishops and regulars in pastoral activity, relaxing the Tridentine insistence on episcopal regulation of preaching and hearing of confessions by regulars which the popes more consistently sustained in Europe; whereas overseas they were thus tending to revert to the

11 A.S.V. Spagna, XXX, 376r ff., 414r ff., 440r ff., 496r ff.; XXXI, 54r ff., 257r ff.; XXXIII, 85r ff., 450r ff.; XXXIV, 69r ff., 100r ff., 247r ff.: 1584–88; A.G.S.: Negociación de Roma: Leg. 980: 1605; Comisaria de Cruzada: Leg. 516; A.D. Wright, 'The Institutional Relations of Church and State in the Overseas Iberian Territories', *Hispania Sacra*, XL (1988), 693–9.

pre-Tridentine position confirmed by Hadrian VI. The papacy claimed that bishops overseas were bound, like European diocesans, to pay periodic *ad limina* visits to Rome, though at longer intervals, but in reality the Crown controlled the movement of prelates back to Spain, let alone to Rome. Yet royal supervision did not in fact prevent continued conflict in the overseas empire between seculars and regulars, not least over financial resources, and bishops there came to clash not only with mendicants but with Jesuits too.

Economic and social conditions overseas prevented any successful application, after the Council of Trent, of the papal programme to eradicate private property among nuns and reduce the entry to female convents to that of girls with a genuine individual vocation, duly tested by the diocesan in order to detect parental coercion. The mendicant origin of some of those appointed to overseas bishoprics did not itself prevent dispute between diocesans and regulars. Nor was episcopal authority overseas left for long without the competing presence of the Spanish Inquisition, which, as in Spain itself, was for all practical purposes independent of Roman authority. Such conditions, including the export of a peninsular inquisitorial jurisdiction, were largely replicated in coastal Brazil, not only during the period between 1580 and 1640 when the personal union of the Iberian monarchies was in force, for the papal award of 1493 had specified the jurisdiction of the Portuguese Crown to the East of the crucial meridian.

The Iberian monarchies

The principle and application of such a division were agreed by the two Iberian Crowns between themselves. Yet even between 1580 and 1640 the papacy had to deal with concurrent, not integrated, overseas administrations, since the royal Council of Portugal was continued by the Spanish monarchs, and it preserved its own responsibility for Portuguese overseas territories. This ensured that the Portuguese royal patronage rights overseas, forming the *padroado*, were fully maintained. Control of ecclesiastics' passage overseas was enforced, just as in the Spanish empire; nor was the choice of bishops for overseas bishoprics necessarily always better than that made by the Council of the Indies. Indeed, the development of a clear provincial and diocesan structure in the Portuguese overseas possessions was a slower affair than in the Spanish empire, with damaging consequences in both China and Japan eventually.

Moreover, the personal union of the Iberian monarchies did not alter the distinct nature of Portuguese overseas expansion, which outside coastal Brazil differed from the Spanish pattern of conquest and settlement, found not only in Mexico and the West Indies but from the lowlands at least of Peru to the Philippines. Beyond Brazil the Portuguese empire was rather a series of enclaves, such as those of Goa and Macao, surrounded by vast areas which were in fact under native not European control. From Brazil to the East Indies it was also the Portuguese empire which suffered the most from Dutch attack, and this Dutch antagonism was not much affected by the eventual struggle of Portugal itself for independence from Spain. Above all the post-Tridentine papacy faced a new problem not provided for in the original papal allocation of overseas jurisdiction to the two Iberian Crowns. In the Far East, the expanding Spanish presence, extending Westwards from America across the Pacific, came into conflict with the claims of the Portuguese Crown to control not only the route to the Cape but all that lay to the East of that. The personal union of the monarchies did virtually nothing to reduce this confrontation of two competing jurisdictions. Such national rivalry presented the papacy with an even graver difficulty, as the Spanish missionary presence in the Far East was chiefly represented by mendicants, the Portuguese missions chiefly by the Jesuits, at least initially.

It should not, however, be assumed that the papacy faced an easier prospect in overseas territories where the original papal division of global responsibility between the two Iberian Crowns alone had little practical effect. The post-Tridentine papacy lacked both the financial resources and the personnel to move rapidly towards independent missionary endeavour under directly Roman control. This was seen in those areas of North America and, eventually, other parts of America and the West Indies which came into French possession. What in practice determined missionary conditions there were not Rome's dispositions but the presence or absence of royal support, eventually developed under Louis XIV and subsequent rulers as a *de facto* royal patronage system parallel to the formal rights enjoyed by the Iberian Crowns. When the Catholic monarchies of eighteenth-century Europe extracted from the papacy the suppression of the Society of Jesus, this confirmed the Crowns' expulsion, from all overseas territories under their control, of a missionary force closely connected, at least in theory, with Roman authority.

Papal influence in the overseas missions

The Society's overseas activities, involving complex financial liabilities, added in fact to the allegations used in Europe itself in the anti-Jesuit campaign. The independence of the South American Reductions was also unacceptable to eighteenth-century colonial monarchy. But long before this important element in European overseas missions was eliminated, the papacy had begun an attempt to recover some real influence in the overseas missions. By the beginning of the seventeenth century some ecclesiastics were already well aware of the unsatisfactory state of the Church in such areas as the Spanish overseas empire. This stimulated the planning of a body of missionary clerics who would be subject to Roman not royal control, and who might be free from the counter-productive rivalries between the religious orders.

Tentative designs begun under Clement VIII produced more coherent proposals under Paul V. These were at the origin of the papacy's creation of its own organ of supervision, the Roman Congregation De Propaganda Fide, instituted by Gregory XV in 1622, and the subsequent erection of a special seminary for the work of the Congregation by Urban VIII in 1627. But the reaction of the Iberian Crowns was distinctly negative, as was suggested by the timing of the new oath of loyalty in the Spanish empire. The Spanish Crown continued to insist that reports from bishops overseas be sent to the Council of the Indies, not to any Roman tribunals, whether the Congregation of the Council or Propaganda. Similarly, it remained difficult for the papacy to assert real control, as opposed to theoretical authority, in an area claimed by Portugal as its own, such as India.

A global perspective had in one sense not been lacking at Rome even at the time of the Fifth Lateran Council, since from the early sixteenth century the papacy had encouraged French participation in the discovery of new lands overseas, initially in the North Atlantic, despite the terms of the original papal arbitration between the claims of Spain and Portugal. The reality of French, just as much as Iberian, independence in the overseas missions was evident however, whether in the rivalry of the priests of the *Missions Etrangères* who joined in the North American effort alongside French Jesuits, or in royal support for the subsequent exclusion by the bishop of Quebec of the Jesuits from Louisiana. The succession of Bourbon rulers to the throne of Spain, and control of its overseas possessions, from the early eighteenth century, indeed altered the relations of the papacy and the Crown with reference to the missions. For the Bourbon regime did not recognize the papal grant of jurisdiction as the necessary and crucial foundation of its overseas *patronato*. It demonstrated a conviction of its own independent rights in this sphere by subjecting the Jesuits in particular to closer supervision in the missions, even before the expulsion of the Society from Spanish territories in 1767.

Initial co-operation between the papacy and the French Bourbon monarchy allowed the creation of the bishopric of Quebec in 1674 by Clement X, who also canonized Rose of Lima, as America's first saint. But a century later the suppression of the Society of Jesus in French territory, together with political change in North America, seriously reduced missionary effort. On the other hand, the effect of British Protestant rule was to increase pro-Roman sentiment among the North American Catholic population, despite their traditionally Gallican outlook. Pius VI, faced with the success of the American War of Independence, accepted the local clergy's own choice, a member of the suppressed Society of Jesus, as bishop of Baltimore, and subsequently created another see at New Orleans. Meanwhile Benedict XIII had provided another American saint, Toribio of Lima.

In the Spanish overseas empire, however, royal, subsequently viceregal permission was necessary for diocesan synods, which were to be held in the presence of the viceroy or to have their decrees approved by him and by the king. Irrespective of papal rulings, similarly, a royal decision of 1574 announced support for episcopal authority in conflicts with regulars, but this was never fully implemented. The attempted intervention of the short-lived Pope Gregory XIV on behalf of the native population of the Philippines was equally of limited effect, as indicated by the observations of Spanish regulars about the continued oppressive behaviour of some colonists and administrators there. Knowledge of the real conditions in overseas missions was constantly pursued under the aegis of the Congregation De Propaganda Fide, as was suggested when in 1658 Alexander VII condemned the continuing restrictions on the access of American Indians to the full range of sacraments, specifically communion. Subsequently, Clement IX felt obliged to condemn the commercial involvements of missionaries in both the East Indies and America. His successor Clement X extended protection to the idiosyncratic Portuguese Jesuit Vieira, whose undoubted patriotism had not shielded him from local Inquisitorial authority, in the wake of Portugal's recovery of independence; in part because of his continuation of the Jesuit tradition of denouncing where necessary the ill-treatment of non-Europeans in the overseas colonies.

Following the encouragement in 1682 by Innocent XI and Propaganda of a renewed Franciscan mission in Mexico, Clement XI urged regulars to create training-colleges for each order's missionary work, which could again be seen as attempting to increase missionary manpower more amenable to papal than to Crown direction. However the ancient tensions between the papacy and the Crown in Spanish America continued. A major summary of the regalist theory of the *patronato*, published between 1629 and 1639, had been put on the Roman Index in 1642. But precisely because of the independence from Rome of the distinct Spanish Index and its sole currency in Spanish territories, the Roman prohibition was of no practical effect. Under the Spanish Bourbons indeed the remit of the Council of the Indies extended to appointing visitors to inspect the religious orders overseas. The intervention of royal and viceregal authorities in the eighteenth century, for example, also caused considerable delays to the extension of the Franciscan mission in California. On the other hand, a new hospitaler order founded in Mexico, similar to those of the European Counter-Reformation, was able to secure official recognition from Clement VIII in 1594, while another such specialist order set up in Central America, South America and Mexico received papal recognition in 1672.

The presence in parts of Africa, by the eighteenth century, of other religious orders in addition to the Jesuits, allowed at least limited missionary work there to survive the Society's suppression, and the Italian Capuchins in Angola, for example, looked to the Roman Congregation De Propaganda Fide, even if also making necessary acknowledgement of the Portuguese *padroado*. Rome had eventually confirmed the *padroado* of the Portuguese Crown, following the recovery of independence, but this did not prevent the monarchy imposing a new oath of loyalty on non-Portuguese clerics in those overseas territories which were in fact, not just in theory, controlled by Portugal. Such tensions preceded Portuguese resentment of the papacy's early eighteenth-century condemnation of Jesuit experimental practices in India, which included variations in the baptismal rite and toleration of child marriages. The ineradicable caste system, however, had of necessity to be recognized. But in any case Jesuit work in India would eventually be brought to an end by the cumulative expulsions of the Society from both Portuguese and French territory.

The peculiar problems encountered by Christian mission in the subcontinent were complicated by Portuguese insistence that royal authority was paramount, not only at Goa itself but beyond that enclave. The Jesuit experiment in assimilative missionary methods, directed at the highest caste in India, was begun by Nobili, but eventually, despite initial apparent approval by the Holy Office and Gregory XV, it succumbed to papal disapprobation, confirmed in 1744. For although the missionary problems found in India and China were in fact very different, a common campaign criticizing Jesuit experimental missionary methods was provoked among Catholic opponents of the Society, not least mendicants. The separation of converts from the different castes proved an unavoidable necessity in India, and the papacy's gradual approval of the presence in the subcontinent of a large number of different religious orders, of both pre- and Counter-Reformation origin, reflected the practicality of allowing some social specialization in the orders' work there. Nevertheless the growing campaign against the Jesuits' innovatory missionary methods eventually won a negative judgement from the papacy, despite its earlier sympathy with Italian Jesuits working in India but facing Portuguese hostility to their degree of independence.

At Goa the arrival of the Franciscans, in 1517, had preceded both the creation of a bishopric, in 1534, and, by definition, the presence of the Jesuits after the arrival of Francis Xavier in 1542. The Theatines too subsequently attempted to recognize only the authority of the Roman Congregation De Propaganda Fide, as opposed to the royal *padroado*. But the Portuguese authorities in the East, at least within the enclaves of effective control, could deploy not only viceregal but also Inquisitorial jurisdiction against recalcitrants, given the practical independence of the Portuguese, just as of the Spanish Inquisition, from Roman supervision. A papal envoy, Tournon, was in due course detained by the Portuguese at Macao. By 1704 a papal representative had nevertheless condemned the Jesuit assimilative missionary methods in India, for reasons which can be seen more clearly when the Chinese case is considered, despite, as noted, the very real differences in the conditions encountered in the two areas. But India had also presented another problem to the papacy, following the European encounter there with the native St Thomas Christians.

The peculiar difficulties raised by this confrontation between an ancient Christian Church and the post-Tridentine form of Catholic Christianity were not fundamentally resolved by such plans as those of the Jesuits to educate Malabar Christians in Cochin, in order to inculcate attachment to Roman ways.[12] An attempt was indeed made to Latinize their Church, specifically under the influence of the regular orders, especially after the death of the last native metropolitan of the St Thomas Christians. But this proved at least partly counter-productive, as schism resulted. The Portuguese insistence on maintaining the claims of the *padroado* in the Malabar complicated resolution

---

12 A.S.V. Spagna, XXX, 496r ff.; XXXI, 257r ff.: 1585.

of the schism, quite apart from the disruption caused by Dutch incursions. The division of the St Thomas community between those recognizing and those refusing Roman obedience was thus perpetuated to the end of the eighteenth century, despite the efforts of the popes and of Italian Carmelites working locally on their behalf. The attempted Latinization, pursued not least by the Jesuits, faced native objection in particular to enforcement of clerical celibacy, as reaffirmed for the Western Church at Trent.

As the Tridentine teachings on sacramental doctrine and practice were introduced, fear of subjugation to Portuguese authority interposed. The profession of faith eventually imposed by the Portuguese-appointed archbishop of Goa on the Malabar clergy was essentially the Tridentine one, and the decrees of the Council were indeed declared binding on the Malabar Church, which was also pronounced to be subject to the Portuguese Inquisition at Goa. The see of Goa remained vacant for a long period in the later seventeenth century, in the prolonged tension between Rome and Portugal after its recovery of independence, not least over episcopal appointments. But even previously, when a Jesuit was provided as bishop, subsequently archbishop, for the Malabar Christians from the beginning of the seventeenth century, his jurisdiction was disputed by the Portuguese bishop of Cochin, and criticized by mendicants, who were always opposed, in India as in Japan, to Jesuit enjoyment of episcopal office. The native archdeacon of the Christians, previously the administrative if not liturgical superior of his Church, also remained disappointed, and led a revolt against the new bishop. The Portuguese claimed patronage rights over the new archbishopric, and Vicars Apostolic acting directly on the papacy's behalf were unable to end the schism.

But the more general difficulty for the papacy of asserting an independent authority in the overseas missions was also evident in India, once again in the use of French ecclesiastics as a force distinct from the clergy under the Iberian Crowns. French missionaries, specifically Capuchins in the case of India, opposed the Jesuit assimilative missionary methods in the subcontinent. Criticism had already persuaded the papacy to formulate a condemnation, even before it was pronounced by a local papal representative, once again a Frenchman. The Jesuits' protests against the condemnation combined with the Portuguese objection to the intervention of papal and French authority, which revealed the extent to which the Jesuits' presence in India was integrated into the operation of the *padroado*. Roman confirmation of the condemnation nevertheless followed in 1734 and 1739, while after four decades of uncertainty and dispute such condemnation was only temporarily relaxed by Benedict XIV, who in Europe enjoyed the reputation of an unusually enlightened pope, but here alluded to the necessity of Augustinian rigour.

The arrival of the English in eighteenth-century India created a new obstacle to exercise of specifically papal authority there, however, even if the English were more tolerant of Italian missionaries than of clerics openly avowing loyalty to the Portuguese *padroado*. The Dutch expulsion of the Portuguese from Ceylon, by the second half of the seventeenth century, brought a halt there to the work of Europeans from a number of religious orders, whose activities had been regulated by the Crown not the papacy. Clandestine Catholicism was able to survive nevertheless, despite Dutch penal laws, not least because of the presence of a native clergy. For in the Portuguese East, there was never a total opposition to the creation of native priests, and eventual Jesuit, papal and Propaganda favour towards such a development was not so obstructed, despite the exclusion in India of low-caste converts from membership of some religious orders. The subsequent replacement of the Dutch by the English in Ceylon hardly helped the papacy to contribute to the survival of Catholicism there, while the English came to assert an alternating influence, alongside the Portuguese, over the most senior ecclesiastical appointments in the Catholic Church in India.

Jesuits and other regulars in the missions

Elsewhere in the East the arrival of orders other than the mendicants and the Jesuits went some way to support papal attempts from the mid-seventeenth century onwards to create a missionary presence independent of the Portuguese *padroado*. But while Barnabites came to work in Burma and Theatines in Borneo, as well as Oratorians in India, French clerics of the Parisian *Missions Etrangères* from early in the reign of Louis XIV represented the growing ambitions of the French Crown in the East, initially by their presence in Indo-China. Spanish penetration of the area had preceded this, but a Jesuit mission had been expelled from one part of Indo-China for a while. Moreover, earlier in the seventeenth century the experience of the French Jesuit, Père de Rhodes, had convinced him of the need for a native clergy and missions independent of the Iberian Crowns. Yet the French impetus to criticism of Jesuit missionary methods in the East was eventually to have implications for the Society's work in Indo-China just as in China itself. After the suppression of the Society but before the end of the eighteenth century, the French Crown even made an unsuccessful approach to Rome for formal recognition of royal patronage rights in the area, despite the continued presence of Spanish and other missionaries alongside French clerics.

In the East Indies the papacy was faced with the convergence of both Spanish and Portuguese missions, and the presence of Jesuits and mendicants, old orders and new. By the end of the seventeenth century the pope's authority was represented by an Italian Vicar Apostolic in Borneo. But both Dutch and Islamic encroachment limited the success of the Catholic missions in this area; even before final Spanish recognition of Dutch independence in the mid-seventeenth century, the earlier twelve years' truce had not necessarily been observed by the Dutch in the East. The consolidation of the Spanish *patronato* in the Philippines provided a better defence against the spread of Islam, but it still did not prevent counter-productive tensions between secular and regular clergy, bishops and regulars, Jesuits and mendicants, which the papacy was in practice ill-placed to resolve with any lasting success.

An initial prospect of co-operation between the papacy's global authority and the delegated agency of the Portuguese Crown, in the exercise of its overseas *padroado*, was suggested by the agreement of Gregory XIII in 1576 to create a bishopric at the Portuguese enclave of Macao on the Chinese coast. But such a decision could not prevent later conflict, when the papacy wished to create bishoprics in the interior of China, with responsibility also for areas such as Tonking, Cochinchina and Formosa. This was opposed by the Portuguese, particularly anxious to reassert their Crown's monopoly of ecclesiastical supervision in the East after the struggle to regain independence from Spanish rule in the Iberian peninsula itself. The determination of independent Portugal to defend its ancient *padroado* overseas led, among other things, to protest at Rome over the appeal of the Spanish Dominican Navarrete for confirmation of the decision by Urban VIII to allow missionaries of any origin to go to China and Japan by routes other than the Portuguese-controlled Cape route. For in 1585 a papal brief had given the Jesuits a monopoly of the Japanese mission, conducted within the framework of the Portuguese *padroado*.

Japan

But the papacy recognized, by the end of the sixteenth century, that it could not in fact enforce a Jesuit monopoly of the mission in Japan. The entry of Spanish friars from the Philippines, in addition to the existing Jesuit mission under the Portuguese *padroado*, could not in practice be prevented by rulings from Rome. The tragic effects of the rivalry of the two missionary groups in Japan demonstrated the unreality of Portuguese claims to a monopoly of supervision in the East, Japan included. It also revealed the failure of the papal design to unify missionary endeavour there by bringing it entirely under a local bishopric, as opposed to that of Macao, given the friars' resistance to episcopal authority exercised by a Jesuit. The bishop's authority in any case proved to be ambiguous in relation to the internal command structure of the Society of Jesus itself in Japan and the East.

The papacy was unable to provide more than general encouragement for the Jesuits in Japan, despite the Society's public relations success in leading a Japanese delegation to Italy in the late sixteenth century. The 'embassy' of young and mainly well-born Japanese created a great impression at Rome itself, as well as at Venice, Florence and Milan. Equally evident was the inability of the Portuguese Crown to give substantial financial support to the Jesuit mission in Japan, once missionaries had been shipped out to Macao and across to Japan itself. That was the origin of the Jesuit system of self-support in Japan, which clearly but fatally involved the Society in trading activities between Japan and Macao, and, consequently, even in the temporal administration of an important enclave in Japan. The papacy could not prevent internal political developments in Japan which led to the increasingly anti-Christian policy adopted by the shoguns, who were attempting to reduce the independence of feudal lords, and of necessity to halt the further conversion of retainers of those who had adopted Christianity.

But in 1640 the final exclusion of European Christians from Japan came too soon for the Jesuits' inevitably lengthy preparation of a native clergy to have reached a self-sustaining conclusion. In any case ordination of further generations of such clergy would obviously have been difficult and dangerous if not impossible. The initially uncertain but finally determined waves of persecution within Japan thus enabled only a clandestine lay community to survive in isolation, deprived of the sacraments, except potentially baptism. The slow beginnings of a native clergy in Japan had encountered particular difficulty with the necessary acquisition of Latin, and the problem, to be met also in China, of a suitable terminology for the Christian Deity was resolved in Japan only by the use, in all discourse, of the Latin word for God. Dutch encouragement, though not initial instigation, of Japanese governmental suspicion of Spanish designs, as represented by the friars' arrival from the conquered Philippines, allowed the Jesuits and the Portuguese trading presence to become suspect too, as the union of the Iberian monarchies had not been broken before 1640.

The fact that some of the Jesuits in Japan, as elsewhere in the East, were not themselves Portuguese did not help to save the Japanese mission. Obviously Spaniards would be unwelcome in any case, once the Japanese rulers had realized that the king of Portugal was, at this date, none other than the king of Spain. But whereas Ricci, as an Italian Jesuit, was able to make some initial progress in China, despite having arrived under the Portuguese *padroado*, the involvement of Italian Jesuits in Japan was of no avail. After a peasant revolt involving Christian converts in 1638, the final determination from 1640 to close Japan to European Christians was relentlessly pursued, just as Portugal began its own resistance to Spanish rule in the Iberian peninsula itself.

China

The seeds of the conflicts in China which the papacy sought to resolve were evident from an early date too. The Jesuit Ricci, who introduced an initial version of the assimilative missionary methods favoured by many of the Society's members in China, arrived there in 1583, and a Franciscan friar, Martín Ignacio de Loyola, self-evidently not of Italian or Portuguese origin but Spanish, followed in 1585. His expulsion by the Chinese authorities, however, aroused some suspicion of Jesuit collusion in this reaction. From the Jesuits, on the other hand, Clement VIII in 1600 withdrew any absolute monopoly of missionary activity in China, allowing the use of any routes for missionaries to enter either China or Japan, thereby of course legitimizing the Spanish and mendicant route across the Pacific in addition to the Portuguese and Jesuit route via the Cape. The evolution of conditions inside China, both political and cultural, in any case forced the Jesuits there to reconsider the initial version of their assimilative approach.

In 1628 a meeting convened in Nanking province to review their policy of accommodation revealed a range of internal criticisms. This dissent subsequently became known to one of the Jesuits' most articulate external critics, the Spanish Dominican Navarrete, who learned more of it from François Pallu, bishop of Heliopolis, who had himself been informed by some French Jesuits. The Jesuit Jean Valat, for example, opposed allowing Chinese converts to continue the traditional veneration of ancestors, which caused mendicant critics of the Society to regard him as an ally. But the Portuguese Jesuit, João Rodrigues, known from his virtually political and mercantile activities in Japan as 'The Interpreter', was also opposed in the Chinese mission to Ricci's version of accommodation. The opposition of such a local expert influenced the revisionist position adopted by Longobardi, successor to Ricci as superior of the Chinese mission, above all on the contested significance of a possible Chinese term for heaven or the heavens. This accounted for the frankly critical tone of his treatise composed in 1623–24, which a vice-provincial of the Society, Furtado, accordingly sought subsequently to destroy. But a partial copy reached mendicant hands, when the French Jesuit Valat showed it to the Franciscan Antonio de Santa María who in turn showed it to Navarrete.

Philip IV, who was still at the time king of both Spain and Portugal, ruled in 1632 that all religious orders were free to travel to both China and Japan by either the Pacific or Cape route. The logistic factors of distance, finance and personnel which reduced effective papal initiative in the overseas missions were immediately evident in the reaction of Urban VIII, who responded by repealing in 1633 the already qualified Jesuit monopoly of the Chinese mission. Precisely in 1633 a Dominican, Morales, entered China. By 1638 friars had reached Peking, and their observation of Jesuit methods furnished subsequent allegations that the Jesuits refrained from frank preaching of Christ crucified. A local conference was refused by the Jesuits, however, who sent a member of the Society, Semedo, to Rome to secure papal approval. But this move was complicated by the publication in Manila of a Jesuit defence by Roboredo, who had no direct experience of China; and though this was disavowed by the Society's own superiors, that could not prevent its being used in Europe by Jansenist critics of the Jesuits.

The opportunity which Rome detected for loosening control of the Eastern missions from the grip of the Portuguese Crown was also maximized by the policy pursued by Ingoli, the influential and active secretary of the papal Congregation De Propaganda Fide. Whatever his attitude within Europe to specifically Jansenist critics of the Jesuits, it was symptomatic of his missionary strategy, intended to enlarge papal influence and confine Crown control overseas, that in 1645 he complained to the Dominican Morales that the Dominicans failed to supply systematic reports to Rome on their Chinese missionary work, unlike the widely published Jesuit accounts. The report presented at Rome in 1645 by Morales was on the Jesuits' activities in China, and his adverse criticism caused Innocent X and the Holy Office to arrange a formal response from the Congregation De Propaganda Fide, which Morales served on the Jesuits in China in 1649. But for the time being at least the Jesuits were equally adept at Rome in appealing to the papacy's desire to free Eastern missions from Portuguese Crown control. The Jesuit Martini, like some of the other Italian Jesuits who served in the Eastern missions under the *padroado*, was in fact critical of the Portuguese authorities, and in 1656 he secured, in response to the Morales document, a decree from Alexander VII in the Society's favour, which Navarrete in turn attempted to have revoked but without success. The Jesuits therefore regarded the 1656 decree as authorization to continue with their evolved version of assimilative missionary method in China.

But the Jesuits also appealed to the Portuguese Crown, on more general grounds, requesting its favour for their loyalty to the *padroado*, as they continued practical resistance to papal abrogation of their original monopoly of the Chinese mission, as incidents showed in 1649 as well as later, in 1673. Ambiguity resulted from the ruling secured by Morales, which appeared to prohibit as superstitious the veneration of ancestors and of Confucius, when compared with the subsequent decree obtained by Martini, which seemed to reflect the initially favourable attitude of the Propaganda Congregation towards assimilation, by permitting at least some of the contested Rites. The mendicants, not least as a result of the campaigns of Navarrete, were to counterattack once more, with some apparent success, securing decrees in their interest from Clement IX in 1669 and Clement X in 1673. But while internal discussion of missionary methods continued among the Jesuits themselves to 1665, and indeed beyond that date, they were for the time being careful not to allow members of the Society to publish any criticism of the Riccian principle of accommodation. Once again political and cultural change in China's internal affairs provoked a new set of difficulties, awaiting eventual papal reaction, when from 1664 the imperial authorities ordered a severe confinement of the missionary presence.

While both Jesuits and Dominicans attempted to remain, the former at Peking and the latter in provincial hiding, nevertheless between 1664 and 1670 a group of both was interned at Canton, supposedly awaiting banishment to Macao; and was thus provided with a prolonged and enforced opportunity for fraternal criticism, reminiscent of the painful disputes over correct strategy under proscription which in Elizabethan England had divided clerics such as those Catholic priests incarcerated by Protestant authority at Wisbech. The Dominican attitude in the East had in one respect been arguably very different from the established, even if not the initial, mendicant views in Spanish America. For during the 1664–70 confinement of European missionary activity in China, good work could still be done in the provinces by a native convert, Lo Wên-tsao, known to his fellow Dominicans as Gregorio López, whom the Dominicans in the Philippines had allowed to be priested, before any possible ban on the ordination of natives might be encountered. Indeed, it was the Dominican Navarrete who subsequently urged that this native priest be made the first Chinese bishop, inside China, whatever the implications for the Portuguese claims that the see of Macao possessed comprehensive jurisdiction. In fact the wider missionary problems in the East, including the questionable propriety of assimilative methods, were well known in the Spanish Philippines themselves.

The conjunction of conflicts which the Eastern missions presented to the papacy was further compounded when, in Europe, the personal reign of Louis XIV began. While within France the monarchy was about to disband at least the central organization, as opposed to provincial units, of the movement of *dévot* origin, the *Compagnie du Saint-Sacrement*, the relatively new foundation to promote overseas Catholic mission, the *Missions Etrangères*, opened a seminary to train missionaries at Paris in 1663. This potentially provided, for the papacy, a new reservoir of missionaries for work overseas who would not be bound to the formal patronage systems of the Iberian Crowns, nor be members either of the Society of Jesus or of the mendicant orders. Despite the obvious ambitions of the French Crown to extend its own informal but effective patronage of Catholic overseas expansion, there was some possibility at least that such French manpower might complement the clerical forces trained at Rome itself for mission work under neither Crowns nor religious orders, since the founding of the Propaganda seminary there by Urban VIII in 1627. Thus the original vision among a handful of ecclesiastics in the pontificates of Clement VIII and Paul V, of a body of secular clerics working in the missions under direct papal authority, might be fulfilled.

Bishop Pallu, whom the Dominican critic of the Jesuits in China, Navarrete, encountered on a voyage taking him eventually to Europe after his escape from Canton to Macao, was a founder of the *Missions Etrangères* of Paris, an institution which also adopted a positive approach to the ordination of native clergy. But the bishop's presence in the East also represented the papal use of French ecclesiastics to assert Roman authority in distant locations, by their appointment as Vicars Apostolic, despite the rejection of their jurisdiction by the Portuguese Crown. The bishop had been visiting Paris to enlist the further support of Louis XIV, a reminder of course that the papacy was hardly escaping reliance on European monarchical authority in fact. His own reports to Rome were favourable to Navarrete; and it is not surprising that the Spanish friar expressed his own views in favour of the Vicars Apostolic and against the Portuguese *padroado* in the East. The Spanish Crown naturally aimed to defend its own *patronato* in the East as well, and Pallu, as a papal envoy, was arrested in the Philippines in 1674 and sent to Spain in 1676, though released in 1677.

The papacy was thus facing a competition between three, rather than just two sources of European authority in the East, even if partly as a result of its own initiative, quite apart from the continuing conflicts between religious orders. So it was symptomatic that in 1668 an Italian Jesuit in Canton complained to the General in Rome about his own local superior in the Society, a Portuguese, who was provocatively offensive to Spanish missionaries. Yet while the Portuguese continued to oppose the activities of Spanish friars in the

East, the latter remained critical of the Jesuits not only for their missionary methods but also for their undoubted commercial involvements, intended to support their missions, and their alleged money-lending at high rates of interest thought normal by the Chinese. The Jesuits were even accused of complicity in the Dutch capture of Formosa, which blocked one route for mendicant entry to provincial China, though the frustrations encountered by the Society itself in the Spanish Philippines were caused by secular as well as regular clergy. The degree to which the Portuguese preferred Italians to Spaniards was suggested when Italian mendicants joined in mission alongside the Jesuits, with the arrival of Franciscan Capuchins. But the fact that Italian friars in China owed allegiance not to the patronage of either Iberian Crown but to the Propaganda Congregation did not help the papacy much in the long run. By the seventeenth century Jesuits themselves, both locally and at the Society's Roman headquarters, were occasionally expressing doubts about the implications of the astronomical work carried out for the Chinese imperial authorities by the Jesuit mission at Peking.

The French, as opposed to the Portuguese, mission at Peking might be expected to show more prompt obedience to any eventual Roman ruling on the contested Chinese Rites, because of the French Jesuits' claim not to be subject to the Portuguese *padroado*, but, in fact, when French Jesuits were sent to China in 1685, their scientific purposes were stressed by the government of Louis XIV, intent on securing their independence not only from the existing, nominally Portuguese Jesuit mission, but also in fact from papal direction. French Jesuits praised their own monarch, but also courted the new imperial dynasty in China, as opposed to the mandarins of the previous governmental and cultural elite. But such French Jesuit independence weakened papal control too, as was suggested when Bouvet's visit to Europe in 1697 involved his presenting reports at Paris but not at Rome. Jesuits in the East also expressed criticism even of papal envoys who were French, when Vicars Apostolic sent by the Roman Propaganda to Siam were charged with anti-Jesuit 'Jansenism'.

A crucial factor which, once again, demonstrated the papacy's inability to establish effective control of the missions in the East was that in Europe the French *Missions Etrangères* were developing a markedly anti-Jesuit attitude. This was typified by De Lionne, an early associate of the *Missions* who had worked in the Fukien province of China between 1689 and 1702 and was rabidly anti-Jesuit. Thus, although the Society attributed the hostile attitude of the *Missions* to the influence of Navarrete, the link was more complex and less one-way. The friar's unpublished, though partially printed, 'Controversies', which continued his attacks on Jesuits and their missionary methods, faced both Jesuit obstruction and the delaying action of the (by no means pro-Jesuit) Spanish Inquisition; but though the Society gained possession of the work, another copy reached the *Missions Etrangères* in Paris. By 1689 a prominent Jansenist opponent of the Society, Arnauld, was drawing on the 'Controversies' for his own attacks on the Jesuits. But when Navarrete himself reached

Europe from the East, he was able to respond to the wish expressed in 1672 by Cardinal Barberini for more information on the China mission.

In 1673 Navarrete went to Rome in person and submitted reports both to the Congregation De Propaganda Fide, on the orders of Cardinal Ottoboni, and to the Holy Office. Through the secretary of Propaganda, now Baldeschi Colonna, he obtained a new papal decree confirming that the Jesuits had no monopoly of the Chinese mission. This decree coincided with a ban on further publication of the Jesuits' *Relations* of their activities. However the friar's own memoirs, substantially anti-Jesuit in nature, did not remain hidden in the archives of Propaganda, but achieved wider circulation, bringing awareness of Jesuit activities in China to the attention not only of European Catholic critics of the Society but also, for example, of Leibniz. In some ways this marked a turning-point in Roman reaction to the endless problems presented by the Eastern missions and by the Chinese controversies in particular.

The demise of the Jesuits

At the start of the eighteenth century Clement XI made a glum review of the situation and in 1704 the first clear Roman condemnation of the contested Chinese Rites was issued. This condemnation was repeated in 1715, and again in 1742 when the Bull *Ex Quo Singulari* renewed the obligation of missionaries to take an oath of obedience to the Holy See. European critics repeatedly accused the Jesuits in the East of refusing either to be bound by the papal condemnations, or to co-operate in missionary activity conducted according to permitted methods. The allegations in Europe concerned the Jesuits' conduct not only in the East but also in Spanish America, where the well publicized clash between Jesuits and Bishop Palafox over finance and jurisdiction was added to the controversy, encouraging the campaign for the suppression of the Society. When the papacy finally consented to its suppression, this obviously represented among other things a final end to the distinctive Jesuit endeavour both in the Eastern missions and elsewhere overseas. For the missionary controversies had served to distinguish and divide papal and Jesuit policies outside Europe.

The anti-Jesuit sentiments of the *Missions Etrangères* had also been encouraged by De Lionne, bishop of Rosalia. In 1701 the *Missions* published two treatises of an anti-accommodation nature, relating to the Chinese controversies, one composed by the Franciscan, Santa María, but the other being that written at an earlier date by Longobardi, the internal Jesuit critic of the pristine assimilative policy begun by Ricci. As papal policy evolved, from the initial, open-minded attitude of Propaganda on assimilative methods towards rigorist condemnation, the early eighteenth century saw the papacy fighting for its independence against the pressures exerted by Jansenists and their opponents, by Louis XIV, and indeed by all the parties in the Spanish Succession struggle, which in turn had its own implications for European control of overseas territories, diplomatic influence or trading relations. Tournon, the

French papal envoy, was imprisoned by the Portuguese at Macao, as they resisted his intervention in *padroado* territory, though he was eventually rewarded by Rome with the status of cardinal. However, what he discovered of Chinese conditions suggested, correctly enough, that only a minority among the local Jesuits themselves solidly and unreservedly supported the accommodation policy, even in its evolved and qualified form. This was precisely what critics like Navarrete were themselves alleging. The final papal condemnation of accommodation in China in 1742, and the later consequences of Jesuit expulsions and suppression, affecting both Portuguese and French operations, still in fact left non-Jesuit French missionaries perplexed over the issue.

A fatal mistake, on the part of the Jesuits themselves, was the intervention, at a crucial juncture, of European members of the Society who lacked personal experience, or at least extended and profound involvement, in the Eastern missions. What was presented, in two crucial publications, was an uncritical defence of accommodation, much more crude than Ricci's original position and less carefully refined than the methods in fact evolved subsequently in China itself. These publications became, from the early eighteenth century, the chief target of attack for French critics of the Jesuits, especially those among the members of the Sorbonne. Against the French background of debate about the treatment of the internal minority of former Huguenots, following the Revocation of the Edict of Nantes, a conflict arose involving the head of the *Missions Etrangères*, Brisacier, and the king's future Jesuit confessor, Le Tellier, whose *Défense des nouveaux Chrétiens et des missionnaires de la Chine, du Japon et des Indes* was first published in 1687. The policy pursued in the East by the French clerics of the *Missions* promoted a view that it was they, not the Jesuits of the *padroado*, who were the papacy's agents and allies in the missionfield, and this was influencing opinion in Europe itself before the attack was taken up by the theologians of the Sorbonne.

The Superior and Directors of the *Missions* appealed in 1700 to the pope, submitting for condemnation propositions taken from the two fatal Jesuit publications, one of Le Comte, *Nouveaux mémoires sur l'état présent de la Chine*, of 1696, and the other of Le Gobien, *Histoire de l'édit de la Chine en faveur de la religion chrestienne*, of 1698. This appeal for Roman condemnation of over-confident propositions intended to justify accommodation touched in part on Jesuit expressions of gratitude for a Chinese imperial edict of 1692, supposedly favourable to Christianity. What the papacy at the beginning of the eighteenth century felt obliged to do, however, was to assert its own authority, not only against secular authority, whether Catholic or non-Christian, but also over rival religious orders and other clerics competing in their claims to represent Roman policy. The independence of the Paris theology faculty, in this as in other, more directly European matters, had to be countered once more, in another attempt to reassert the explicit Tridentine pronouncement that the papacy should exercise a monopoly of all post-Conciliar interpretation and decision on issues of doctrine or discipline. The papacy could not afford to appear tolerant of alleged Jesuit laxity, especially in converting non-Christians to the true Catholic faith, when Jansenist and pro-Jansenist critics were so eager to assert their own competence to pass judgement, in breach of Rome's monopoly of definitive sentence.

From the middle of the seventeenth century the papacy had attempted to advance its own control of developments in the East, by acquiring disinterested but well-informed evidence about the significance of the contested Chinese Rites, involving veneration of ancestors and of Confucius. So it was not simply defence of its own authority which led the papacy in 1715 to confirm the decision of its local French representatives, condemning the Chinese Rites as incompatible with Christianity, but papal condemnation of the Chinese Rites contributed to the decision of the Chinese imperial authorities to halt further missionary activity in the provinces of the kingdom. The papacy might send another envoy, Mezzabarba, after the death of its French representative in the East, Tournon, to try to secure obedience to the Roman decision, but that could not alter the independent policy of the Chinese imperial authorities, which even more fundamentally determined the fate of the Chinese mission. Despite the maintenance of some clandestine missionary work in the Chinese provinces, this imperial policy also limited, of necessity, the opportunities for the products of an independent Italian initiative of the eighteenth century, a college at Naples designed to train clergy for the China mission. The papacy, moreover, had only made reluctant concessions over the use of the vernacular, as opposed to Latin, in China. Nor could the effects of condemning the Jesuits' assimilative missionary methods in the East be offset by the condemnation, within Europe, of their Jansenist opponents, by the Constitution *Unigenitus* of 1713.

Enforcing obedience in the East to the papal ruling against the Chinese Rites allowed by the Jesuits to their converts proved difficult, as was suggested by the decree of Propaganda in 1723, which ordered the Society's General to ensure Jesuit compliance with the anti-accommodationist decision of Clement XI in 1715 and provide written evidence of submission. Such tensions, even within the Society, were far removed from the ambitious post-Tridentine plans of the Jesuit Possevino for evangelization and Christian union on a global scale under papal leadership. Yet the papacy's decisive stance against the Chinese Rites, after 1700, took its place in the long campaign, from the time of Gregory XV onwards, to recover some independent control of the overseas Catholic missions. The apparent logic of this step was in fact clearer in relation to European Catholic secular powers than it could possibly be with regard to the non-Christian imperial authority in China. The reaction of that authority to the fact, rather than just to the content, of papal adjudication on the contested significance of the Chinese Rites was equally decisive and predictably negative. Such barbarian intervention and naturally ignorant 'interpretation' was final proof of the unacceptable nature of any missionary activity in China. The Jesuit presence at Peking was firmly confined to scientific work at Court even before the papacy's suppression of the Society.

With such an outcome there also vanished of necessity any last trace of an earlier ambition to see Islam encompassed by the presence of Christianity to its rear, on a second, far-Eastern front. Yet by the later eighteenth century it was arguable that the Islamic power of the Turks no longer represented so positive a danger to the survival of Christendom, though this reflected the internal evolution of the Ottoman Empire rather than any papal success in establishing a common front with the Eastern Orthodox Churches. Nevertheless, if that were so, the pressing need for a close watch on the unassimilated presence of Jewish communities within the frontiers of Western Christendom had certainly diminished, while the urgency of co-operation with the non-Catholic Christians of the West had also decidedly declined. By the later eighteenth century the papacy could not fail to be aware that the attempt to recover its own independent control of the global extension of Catholic Christianity, in the face of Catholic secular authority, had only had limited success; while the most obvious challenge, from those same Catholic secular powers, to the integrity of Catholicism and, within that, to Roman authority seemed by then to confront the papacy within Western Europe itself.

CHAPTER 7

'The Papal Prince'

During the last four decades of the present century the temporal government of the papal states between the end of the Council of Trent and the outbreak of the French Revolution has been at least partly reassessed. An older, largely Italian but more generally also anti-clerical view, of an unmitigated decline, has been the subject of historical revision based on still far from comprehensive new research into such questions as papal finance. The partial nature of such research naturally accounts for the variety of interim judgements. One recent review of essentially eighteenth-century papal government in the city of Rome defined the truly post-Tridentine age, with respect to that government, as beginning only with Innocent XII, at the end of the preceding century, but continued to distinguish this newly identified post-Tridentine period as one of gradual decline (though not conscious retrogression) and of relative secularization (as opposed to unwavering clericalism). Such a view was presented as being in line with the major arguments about papal sovereignty put forward by the Italian historian Prodi, according to whom one of the clearest contemporary analysts of that sovereignty and its post-Tridentine evolution was Cardinal De Luca, influential during the pontificate of Innocent XI from its start, and especially after his elevation to the college of cardinals in 1681 until his death in 1683.

Yet, as has already been noted, Prodi's own arguments have been further developed, though not necessarily in a context familiar to all English-speaking readers. For Prodi's later thoughts involved recognition that De Luca acknowledged the singular and anomalous nature of papal government in central Italy, which remained distinct from that of secular states and retained internal contradictions in its functioning. More recently still, another Italian historian has made a new study of De Luca and the government of the papal states. In this the popular joy expressed at the death of the cardinal is interpreted as indicative of hopes for an end to the austerity and rigour imposed in the name of Innocent XI with regard to public finance and public order. In the case of law and order, the cardinal was certainly faced with a confusion of competing Roman jurisdictions, as he attempted to distinguish the temporal authority of the pope and establish the clarity and certainty which ought to characterize good government and just rule.

PAPAL SOVEREIGNTY

There were indeed competitive expressions of public justice found at Rome, though this was arguably not in fact unusual in the so-called 'absolute' regimes of early modern Europe, which were rather more manifestations of distributive justice than of real autocracy. Thus the cardinal attempted to limit the ordinary tribunals involved in the secular government of the papal states 'merely' to those of the auditors of the Apostolic Chamber, of the Cardinal Vicar, of the papal Governor of Rome, of the Roman capitol, of the Roman Rota, and the specifically financial tribunals of the Chamber, the Cardinal Camerlengo, and the papal Treasurer. But then, even so, the peculiar jurisdictions had to be added of the Cardinal Archpriests of the three most major Roman basilicas, of the judicial conservators of charitable institutions, of monasteries, of the military judge advocates, of the keeper of Castel S. Angelo, of the Roman port of the Ripa Grande, and of many others. The immediately post-Tridentine popes, moreover, had not in fact ended entirely the legal pretensions of the leading Roman baronial families, while notoriously the Roman embassies of Catholic rulers claimed diplomatic immunity within extensive quarters of the city. Despite the public clashes over such immunity, which had often humiliated the papacy from the start of the personal reign of Louis XIV, the cardinal was intent on renewing the struggle to limit the physical extent of the claim, since contraband as well as criminal disorder flourished in the extended enclaves, representing an estimated annual loss to the papal customs of 50,000 écus.

Though Innocent, fortified by his own clear austerity, resumed the campaign for reductions of the quarters early in his pontificate, from 1677, the cardinal's triumph in this respect was only posthumous, achieved under Innocent's successor. Yet Alexander VIII, in his short pontificate of 1689–91, also represented a posthumous defeat for the cardinal, in reviving a conspicuous nepotism which the cardinal had attacked as unjustifiable. Innocent had equally taken this view, and prepared a bull to outlaw such papal practice, but it was blocked by the opposition of the college of cardinals, alleging that implicit condemnation of previous popes was improper, and apparent substantiation of anti-Roman criticism was impolitic, though the pope never made his own nephew a cardinal. However, a posthumous victory for De Luca was eventually achieved, when the successor to Alexander VIII, Innocent XII, was able to use a moment of reaction, early in his own pontificate, to publish such a bull in 1692. Indeed, such difficulties might imply that De Luca's analysis of the complications engendered by the multiple roles of the pope did not go far enough.

As has been suggested so far, the pope's function as a secular ruler was added not just to his roles as bishop of Rome, patriarch of the West, and 'bishop of the universal Church', but also to his intermediate ones as metropolitan and *de facto* Italian primate.[1] The status of cardinal eventually acquired by De Luca himself proved less than full protection at the Roman Court as he pursued his reforms, and it has been argued that he had already lost the pope's confidence at the time of his death. He had, after all, also criticized the legal immunities of familiars of the Roman Holy Office, and left himself open to attack for alleged failure to support the papacy whole-heartedly in the conflict with Louis XIV over the *régale*. Some of the cardinal's writings were even subjected to posthumous disparagement, when they were reviewed in 1690 by the Congregation of the Index, though not in the end condemned. Yet for all his typical Curial foundation as a lawyer, De Luca, in the most comprehensive of his legal publications, recognized the importance of the Tridentine decrees within the complex systems of law operative in the papal states.

The creation by Clement VIII in 1592 of a Curial Congregation specifically for the temporal government of the papal states, the Congregazione del Buon Governo, might seem an important step in the consolidation of a centralized and more 'absolute' regime, irrespective of Tridentine ideals of limiting the intrusion of papal governors in ecclesiastical affairs at least, but even here it is important to note that, as in many other respects, one major part of the papal states, Bologna, remained independent, in this instance from the uniformity pursued by the Congregation. Papal Legates at Bologna might indeed override the immunity of local ecclesiastical courts and the sanctuary of ecclesiastical property, in the pursuit of good order. But first, it is important to recall that this was not in breach of the Tridentine ideal, that clerics should be judged and sentenced by ecclesiastics, and that immunity should only be waived by ecclesiastical authority. Secondly, it is striking that, precisely to preserve this principle and avoid setting unfortunate precedents for secular rulers elsewhere to follow, the waivers issued to a Legate there by the Curial Congregation for Immunities were limited in duration and were not to be made public.

The range of responsibilities of papal government might be illustrated by the prison reform undertaken in Rome by Innocent X, whose new prison building (1652 onwards) allowed the segregation of different categories of inmate. Such improvement was based on the ideas of Bishop Scanarolo, whose mid-seventeenth-century experience as an inspector of prisons, in the Tribunale della Visita, eventually inspired his treatise *De visitatione carceratorum* (1655). The revenues available to the papacy were obviously crucial for any such social provision, so the financial systems of the papacy must be reviewed. Within these, sources of revenue must first be identified.

---

1 H. Gross, *Rome in the Age of Enlightenment. The Post-Tridentine Syndrome and the Ancien Regime* (Cambridge 1990); cf. A. Lauro, *Il cardinale Giovan Battista De Luca. Diritto e riforme nello Stato della Chiesa (1676–1683)* (Naples 1991).

PAPAL FINANCE

By the time of De Luca the venal offices of the Curia and papal states (which must be distinguished from ecclesiastical benefices) were fully evolved as a central part of the papacy's finances. Notional shares in these offices, as well as sole title to a nominal office, were regularly traded in a market made by the Roman banks, with an average expectation of an 8 per cent return on such investment. But with the evolution of a further venal right to make transfers of office (partly akin to the French *paulette*), the papal administration, by De Luca's time, had lost any real disposal of the offices, bar a tiny proportion still available for re-allocation. Furthermore, of the 3,762 offices disposable in his time, only a small number involved a personal obligation to perform the associated duties, which were usually left to a nominee. Consortia were formed to invest capital in the acquisition of office, with profits shared *pro rata*, even if by the second half of the seventeenth century alternative forms of investment in papal finances were becoming relatively more attractive, and a consortium might also be used as a shell for other private financial operations which were not regarded as licit by Roman authority.

The papacy's temporal revenue from within the papal states was certainly increasing in the sixteenth and seventeenth centuries, involving income from the alum mines, the grazing rights (which were thought of as part of customs), the salt monopoly and the postal franchise. By about 1600 these revenue sources were farmed by financiers, with a farm of nine years, but the extent of the farm might vary geographically, to cover sources throughout the papal states, or in a single province, or in a more limited locality still. However, the returns made directly to the papal exchequer were small, as administrative costs and the management of the accumulated debt accounted for the majority of the income. Moreover, more truly ecclesiastical revenues, from levies on the clergy, the estate of deceased prelates and clerics, payments made by newly appointed bishops or revenues from vacant sees for example, could no longer add that much to the papal budget.

In the first place, even where Apostolic Collectors were still operative, in Italian and Iberian states, there was frequent contest over their exactions, as events in Spain, Portugal and the kingdom of Naples show. Secondly, such income did little more than support the papal debt, by providing for payments to the papacy's creditors, above all investors in the venal offices already mentioned. The administration of the Apostolic Chamber was, for practical purposes, in the hands of a banker, appointed by a pope to be the *Depositario generale*. Again high administrative charges, mostly staff costs, reduced the papacy's real income in the Chamber. At the end of the second decade of the seventeenth century a quarter of the Chamber's expenditure was for the upkeep of the papal Court, a quarter for the maintenance of cardinals and payment of expenses to nuncios, a third for military garrisons at Rome itself and Avignon, and only 3 per cent for the administration of the city of Rome.

A more flexible source of income therefore was the papal Datary, since the flow of proceeds deriving from provision to certain types of benefice, or provision in certain circumstances, and from dispensations was not fixed. The Datary thus handled such more truly ecclesiastical income as well as the revenue generated by the venal office market, the latter certainly making papal government more rather than less typical of continental European systems of state finance in the Ancien Régime. Variable income deriving from the occasional grant of privileges by the papacy also involved less clearly ecclesiastical payments, such as fines paid to compound for criminal sentences or fees paid for derogation from sumptuary restrictions for example. But in the same period, three-quarters of such income merely went to service the papal debt. The disposable income of the pope, administered by a Secret Treasurer who was commonly the *Depositario generale* himself, was thus reduced to an annual sum measured only in tens of thousands of scudi.

Not only was accumulation of a reserve out of the question, but so was any large-scale formation of policy, if expense was involved. This is a most important consideration when the actions of the post-Tridentine popes, often seeming increasingly reactive and unco-ordinated, are viewed more generally. Thus the nominal increase of the papal budget even after the inflationary pressures of the sixteenth and first half of the seventeenth century had eased should be read as a continued accumulation of debt, even as prices stagnated and fell. Already in 1623 direct and indirect taxes accounted for 95 per cent of the revenue generated in the papal states, a fiscal pressure which again made papal government akin to, not different from, other continental European states in the seventeenth century.[2] Thus servicing the papal debt required over half the papacy's income by 1599 and, after short-lived reductions, it required two-thirds by 1673.

To manage this debt and avoid bankruptcy the papal investment funds, the *monti*, begun before the Council of Trent, remained crucial. A *monte* could be sold to bankers, who then sold shares, which could be expected at the end of the seventeenth century to entail interest charges of only 3 per cent for the papacy. Nevertheless in 1667 papal debt already amounted to 36.5 million scudi, against annual revenue of only 2.6 million, of which 1.5 million was required for interest payments. The various *monti* at that time represented a capital of 33.8 million scudi and investment in venal office amounted to 2.7 million. But, as was obvious by the beginning of the next century, military expenditure for the attempted defence of the papal states could on occasion rise, to account for over half the papacy's outgoings. Subsidies to Catholic powers involved in war against the Turks or against heretical opponents are calculated to have amounted to a total of 19.6 million scudi between 1542 and 1716.

2 P. Partner, 'Papal Financial Policy in the Renaissance and Counter-Reformation', *Past and Present*, LXXXVIII (1980), 17–62; J. Delumeau, *Vie économique et sociale de Rome dans la seconde moitié du XVIe siècle* (2 vols, Paris 1957–59).

The ability of the papacy to maintain relative stability and avoid bankruptcy for so long was nevertheless based on some well-judged foundations, and was not simply good fortune; it also of course represented avoidance of the financial and political shipwreck which overtook, for more or less extended periods, other European regimes of the early modern period. First, the papacy after the Council of Trent insisted on payment calculated in gold scudi, reckoning on the basis of real currency and not just units of account, while confining all but rare, extraordinary expenditure to disbursement in silver scudi. Secondly, this was clearly advantageous, since already in the second half of the sixteenth century the value of silver in relation to gold was falling. By 1599 the approximately 2,900 venal offices were valued at around 3.8 million gold scudi, according to one source. But the charge to the papacy in the form of interest payable declined from under 6 per cent to roughly 4.8 per cent even between the end of the sixteenth century and 1619. Even in 1590 the proportion of papal revenue devoted to such payments may have been as low as one-sixth.

The income enjoyed by office-holders, more generally, obviously represented a positive element in the Roman as opposed to strictly papal economy, even though such recycling of wealth may be judged to have been as ultimately unproductive as the equivalent operations in Habsburg Spain or Bourbon France in the early modern period. The multiplication of the papal *monti*, as a system of funded debt, inviting investment against the security of what were effectively government bonds, made Rome an attractive money market for most of the period from the end of the Council of Trent until well on in the seventeenth century. The institutional continuity of the elective papacy in one way represented greater security than the uncertainties of an hereditary dynasty. Reduction of the interest paid on such loans was not only planned, as under Paul V, but gradually achieved. Yet the market remained active, with an estimated annual exchange of shares, calculated for 1619 as 15,000 shares of 100 scudi each, representing one-sixth of the debt being bought and sold each year.

The importance of the early seventeenth-century borrowing of Clement VIII and Paul V was thus in consolidating papal debt in long-term funds allowing low interest rates to be maintained. Such foundations allowed the papacy to survive the doubling of its indebtedness under Urban VIII, and to continue to attract Genoese investors, even when the finances of Catholic Spain were faltering. It has been calculated that papal income was rising from 1599 to 1672, and slightly declining to 1691, while within this period the percentage of papal income devoted to interest on the total debt declined from 53 per cent odd in 1599 to 46 per cent odd in 1619. Then, after rising to 59 per cent odd in 1654, and perhaps distinctly higher by 1673, it supposedly declined again to 56 per cent odd in 1691. However papal debt was not the sum total of Roman debt.

Like other European municipalities in the early modern period, the city of Rome accumulated its own debt, estimated for 1599 at 800,000 silver scudi. Economic difficulties elsewhere in the papal states in the last decades of the sixteenth century led to greater papal regulation of communal debts. In 1592

Clement VIII limited the rate of interest on such communal loans and loan-bonds to 7 per cent, and in 1604 established yet another papal *monte*, in this case intended to underwrite some of the communal debt. Such debts in the papal states, other than in Rome itself and financially self-regulating Bologna, were supposedly reduced under Paul V, but remained a distinct feature of Urban VIII's pontificate and the associated upheavals in central Italy. To maintain order in Rome itself, papal responsibility for regulating the grain supply obviously remained crucial as well.

The immediately post-Tridentine popes, however, created new *monti* specifically to raise funds for extraordinary needs, whether contributions to the struggle against the Turks in the Mediterranean and in Hungary, or the administration of the papal states and their enlargement by the incorporation of Ferrara, for example. Such specific borrowing has to be set against that part of papal expenditure over a whole pontificate which may be classed as nepotism, as with the total outlay of Paul V under this heading, which has been calculated as the equivalent of over one million silver scudi. Yet it was Paul V who also took steps to restore the papacy's ultimate reserve, the gold deposits originally housed in Castel Sant' Angelo by Sixtus V, who thus took his place among the most 'bullionist' of early modern European rulers. The gold reserves accumulated by Sixtus V rose from 350,000 gold scudi to one million by 1586 and to 3 million gold scudi by 1590. This was achieved by the sale of shares in funded debt, to the value of almost 2.5 million silver scudi, and the sale of new venal offices, in addition to other income.

The rare withdrawal of 150,000 gold scudi from the reserves by Clement VIII, at the time of the annexation of Ferrara, was made good by Paul V, even though successors of Sixtus V spent the original additional reserves of over one million silver scudi. It was consistent with papal financial policy to maintain the very strict criteria laid down by Sixtus V for any drawing on the gold reserves, and to decline to meet even the most pressing demands of Catholic rulers supposedly fighting in the interests of the Catholic faith from this resource. Financial accounting at the papal Court seems in some ways to have been improved from the start of the pontificate of Clement VIII, with effects visible into the seventeenth century. But the resulting records, which allow, for instance, a clear understanding of the marginal or even negative results on turn-over of the 'ordinary' papal revenue, do not in fact reveal much about the flexibility of the papal finances at the death of Clement VIII for example. For, as already noted, while the mixed nature of the revenues handled by the Datary introduced such flexibility as there was, the responsibilities of the *Depositario generale* were not confined to the Datary alone.

Extraordinary expenditure

Extraordinary expenditure, such as that for the building operations of Paul V in Rome and elsewhere in the papal states, calculated to have cost 2.5 million scudi, had by definition to be supported in other ways. Nor, as has already been suggested, should papal nepotism be seen as necessarily different from the proprietary or patrimonial understanding which early modern European rulers habitually had of their inheritance. In any case, the variable element in the Datary contribution to total papal revenue means that the more accurate overview attempted under Clement VIII can only give retrospective plausibility to estimates for the immediately post-Conciliar pontificates. According to this, Datary income increased from 80,000 silver scudi annually under Gregory XIII and 200,000 under Sixtus V to 300,000 under Clement VIII, as also under Paul V. But even so, not all variable income passed through the Datary and the combined sums of this nature might account for as much as a quarter of total papal revenue in the late sixteenth century.

The importance of variable income is increased when it is remembered that the relation of papal silver currency to gold was changing, from 1:1.2 in the 1590s to 1:1.3 in the early 1620s and 1:1.4 in the 1650s. Allowing for such complications, it has been asserted that the temporal revenues of the papacy doubled between 1565 and 1592, and that, even after the recession of the 1590s in the papal states, recovery in this type of revenue was evident by 1605. Nor was the papacy forced into planned devaluation of its currency until 1684, and then only by under 5 per cent. On the other hand, Sixtus V had effected economies within papal government, reducing the cost of staffing the temporal administration of the papal states to almost half the figure of 8 per cent of temporal revenue for the 1570s, but these were not maintained; and such staff costs had returned to about 9 per cent between 1619 and 1623. Such calculations are necessarily partial, and do not represent the total cost of all administration which might be classed as temporal throughout the papal states. Similarly, it has been suggested that taxation in the papal states quadrupled, while prices doubled and wages may have failed to double. But such estimates are for the whole of the sixteenth century and do not purport to give a picture confined to the post-Tridentine decades of the century.

If it is taken that a scudo represented 100 *baiocchi*, then it may be relevant to note, as a measure against which to assess papal revenue and expenditure, that in the last decade of the sixteenth and the early decades of the seventeenth century wages in the Roman construction industry were 40 to 50 *baiocchi* a day for builders and 25 to 30 a day for their assistants. In fact, however, as research on the building of Roman palaces under the popes of the Baroque has suggested, conditions varied greatly, depending on whether workers were taken on as merely casual labour or hired (and fed) in teams to complete major projects.[3] The papacy also obtained a modest return from the monopoly of the alum mines of Tolfa. In the 1560s the monopoly for the production of 36,000 *cantari* cost a member of the Pallavicino family nearly 28,000 silver scudi. In the 1590s a monopoly right to produce the same amount cost the Olgiati over 35,000 silver scudi, and by 1626 a member of the Sacchetti paid more than 38,000 silver scudi to produce 34,000 *cantari*.

3 J.B. Scott, *Images of Nepotism: the Painted Ceilings of Palazzo Barberini* (Princeton, NJ 1991).

In 1592 the papal budget was finally rearranged to reflect more accurately the limitations of the papacy's non-temporal revenues, as they had evolved by then. However, the Tridentine reforms did not in the long term seriously undermine the income received through the Datary, partly for the issue of papal bulls and partly also for dispensations, so that this source of income amounted to possibly 166,000 gold scudi under Sixtus V, increasing to more than 200,000 gold scudi by the early seventeenth century. The proportion of land owned by ecclesiastics in the immediately Roman area may have remained fairly constant, at 28 per cent in the late sixteenth century and still 25 per cent at the end of the eighteenth century, but papal taxation on the clergy of the papal states did not produce a great income. Though the papacy certainly sought to levy sums on clergy and ecclesiastical institutions elsewhere in Italy at certain times, the resistance of secular government was often evident, as also over papal exactions from the estate of deceased clerics in certain instances. Thus even if by 1619 monastic institutions in the Italian peninsula were being required to produce for the papacy an annual total of 80,000 silver scudi, the larger figure of an additional annual return between 1619 and 1623 of 100,000 silver scudi must be assessed in the light of the fact that the Apostolic Collectors, who pursued for example the temporalities of vacant sees as well as the estate of deceased ecclesiastics, were at work in the Iberian as well as the Italian peninsula in order to produce this. Their activities (and those of sub-collectors) were in fact much contested in the Iberian kingdoms, and the position of Apostolic Collector in Spain had eventually to be merged with that of nuncio, as supposedly affording greater diplomatic protection.

This was the background to developments which have been calculated to represent less than a doubling of non-temporal papal revenue by 1623, compared with a century previously, as opposed to a quadrupling of temporal revenue over the same period. When an attempt is made to estimate total papal income, the proportion spent on the papal household is assessed as having risen to 13 per cent only under Clement VIII, returning thereafter to a figure of 9.5 per cent, much nearer to the previous level of 8 per cent. If by 1619 military and naval expenditure represented *c.* 15 per cent, this reflected the annual cost of the papal galley fleet, 60–70,000 silver scudi by the end of the sixteenth century, roughly equivalent to that of the defence of Avignon. Expenditure by Clement VIII of over 600,000 silver scudi in the Hungarian campaign, in 1595, and of 750,000 silver scudi for the annexation of Ferrara in 1597–98 was precisely extraordinary. The use by Gregory XIV of 400,000 gold scudi, from the gold reserves, to subsidize the Catholic struggle against the Huguenots in France, in 1591, was equally exceptional. On similar subsidies to Catholic powers in Europe Paul V spent only 335,000 silver scudi, and Gregory XV, at a time of increasing tension, 500,000 silver scudi.

By way of comparison, Sixtus V and Paul V are thought to have spent more than one million silver scudi each on building works, a large proportion in either case being for the continued work on St Peter's. Paul V is also reckoned to have spent 4 per cent of his whole income during his pontificate, once again over one million silver scudi, on his family, enabling them to invest more than two million silver scudi in real estate. As a result of theological advice on the disposal of papal revenues, Urban VIII was assured that an outlay on his relatives of 5 per cent of total papal revenue would be proper. Despite changes in the business and hence character of the nunciatures after the outbreak of the Thirty Years' War, the papacy between 1576 and 1648 managed to stabilize the monthly allowance to nuncios at Courts outside Italy, at 230 silver scudi. Only later in the seventeenth century were nuncios' allowances recalculated upwards, though still paid in silver scudi. Charitable expenditure, excluding the purchase of grain, has been estimated at 4.5 per cent of all papal revenue in 1619, an apparent increase on a figure of 3 per cent under Clement VIII. Papal revenue and expenditure are, however, less than perfectly defined concepts. The income of a new papal initiative like the Congregation De Propaganda Fide might be separately provided and, hence, accounted for, while the total income of the cardinals and Curialists might exceed that attributed to the pope himself. The economy of Rome, moreover, was distinct from that of the papal states beyond the city, as was also demonstrated by the devaluation of the currency struck by mints elsewhere in the papal states relative to that issued at Rome itself.

Customs revenue

One important source of income was that derived by the papal government from the customs revenue at the main port of Rome, at the Ripa Grande. The importance of maintaining and securing maritime communications was clear to the papacy. To guard the coast of the papal states the fortifications at Civitavecchia were strengthened by Clement VIII in 1604, Paul V in 1616 and Urban VIII in 1630. While Urban's fear of military attack during the later War of Castro accounted for his creation of bastions around the Janiculum, the resiting of the Porta Portese and associated reordering of the Porto di Ripa Grande, he had economic considerations in mind as well, when he gave customs concessions for Civitavecchia. Papal attempts to boost the economy of the main port on the eastern side of the papal states, Ancona, led to its eventual opening as a freeport in 1732.

For the crucial supplying of Rome itself, the Ripa Grande was essential. Grain had to be imported, sometimes from Sicily, as indicated by the repeated negotiations with Spain, not confined to the pontificate of Clement VIII, over such imports and charges to be paid for them. It also had to be imported, at least until the disruption of the Thirty Years' War, from Poland and Germany, via Dutch intermediaries, or even from Turkish territory, through the agency of the Knights of Malta. Roman grain prices had already risen in the sixteenth century, but fluctuated further in the first half of the seventeenth century, starting from the base line of one scudo per *rubbio* in 1603 and 1608, reaching a minimum of 42 giulii per *rubbio* in 1640, but maintaining an average of 70 giulii which was a sign of relative scarcity. During the seventeenth century the golden scudo rose from an initial value of 10 giulii, which remained the value of the silver scudo, to 16.5.

Despite the import of 15,000 *salme* of Sicilian grain between 1604 and 1608, in addition to 15,000 *rubbia* from the papal Marches in 1601–2, there were grain shortages in Rome in 1606, 1617, 1623, 1627, 1635 and again in the 1640s. Shortages of another basic necessity, oil, in 1626 and 1630 caused tax to be waived on its import. Provisioning for Rome involved supply for a population estimated at 110–120,000 *c.* 1640, peaking at 120–130,000 *c.* 1650, dropping with the 1656 epidemic to *c.* 100,000 and recovering only gradually at first from 1657 to reach *c.* 130,000 by 1697. But the Ripa Grande port was also the point of entry for the substantial supply of fine wines, which in this period were considered to be some of those from the kingdom of Naples, Tuscany and Corsica. It has been estimated that under Sixtus V an annual 11–12,000 *botti* of wine were imported through the port, and perhaps no less throughout the seventeenth century.

The price of wines, varying even for a given type, was fixed from time to time at the seat of Roman municipal administration, the Capitol. Since local wines, and those imported wines which were less appreciated, were priced more cheaply, there was a risk of contraband, involving adulteration of fine wines, which could only be countered by increasing the salary of the customs officials at the Ripa Grande, in the hope of making them less exposed to bribery. The tax on retail sales of imported wines, administered by the Roman municipal authorities, was dedicated to the support of the papal university, La Sapienza. The Genoese and Florentines, rather than native Romans, who tended to monopolize the farm of the Rome customs and the affairs of the papal treasury, thus dominated the wine and grain trade via the Ripa Grande, but marble was also imported from Carrara. By the end of the seventeenth century, however, the Roman alum export trade was suffering from the competition of the alum mines of Lipari and Pozzuoli in Spanish-ruled territory. Textiles were imported from the Netherlands after 1640, by permission of the Cardinal Nephew, Antonio Barberini, in his role as Cardinal Camerlengo.[4]

The customs at Rome, not just at the Ripa Grande port alone, were farmed on a nine-year cycle in the period between the mid-sixteenth and the mid-seventeenth century. During this time the yield doubled, to reach, by 1657, 234,000 scudi, partly because of rising rates of customs dues but also because of devaluation of the silver scudo. Thus, at face value, the yield was already rising from 180,000 scudi in 1600 to some 209,000 scudi in 1624 and 1626. At the Ripa Grande customs dues on wine were 4 per cent, but 10 per cent on other goods, though wine remained the most important single import at this customs post. The customs farmers were allowed 3 per cent of the returns at the Ripa Grande and 2 per cent of the total returns at the customs posts

4 D. Busolini, 'Il porto di Ripa Grande a Roma durante la prima metà del XVII secolo', *Studi Romani*, XLII, 3–4 (1994), 249–73.

elsewhere, as at the city gates, but they had to find the wages of the customs officers at the gates and quays, and were obliged to respect the customs exemptions granted by the Apostolic Camera. Thus for a nine-year farm between 1612 and 1621 the farm was calculated at 190,500 scudi per annum.

Exemptions sustained Roman life in other ways, but obviously reduced this source of income. The papal household had a right to 3,700 *botti* of wine a year, cardinals and lesser clerics enjoying smaller allowances tax-free, from twelve to five *botti* each, while the mendicant orders were exempted from taxes on food-stuffs but not wine. Thus, at face value at least, the total customs revenue at Rome, not just from the Ripa Grande, was reckoned to be 360,877 scudi in 1639–40, 458,507 scudi in 1654–55, 512,678 scudi in 1690–91, but then 455,544 scudi in 1696–97, and only 270,407 scudi in 1697–98. Despite a fluctuation associated with epidemic in 1656–58, much of the second half of the century, until the very end, thus suggested a relative prosperity, allowing the resumption of rebuilding and town planning which marked the pontificate of Alexander VII, and which arguably reflected a determination by the papacy to reassert locally an authority and grandeur which the Peace of Westphalia might seem to have challenged on a wider stage.[5] The seventeenth century, after all, saw a small growth in the Roman population, despite the epidemic of 1656.

The statutes governing the Ripa Grande and the subsidiary quays at the Ripetta, both of which were under the supervision of the Apostolic Camera, were reconfirmed by Urban VIII in 1639. According to the statutes, the officials of the Ripa and Ripetta, forming the Presidenza delle Ripe, were in charge of the provisioning of Rome, while the associated tribunals of the Ripa Grande and the Ripetta dealt with relevant criminal and civil cases. The Presidente delle Ripe himself was always a cleric of the Apostolic Camera, thus a characteristic Roman clerical bureaucrat, subject to the Cardinal Camerlengo and the President of the Tribunal of the Ripa Grande. Although his appointment was only annual until 1725, he ensured continuity of administration by delegating responsibility to the Judge of the Ripetta and the Camerlengo of the Ripa Grande, under whom, in turn, were subordinate magistrates and officials. As Cardinal Camerlengo Pietro Aldobrandini revised the wine customs in 1607. But the epidemic of 1630 represented the type of emergency which might necessitate special regulations affecting the whole working of the port of Ripa Grande.

A more prolonged effect on the working of the port and its trade was caused by papal attempts to maintain and improve the navigability of the Tiber. Clement VIII had the river dredged in 1602, and by 1612 Paul V had achieved the reopening of the navigable channel of Fiumicino, under Carlo Maderna, at a cost of 80,291 scudi. But both interventions had damaging consequences in the longer term, as continued flooding suggested. Costly maintenance work on the river was continued but proposals for major

---

5 R. Krautheimer, *The Rome of Alexander VII, 1655–1667* (Princeton, NJ 1985).

improvements during the seventeenth and eighteenth centuries were never realized. In any case, incoming shipping had to be drawn upstream to the Ripa Grande, against the flood, by buffalo. The monopoly supply of buffalo traction benefited the see of Ostia, but profits were fixed by Clement VIII in 1594, and regulated by confirmations of 1611, 1639 and 1643.

The corporation of mariners at Rome, like other similar bodies, maintained social funds to relieve members during illness or provide marriage dowries for members' daughters. Such provisions were reproduced by the fishermen and fishwives when they separated to form their own corporation from 1618. Specialist wine merchants formed their own organization only in 1731, but long before then the closed corporation of brokers, who controlled the supply of imported goods, including wine, was all-powerful. Their number was fixed by Pietro Aldobrandini in 1611–12, after being reduced to a dozen by Paul V. Each broker's position was venal, and cost more than 700 scudi, of which part went to the Apostolic Camera.

Fixed payments raised by the brokers among themselves provided a common fund, which formed the guaranteed reserve for one of the papal investment funds, the *Monte dei Sensali* created by Sixtus V. An interesting suggestion of stability, but of course at face value, so hardly indicative of economic growth or financial gain, is provided by this *monte*. While its accumulated funds under Sixtus V represented 40,000 scudi, with an expectation of 10 per cent interest, the same figures occur for the last decade of the seventeenth century. Such lack of dynamism may also be related to the evolution of the brokers' corporation, for during the eighteenth century they became truly public officials on a fixed salary. The Roman customs dues were thus in any case only one part of total papal income, even within the papacy's non-ecclesiastical revenue.

Ecclesiastical revenue

By contrast, the resulting burden on the rest of the papal states generally can be appreciated when it is observed that already in 1619 even the more clearly ecclesiastical revenue handled by the Datary, and supporting then a quarter of the total papal budget, was derived largely from Italy, and above all the papal states. Levies on certain religious orders were made by the papacy in Lombardy as well as in the papal states, but clerical levies elsewhere in Italy were either shared between Rome and the local secular government, as in Tuscany and the kingdom of Naples, or represented subsidies conceded by the papacy to the state in question, as in Piedmont and the Venetian Republic. Thus one estimate has alleged that of a total income from 1570 to 1660 of 258.4 million scudi, the papacy derived 118.5 million scudi from ordinary revenue raised in the papal states as against 100.4 million from clearly ecclesiastical revenues. However, such a calculation has to be assessed in the light of the realities of Curial funding. The staff costs of the Roman Curia remained, in a sense, self-funding, even after the Council of Trent, because of the number of benefices, located throughout the remaining parts of Catholic Europe and not confined to Italy or the papal states, which could still be used to remunerate Curialists, depending on the type of benefice and circumstances of provision.

The 'simple benefices' without the pastoral responsibilities of the *cura animarum*, which might allow non-residence or dispensation from residence, were one resource, and the fact that such benefices without cure of souls could be held in plurality gave them an added value. Papal authority could also allow someone other than the benefice-holder to benefit from pensions imposed on a benefice and could permit certain benefices to be held by commendators, who were not obliged to reside or perform in person the duties attached. Such benefits could be accumulated within networks of patronage at the Curia, since the papacy could also authorize the transfer of pensions to a new beneficiary. Above all the papal indult, which allowed favoured ecclesiastics to transmit their ecclesiastical income by testamentary disposition, meant that this elite could bequeath their accumulated estate to lay relatives, which was an essential mechanism by which papal nephews could provide for the socio-economic maintenance of their family beyond the lifetime of the pope himself and beyond their own. On the other hand, it could well be accepted that throughout the papal states the holders of the best benefices, not least bishoprics, were mostly connected to the Curia, in which case, it might be said, the net effect of the revenue cycle was neither to withdraw wealth from the area of papal temporal government nor to add to it.

In the case of such papal nephews as have received close financial investigation, another balance of interest emerges. Cardinal Scipio Borghese was notorious even among contemporaries for his accumulation of commendatory abbacies, which between 1605 and 1633 accounted for 1,976,427 odd scudi, or 30.3 per cent of his total income of 6,525,100 scudi. Of this commendatory revenue, one-third derived from positions within the papal states, while two-thirds was drawn from institutions in other parts of the Italian peninsula under Spanish rule. When the former papal nephew, Cardinal Ludovisi, died in 1632 his annual income from commendatory office amounted to 67,723 scudi, or 73 per cent of his total annual revenue of 91,728 scudi. The relevant institutions situated in the papal states contributed 28 per cent of the sum, those in Spanish-ruled Italy about 36 per cent, and French establishments 7.4 per cent.

By the time of the death in 1671 of Cardinal Antonio Barberini, however, his commendatory income of 49,500 scudi, representing 76 per cent of a total revenue of 65,133 scudi, was made up largely from within the papal states, 68 per cent, and only 6 per cent was produced by Spanish-ruled Italy. Here again, though, revenues recycled to such a large extent within the area of temporal papal rule may be seen as disadvantaging the greater part of the papal states, but the cardinal's famous expenditure within Rome can hardly be viewed as damaging the capital. Even when the other prelates' income was more substantially from Spanish-ruled territory, it should be added, this was not necessarily the southern areas of Naples and Sicily.[6] It would therefore be incorrect to suppose that relative relief of the financial burden which papal nepotism represented for the papal states was only achieved at the expense of the Italian *mezzogiorno*. But it remains clear that, at times, Spanish-ruled Italy could make a useful contribution to this aspect of Roman finance.

The eventual changes of regime in both Lombardy and Naples were thus crucial for the papal system of finance, because from the early eighteenth century onwards administrations which were increasingly intent on excluding Roman influence and exploitation came to rule these areas. Such a development, together with the revival of a resident royal (as opposed to viceregal) Court in mid-eighteenth-century Naples, must therefore be kept in mind when the seemingly ever greater weakness of the eighteenth-century papacy in the face of Catholic secular authority is considered. In any case, despite momentary suggestions to the contrary, as in the Barberini pontificate, the nepotism of the post-Tridentine popes essentially settled into a pattern of financial establishment rather than territorial extension to secure the future of their families. Lay members of papal families might marry into baronial dynasties, or acquire new properties which bestowed feudal rights; but truly dynastic principality-building was no longer possible. The income of Cardinal Nephews might indeed depend heavily on ecclesiastical resources, but the revenues of the papacy itself, as already noted, could only be maintained by combining local temporal exactions with wider and ecclesiastical contributions.

ROMAN CIVIC ADMINISTRATION

The Roman Court, as a financial as well as an administrative capital, remained a centre of attraction for those beyond the papal states too, as was shown by the Florentine and Genoese families who became in due course a part of the 'Roman' aristocracy. Such immigration, at all social levels, helped to account for the rise in Rome's population from about 85,000 in 1566 to about 115,000 in the 1620s, and on to about 138,000 by 1700. The clerical composition of the population was, however, average enough for Italian cities of the time, at about 2 per cent, representing in the 1620s and 1630s for example between 1,500 and 2,300 persons. By 1630 the population of Rome's male and female religious houses was over 5,600 in total. Employment for manual labourers in the construction and building trades continued, even if at fluctuating rates, into much of the seventeenth century and parts at least of the eighteenth. Domestic service was naturally a permanent prospect, and a serving-maid's monthly wage in the seventeenth century would purchase fifty of the standard-issue bread-loaves.

6 W. Reinhard, 'Finanza pontificia, sistema beneficiale e finanza statale nell' età confessionale', in *Fisco religione Stato nell' età confessionale*, ed. H. Kellenbenz and P. Prodi (Bologna 1989), pp. 459–504; M. Völkel, *Römische Kardinalshaushalte des 17. Jahrhunderts: Borghese, Barberini, Chigi* (Tübingen 1993).

The stability of grain provision for Rome was assured by the papal government, if necessary at the expense of other areas of the papal states. Yet the agrarian basis of the economy of the papal states, which was still fundamental to that of Rome, because of the sources of clerical income, was ultimately insufficiently elastic. This constraint was further increased, especially after 1620, because the growth of pasture at the expense of crop cultivation continued throughout the seventeenth century, despite rising grain prices. This change reduced agricultural employment and encouraged malarial marshland. It is arguable that in Rome itself structural or chronic poverty increased and became ineradicable during the seventeenth century. The relatively extensive provision in the city for institutional relief of poverty also arguably attracted the itinerant poor from other parts of the peninsula, as general economic distress overtook much of the latter. But the maintenance of such public order as any early modern European regime could impose could not be left to chance.

Under Urban VIII, whose knowledge of the evolving government of Bourbon France, for example, went back to his nunciature there early in the seventeenth century, his Cardinal Nephew, Francesco, occupied the Cancelleria palace, after he became vice-chancellor in succession to Ludovisi in 1632. He also had quarters at the papal palace itself, where indeed the areas adjacent to the Quirinal, in that other part of the city, became something of a Barberini territory. The new Palazzo Barberini, on the slope below the Quirinal, reflected the power and glory of the whole family, including both the other papal nephew, Cardinal Antonio, Cardinal Camerlengo from 1638, and the lay nephew, Taddeo, who was General of the Church from 1630, in succession to his own father, and governor of the Borgo, across the Tiber, from 1632. The papal insistence on awarding to Taddeo the hereditary title of Prefect of the City, on the extinction of the Della Rovere of Urbino in 1631, heightened endemic tension in Rome between representatives of foreign powers and papal government within the walls. This was so despite the fact that Urbino was peacefully incorporated into the papal states, and not made a family inheritance. But particular Barberini dominance of the area near the Quirinal was itself further enhanced by the association of the pope's Capuchin brother, the elder Cardinal Antonio, with the adjacent church and convent of that order.[7]

Such evident control of an identifiable zone of the city was in turn reflected after the succession of Innocent X and the flight, for a while, of the Barberini to France. The pope's determination to employ equally eminent architects and sculptors to create a visual display of family eminence at Piazza Navona marked dominance of a different area of the city, further enhanced by the subsequent exclusion of trading from the piazza (except on specific market days) and its increased use as a theatre for public ceremony and celebration. The Pamfili presence within the city was thus distinct from the Francophile and Florentine

---

7 L. Nussdorfer, *Civic Politics in the Rome of Urban VIII* (Princeton, NJ 1992).

connections of the Barberini, which looked back, as Gregory XV had also done, to the Aldobrandini pontificate at the turn of the century. Yet papal power in Baroque Rome could also reveal itself momentarily nervous, as with the fierce reaction of Urban VIII to astrological speculation on the end of his pontificate, though that indeed was not unconnected with the rising tide of Spanish hostility towards him. Thus power was not solely related to wealth in papal Rome, but potential financial strength was necessary to consolidate real power, as for example in the post of Cardinal Camerlengo, which at this date was a venal office, calculated at the beginning of the 1630s to cost between 50,000 and 70,000 scudi. Under his jurisdiction, officials, mostly clerical, occupying posts which were again mostly venal, had responsibility not only for the grain supply, the supply of meat and oil, the port of Rome and the customs, but for other urban spheres too, such as the mint and the coinage, most of the prisons and maintenance of the main streets. The judicial authority of the Apostolic Chamber, however, extended beyond the city, to cases arising elsewhere in the papal states as well, but many of the functions of the Chamber had some partial extension beyond the city.

Such responsibilities were exemplified by supervision of the Roman water supply from the seventeenth century. Within the city some of these functions involved co-operation with the surviving municipal officials, while intervention by Curial Congregations headed by cardinals occurred spasmodically rather than systematically, or was naturally prominent at specific moments, as when the city was threatened by plague between 1629 and 1632. Some Curial Congregations indeed were responsible for the affairs of the papal states only outside Rome itself, as with the Congregation of Buon Governo and the Consulta. The suspension of inferior authority, which in Rome followed a pope's death, was not without parallels in the autocracies of the old European order, though the categories of prisoner released by the cancellation of office-holders' personal authorization were perhaps unusually extensive there. Ritual humiliation of statues of newly deceased popes was also an interesting counterpart to the often belated commemoration of the more considered virtues or achievements of the pontiff by a papal family's expenditure on an elaborate tomb.

Hereditary princely authority was also exerted in maintaining authority during a vacancy of the Holy See, in that the Savelli monopolized the position of Marshal of the Church, in effect controlling access to the conclave; while the college of cardinals claimed at least partial interim powers in the government of the papal states, as well as, more dubiously, in the diocesan supervision of the Rome bishopric and even oversight of the patriarchate of the West. The maintenance of public order in the city during a vacancy of the Holy See allowed a more unfettered authority to be claimed, in these abnormal circumstances, both by the college of cardinals as a whole and by the municipal officials. But even in supposedly normal conditions, overlapping jurisdictions within the city, typical enough of pre-Revolutionary European regimes, occasionally required an imposed demarcation, such as that attempted by Paul V in 1612; one constant, however, remained the fact that tribunals presided over by lay magistrates had no jurisdiction over clerics. Even during ordinary times lay employees of the papal Court were subject to a special tribunal, the so-called Corte Savella. But during a vacancy of the Holy See the governorship of the Borgo, the quarter where the Vatican housed the conclave, was entrusted to a cleric, in place of the lay governor who held responsibility under each pope.

At the seat of the municipal administration, the readopted Capitol, papal authority promoted or permitted the elaboration of buildings, planned from the sixteenth century but only gradually completed in the seventeenth, which nevertheless included prominent reminders of ultimate pontifical sovereignty. In parallel with this visual reordering, revised statutes of the Roman municipality, from 1580 onwards, were operative by virtue of papal approval. That confirming authority was what ultimately determined the spheres of action of the Senator, the three Conservators, the larger public council and the smaller secret council, and the other municipal magistrates and officials. The Senator's subordinate judges, indeed, sought appointment directly by Curial not municipal favour, while the fact that the Senator himself could not be a native of the city emphasized the dependence of his judicial office on papal sovereignty. The agrarian basis of Rome's urban society was also recalled in the use of the Conservators' Capitoline palace not only by the civic administration of the three Conservators themselves, the urban notaries' corporation and the tribunals of the artisan guilds, but also by tribunals acting in the interests of great landlords. The cult of local saints specifically associated with Rome was also celebrated at the palace, to be complemented before the end of the seventeenth century not only by another 'Roman' saint, S. Francesca Romana, and the 'adopted' Roman, St Philip Neri, but also by the candidate successfully promoted for beatific status by a family of Baroque Rome in the case of Ludovica Albertoni.

While Innocent X, himself a Roman, encouraged the completion of the Capitoline buildings, he counter-balanced this by the suppression of some minor municipal offices in 1644. After 1669, formal meetings of the Capitoline councils appear to have ceased on any regular basis, leaving only occasional gatherings and specifically those held when the Holy See fell vacant. Commissions continued to have specific functions, such as partial involvement in the maintenance of Rome's water supplies and oversight of aspects of the annual Carnival, quite apart from delegations to superintend specific ceremonies or to make representations on particular issues to the pope. But a permanent representative of papal authority was also present in municipal business, the Procurator Fiscal of the Capitol, whose income in part depended on the efficient administration of justice in the civic tribunals. So too the municipal finances were in no sense wholly independent of papal finances administered by the Apostolic Chamber, and municipal officers handled, in addition to the tax on wine, a tax on meat and certain payments from the Jewish community of the city, among other revenues. The main customs dues, including an initial levy on wine, did not pass through municipal accounts *en route* to the papal coffers.

As with other European municipalities of the early modern period, the Capitoline authorities entered into consolidated debt, to the extent that eventually over 70 per cent of municipal income at Rome was devoted to interest payable on bonds in the papal *monti*. Increases in the meat tax were particularly directed towards servicing such debt, which was in addition to payments owed by the Capitoline magistracy to investors in papal venal office, over and above holders of municipal venal office. Expenditure also involved the presentations of altar plate or candles to certain Roman churches and provision of organ music at S. Maria in Aracoeli, adjacent to the Capitol, which still continued in the present century. Roman municipal authority was thus indubitably dependent and also essentially dispersed, especially by contrast with the concentration of local power allowed to the civic elite in the politically more uncertain city of Bologna, within the papal states. Equally, after 1700, non-Romans continued to enter the Curia, sometimes using the Roman University of La Sapienza to acquire the necessary legal formation, although a fixed schedule of Roman nobility was finally drawn up in the eighteenth century, under Benedict XIV, in 1746. While papal officials regulated the crucial weight and content of the basic Roman bread-loaf, the Roman municipal authorities, like those in other places in the papal states, retained responsibility for enforcing the price and quality of other food-stuffs and for supervising weights and measures. But by the seventeenth century papal officials set the price not only of meat, cheese and oil, but of other comestibles too.

Guilds

Under normal conditions oversight of the urban artisan guilds at Rome remained a municipal affair, but as the seventeenth century progressed, direct papal levies on the guilds became a regular financial measure. While an ordinary civic militia was directed by subordinate Capitoline officials, the guild network of organized labour was specially deployed on occasion, for example in maintaining anti-plague measures. Outside the walls, by contrast, the advance of papal sovereignty at the expense of intermediate authority had arguably made least progress close to Rome itself, for precisely feudal powers had been retained by the greatest baronial families, like the Orsini or the Colonna, while the Barberini had indeed married into the latter and so helped their acquisition of similar rights. Fiefs were also owned by Roman institutions, like the Santo Spirito hospital, but the feudal jurisdiction of the Capitol, beyond the city walls, was no longer of vast importance, though the fief of Magliano in Sabina took civic temporal jurisdiction into one of the Suburbicarian Sees held by the Cardinal Bishops.

Epidemics, on the other hand, represented a threat to Rome from all other territory in the Italian peninsula. The special papal Congregation with ultimate responsibility for measures against plague was revived in 1629–34, more successfully, in terms of the preservation of health, than in 1656–57. But for even relative success co-operation of Curial and Capitoline officials was essential, especially as the latter exercised much practical oversight of the measures, including those against itinerant beggars, which in turn demanded the involvement of exceptionally extended categories of adult male inhabitants of the city. Lay activity thus complemented the work in quarantine centres of regular clergy, like the Theatines and the Ministers of the Sick, which was again financially supported by the Capitol. As a precaution against plague within the city, the poor and unemployed were pursued with unusual vigour, and attempts were made to confine categories of both male and female in existing or specially adapted institutions. A plan for the latter had already been drawn up in 1627, and a systematic investigation of the poor of each parish was already conducted in 1629, but was not immediately repeated.

The character of papal government at Rome nevertheless led to some distinctive features, not perhaps entirely paralleled in other early modern European examples of anti-plague legislation and practical measures. The complementary care provided by the regular orders during the threat of epidemic at Rome was separately supervised, for once by the Congregation of the Consulta. The special devotions designed to avert divine wrath and punishment were led by the pope in person, when Urban VIII headed repeated public processions to the basilica of S. Maria Maggiore, and when he said Mass at the church of St Sebastian, the great protector against plague, which he had restored on the Palatine. Papal authority enforced the cancellation of Carnival festivities; and the end of the plague threat was marked by a papal visit to S. Maria in Aracoeli, adjacent to the Capitol. Papal authority was obviously just as crucial in more normal times too, in the regulation of lay devotion within the city.

Despite the repeated restrictions on unauthorized cults during the pontificate of Urban VIII, civic support enabled the Albertoni family to promote popular veneration for Ludovica Albertoni, a Roman matron of the early sixteenth century. But only with the succession of Clement X, from the Roman family of Altieri, which became linked with the Albertoni through the pope's choice of Cardinal Nephew, could formal beatification of Ludovica be pursued, 1670–71, and Bernini's recumbent statue be erected, 1671–74.[8] The success of the Hieronymites in fostering the cult of another Roman saint, St Alessio, depended on the conjunction of favour shown both by the municipal authorities and by the Barberini family, as witnessed in the latter case by the famous music drama about the saint, performed in the Barberini palace in 1632. The earthly power of the pope himself was equally recognized by municipal activity, whether in public celebration of Taddeo Barberini's elevation to the Prefecture of the city, in the face of diplomatic envoys' hostility, or by memorial inscriptions to commemorate the pope or members of his family,

8 S.K. Perlove, *Bernini and the Idealization of Death: the 'Blessed Ludovica Albertoni' and the Altieri Chapel* (London 1991).

culminating in the commissioning of a Capitoline statue of Urban VIII, completed by Bernini in 1640. The commission to rebuild the Trevi fountain, beneath the Quirinal rather than the Capitol, originally awarded to Bernini, was a project controlled by the pope and members of his family however; for popes often sought to commemorate themselves by monumental fountains as much as by the erection of obelisks.

Papal intervention also diverted funds normally controlled by the municipality to improve drainage or contribute to the cost of housing pilgrims during the Jubilee of 1625. Repair of the Pantheon, whatever damage popular sentiment attributed to Barberini involvement with the monument, was also undertaken with redeployed funds normally managed by the municipal authorities, as a result of papal orders. Papal policy again caused the systematic debt of the municipality to increase, in the case of financial contribution to work intended to control water flow in the Tiber river system, upstream of Rome, where flooding remained a recurring problem. But the pope was not, in turn, willing to contribute himself to the costs of celebrations for the 'local' saint, S. Francesca Romana, in 1638. He, after all, was faced with the need to double the systematic debt of the papacy itself during a period of twenty years, with obvious implications for the tax burden on his temporal subjects, a burden which was evident in indirect as opposed to direct taxes even more in Rome itself than in the rest of the papal states. That balance, in fact, reflected the interests of the upper classes rather than the artisans at Rome, and gave formal recognition to the civic consent supposedly involved in the raising of secular revenue.

An equally formal municipal participation was indeed required when indirect taxation was increased in Rome on the occasion of the second War of Mantuan Succession in 1628. This way of collecting extra revenue for special needs had its own precedents, as when Pius V was raising funds for the struggle in France in 1567 or Sixtus V was reinforcing the papal fleet in 1588. The parallels in the pontificate of Clement VIII involved funds for the war in Hungary against the Turks, but also contributions towards the cost of supplying grain which, after all, benefited Rome and its population themselves. Despite potential civic benefit, however, proposed alteration to the way in which money was raised for road repairs and street improvement within the walls was successfully resisted. More popular disquiet greeted further increases in indirect taxation at Rome by 1629. The authority of parish priests was ordered into action, ostensibly to assess the realities of wealth and poverty in the city. But papal expectation of a direct, even if voluntary grant from the better-off in Rome met with repeated resistance in 1630, despite the efforts of civic and papal officials, and criticism of papal nepotism began to be heard.

The War of Castro

Such tension increased in the final years of the pontificate of Urban VIII, as the pope reasserted papal suzerainty over a possession of the Farnese, in the

War of Castro, extending from 1641 to 1644. Although the interests and security of the papal states were nominally at issue, there was a feeling that rather more at stake was the family ambition of the Barberini, at odds with the Farnese, as the last papal dynasty openly to create a princely patrimony, in the full territorial sense. Financial distress was real enough as a result of Urban's far from successful war, so that the tensions in Rome common during the vacancy of the Holy See, in this case following Urban's death, were abnormally enhanced. Civic reaction, even before the pope's death, began to suggest that a distinction was sensed, between pontifical and proprietary interests. Yet initially the sovereignty of the papal states might have been considered a genuine issue, since Paul III had to a degree impaired this by his creation of the Farnese duchy of Castro, as an enclave in Lazio itself, north of Rome.

The further instability, threatened by Farnese financial difficulties affecting the papal system of finance itself, also appeared to involve the rival ambitions of Taddeo Barberini. In the escalation of calculated discourtesies in Rome between the Farnese duke of Parma and members of the Barberini family, the duke shockingly forced his presence on the pope in 1640, in a more serious breach of essential pontifical protocol. Financial pressure on the duke could be increased in response, not least by diverting profitable grain exports from the duchy of Castro. The conduct of the war against the duke became very much a family affair, involving the Barberini cardinals as well as Taddeo, despite initial stress on the defence of the patrimony of St Peter. Extra indirect taxes had an immediate impact, before the question of military enrolment in Rome was raised, while exaction of some taxation became more openly a Curial rather than a civic operation.

Popular resentment, however, forced the speedy abandonment of an innovatory tax on common as opposed to fine wine. For the questions at stake in the conflict were constantly expanding, as the expulsion of some regular clergy from Parma and Piacenza suggested, and Barberini ambition was also suspected to extend to the Parma duchy itself, not just the Castro enclave, giving rise to defensive agreement between other Italian and European powers. With such implicit support, and further practical help, the duke of Parma was thus able to reverse the thrust of the war, invading the papal states in 1642, arousing the spectre of loss of the never perfectly certain city of Bologna. The municipal offer to organize a civic militia for the defence of Rome itself was therefore not entirely disinterested, as Bologna, Imola and Faenza surrendered in turn, but capability was another problem, for both mounted and unmounted militia. The point could not be concealed, when the pope himself retreated from the exposed Quirinal to the Vatican, within its own system of walls, however old.

Because the costly war seemed to have endangered so much and achieved so little, except the survival of Rome without sack, it was impossible to prevent criticism of the Barberini nephews, which the pope in effect recognized by his establishment of the 1642 theological commission to advise him on the permitted limits of family favour. While Roman artisans, as militiamen, achieved unusual rights to go about armed, indirect taxes at Rome continued to rise, as troops of other Italian states openly entered the war against the pope by 1643. Papal attempts to confiscate silver in Rome in return for bonds in the papal debt were almost as much of a fiasco as the conduct of the war itself. More important was the prospective loss of support for the pope from the Florentine community within Rome itself, given the crucial involvement of Florentines as well as Genoese in the workings of pontifical finance. Money shortage was experienced at popular level in the city too, yet, with a certain logic, further financial demands were made by the papal government on the municipality even as the need for peace negotiations was at last being addressed by the pope.

Prospective resistance to a direct poll-tax was recognized to be beyond the ability of even the parish priests to surmount, and Curial clerics were supposed to ensure collection, in the face not only of refusal by armed artisans but of opposition from some parish priests too. By early 1644, the papal poll-tax experiment had been rapidly abandoned, followed by a peace treaty which was unproductive for the papacy, but indirect taxes continued to increase in number and to rise, almost until the death of the pope in mid-summer. Encroachment on the gold reserves had even been necessary, when papal innovations in taxation met the resistance of the normally privileged classes and the unusually armed populace. The débâcle of the Castro War certainly contrasted with the final uncontested enlargement of the papal states, in the case of Urbino. But it also ensured that nepotism remained an issue for the rest of the seventeenth century.

Urban improvements

The bull of 1692 against nepotism had been partly the work of Cardinal Albani, who subsequently became Pope Clement XI. His heraldic arms, the star and *monti*, are ubiquitous in Rome, visible in sculpted or other form on many monuments. But what his arms celebrated was hardly family aggrandizement on the Barberini model, but rather the pope's princely care for the city and its people. Urban improvement, in the clearing and levelling of squares for example, in one sense took up a programme promoted earlier by Alexander VII, in the mid-seventeenth century, as well as by immediately post-Tridentine papal road construction. The installation of further granaries in part of the Baths of Diocletian, the encouragement of manufactures in the work-house of San Michele, the provision of a proper quay at the Ripetta, were all part of the work of Clement XI in this sphere.

The improvement of sewerage and the creation of new fountains, not only revival of earlier projects for the Trevi fountain, all had an obvious importance for the health of the civic population, and were not just a response to the periodic flooding of the Tiber, experienced once again at the beginning of the pontificate. So too the building works that were continued throughout his pontificate were more than just a reaction to earthquake damage at its start or promotion of urban employment in the construction and decorative trades. Intervention to preserve or restore many churches, including some relatively minor and obscure ones, was clearly part of a programme to demonstrate the unbroken traditions of the Roman faith and papal authority, stretching back to the early Christian centuries. That this had an ecclesiological purpose is obvious, though the relative sensitivity to archaeological evidence shown by Clement and the scholars and artists who worked with him and for him should not obscure the fact that the essential aim was not a novelty; for a devout if comparatively less scientific archaeological approach to Christian antiquities above and below ground had been conspicuously displayed by Baronius and even on occasion by the Barberini.[9] Thus the projects instigated under Clement which subsequently, by the end of the eighteenth century, produced newly systematic collections of Roman antiquities, made available to the public by the papacy itself, and not just by individual cultured cardinals, eventually helped to encourage the non-Italian and often non-Catholic tourism which began to contribute to the Roman economy.

But classical antiquity as such, except as a testimony to Christian triumph, was not at the heart of the Clementine programme. For once again it is crucial to note the continuity as opposed to novelty in the pope's outlook. After the conspicuous celebration of papal power in Barberini Rome, the pontificate of Innocent X saw a variation, in terms of projects and favoured artists, rather than a rejection of such visual display. With regard to both projects and artists, the pontificate of Alexander VII also represented in many respects a resumption of the Barberini ambitions for the physical state of Rome. It has been noted, correctly enough, that the pontificates of the later seventeenth century were relatively restrained, by contrast, in some cases even austere, as far as conspicuous display and papal expenditure were concerned, as opposed to the personal taste or learning of Odescalchi or Ottoboni, or the alternative cultural centre of the Court of Christina of Sweden.

As has been argued throughout the present work, commitment to pastoral duty in the Rome diocese was not a peculiarity of the later seventeenth-century pontificates, but rather a continuity largely maintained, with the possible exception of Innocent X, throughout the century; and so it was natural enough that this should still be demonstrated in the first pontificate of the next century by Clement XI. What altered the means employed for emphasizing that pastoral role and responsibility were exterior circumstances. The conspicuous austerity of the late seventeenth-century popes had not in the end achieved so very much against either Jansenist dissidence, chiefly in France, or the fluctuating but related regalism and Gallicanism found in the kingdom of Louis XIV. Many of the specific Roman projects undertaken by Clement

9 B.A.V.: MS Barberiniani Latini 7819, fo. 59r: 3 Apr. 1624; cf. Biblioteca Vallicelliana, Rome: MS Q. 35; C.M.S. Johns, *Papal Art and Cultural Politics. Rome in the Age of Clement XI* (Cambridge 1993).

were devised to limit costs, while some major achievements, such as new façades for the basilicas of St John Lateran and S. Maria Maggiore, were postponed, to be accomplished only later in the century. Financial constraint was not however the chief difficulty under which Clement laboured.

As already noted, the opening of the Spanish Succession contest coincided with the start of his pontificate, and he struggled with only limited success to resist both the pressures applied by the competing powers of Catholic Europe to secure his support and recognition of their claims, and even the invasion of papal territory. Furthermore, the papal response to the French Crown's demands for doctrinal as well as political pronouncement hardly proved more successful, given the sustained opposition among French and other Jansenists to the issue of *Unigenitus*, intended to impose a final resolution of the disputes involved. Clement's building, restoration and decorative schemes in Rome were thus a complex response to very difficult circumstances, and cannot truly be seen as a simple reaction. So while it may be correct that the works he promoted were not just a conscious substitute for successful displays of either political or doctrinal authority which were beyond his ability, the identity of the projects does suggest determined demonstration of papal claims to an ancient and continuous power in the face of hostile forces. The city of Rome over which the papal prince ruled, the diocese of which he was the resident pastor, was to provide the theatre in which the claims of the papacy to wider jurisdiction could still be shown.

Whatever the regalism of Catholic rulers elsewhere, within the city the supremacy of the sacred over the secular could be emphasized, by the provision of gates and railings to prevent the profanation of the narthex of a church or basilica, and the sacred status of the Coliseum, as a chief place of Christian martyrdom, was preserved by similar means. While relics and the constancy of martyrs, in the face of secular rulers' hostility, were given ceremonial and visual exhibition, the responsibilities of the reigning bishop of Rome were also underlined. One relatively major project resumed by Clement was embellishment of the cathedral, St John Lateran, begun by Clement VIII, and subsequently renewed by Innocent X, after restoration of the Baptistry by Urban VIII. Still wider spheres of papal jurisdiction were recalled not at the Lateran basilica, traditionally associated itself with the French Crown, but at St Peter's. Substantial work on the interior decoration of the basilica was set in motion, even if major external projects, such as revival of the plan for a third section of the colonnade, to define the Eastern limits of the piazza, or the creation of a new sacristy adequate for the needs of the basilica were, in the one case, not pursued, or, in the other, postponed to later in the century.

While St Peter's was traditionally associated with the Emperors, among secular rulers, the dutiful subordination of Catholic princes to the needs of the Church and the authority of the papacy was represented, in the face of the hostile pressures which Clement was encountering from both Bourbons and Habsburgs, by the completion of the monument to Christina of Sweden and the placing of the equestrian statue of Charlemagne in the narthex, opposite

Bernini's mounted Constantine. The work at S. Maria Maggiore, traditionally associated with the Spanish Crown, was less extensive, but the pope's resistance to Crown claims to legatine jurisdiction in Sicily, a chief focus of dynastic struggle at this very time, was given further expression by interventions in the fabric and decoration of the Sicilian 'national' church in Rome. Continued conflict between the Catholic secular powers of Europe was also an obstacle to the pope's entirely traditional desire to unite Catholic Christendom in a campaign against the Turks, especially given the opportunity which the failure of the Turkish siege of Vienna had provided before the beginning of the new century. While the anti-Turkish campaigns might only resume with the greatest success as peace in Europe was at last achieved, Clement could approve the completion at St Peter's of the monument to Innocent XI, under whom Vienna had been relieved. Equally traditional was the pope's interest in displaying the ultimate headship of Rome over the ancient Eastern Churches.

Clement's involvement in the conservation and restoration of the venerable Roman church of San Clemente was more than a tribute to the first of that name to hold the Petrine office, a martyr at the hands of oppressive secular authority. The decorative scheme showed both the martyr and the subsequent exercise of papal responsibilities, including, in conspicuous but subordinate positions, Cyril and Methodius, the apostles of the Slavs, associated also with the Balkan areas which Clement XI hoped to see recovered for Christendom from Turkish control. But to regard any of Clement's projects in Rome as angry gesturing, or displacement of energies which could not be successfully employed outside the city, would be mistaken. They were not a negative complaint, but intended as a positive means of instruction. The involvement of the Catholic secular powers was consciously sought in all this, and not simply because of the pope's own financial limitations.

Participation in Roman restorations and rebuildings was to encourage the unity of Catholic rulers and their sense of solidarity with the Roman Church, under papal leadership. So the great series of statues of the Apostles at the Lateran, the papal cathedral, was accomplished with subsidies from Spanish and German prelates and princes, and French sculptors were included prominently in the commissions for individual statues, even though this failed to excite a financial contribution from Louis XIV. The papal plans for the Lateran thus particularly renewed the restoration begun there by Clement VIII, which was intended to celebrate and consolidate the harmony of Catholic Europe following the reconciliation of Henri IV of France and Franco-Spanish peace. The continuing delicacy of the papacy's relationship with the Portuguese Crown, after the mid-seventeenth-century recovery of independence, suggested the value of involving the Portuguese kings in the Lateran series of the apostles too. But while a financial response was indeed forthcoming in this case, the relative wealth of the Portuguese Crown, increasing at this time, made relations with Rome over control in the foreign missionfields more rather than less strained; and ceremonial concessions for the Church in Portugal itself, during the eighteenth century, could not in fact prevent a fierce regalism, in which Portugal led the attack on the Society of Jesus against a faltering defence of the Jesuits by the papacy.

Once again, as far as the pontificate of Clement XI was concerned, it was in Rome itself that the pope could try to promote co-operation in place of conflict among the Catholic secular powers of Europe. The pope as ruler of the city could involve other Catholic rulers in urban improvement, and thus it was that the scheme was revived to create a monumental stairway down from the Roman convent of the French branch of the Minims to an area of the city associated with the power and presence of the Spanish, once Louis XIV was dead but Spain was now Bourbon. Even though not all of Clement's urban projects were completed before his own death, visible memorials of his princely care remained, combined with displays of his assertion that papal authority was traditional, continuous and indivisible. The use of an antique obelisk in one of his major fountains looked back to similar use of obelisks at the centre of newly developed spaces in papal Rome, whether in the evolution of St Peter's square, or in Bernini's work elsewhere for Alexander VII, and suggested the triumph of the Roman faith over the wisdom of the ancients. In this sense Clement did far more than simply renew papal concern, found so clearly under the Barberini, to demonstrate monumentally on the Capitol itself the claims and achievements of papal authority.

More important, in symbolic terms, was Clement's canonization in 1712 of Pius V, who had united Catholic Christendom, however briefly, against Turkish Islam. The encouragement of a revived tradition of mosaic work in the interior decoration of St Peter's also had a more than practical value, in that it represented the continuity of Roman tradition and papal leadership from even earlier ages of Church history; this suggested a reclaiming of devotion to Christian antiquity from the monopolizing claims of Jansenist critics of Rome. Repairs and reordering at the Pantheon underlined a still greater Roman antiquity, but one crucially sanctified by the lives and deaths of Christian martyrs. Ancient Christian images that were supernaturally sacred, because of miraculous powers, were also preserved, in Clement's projects, irrespective of aesthetic priorities; but this again was not innovation, but a tradition already found, for instance, at the Chiesa Nuova of Baronius and the Oratorians. The punctuation of space within the city of Rome by the re-erection of obelisks in fact continued to the very end of the papal Ancien Régime, involving those at the Quirinal and elsewhere as late as 1782, 1787, and 1789 itself onwards.

Papal intervention to conserve and reorder the displays of classical antiquities on the Capitol was matched by the addition of a picture gallery there, as part of the programme of Clement XII and Benedict XIV. Under the latter, conservation was also undertaken on the Coliseum, following restoration of the Arch of Constantine begun under Clement XII, while at the mid-point of the eighteenth century a major repair of the ancient city walls overtook previous piecemeal restoration. Such programmes should not be seen solely as promoting a tourism attracted to classical remains or as demonstrating a fashionable adherence to ideals of good government and enlightened rule. While such aspirations were alluded to, for example by the final form of the Trevi fountain, the precise context should be remembered in which, for instance, the Capitoline authorities oversaw the cleaning and repair of almost all the city fountains at the same mid-century point of time. The approach of the Holy Year of 1750 thus stimulated a demonstration of papal authority which was not to be confined, any more than under Clement XI, to a purely secular or princely dimension.

In the case of the ancient church of SS. Pietro e Marcellino, for instance, Benedict XIV decided on major reconstruction, going far beyond more limited interventions in the fabric under Clement XI and Benedict XIII. But he permitted the new construction to be delayed by archaeological investigations, which were precisely part of his resuscitation of study of early Christian antiquities and history, conducted at the Chiesa Nuova of the Oratorians, once the centre of the work of Baronius. Moreover, Benedict originally intended the reconstructed church to remain the residence of the Maronites, in whose troubled affairs he had intervened, demonstrating the ultimate papal headship and care of the non-Latin-rite Churches in communion with Rome. Furthermore, the attention paid to this particular church building was increased by its location, on one of the connecting routes, which Benedict was intent on improving for the Jubilee year, linking the basilicas of the Lateran, S. Maria Maggiore and S. Croce in Gerusalemme. The new façades for the last two of these, completed under Benedict, complemented the monumental main façade finally added to the papal cathedral, at the Lateran, by 1737.

Thus the preservation of classical antiquities certainly remained one priority of the eighteenth-century papacy, from edicts of Clement XI in the first years of the century to the elaboration of a museum collection at the Vatican completed by Pius VI, via the appointment of the famous classical scholar and antiquarian, Winckelmann as Superintendent of Antiquities, even if the latter's direct impact on the collection was marginal. But even the short pontificate of Innocent XIII (1721–24) had equally seen the continuation of the projects not only for the Lateran façade and the Trevi fountain but also for the 'Spanish Steps', though the care of Benedict XIII for his episcopal and indeed metropolitan roles did not, admittedly, contribute much to conclusion at the Lateran. Obviously the culture of eighteenth-century Rome was open to international influences, especially in the visual arts, whatever the priorities of such a pope. Papal patronage was only one possible, local influence on adoption of more classicizing styles in the visual arts. This increasingly independent evolution of Roman culture was also suggested by the development in the city, from the late seventeenth century onwards, of theatres which were essentially public, whatever their patrimonial origins or ownership.

THE PAPAL STATES: BOLOGNA

Even less effective, arguably, were papal attempts to direct economic and social change in the central papal states, beyond the walls of the city, but on which, however partially, the urban economy itself depended. The movement of capital into investment funds, the *monti*, contributed to the conversion of arable land to pasture, so that under Innocent XI, for instance, only a tenth of the surface area of the region immediately around Rome, the *Agro Romano*, was devoted to agriculture as opposed to pasture. These developments resisted papal intervention, such as that of Alexander VII, designed to promote an export trade in grain. The papal commission responsible for maintaining the grain supply to Rome, the Annona, was, after all, intimately connected to the interests of land-owning families; nor was this seriously affected by the attempt of Benedict XIII, in 1725, to create a supervisory Congregation for the Annona. Equally limited in impact and in duration was the partial relaxation by Benedict XIV, from 1743, of the regulations governing the grain supply, removing a crucial tax in preparation for an intended freeing of the grain trade between the different provinces of the papal states from 1748.

The local monopolies maintained by landlords, at the expense of the general population of a given area, were indeed reinforced by the transfer of estates from the most ancient baronial families to relatively new dynasties, chiefly associated with popes of the Ancien Régime. This was true despite papal governmental attention to restoring or opening up the seaports, at Civitavecchia, Terracina, Anzio and Corneto. Similarly, the rebuilding of parish churches in the central papal states, during the eighteenth century, might often reflect more the reassertion of baronial authority than the solicitude of papal government itself. The latter was however active, in as much as the papal Congregation del Buon Governo intervened north of Rome to provide aqueducts at Civitavecchia, Corneto, Nepi and Sutri, while improvement of the Via Flaminia involved an important viaduct. Symptomatic nevertheless was the succession to Colonna ownership of estates at Palestrina by the Barberini, at Valmontone by the Pamfili, by the Rospigliosi and Borghese elsewhere, to Savelli ownership of estates at Ariccia by the Chigi.

New construction was undertaken by such families, all the same, which in some sense benefited the wider communities, as with works for the Albani at Soriano, the Ruspoli at Vignanello, the Pamfili at Valmontone and S. Martino, the Altieri at Monterano and Oriolo, the Rospigliosi at Zagarola, for example. Even a non-papal family favoured by a papal dynasty, like the Bolognetti for instance under Clement XII and Benedict XIV, might be the ultimate owners of part of the once extensive baronial possessions of an ancient lineage such as the Orsini; but these changes in ownership could not deflect the impact on the local population of events like the epidemic of 1665 or the food shortage of 1691. Over a long period, despite such interruptions, the population of a given locality might nevertheless increase, as it did for example at Vicovaro, to the extent of being nearly three times in 1782 what it had been in 1656.[10] But for all that the sector of the papal states nearest Rome, the *Agro Romano*

10 M. Spesso, *La cultura architettonica a Roma nel secolo 18: Gerolamo Theodoli (1677–1766)* (Rome 1991).

and Lazio, largely remained in a state of agrarian stagnation during the eighteenth century. This was despite the involvement of what by this time was an essentially urban element, the so-called *mercanti di campagna* in the leasing of many estates.

Such stagnation did not allow the port of Civitavecchia to compete successfully with the new Tuscan freeport of Livorno, which in turn also managed to eclipse in importance the Adriatic papal port of Ancona, despite the decision of 1732 to make that too a freeport. Ancona indeed continued to suffer further from Venetian competition, whatever the relative quiescence of eighteenth-century Venice. In the more distant parts of the papal states some manufacture, especially of silk and textiles, attempted to promote itself in the eighteenth century, but quality was both poor and variable, as a result of a poorly controlled putting-out system. Yet where larger units of manufacture were found, papal policy tolerated obstructive guild privileges because of a desire not to disturb local interests among the population of the papal states. Whereas exceptionally at Bologna, despite the existence of the papal Legate, local self-government remained relatively extensive, because of traditional Roman awareness of the political sensitivity of the city, elsewhere in the papal states such powers were much more limited.

Indeed, the powers of a Legate were further enhanced in specific cases, as for instance at Ravenna by Cardinal Alberoni during the pontificate of Clement XII. Yet even close to Rome the impotence of papal government was vividly revealed to the unfortunate population, as foreign armies occupied places near the capital; nor was this only a reflection of the weak position in which Clement XI found himself at the beginning of the eighteenth century, epitomized by Alberoni's diversion of the Spanish fleet from supposed co-operation in the relief of Corfu from Turkish blockade. In the European conflicts with direct repercussions for Italian territories during the pontificates of Clement XII and Benedict XIV, places as close to Rome as Ostia, Velletri, Palestrina, experienced occupation or devastation by foreign troops. Such damage to areas of the papal states nearest the capital further ensured that the economy of this sector remained depressed, a stagnant agrarian economy which had virtually no elasticity which might stimulate consumption of manufactures from other parts of the papal states. Calls for the papacy to adopt a more protectionist policy towards manufactured imports also failed in the face of the eighteenth-century popes' evident vulnerability to pressure from the major powers of Catholic Europe.

From the beginning of the eighteenth century, with the creation of a new Curial Congregation for the Economy, Clement XI attempted to rationalize the fiscal system in the papal states, pursuing tax reform, but with only modest results. Another new Congregation, founded in 1701, was intended to review and then improve the agrarian economy of the *Agro Romano* and the grain supply to Rome, encouraging commerce and manufacture more generally too. But though a wholesale reform programme was drawn up, the competing interests of traditional agencies, both within and without the Curia, prevailed;

and the new Congregation had effectively ceased to function by 1706, before being suppressed in 1715. The subsequent dominance of Cardinal Coscia, during the pontificate of Benedict XIII, did nothing to improve the temporal government of the papal states, but rather the reverse, with a considerable increase in papal debt. This was the net effect of the attempt by Benedict XIII to deregulate the grain trade and promote economic expansion by means of another new Congregation, nominally for Agriculture.

As a result, the real work of yet two more new Congregations, instituted by Clement XII, was confined to investigating and attempting to redress the financial disorders of the Coscia regime. In addition to the public building works undertaken in Rome itself, the pope also promoted major works outside the capital, such as a land reclamation scheme at Ravenna, in which Cardinal Alberoni invested some of his surplus energies. By contrast, the plan of Benedict XIV to stimulate the textile industry in the papal states, as one means of revitalizing the feeble papal finances, had little success. But from 1748 Benedict began the deregulation of the grain trade, confirmed and extended by Clement XIII in 1766. Despite an interruption to this policy subsequently, Pius VI renewed it for Bologna in 1780 and then for the rest of the papal states; but many controls in fact remained in force.

The pope also undertook land reclamation, but essentially at the expense of papal finances and to the ultimate benefit of a few land-holders. Papal nepotism under Pius VI, not confined to the creation of Palazzo Braschi, contributed to the limited results of drainage schemes in the Pontine Marshes. Once again a new Congregation was formed, in 1776, intended to achieve a systematic tax reform and revival of the economy. Internal customs dues were in fact effectively suppressed in 1777, and this was complemented in 1786 by new regulations for the external customs of the papal states. Though the pope's experience in the management of papal finance was clearly important, political considerations still made their impact, so that Bologna was excluded from the general suppression of internal customs barriers.

Local interests and private privileges in fact more widely impeded the economic reforms of the pontificate. In the case of Bologna, the city and surrounding territory remained constantly able to defend its own advantages, as for example with edicts expelling 'foreign' (that is non-Bolognese) beggars from its territory, issued in 1586, 1607, 1617 and 1633. The population of Bologna itself fluctuated between 60,000 and 70,000, from the sixteenth to the eighteenth century. The supply of the basic form of bread was in one sense left to market forces, but with ultimate oversight by a municipal tribunal, which freed specifically papal authority from any danger of popular criticism, as was shown even in riots of 1671 and 1677. But the system was defended chiefly because it suited local interests, as was demonstrated by the attempt of the Bolognese Senate to resist the deregulation of the grain trade declared by Benedict XIV, despite his own Bolognese background.

The adjustment to the bread supply made in 1772 was indeed introduced by local authority. Arguably Bologna maintained an easier equilibrium, in social and demographic terms, than, say, Ravenna, which certainly felt the effects of both food shortages and epidemics, in 1709, in the 1730s and 1760s. In that part of the Romagna an agrarian crisis, from about 1764 onwards, contributed indeed to cumulative peasant indebtedness and eviction of crop-sharing tenants. At Bologna the attempt to enclose beggars in a workhouse situated outside the city walls began as early as 1563; though the lack of efficacy contributed to a project for the enclosure of the city's beggars in 1726, under local leadership, both clerical and lay. Papal authorization was ultimately necessary, all the same, while financial difficulties impeded the realization of the 1726 plan.

A renewed project of 1756 noted that Benedict XIV had meanwhile diverted some potential funding to local educational needs. Benedict's knowledge of Bologna was of course personal and direct; but the relatively extended self-government allowed at Bologna could not, on the other hand, free the popes from ultimate responsibility in popular opinion. In the mid-eighteenth century it was to the Legate that workers in the city complained when the combined effects of taxes and excise charges threatened their ability to purchase basic foodstuffs: not only bread, but oil, wine and certain cuts of meat. In this case, it was implied, municipal regulation of supply and prices was failing the poor. The Bolognese municipality had over a long period had to contend with the effects of economic crisis in the 1590s, itself triggered at any rate by a food shortage.

Some success was achieved, in that Bologna's economy recovered during the seventeenth century, at least by comparison with the continued stagnation or decline of other Italian cities during the same period. But by 1730 new problems were presenting, which endangered the traditional combination of a largely market-regulated food supply with ultimate municipal control as far as basic foodstuffs were concerned. From that date the local authorities attempted to respond by adopting more interventionist, mercantilist policies, even if without much success, whereas previously traditional procedures had sufficed, even for instance during food shortages such as that of 1648. By 1763 the local authority at Bologna was attempting direct price regulation for an extended list of foodstuffs and animal products, while continuing to ensure that among these the basic form of bread appeared to remain at a low price. In the case of porkmeat products, a Bolognese speciality after all, a system of supply and pricing originally established in 1662 collapsed in mid-eighteenth century, precisely in 1749–50, after the evident difficulties from the 1730s.

The result was tension between the different sectors of municipal government. In the specific case of Bologna, then, despite its distinctive position within the papal states, a clear contrast can be seen between a temporal concern such as food supply, and an ecclesiastical competence, such as the regulation of matrimony, which was firmly pursued after the Council of Trent by the archiepiscopal tribunal, as the Conciliar decrees had intended. Indeed, local Bolognese statutes, of civic origin, supported the aim of the Tridentine marriage legislation by threatening loss of dowry against females who attempted to persist in clandestine exchange of vows.[11] Similarly, at Rome itself the authority of the Cardinal Vicars in the eighteenth century increasingly extended to affairs which had both religious and social dimensions, such as control of midwives. From about 1786 formal medical instruction for Roman midwives was provided.

GOVERNING THE PAPAL STATES

At Rome, however, provisioning of the city, and hence demographic growth and even law and order, were all undermined in the 1730s by the impact of European conflict in the Italian peninsula. To a degree this was to stimulate a more coherent and conscious attention to the government of the papal states as a whole under Benedict XIV. But even so the papal states remained in fact a collection of provinces and cities rather than an organic political unit, and the interplay of peninsular and international influences at the Roman Curia, as the one potential source of unified direction of papal temporal government, made this situation liable to persist. On the other hand, the peculiar conditions in the papal states should not be overestimated. Even during the upsurge of banditry in the last decades of the sixteenth century, this was not in fact confined to the central papal states, but was simultaneously marked in the Veneto, in Spanish-ruled Lombardy, in the kingdom of Naples, with parallel disorders in Sicily as well as Calabria.[12]

As far as a coherent interest bound the various provinces under papal temporal rule to the capital city, or rather Court, it was that of local elites whose members pursued parallel careers at the Roman Curia or exploited contacts there to gain provincial benefices. But that, of course, failed to distinguish such elites from those in other parts of the Italian peninsula, outside the papal states. This is, indeed, another way in which it could be argued that, for the late sixteenth and the seventeenth century at least, if less clearly in the eighteenth century, a *de facto* primatial leadership of the Church in peninsular Italy was more evident and perhaps more important than any real development in the papacy's role as temporal ruler of a part of the peninsula. Such an interpretation could be further supported by the observation that, even in the second half of the eighteenth century, attempts to achieve a more unified direction of the affairs of the papal states largely foundered on the obstacle of local privileges and interests which had, indeed, remained essentially unchallenged throughout. While eighteenth-century Rome was ever more a centre of international interests, no longer purely religious and therefore no longer denominationally restricted, it was not developing as the political capital of a state, in

11 A. Guenzi, 'La tutela del consumatore nell' antico regime. I "vittuali di prima necessità" a Bologna', in *Disciplina dell' anima, disciplina del corpo e disciplina della società tra medioevo ed età moderna*, ed. P. Prodi (Bologna 1994), pp. 733–56; cf. L. Ferrante, 'Il matrimonio disciplinato: processi matrimoniali a Bologna nel Cinquecento', in ibid., pp. 901–27.
12 A.D. Wright, 'Venetian Law and Order: a Myth?', *Bulletin of the Institute of Historical Research*, LIII (1980), 192–202.

the sense that Lisbon and Madrid, Paris and Vienna, even Turin and Florence, or Naples were, to take only examples from Catholic Europe. That this should remain the case had already been an explicit contention of Louis XIV.

One result of this was arguably to consolidate the economic, and not simply political dominance which other cities in the papal states had over their surrounding countryside. But this could equally be interpreted as confirming a long-standing tendency in the central and Northern parts of the Italian peninsula, rather than as a peculiarity either of the papal states or, within them, of the post-Tridentine period. Rural depopulation and movement to the cities in the Romagna was already under way during the sixteenth century. Accumulated debt in rural communities of the Romagna might in certain instances produce a belated surrender of vestigial local rights to urban control as late as the 1770s. But in other cases urban debt, in the same region, could by the eighteenth century allow a revived rural challenge to such civic dominance.

The resulting conflicts, however, certainly impeded any progress towards a more 'enlightened' administration projected at Rome, as much as they had obstructed plans for land reclamation in the late sixteenth and early seventeenth centuries. It might also be suggested that, in such circumstances, the Legatine tribunal at a regional centre, such as Ravenna, can best be seen not as a largely unsuccessful example of a would-be 'absolute', or, later, 'enlightened', provincial intendancy, as understood in traditional historiography, but rather as a tolerably efficient mechanism for local application of that not arbitrary but arbitrating or 'distributive' autocracy which the most recent scholarship has detected, instead, in the classic models of seventeenth-century Bourbon France and of at least Habsburg Spain. Nevertheless in the second half of the eighteenth century the Cardinal Legates at Ravenna were certainly trying to reform the working of their tribunal, in civil and criminal proceedings, but with apparently imperfect success. Papal favour towards land-owning monastic institutions, as in the Romagna, still maintained at a time when papal protection was failing against Catholic states determined on programmes of secularization and expropriation elsewhere in Europe, was also a complication. But the secular clergy of the Romagna, and much of their land, also sustained fiscal exemptions on an important scale, whatever theories may be advanced about papal temporal government supposedly overriding such privileges in the face of Tridentine reassertion of ecclesiastical liberties.

At Ferrara, economic stagnation, not unconnected with the silting up of previously navigable waterways, and manifesting itself in the decline of the silk industry, was already evident in the last decades of Este rule in the sixteenth century. But after the incorporation of Ferrara into the papal states in 1598, the plans of Clement VIII and Paul V for general land reclamation, involving regulation of the water systems, failed in the face of the multiplicity of competing local interests. In this case, involving control of water systems, which some recent historians have seen as a key characteristic of at least some authoritarian regimes, there was certainly no advance towards an 'absolute' temporal regime. On the contrary, after the food shortage of the 1590s, ecclesiastical and some lay land-holders in the area managed to increase the yield from their possessions. But this was at the expense of the productivity of the Ferrarese as a whole, since such landowners gained papal exemption of their labour-force from the common obligation to work as necessary on the conservation of the waterways which dominated the territory. Indeed, as a result, papal government was forced by the mid-seventeenth century to commute this remaining obligation into a fiscal charge, since as a direct labour imposition it had collapsed.

Yet local papal administration, based in Ferrara itself, was in turn hampered by the decision to make minor centres in the territory no longer dependent on the former ducal capital, but subject to a Roman tribunal for the supervision of temporal government, the Consulta. For all that, the projected co-operation on general land reclamation, involving Ravenna as well as Ferrara, was not achieved, as has already been noted. Deterioration of the water systems throughout these parts of the papal states, with damage to manufactures and commerce as well as agriculture, thus continued, as municipal schemes for repairs and improvement remained competitive rather than co-operative, and, being partial, almost bound to fail, even if ever attempted. That was certainly in contrast with the efforts of papal temporal government from the 1590s, extended to Ferrara in the early seventeenth century, to achieve an ultimate control of grain supply throughout all parts of the papal states. This was, however, an obvious response to particular circumstances and needs, the food shortages of the 1590s and the priority of ensuring that Rome itself was always adequately supplied with grain, even if this impeded a market in grain between the various provinces of the papal states themselves. Only the papal Legates could grant specific permission for grain sales between provinces, providing of course that the authorities in Rome itself were not maintaining an absolute prohibition at the time.[13]

At Ferrara, after the imposition of strict regulation from 1603, a Legatine control, stabilized in 1617, was partially relaxed in mid-century by Cardinal Spada, who opened the way to the sale of licences for export of grain, dependent of course on the Legate's good-will. At Ravenna accusations of improper traffic in similar licences were made against Legatine officials to the end of the papal Ancien Régime. In seventeenth-century Ferrara a virtual market in licensed exports developed, involving Genoese and Florentine businessmen, Curial prelates and major ecclesiastical institutions, and even once again officials of the Ravenna Legatine tribunal. This was in addition to contraband movement of grain; by such ways, in certain years, the Ferrarese and Romagna were in fact supplying grain to Bologna and not simply to Rome. Giving priority to grain supply and control was not, though, a peculiar obsession of the papal government, among early modern European regimes, even if, at ·

13 C. Casanova, *Le mediazioni del privilegio: Economie e poteri nelle legazioni pontificie del Settecento* (Bologna 1984).

Bologna, the relative favour shown to landowners indirectly damaged the silk industry, on to which fiscal burdens were disproportionately shifted.[14]

Damage to the silk industry at Ferrara, not least because of conflicts between groups involved in basic silk production and those interested in promoting high-quality silken fabrics, was already visible in the last years of Este rule, but was not reversed by papal attempts to intervene. Difficulties in the once leading silk industry at Bologna were largely self-induced, or compounded by advances made in production outside Italy, or even within, as in Piedmont. In the latter case, close government control thus contrasted with a lack of papal intervention at Bologna, rather than over-regulation. Similarly, the Romagna remained free to raise cattle for supply to other territories of the papal states, such as Ferrara and Bologna. But at Faenza the silk industry was only temporarily rescued from constant difficulties, between 1670 and 1720, by the intervention of French investment.

The limitations of papal government itself were certainly revealed by the early eighteenth-century attempt to collect a new, uniform tax across the papal states, supposed not least to meet the problems caused by war and foreign invasion. Despite the aim of including all privileged persons and institutions, ecclesiastical as well as lay, in the scope of the tax, the returns were in fact well below what was anticipated. Even in principle Ferrara was exempted, and Bologna successfully defended its right to make a 'voluntary' contribution, essentially on its own terms. The episode indeed strengthened Bolognese local autonomy, and in 1719 the Legate faced the possibility of armed revolt, while anti-Curial sentiments had begun to be expressed even under his predecessor in office. A successor defended the fiscal privileges of the clergy from the attempts of the civic authorities to limit these, so far was papal temporal government, even at Bologna, from reducing clerical rights in the interests of sovereign power. While bishops in the Romagna had to keep an eye on conflicts between secular and regular clergy, the disputes over financial contributions or management of charitable institutions, involving local lay authorities on the one hand and the clergy on the other, were not entirely new at the time of early eighteenth-century occupation by foreign troops. But from the later seventeenth century, and then on into the next, bishops were clearly intervening in such disputes, with some success in defending the rights of the clergy reasserted at the Council of Trent.

Once again this was not the subordination of ecclesiastical interests to those of temporal government; nor, apparently, the subjection of episcopal authority to Legatine or Curial power. At Cesena the intervention of Benedict XIII, himself a former bishop of the place, ensured in fact, whatever his original intentions, that episcopal defence of clerical fiscal exemption was confirmed in 1727. A question of a new cadastral survey of the area still remained, and in 1731 the Roman Buon Governo Congregation agreed that the clergy should

14 A.S. Ven.: Secreta Archivi Propri Roma, 17, fos 54v ff., 60v f., 61v ff., 68v ff., 71r ff.: 4 Aug.–8 Sept. 1565; 18: 19 Jan.–24 Aug. 1566.

contribute to the costs of this. Only the energy of Alberoni finally got the survey under way in 1739, though this did not culminate in a reapportioning of fiscal burdens. This was thus little different from the outcome of previous papal interventions in the same question, by Alexander VII in 1662 and Innocent XI in 1681.

International complications, at a time of foreign invasions, were more involved when Clement XI in 1719 attempted to revive the economy of the Romagna by negotiating favourable terms for imports of cloth from Habsburg territory, via the province, but encountered French opposition and threats of retaliation. Failure of such a scheme affected both Ferrara and Bologna too. The declaration of freeport status for Ancona was similarly to face Venetian opposition, the effects of international war and poor grain harvests in the Marches. Customs officials in the papal states equally had their own reasons for resisting any reduction in the network of customs barriers. But the acknowledged Roman priority of ensuring an adequate grain supply to the capital city at all times was what meant that the Marches could not balance years of poor harvest against a free trade in surplus grain in good years.

Under Clement XII, nevertheless, some progress on long-debated projects was made, not least on the diversion of waterways at Ravenna, discussed ever since a particularly bad flood in 1636. The project of a general land reclamation in the eastern provinces of the papal states was revived from 1692 and again in 1709. Benedict XIII attempted to resolve the continuing local disputes within the provinces over such a plan. But Clement XII, stimulated by further floods in 1731, encountered similar obstacles to those faced by Innocent XIII. Alberoni's ability to make progress at Ravenna was the more outstanding, and reflected his good relations, on this issue at least, with Rome itself. He was also able to make use of unemployed labour, in a way which complemented ideals of ending vagrant mendicancy.

At Bologna, the encouragement by Benedict XIV of local financial reform, from the start of his pontificate, produced little profound change, despite his close links with the city. By 1754 what had chiefly been gained was a more orderly and efficient accounting in the city's magistracy. Parallel Legatine intervention at Ferrara from the 1740s resulted only in a reordering of the civic debt; but improvement was not long-lasting, as was revealed during the food shortages of the 1760s. The Buon Governo Congregation at Rome ordered better financial procedures in the Romagna from 1755. At Ravenna, however, the continuing conflicts between lay and ecclesiastical interests were not resolved before the 1770s. Faenza benefited from the remission of certain debts owed to Rome, between 1748 and 1754, on account of the damage incurred in the occupation by foreign troops; and in 1755 the Buon Governo intervened to reorder the public debt there. The question of a new cadastral survey there became dormant until 1786, but at Cesena such a survey remained a matter of controversy, despite the intervention of the Buon Governo, from the 1750s and 1760s, until 1779. That was merely the start of a new round of dispute, despite the intervention of the Legate in the early 1780s.

Local opposition, not confined to clerical defence of fiscal privileges, impeded the progress of a new cadastral survey at Rimini beyond 1768 and an appeal in 1769 to the Buon Governo against the findings of the survey. In 1778 the finally completed survey was again challenged. At Imola the interventions of Benedict XIV over the local public debt still left a disastrous situation facing the government of Clement XIII in the food shortages of the 1760s. The crisis of the 1760s, at Faenza, saw speculative loans of grain to peasants extracting interest at an effective rate of 10 per cent, despite traditional Catholic opposition to such levels of usury. The intervention of the Legate only managed to reduce the rate demanded to 8 per cent.

With the failure of the general project of land reclamation promoted by Benedict XIV, renewed pressure for local drainage and embankment schemes might be felt. In the case of Faenza litigation between affected local interests delayed proceedings at least until 1757; for the Roman Curia was the seat of legal tribunals ready to hear such cases, as well as of administrative agencies such as the Congregation overseeing water and waterways or the Buon Governo. Moreover, the undoubted efflorescence in eighteenth-century Italy of a more critical genre of antiquarian studies, not least among ecclesiastics, provided in fact new resources for the defence of clerical immunities, in the papal states as well as elsewhere in the peninsula. Such considerations were inevitably part of the background to the crisis of the 1760s, in the papal states in general and the Romagna in particular. The initial food shortage of 1763 led to price rises, popular unrest, increased public debt, and an inability to overcome the effects of successive years of poor harvests, with rural depopulation and epidemic affecting demographic levels.

The first shortage of 1763 was not in itself too severe in the Romagna, but its effect was obviously aggravated by the inflexible demands of Rome for the supply of the capital. Accusations of local speculation also naturally arose, and the involvement, among alleged speculators, of Jewish businessmen may perhaps shed a little light on the otherwise puzzling recrudescence of anti-Jewish sentiment in eighteenth-century Italy. In any case, though the 1764 food shortage throughout the papal states was, once again, not so particularly acute in the Romagna, the poor harvest of 1765 was further threatened there by the effects of flooding, the outcome of unresolved dispute over water management and land reclamation. The papal response was partial and remedial, involving a minor relaxation of regulations and an approval of bread distributions to the poor, rather than fundamental and radical; yet the damage caused by the crisis to the already weak papal finances was obviously profound. Only from 1766 was the papal plan for a general land reclamation in the eastern papal states revived and the project revitalized. Once again, though, lay and clerical interests in the Romagna opposed a more general plan, which of necessity involved Bologna too. Conflicting local interests impeded even the extension of rice fields, and Romagna opponents of the general project for a while received Legatine support against Rome.

Nevertheless, elements at Rome had not forgotten the alternative ideal of a free market in grain. This encouraged some extension of cultivated land in parts of the papal states, even if no improvement in grain yields. In the Marches and at Urbino, grain was released for sale by the growing of maize as a new, alternative source of basic nutrition for the peasants. For all that, public debt at Urbino escalated during the food shortages of 1763–67. Criticism of Rome grew in fact, because the crisis years intensified Curial reliance on local monopolists to ensure the capital's grain supplies, while licences for private sales of grain by such interests were only belatedly halted. From the Romagna too came pleas to Cardinal Rezzonico, Chamberlain of the Roman Annona, which supervised the grain supply, for the suspension of grain export licences.

Food shortage threatened again in 1772–73, when the Legate at Ferrara, Cardinal Borghese, revealed that the poor were dependent for their survival on the import of maize from the Marches, a supply in which Jewish agents were also involved, at Ancona as well as Ferrara itself, in conditions where local civic finance was unable to make adequate provision. In the Romagna local public debt increased greatly during the 1760s. Private debt naturally grew alongside this, with confiscations of property. At Ravenna an attempt to stabilize the public debt was undermined in the 1780s, and the debt in fact began to increase again from 1786. This was the result not only of recurrent difficulties in the papal states, such as bad harvests and degradation or shortage of coinage, but also, by an irony, of the abolition by Pius VI of local imposts. In such circumstances, at Faenza, peasants were abandoning their holdings.

While the local economy of Faenza showed some signs of recovery in the second half of the eighteenth century, the rest of the Romagna stagnated, despite the attempts in the mid-1760s of the Legate, Cardinal Crivelli, to stimulate the silk industry at Ravenna, which collapsed after his tour of duty. Disputes over the administration of charitable institutions in the Romagna naturally revived in these circumstances, but investigating clerical authorities, as at Cesena in 1752, found for the Tridentine priority of episcopal control, not for any consolidation of temporal management. Equally, the Roman Congregation del Buon Governo confirmed episcopal supervision of certain charitable foundations at Faenza, which were in dispute in the second half of the eighteenth century. By 1769, even in papal Ravenna, the privileged position of monastic houses as extensive property-owners there was under attack. But the originally anonymous criticism was only briefly supported by other local interests, and was not in the end adopted by the Legate.

The initial papal project, of 1777, to eradicate the internal customs dues within the papal states was accompanied by a plan for a general cadastral survey. But the government of Pius VI did not complement this with a re-ordering of the customs at the external frontiers of the papal states, on protectionist lines, until 1786; while no major reallocation of tax burdens in the event followed from the earlier provisions. Papal temporal government had simply proved incapable of such an enforced reorganization, in fact, in the face of persisting local resistance. At Ravenna the complete deregulation of the grain market from 1780 did not long survive the shock of the French Revolution. The abolition of local customs dues tended, in any case, to destabilize the precarious public debts of civic communities in the papal states. Despite momentary signs to the contrary, the 1780s finally saw the Legate at Bologna, as promoter of the papal reform plans, lose even partial noble support, as the aristocratic interest reverted to solidarity with civic authority in defence of traditional local privileges.

Nor was Pius VI at all well placed to reduce Bolognese independence, finally, as he visibly struggled to resist the pressures of Joseph II on the institutional Church throughout his possessions. Least of all in such circumstances could the pope proceed by persuading the lay leadership of Bologna to reduce its long-standing degree of autonomy in exchange for a corresponding reduction in the privileges of the local secular and regular clergy. This was the reality behind the ultimately limited confirmation to the Legate, at this last stage of the Ancien Régime, of a jurisdiction overriding that of the archbishop of Bologna in the trials of clerics. Equally, the papal government proved impotent to prevent breaches of the new external customs barriers of the papal states by systematic contraband. Even the mid-century and late eighteenth-century popes who had particularly close links with the papal states – Lambertini, Ganganelli, Braschi – were unable to enforce major change in temporal administration. To the end of the Ancien Régime the temporal government of the papacy revealed its very real limitations, not an extension of genuine sovereign power.

CHAPTER 8

Conclusion

The occupants of the papal throne in the years from 1564 to 1789 inclusive were all in one, simple sense post-Tridentine popes. While the absence of any further General Council certainly marked this period, those popes headed a Church which was equally certainly post-Conciliar. That this was true in more than a negative or purely chronological sense was effectively ensured by the action of Pius IV, pope at the termination of the Council of Trent, in fulfilment of the Council's own final wishes. His confirmation and promulgation of the Conciliar decrees, before 1564 was over, followed the creation of a commission of cardinals and Curialists to review the Conciliar decrees. The application of the decrees thus became an exercise of papal, no longer solely or directly an expression of Conciliar, authority.

THE TRIDENTINE PAPACY

The commission, acting by papal authority, evolved during 1564 and 1565 to become a larger, permanent Congregation for the interpretation of the decrees, exercising that final arbitrating power which the Council itself had passed to the papacy, and which the popes thereafter defended as a monopoly of decisive judgement, even in the face of Gallican and Jansenist dissent. In confirming the decrees of the Council so promptly, Pius IV had also looked not to the ambiguous wording of the passages which had finally attempted to resolve the long Conciliar conflicts over the relations between bishops and the papacy, leaving at least some of the former still dissatisfied, but to one of the last declarations made by the Council, as it dissolved: that in all respects its own decisions were to be understood to leave intact the authority of the papacy. The formal acclamations which concluded the Council were led by the French Cardinal of Lorraine, and included a reference to Pius as 'pontiff of the holy universal Church', whatever reserve French and Spanish bishops might have felt previously about so explicit a statement of the universality of papal jurisdiction. Accordingly, the bull of confirmation, dated January 1564, was signed by Pius using the formula 'Bishop of the Catholic Church', and reaffirming the papal monopoly of authoritative interpretation of the Conciliar decrees. That the Congregation of the Council remained a permanent vehicle for papal direction of the post-Conciliar Church was thus logical, but still depended on the events following the death of Pius IV in late 1565. Cardinal Ghislieri, who succeeded as Pius V at the beginning of 1566, had been a member of the evolving Congregation. Application of the decrees, involving the Roman authority of the Congregation, was thus to be secured as a continuing papal objective, not simply a temporary goal of Pius IV, or a subsequent campaign, outside Rome, conducted by his nephew, Charles Borromeo, in the Milan which soon became the latter's residence. In a chronological sense at least, Pius V was obviously the first of the wholly post-Tridentine popes. But it might still be asked whether in more profound senses it was not so much this immediately post-Conciliar pope who determined the direction of the papacy within the post-Tridentine Church as one of his direct successors, either Gregory XIII or Sixtus V.[1] Since one line of historical interpretation would even deny that the impact of the Protestant challenge or the decrees of the Council of Trent was particularly decisive in the long-term evolution of the papal office, the question may perhaps be better taken up here at the conclusion of a serial analysis of the various aspects or dimensions of that office throughout the period from 1564 to 1789.

A TEST-CASE: PIUS V

As has been noted, Charles Borromeo, both as archbishop of Milan and by virtue of powers delegated from Rome, was to a degree used by the papacy to begin a reform of the Church in the Italian peninsula, especially on its Northern borders; and this involved for a while at least the establishment of an effective papal primatial leadership, an ultimately Roman rather than Milanese affair. That later evolution, not immediately clear in all respects, was at least suggested by the review and eventual, even if less than instant, approval by Pius V of Borromeo's provincial decrees. While the Council of Trent had envisaged that regular provincial councils would provide another mechanism for the resolution of doubts or difficulties in the local application of the Tridentine decrees, it is nevertheless striking that Pius V made this use of Milanese initiatives at the time. For whatever plans he may have had to call by his own authority an immediately post-Tridentine council of the bishops of the Italian peninsula, in fact the papacy waited until the early eighteenth century before even a metropolitan assembly, relating only to a specific provincial constituency of bishops, was summoned to Rome. But Pius V did initiate, by his own authority, Apostolic Visitations in many parts of the Italian peninsula, including the papal states themselves, and not solely in the North.

So this only indirectly contributed to general centralization under Roman control, sometimes regarded as the most outstanding characteristic of the

1 N. Lemaitre, *Saint Pie V* (Paris 1994).

post-Tridentine Church. But arguably it was already a step towards effective primatial direction of a distinctively Italian Church on the peninsular mainland, subsequently reflected in the decoration for Gregory XIII of the Vatican Gallery of Maps and Views of Italy. Such an evolutionary interpretation of the post-Conciliar papacy might also be supported by the fact that it was subsequently, under Sixtus V, that the obligation for both Italian and non-Italian bishops to pay regular *ad limina* visits and lodge reports at Rome with the Congregation of the Council was systematized. It was also under Gregory XIII that the network of resident nuncios representing the papacy at Catholic rulers' Courts was first clearly established. The personal attention paid by Pius V to the business of the Holy Office, however, was another facet, both cause and symptom, of the emergence of a distinctive papal primacy, effectively directing the Church in most of peninsular Italy; even if the most marginal areas, like the Tende valley, needed the anti-heretical intervention of a Catholic secular ruler such as the duke of Savoy.

Roman examination of candidates for Italian bishoprics, taken up with vigour by Clement VIII at the end of the sixteenth century, had also been called for by Pius V as early as 1567. Yet the need for more systematic information on the suitability, by Conciliar standards, of those nominated to other bishoprics, as in France, was already recognized too. The action of Pius V, from 1572, to establish a Roman commission which would become the Congregation of Bishops, was intended to further such an aim, as well as reasserting the pope's view that bishops facing accusations should properly be judged at and by Rome. This was obviously of particular importance as the Dominican pope tried to insist that the Spanish Inquisition relinquish to the Roman Holy Office his fellow Dominican, the Spanish primate, Carranza, for definitive investigation and judgement, finally achieved in 1567, as far as transfer to Rome was concerned. Once again, however, systematizing the Congregation of Bishops had to await Sixtus V, who thus reinforced Roman control over bishops generally, but most effectively in the case of Italian bishoprics, many of which were subject to direct papal provision not to royal nomination as in France or Spain.

Similarly, general reform of the Roman Curia was planned by Pius V from 1566–68, even though the major reorganization was that subsequently made by Sixtus V. But certainly in the case of the Penitentiary, the reform achieved in 1569 by Pius himself was radical and decisive, reducing the size and remit of the tribunal and excluding members not in priest's orders. From the same year, the vital reordering of Curial archives was also begun, starting with those of the Apostolic Chamber, though major initiatives in this sphere more generally awaited subsequent pontificates. Pastoral visitations conducted in person by Pius V established the diocesan care of Rome which was to mark most post-Tridentine pontificates, complementing in this case the inspection of other churches and foundations delegated to the specialist, Ormaneto, supplied from Milan by Charles Borromeo. Furthermore, the visitation by Pius of the seat of the Dean of the College of Cardinals, the Cardinal Bishop of Ostia, could be described as the exercise of a distinctly metropolitan oversight.

In the case of the delegated episcopal visitation within Rome, Ormaneto's employment once again demonstrated the identification of Pius with the priorities of Pius IV and Charles Borromeo, even when the latter left Rome for residence at Milan. An extension of this diocesan reform at Rome was the examination from 1567 onwards, first under Ormaneto and subsequently under other delegates, of the competence of confessors. The reorganization of the parochial structure of the Rome diocese was obviously complementary too. Aspects of the renewed Marian cult in the Counter-Reformation, including the already popular rosary, were officially recognized, systematized and promoted by the Dominican pope, even if a post-Tridentine concern for clerical direction of lay confraternities was also involved; and even though some of his projects in this respect were only accomplished by Gregory XIII. On the other hand, the extensive privileges obtained under Pius by the Dominicans, and to a lesser extent by other, chiefly mendicant orders, ran counter to the spirit of the Tridentine decrees passed by an assembly of bishops, who had been intent on restoring episcopal control over at least the pastoral functions of the regulars.

The partial reduction, under subsequent popes, of such exemptions, and the parallel reversal of the mendicant pope's attempts to make the Society of Jesus conform more to a traditional monastic pattern, were better indications of the general direction of post-Tridentine papal policy in this regard. Though, of course, in the case of the Jesuits, conflict over both activities and constitution continued to the end of the sixteenth century and beyond. The promotion of reformed and observant branches of religious orders, at the expense of conventuals, however, was already indicative of the main trend of post-Conciliar papal policy, as was the campaign to reduce groups of females who pursued a communal existence to the status, vows and enclosure of fully professed nuns. Moreover, the restoration by Pius V of the pastoral liberties of the mendicants, after the Conciliar limitations, at least in part reflected his concern for adequate pastoral provision in the overseas missions, and in this context, as opposed to that of Catholic Europe, his relaxation of strict episcopal control was more in line with subsequent papal policy. Post-Tridentine bishops in Europe also encountered resistance from regular orders to contributing to the costs of diocesan seminaries for the training of secular clergy, and this objection was sustained long after exemption in the matter was initially granted by Pius V to the mendicants. This was despite the Conciliar permission for communal property to be held by most of the mendicant orders, with further concessions for other orders such as the Jesuits.

But the papal declaration that a medieval, and precisely a Dominican theologian, Thomas Aquinas, was to be accorded the previously patristic status of Doctor of the Church suggested the further, long period of difficult relations between the Order of Preachers and the Society of Jesus. It certainly did not in fact establish any monolithic theology in the post-Conciliar Church, and the long doctrinal disputes internal to post-Tridentine Catholicism clearly implied quite the reverse. At the disciplinary, as opposed to the doctrinal level, both Pius V and Gregory XIII, together with the Congregation of the Council in its interpretations of the regulations for regulars decreed by the bishops at Trent, allowed some relaxation of the otherwise severely restrictive conditions governing female religious communities. In the case of those male communities which were habitually subject to the imposition of commendatory abbots, Pius V attempted to reassert the intentions of the Council, by stressing to secular rulers the necessity of nominating commendators who were at least adults and in minor clerical orders, however long the achievement of even such minimum qualifications took in France for example. The pope's decision to suppress the decadent Humiliati entirely showed that, on occasion, papal judgement on a specific order could be even more radical than what the Council of Trent had finally decided for the orders in general, before seventeenth-century papal dissolution of convents or conflation of religious orders preceded the eighteenth-century suppression of the Jesuits. The suppression of the Humiliati, moreover, reinforced the authority of Cardinal Protectors over religious orders, in a way generally followed by post-Tridentine popes, in the interests of continued reform of regulars; while in the specific circumstances of the failed attack by Humiliati on Charles Borromeo, archbishop of Milan, the authority of diocesan bishops was also reasserted.

The Council of Trent had transmitted to the papacy responsibility for completion of a catechism and an Index of prohibited literature, together with revision of the liturgical books, most importantly the missal and breviary. The action of Pius IV, and in the case of the catechism the particular attention of Charles Borromeo as well, had ensured that this responsibility would be discharged by Roman commissions, but the subsequent determination of Pius V was again important for the achievement of the task. While possible models for a Catholic catechism already existed, such as those of Canisius in Germanic lands or of Auger in France, the use by the Tridentine preparatory commission of the contested catechism of Carranza as one of several sources made it more than ever important that the pope secured the transfer of the Spanish primate to Rome, since the Spanish Inquisition, in its protracted proceedings, was essentially assuming the inherent culpability of passages in his text. To control the spread of ideas through the medium of print, or even establish a virtual monopoly for Roman liturgical standards in the Western Church was, however, more difficult, even under Pius V, given that interim privileges for Roman printers could only achieve so much, until the later foundation under Sixtus V of the Vatican Press. Indeed, even in the case of the Roman Catechism, whether in Latin or in approved translations, the text had its own evolution, which extended through editions and printings long after the first published version, authorized by Pius V, of 1566.

So too, in a less dramatic way, the issue of the Roman breviary under Pius V could not extend with quite the desired simplicity, in the envisaged stages of adoption first in Rome, then in Italy, and thereafter elsewhere, while the

Roman printing presses were unable to supply the whole of the Western Church; and local variations in fact set in with the involvement of other printers. This was quite apart from modifications introduced by subsequent popes themselves, not least of course with the reform of the calendar by Gregory XIII. In the case of the revised missal, initially proposed by the Council of Trent, the form authorized from 1570 by Pius V included a new set of general rubrics, intended to promote uniformity in the celebration of the Mass. Effective Roman supervision of such uniformity could only be begun to any extent after the creation by Sixtus V in 1588 of the Curial Congregation of Sacred Rites. This real but lengthy projection of a Roman, and above all papal, direction in strictly ecclesiastical affairs in any case also awaited the later complement of the Roman *Rituale*.

By contrast, the energy of Pius V in taking a lead in politico-religious affairs internationally, whether in conflict with heresy or confrontation with Islam, was something which few of the subsequent post-Tridentine popes proved able to match. The later incorporation of Ferrara within the papal states, together with the eventual addition of Urbino, would in due course increase by about 600,000 the population of the late sixteenth-century papal territories, of around 1.5 million. But the subordination of the Este of Ferrara was in a sense anticipated by Pius V, in his elevation of the Medici of Tuscany, as a potential, semi-independent ally in the Italian peninsula, to the status of grand-dukes. The timing of the papal initiative was also instructive, in that it accompanied a momentary royal victory over the Protestant heretics in France, to which the Medici had contributed at papal prompting, thus further reducing the effect of Imperial protest at the pope's innovation. While Pius V was capable of such strokes of Italian and European diplomacy, he proved incapable of reversing the reduction of agriculture, as opposed to pasture, in the areas of the papal states nearest Rome.

In this he arguably showed the real limitations of papal temporal government over a very extended period, beginning indeed in a pre-Tridentine era, rather than indicating a potential transformation of that government which one or another of his immediate successors might eventually begin. Within the limitations which would, in fact, become enduring, Pius V continued the attempt to consolidate and reorder the finances of the papacy and the papal states, begun by Pius IV in 1564 with regard to the relations between the Apostolic Chamber and the provinces under papal temporal government. Thus such prevailing conditions were arguably little affected by the advent to the papal throne of a mendicant from a non-noble family, whose nepotism was distinctly confined, as the first wholly post-Tridentine pope.

In a sphere such as criminal justice the direct authority of the pope over all in the papal states, even papal governors and nobles, might seem to be intensified by Pius V, but the growth of banditry in the papal territories in fact suggested once again the real limitations of papal government which were already evident. These realities, which would not be fundamentally altered by the creation under Clement VIII of the Roman Congregation of Buon Governo, thus give perspective to the undoubted lamentations of Paleotti, as the immediately post-Conciliar bishop of Bologna, about Roman support for the Legates who governed the papal states, despite the priorities pronounced by the Council of Trent. That Roman decisions concerning Bologna under Pius V in fact represented a comprehensive development affecting all the papal states to the end of the Ancien Régime is indeed dubious.

Rather more within the capabilities of papal rule, from the pontificate of Pius V onwards, was a tolerably efficient administration within the city of Rome, conducted conjointly with the municipal authorities, and allowing improvements in such urban affairs as the paving of streets and the cleansing of roads between the seven Major Churches, priorities of the pope even before a shared concern for pilgrim access stimulated Sixtus V to undertake his more famous and drastic interventions in the city's circulation. In fact Pius IV had already begun alteration in the lay-out of the city during the Conciliar years, while under Pius V a papal control of classical antiquities in Rome and their disposal, which would last throughout the papal Ancien Régime, was initiated, despite the apparent disparagement of such antiquities by the pope in person. In the case of Christian monuments, both Pius V and Gregory XIII resumed the search for architects capable of continuing the main structure of St Peter's, left incomplete following the deaths of both Michelangelo and Pius IV, in pursuit of a project whose last additions were made precisely in the final pontificate of the old papal regime, under Pius VI. A personal care of Pius V, however, reflecting his previous career, was certainly the state of the Holy Office palazzo. His attempts to banish social disorder from Rome were also characteristic of his zeal as mendicant and inquisitor, though such priorities were to reappear in later pontificates, as late as the end of the seventeenth century for example, with an accompanying distaste for the licence of the Roman carnival.

Similarly, he attempted to circumscribe the legitimate forms of credit which would be tolerated, restrictions which again reappeared a century later, but which were in reality eclipsed by the forms of papal finance, above all the *monti*, which in all pontificates depended on interest-bearing loans. On the other hand, renewal of the charitable funds from which loans to the poor were made from the Roman *Monte di Pietà* was an initiative of Pius V which certainly set the trend, for many subsequent pontificates, of actively promoting charitable provision within the city. This did not exclude attempts to restrict, to a greater or lesser degree, vagrant beggars in the city and its churches, as was immediately evident in the pontificate of Gregory XIII. Both these immediately post-Conciliar popes also shared a preoccupation with further restrictions on the Jewish community in Rome, certainly as to prohibiting exchange of midwives between Christian and Jewish households, although the preoccupation in fact became decidedly less marked in pontificates beyond the end of the sixteenth century. The physical bounds of the Roman ghetto, enforced though not inaugurated by Pius V, were however maintained, though expanded by Sixtus V.

It was Sixtus too who gave definitive regulation to the financial contribution which was imposed on the Roman Jewish community, but only the more 'puritan' climate of some later seventeenth-century pontificates produced the abandonment, under Clement IX from 1668, of the enforced competition between Jews, among the races run in the Roman Carnival. The public baptism, by Pius V himself in 1566, of a converted Jewish family set the precedent both for papal celebrations of certain sacraments in public and in person, to mark a particular triumph of the faith, and in particular for conspicuous papal attention to the conversion of non-Christians, above all Jews. The promotion under Pius V of both hospices for Jewish converts and compulsory sermons to be attended by Roman Jews was again not new, but confirmed the direction of policy adopted under subsequent popes, starting with Gregory XIII. The latter also continued the concern shown initially by Pius IV for a secure union with ancient, Eastern-rite Churches, in the search for a common front against Islam. The post-Tridentine popes, within Catholic Europe itself, attempted to enforce the prohibition of continued medical attendance on patients who would not make their confession.

The attention paid by Pius V to the affairs of the Holy Office certainly drew on his previous experiences as Inquisitor, but also set a pattern for those post-Tridentine pontificates, already noted, in which a pope had passed an important part of his earlier career in the service of the Holy Office. Outside the Italian peninsula, however, the pontificate of Pius V already showed the difficulty of making Roman interventions in questions of faith effective and binding. The case of the Catholic Augustinianism, taught at Louvain by Baius but contested by other Catholic theologians, foreshadowed the later constraints which the papacy would face in tackling the dispute 'De Auxiliis' and the long-running Jansenist controversy. To enhance the desired unity of Catholics in the Netherlands against the growing threat of Protestantism there, the initial condemnation by Pius V of views attributed to Baius was made secretly and without naming him. Eventually, however, both a public condemnation of such views and a formal submission by Baius proved impossible to avoid.[2]

In encouraging sovereigns elsewhere to armed conflict with both Protestant heresy and Islam, Pius V began two initiatives which remained characteristic of subsequent post-Tridentine pontificates but not for equal lengths of time. While encouragement of a struggle against Islam persisted at least to the early eighteenth century, serious involvement in military campaigns avowedly for the defence of Catholicism and suppression of heresy was a much more strictly post-Conciliar affair, hardly evident after the mid-seventeenth century it might be suggested. On the other hand, for all his zeal in the fight against heresy, Pius V was intent on using the presence of nuncios at rulers' Courts to encourage also local episcopal implementation of the Tridentine reforms. In

---

2 A.M. Artola, *De la revelación a la inspiración. Los orígenes de la moderna teología católica sobre la inspiración bíblica* (Bilbao 1983); M. Biersack, *Initia Bellarminiana. Die Prädestinationslehre bei Robert Bellarmin SJ bis zu seinen Löwener Vorlesungen 1570–1576* (Stuttgart 1989).

this use of nuncios he was setting a pattern of a different sort for the more immediately post-Conciliar pontificates, which was only overtaken from the 1620s onwards by the pressure of more strictly diplomatic business involving the nunciatures, in a war-torn Western Europe. At any period however, a proposed nuncio to a Catholic Court had, in the end, to be *persona grata* to the ruler concerned.

Pius V was thus naturally enough opposed to any doctrinal compromise with the French Huguenots, despite the attempts of the French Crown to pursue such negotiations, but also himself began the policy, continued by Gregory XIII, of urging the Catholic hierarchy in France to make its own adoption of the Tridentine decrees, as the Crown refrained from such an official declaration. On the other hand, the initial enthusiasm of Pius V for the violent repression of Protestantism in the Netherlands attempted by the duke of Alba was only gradually tempered by papal fears that extreme measures were proving counter-productive, but did not prevent the pope's protesting strongly against what he, like many of his immediate successors, denounced as the oppressive policies pursued by Philip II towards the Church in Spain itself. Yet a special papal envoy sent by Pius V to the Spanish Court had as little success as most subsequent special representatives of Rome charged with moderating the direct and autonomous involvement of the Spanish monarchs in the affairs of the Church in the Iberian peninsula. Further east, Pius V began two other policies continued by his successors but, once again, over very different time-scales. His encouragement of the necessarily long and at first slow recovery of Catholicism in Poland set in operation a policy which was to have major success under Clement VIII but would still need to be pursued into the later seventeenth century. His intransigence over royal approaches about a Catholic restoration in Sweden, which were in any case ambiguous as well as tentative, paved the way for the ultimate consolidation of Protestantism there at the end of the sixteenth and beginning of the seventeenth century, an evolution which was not seriously altered by the later spectacular conversion to Catholicism of Queen Christina.

This was true despite the Roman commissions set up by Pius V and Gregory XIII, particularly for the affairs of the German lands and of the Northern kingdoms, and was consistent with the concern of Pius to prevent a new religious settlement in the Empire being made by the authority of the Emperor and Diet. Similarly, it was logical that the pope should use nuncios to urge the Catholic prince-bishops of the Empire to begin in their territories the highly necessary application of the Tridentine reforms, irrespective of the state of internal Imperial politics, which remained uncertain enough under the Emperor Maximilian. Such a programme was gradually to have some limited success, for example eventually in the case of Salzburg, before the seventeenth-century disruption of the Thirty Years' War intervened. The pontificate of Pius V also saw the first fruits of the particular contribution of the Jesuits to Catholic recovery in German lands as in Poland, not least through education of boys destined for both clerical and lay life. Catholic secular princes of the

Empire, above all the dukes of Bavaria, were also henceforth to be encouraged in their own territories.

By contrast the policies adopted by Pius V towards the kingdoms of Scotland and England arguably led to the consolidation of Protestantism and the beginning of unambiguously penal treatment of Catholics there. The pope's misjudgement of the situation in which English and Scots Catholics found themselves at the start of his pontificate was compounded by his misjudgement of both Elizabeth I and Mary Queen of Scots. His eventual intervention against Elizabeth, contrary to the wishes of Spain at the time, caused English Catholics to be defined as potential traitors, since his bull of excommunication and declaration that Catholics owed no obedience to the occupant of the throne could not subsequently be removed from national consciousness, however little effect such positions came in time to have among many English Catholics themselves. In these ways Pius V arguably began a mishandling of the case of England, damaging the interests of Catholics there, which continued at least into the first half of the seventeenth century. Nor did papal policy towards English Catholic exiles initially provide much compensation, since only after his pontificate was a Roman training-centre for priests who would return to minister to the persecuted Catholic community in England set in operation.

Yet, however ineffectually, Pius V was willing to try to gain the support of the schismatic Russian ruler for the anti-Islamic league which the pope was forming at the same time, in 1570–71, in this case subordinating Christian division to the greater demands of confronting Islam. The victory of Lepanto may have indeed been distinctly limited in its effects, failing after all to alter the fact of the Venetian loss of Cyprus, but less directly it marked papal commitment to uniting at least Catholic rulers, in order to present a common front against Islam, which was a policy pursued beyond the end of the seventeenth century, despite the long wars precisely between the Catholic powers of Europe themselves. In the specific case of the immediate allies of Pius V, Spain and Venice, however, subsequent popes were unable to prevent the replacement of temporary alliance by more enduring tension and distrust between the Spanish monarchy and the Republic. By 1572 it was evident enough, if not yet to Pius V, that his plans for the League to carry forward the offensive, in a full crusade aimed at final liberation of the Holy Land from Islamic rule, were unlikely to be put into effect.

CONTINUED EVOLUTION

Nevertheless, the sense that Pius V was the model in many ways for his post-Tridentine successors on the papal throne was rapidly demonstrated by Sixtus V, in extending evident approval to the growth of a cult, even though the earlier pope's beatification and canonization were only achieved in 1672 and 1712 respectively. Naturally that did not mean that all the policies pursued by Pius V had been, even in their own time, successful. In the single year 1570, for instance, he elevated the ruler of Tuscany to the rank of grand-duke without reference to the wishes of the Emperor, prepared the bull of excommunication against Elizabeth of England despite the policies of Philip II, but proved unable to prevent the French Crown making peace, for the time being at least, with the Huguenots. Yet a similar contrast between grand aims and practical limitations was again experienced under Gregory XIII. On the one hand, in 1582 his revision of the code of canon law suggested universal norms for the post-Tridentine Church under papal authority, but on the other, he proved incapable of halting the continued growth of banditry in the parts of the papal states nearest Rome itself.

Sixtus V made more progress on the latter score, as well as improving the city water supply and providing a stable establishment for the Vatican Library. But in publishing the revised code of canon law, Gregory was bringing to completion work which he had begun as a cardinal, along with others, precisely under Pius V himself. His greater flexibility, compared with Pius V, in responding to Swedish approaches also for a while raised hopes of a Catholic restoration in Sweden, but even this in fact was not to prove possible, though there was an indirect contribution to the gradual recovery of Catholicism in Poland. The short-lived popes, Urban VII, Gregory XIV and Innocent IX, had all had some personal experience of the work of the Council of Trent, but with the death of Innocent in 1591 a directly Tridentine sequence of popes, in this personal sense, came to an end. Though the opposition of Sixtus V to any prospect that Henri of Navarre should become king of France was continued by Gregory XIV, this again proved effectively the end of a particular stage in papal policy, once Clement VIII overcame his own initial resistance to accepting Henri's reconciliation to the Church. Clement's relatively more relaxed view of the Protestant monarchy in England, once the new Scots dynasty had succeeded in the person of James Stuart, also opened up at least a slight chance of easing the situation of the English Catholics.

Spanish sensitivity to papal post-Tridentine policy was, however, evident even before Clement VIII accepted the reconciliation of Henri IV. Philip II supported Imperial objection to the elevation of the Medici to the rank of grand-duke by Pius V. He was also firm in excluding in fact, even if not by public rejection, the intervention in the Portuguese succession question intended by Gregory XIII in 1580. On the other hand, it was at the request of the Spanish monarch that Gregory renewed the condemnation issued by Pius V of the views attributed to Baius, even though this again advertised the less than perfect harmony among the embattled Catholics of the Netherlands. Philip's lack of enthusiasm for the election of Jesuit Generals who were non-Spaniards, whether Netherlandish or Italian, did not however deter Gregory from his favour to the Society of Jesus, reversing the changes within it which Pius V had attempted to impose.

But the pope could not persuade Philip to rejoin a league against the Islamic Turks, while Sixtus V had to renew papal defence of the Jesuits in Spain, against not only Dominican critics but also the all-powerful Spanish Inquisition, which was assured of royal support. The patience of Sixtus himself with the extended troubles of the Society, chiefly but not exclusively in Spain, was nevertheless taxed by reports alleging that Jesuits had criticized his supposed relaxation of absolute opposition to Henri of Navarre. This indeed was the context in which the defence of the plenitude of papal power by the Jesuit Bellarmine, considered inadequate by the pope, suffered the short-lived indignity of inclusion in the Index of prohibited literature, and in which the pope was considering forcing the Jesuits to alter their own order's name, the Society of Jesus. Nor could Sixtus take much pleasure from a further outbreak of the dispute at Louvain over Baius, which now very much involved conflict with the Jesuits there. Papal authority itself was also touched on by the prohibition in Spain of a life of Pius V, dedicated to Sixtus, because of its reference to the earlier pope's disputes with Philip II.

The royal plans for a more aggressive Spanish policy towards Elizabeth of England also raised more doubts than enthusiasm in the mind of Sixtus V. Gregory XIV defied Spanish opposition, in a way not otherwise characteristic of his short pontificate, to confirm the peculiar privileges of the Society of Jesus, which had been in question by the end of the pontificate of Sixtus. In the case of Clement VIII, tension with Spain was not simply the result of the final papal acceptance of the reconciliation of Henri IV. For Clement's own previous experiences led him to state clearly that the Spanish Church, including both bishops and cathedral chapters, was far from the model of Tridentine Catholicism, and was in need of further internal reform.[3] The succession of Philip III in the last years of the sixteenth century made such tension if anything worse, while at this time Clement was demonstrating his independence by the annexation of Ferrara, carried out with the diplomatic support of Henri IV. Philip III was not unconditionally willing to agree to the pope's desire for continued support to the Emperor, to further the anti-Turkish campaign.

On the other hand, Clement had his own reasons for a reserved attitude towards the Jesuits, despite his efforts to have the Society readmitted to the whole of the kingdom of France, after Gallican attack on them there. The pope did not in the end, however, persist with all the adjustments he had wished to see introduced in the constitution of the Society. But equally he was known to be opposed to the canonization of Ignatius Loyola, long wished for by the Jesuits. Clement did, nevertheless, praise Jesuits for their contribution to the union of the St Thomas Christians of India with the Catholic Church, supposedly effected by a special archiepiscopal synod of 1599, whose decrees he confirmed. This did not in fact remove the threat of schism, rather than union, and Paul V had to alter the previous arrangements for Jesuit supervision of these Christians. Clement meanwhile had himself removed the Jesuits from direction of the Greek College in Rome, reversing his own previous decision in this instance; their direction was restored only under the favourable Gregory XV.

3 A.S.V. Spagna, XLV, 527r–v, 597r ff., 628r ff.: 8, 20 Oct., 5 Nov. 1594.

Paul V had to resist Spanish pressure designed to force him to give a definitive ruling in the 'De Auxiliis' dispute, instead of imposing silence in the controversy, but he also had to prohibit the reciprocal accusations of heresy which opposing parties in Spain, not least once again Dominicans and Jesuits, were making in the related conflict over the Immaculate Conception. This was not, though, the end of Spanish royal requests to the pope for a positive, definitive declaration of the latter doctrine. But, apart from other considerations, there was little prospect of France accepting such a declaration, not out of objection to the doctrine itself, but because of confrontation with Spain, and unwillingness to see papal authority applied in the kingdom in this way. Spanish candidates for canonization did not make swift or easy progress either, even after Clement's earlier resistance to canonization of Loyola was no longer an issue. Gregory XV did canonize Loyola at last, together with other Spanish candidates, but, while resisting renewed pressure over the Immaculate Conception, he faced a resurgence of Spanish jurisdictional intransigence, following the succession of Philip IV. As a cardinal, he had previously favoured Clement's policy towards Henri of Navarre, while his reform of conclave procedure and his foundation of the Roman Congregation De Propaganda Fide, extending papal supervision over all missionary territories overseas, were bound to cause the pope difficulties with the Spanish monarchy. The prolonged discussions over the necessary conditions, above all affecting the situation of the English Catholics, which the papacy would require were a Spanish bride to be granted to the heir to the English throne, Charles Stuart, were also not at an end, despite the deaths of Paul V and Philip III, and subsequently Gregory XV himself.

The formal remonstrations against Habsburg interference with ecclesiastical liberties, which had seemed necessary in the pontificate of Gregory XV, encouraged the use by Urban VIII of a special Congregation of cardinals charged with defence of ecclesiastical jurisdiction. The infringements of those ecclesiastical rights which the Council of Trent had reasserted caused friction between Urban and both Piedmont and Tuscany. In a parallel to the disputes of the pontificate of Paul V, the pope confronted the republics of Venice and Lucca on essentially similar grounds. Indeed, in 1640 Lucca was placed under Interdict, until 1643. The pope also still felt the necessity of defending ecclesiastical interests against unjustified Habsburg domination in Spain, in Sicily, Naples and Milan. The Portuguese search for independence, from 1640, naturally complicated this problem, which was further compounded, while Naples and Catalonia were also in revolt, by French intervention, ostensibly in favour of the Church in those territories.

Paul V had secured the adoption of the Tridentine decrees by the French Church, though still not by the kingdom's royal administration, but the need for papal intervention against Jansenist teaching first became evident under Urban VIII. In Spain, after considerable difficulties, Urban managed to preserve the authority of the nuncio's tribunal, independent of any royal supervision. However, tension with the newly installed independent regime in Portugal was not in reality much helped by French intervention, pursued by Cardinal Mazarin, though he also represented his policies in France itself as designed to reduce the Gallicanism which had, at times, been given some effective encouragement by Richelieu. For the overseas mission territories, including of course those in which the Iberian Crowns still claimed exclusive patronage rights, the College of the Propaganda, set up by Urban VIII, received the privilege of having its seminarians priested 'ad titulum missionis'. This was a crucial innovation, in the creation of a flexible supply of secular priests for missionary activity, freed from the constraints which the Tridentine decrees had, for other reasons, imposed on ordinands. These ensured that those ordained had adequate beneficed or family income, but had, for instance, complicated the movement of secular priests serving the Catholic community in Protestant England.

The care which had been taken to secure financial support for the work of the Congregation De Propaganda Fide itself allowed its income to grow rapidly between 1633 and 1638, and again thereafter. The universality of papal authority and responsibility was also expressed by Urban's instigation of Apostolic Visitations of the Greek-rite communities of Southern Italy and Sicily. Papal as opposed to Iberian Crown responsibility for missions was again emphasized by the sending from Rome of Capuchin reinforcements for the admittedly tenuous Congolese mission; though a mission to Morocco failed despite French support, supplied by Richelieu and Père Joseph. However, the continuing tensions in the overseas missions between bishops and regulars, not least Jesuits, could not simply be solved by the creation of the Propaganda Congregation. Its first, influential secretary, Ingoli, was certainly hostile to the Society of Jesus for its supposed independence, even of the new Congregation.

That a war on Italian soil over the temporal government and relations of the papacy dominated the last stages of the pontificate of Urban VIII was thus at odds with many of the priorities and objectives which had more largely been pursued under this pope. The belief that Pamfili had strongly advised against the War of Castro helped his eventual election, despite initial opposition from more than one quarter; and despite the fact that his renewed attack on Castro contrasted with Urban's successful incorporation of Urbino. Whatever the limitations which his pontificate subsequently demonstrated, then, an essential continuity of aims and ideals, though not of detailed policy on all fronts, had arguably characterized the post-Conciliar pontificates from that of Pius V to the greater part of that of Urban VIII. As has also been suggested already, the pontificates subsequent to that of Innocent X manifested a renewed attention to many of these Tridentine priorities too. The Tridentine programme had at any rate not been a characteristic only of a few, immediately post-Conciliar pontificates.

THE IMAGE OF PAPAL ROME

A renewed confidence can accordingly be traced in official preaching before the popes, in the decades before and after 1600, both about the papal headship of the Church and about the image of Rome itself. In the period between the end of the Council of Trent and the end of the sixteenth century such sermons delivered in the papal presence called for necessary conflict, a sacred struggle. Thereafter they more often celebrated a triumph of the faith under papal leadership. After that date too these sermons were more likely to reflect on the virtues of Rome as the microcosm of that universal ideal. But already, at the death of individual popes of the immediately post-Conciliar period, their specific achievements could be eulogized in a similar way. Sixtus V not least was praised for restoring visibly the true image of Rome as the central example of Catholic order, not only by his reordering of the street-plan of the holy city but by the complementary christening of ancient obelisks and classical columns.

This too formed a larger, concrete monument to the consolidation of the Catholic faith, clarified and reasserted at Trent, which Pius V had epitomized in the post-Conciliar order for the Tridentine Profession of Faith, to be sworn not only by prelates but by those teaching or taking doctorates in Catholic educational establishments. To enforce perfect compliance with the latter proved less than simple for the popes, since even in the Italian peninsula itself, at the Venetian state university of Padua, some doctoral candidates from north of the Alps evaded the obligation, with Republican connivance, despite the nuncio's protests. But celebration of papal leadership in the reaffirmation of Rome's true image could continue, as for example at the death of Paul V, who had had such difficulty, outside the city, in the case of the Venetian Republic in fact. Indeed, the essence of this triumphalism was already occasionally expressed even sooner after the Council of Trent, as during the pontificate of Gregory XIII. Such celebration of the papal office included reference to the authority exercised in implementing Conciliar decrees.[4]

The popes were, of course, but one source of patronage for the visual arts in Rome, even though papal nephews also naturally featured among leading patrons. The attraction of Rome as a centre for commissions derived not from the papal Court in isolation, but from the cultural life which the presence of that Court encouraged. Alternative sources of patronage, after all, included the households of some cardinals or of a figure of the regal stature of Christina of Sweden. But architects who worked on projects where direct papal commission or supervision was involved, such as della Porta, Fontana or Rainaldi, were ultimately eclipsed by the long career of Bernini, who worked for all the popes from Paul V to Clement X inclusive, before his own death, aged over eighty, in 1680. While his most conspicuous papal patrons were doubtless Urban VIII and Alexander VII, he was not totally deprived of papal work in the intervening pontificate of Innocent X.

Bernini, despite his Neapolitan birth, might be regarded as a Roman artist, since his family settled in Rome during his childhood. Architects who received

4 F.J. McGinness, *Right Thinking and Sacred Oratory in Counter-Reformation Rome* (Princeton, NJ 1995).

commissions for work initiated or supervised by popes also included Borromini (1599–1667) and Maderna (who died in 1629), both of whom had origins in Northern Italy, and Pietro da Cortona (1596–1669), who was Tuscan. The attraction of Roman patronage obviously brought non-Italian artists to the city too, and the sculpture of the Southern Netherlander Duquesnoy (1594–1642) also found a place in the interior of St Peter's, for example. The work of architects on palaces, monuments, fountains, gates and fortifications, deriving from papal commissions, complemented purely ecclesiastical projects. In this way the image of papal authority, in all its complexity, was projected.

That was recognized even in the diplomacy by which secular rulers sought papal agreement that Bernini might accept commissions from them. But without the distinctive ecclesiastical role of the papacy, the papal Court might more swiftly have seen the focus for artistic fashion shift to France, a relative alteration of balance encouraged by less active papal patronage in the last decades of the seventeenth century. For long, though, artists were still attracted from outside Rome to work in the papal city, finding papal commission for fresco work, for example, like the Cavaliere d'Arpino, or Guido Reni, who was from Bologna, in the first part of the seventeenth century. Other specifically papal projects during the century involved fresco work by Guercino, and, in the Palazzo Barberini, by Sacchi as well as da Cortona. The triumphalism of the latter's ceiling in the *salone* of the palazzo can be contrasted with work on papal monuments in St Peter's by a sculptor of the standing of Algardi.

Papal monuments, generally, alluded to the range of responsibilities of a pope, going beyond the mere commemoration of family honour. Papal honour was institutional, not simply personal.[5] Papal favour, nevertheless, contributed to the resurgence of the career of the musician and composer, Palestrina, from the time of the last stages of the Council of Trent onwards, after earlier difficulties. His positions first at the papal basilica of S. Maria Maggiore and then at the Roman Seminary culminated in his direction of the choir of St Peter's from 1571. His clarified polyphony was thus amply demonstrated to meet post-Conciliar liturgical demands, above all that for unimpeded hearing of the exact text.

THE REALITY OF PAPAL AUTHORITY

The application of Tridentine reform raised the larger question of papal authority itself, certainly beyond the Italian peninsula. This was true not least in the crucial period between the attempts of Pius V and Sixtus V to determine the legitimate succession to European thrones on the one hand, and the ending of the Venetian Interdict of 1606–7 on the other. After that episode,

5 E. Cochrane, *Italy 1530–1630* (Longman History of Italy) (London 1988); R. Wittkower, *Art and Architecture in Italy, 1600 to 1750* (Harmondsworth 1958); L.H. Heydenreich and W. Lotz, *Architecture in Italy, 1400 to 1600* (Harmondsworth 1974); S.J. Freedberg, *Painting in Italy, 1500 to 1600* (Harmondsworth 1970).

chiefly concerned with ecclesiastical property and clerical judicial immunity, Paul V and his successors arguably had to exhibit supreme papal authority in more cautious ways. However, as has been seen in the case of Urban VIII and Galileo, that did not mean that decisive use of such authority, in defensive response to external challenge, could be or was avoided on occasion. The decision by Clement VIII to allow the reconciliation of Henri IV to the Church had itself involved the exercise of supreme authority, but this did not alter widespread French conviction that the Gallican nation and Church had adopted the king, as a convert, on their own not Roman terms.

The practical co-operation between Henri and both Clement and then Paul V subsequently still did not bring about official legal reception of the Tridentine decrees in the French kingdom. The occasional embarrassment of James I of England when repudiated by a king he insisted on viewing as a natural ally against unjust Roman claims, despite his own interest in a Catholic marriage for his original heir to the British thrones, Prince Henry, was self-inflicted. Catholic, Bourbon France was useful enough to the papacy as a counter-weight to Habsburg dominance and a still considerable Spanish military and political power in Europe, but the new, officially Catholic dynasty in France was weakened not only by virtue of its necessary concessions to the Huguenot minority. The assassination of Henri realized the internal tensions, not fully resolved, which astute contemporaries had feared might lead to a renewal of civil war. The precarious nature of the regency under Marie de'Medici, with her disposition to accept Italian influence, including papal, combined with the fact of the assassination to strengthen the determination of some French Catholics to pursue a specifically Gallican Catholicism.

This could be seen in the subsequent evolution of Richelieu himself, from pastoral application of the Tridentine reforms in a diocese adjacent to a Protestant stronghold and initial advice to the queen, to co-operation with the young king and eventual triumph over the Huguenot enclaves militarily and politically. But the latter was achieved without necessarily implying greater compliance with specifically Roman objectives, and it was no accident that internal Catholic controversy over papal authority remained acute in France in the first half of the seventeenth century. Nor was it surprising that after another challenge to Bourbon stability, in the mid-century Frondes, the personal reign of Louis XIV initiated a long period of practical challenge to manifestations of papal authority. Yet this confrontation complicated any definitive papal resolution of the growing Jansenist dispute, even when the king himself eventually sought Roman intervention in that new internal threat to French religious cohesion. Equally, it was not accidental that from 1594 onwards revival and consolidation of Gallican assertions of substantial French independence from papal authority merged with specifically anti-Jesuit polemic. French Catholicism was anxious to shed all trace of arguments for tyrannicide, which had surfaced at the time of the League in the later sixteenth century, and attack on supposed Jesuit retention of such theories provided a ready way to demonstrate loyalty to the Crown and Bourbon dynasty.

In turn, a conspicuous tendency within the French province of the Society of Jesus came to place greater practical value on support for and from the Bourbon kings than on open devotion to Rome, if conflict could not be avoided, as was certainly shown in the reign of Louis XIV, after both the assassination of Henri IV and the mid-century anarchy.[6] The extent to which the literary warfare carried on by James I became entangled with an otherwise internal, Catholic conflict in early seventeenth-century France further explains the attempts of the Roman leadership of the Society to prevent Jesuit involvement in questions which might be described as political. But the divisions among English Catholic Recusants, not least over regulars' exemption from the powers of an ordinary hierarchy, again affected French controversy, as early Jansenist attack on the Jesuits was launched in the name of episcopal rights, thereby ensuring that papal authority still remained a point of dispute. The same effect was seen in the beginnings of troubles in the Northern Netherlands, well known in France, which would eventually lead to the Utrecht schism. Richelieu, while using his patronage of Gallican theorists in manoeuvres partly aimed against Rome, avoided French schism; but the ideas which he was willing to patronize provided future support for Jansenist anti-Romanism.

The history of the papacy between the end of the Council of Trent and the outbreak of the French Revolution thus reveals a paradox. On the one hand, the defence of doctrinal unity among Catholics necessitated a fundamentally conservative stance: definitive positive promulgation even of a popular belief such as the Immaculate Conception was avoided in this period. But the defence of such unity involved conservatism not reaction. The Tridentine formulas, the necessary result of compromise between different orthodox traditions, were defended, against the reaction of the Jansenists, who claimed a priority for an Augustinianism based on patristic texts. In pursuit of their own priority, the post-Tridentine popes were largely successful, despite the long and wearing Jansenist controversy that dominated so much of this period.

Formal schism, even in the Northern Netherlands, was kept to a minimum until 1789, and popular religious belief and practice in Catholic Europe were maintained substantially intact. But this doctrinal conservation involved a related but distinct question, which inevitably arose over papal authority, and extended much further than the occasional debates in seventeenth-century France over a personal infallibility of the pope, as opposed to that of the Holy See. The properly Tridentine, that is Conciliar position that the papacy should exercise a definitive and exclusive judgement in interpreting the doctrinal and disciplinary decrees, when subsequently required, was indeed challenged, and increasingly so in two senses. It was clearly the case in geographical terms, since varieties of Jansenism affected not only the Netherlands and France, but Italy itself, Spain and Portugal, and German-speaking Catholic territories. It was also evident in the sense that versions of Jansenism in the end contested not simply specific doctrinal issues, nor in addition only pastoral questions like

6 H. Hillenaar, *Fénelon et les Jésuites* (The Hague 1967).

the frequency of lay communion, but increasingly, and eventually above all, the exercise of papal authority itself in Catholic Europe and its global extensions.

Indeed, the Febronianism of the German-speaking lands, partly under the influence of the Church of Utrecht, came explicitly to challenge papal authority. This was also why the fate of the Society of Jesus, with its apparently intimate relation to the papacy, became so central to the Jansenist conflict. From the decisions of the Council, however unexpectedly, the popes had derived a potentially firm support for the exercise of their authority within the Catholic Church, an authority which supposedly overrode in the final instance all competitive authority in ecclesiastical questions, whether asserted by secular rulers, by royal councils or *parlements*, or by theological faculties. But the popes between 1564 and 1789 found it hard enough in purely doctrinal matters to have their rulings accepted as conclusive and binding. Their whole authority was then increasingly challenged, at first on specific disciplinary issues, but ultimately on wider grounds of ecclesiological principle.

Yet in conflicts with Catholic secular rulers, for example, the popes of this period were not in fact attempting to defend their own authority in isolation. The Council of Trent had reaffirmed certain earlier principles of ecclesiastical right, such as the fiscal and judicial immunities which clerics should properly enjoy. These rights were what the post-Tridentine papacy was attempting to preserve more generally. After 1565, and, despite the efforts of Clement VIII, Paul V and Gregory XV, increasingly after 1625, the popes were shown to lack a coercive power adequate to establish their proclaimed authority when resisted by Catholic secular governments. This was even more evident after 1648, and above all after 1700.

It might indeed be that such Catholic regimes were gradually applying lessons in the consolidation of administrative authority which the precocious example of the high medieval papacy had suggested. But, even if that were the case, it involved precisely the pre- not the post-Tridentine papacy. Nor would such an evolution demonstrate that the papacy between the sixteenth and the eighteenth century was more affected by a common concentration of state power, gradually extending over a long period throughout Europe, than by the precise effects of Protestant challenge and a partly corresponding effort for Catholic revival. The aims of the post-Tridentine popes, it has been suggested here, substantially involved the maintenance and improvement of Roman diocesan oversight, a momentarily distinct restoration of metropolitan leadership, the establishment until *c.* 1700 of an effectively primatial direction of the Church in mainland Italy, and an increasingly challenged assertion of patriarchal headship of the Church in non-Protestant Western Christendom. Also involved, it has been argued here, were an attempt, more not less conspicuous after the 1620s, to act as supreme pontiff on a truly global stage, including the non-European missionary areas, and only finally the exercise of sovereignty over the limited territories of the papal states.

It was not the last of these roles, any more than the first, but the intermediate ones which aroused conflict with Catholic secular authorities. For in pursuing a patriarchal control within non-Protestant Europe, or in extending pontifical oversight beyond Europe, more than in merely giving directions to the Church in all or part of peninsular Italy, the popes encountered governmental resistance, whether over effective supervision of local ecclesiastical life or over clerical and not just papal privileges. Such conflicts, not doctrinal so much as disciplinary, raising issues of ecclesiastical appointments and finance as well as judicial concerns, were, after all, those which in turn marked the dwindling ability of the eighteenth-century papacy to give coherence to the Church on the Italian mainland under its own practical primacy. But such issues were essentially Tridentine, not the product of controversy over the pope's sovereignty within his own states.

In the performance of their multiple roles, therefore, the popes between 1564 and 1789 were evidently not successful in all their aims. Not only were they unable in the end to resist demands for the suppression of the Jesuits, for example, but they also proved incapable of preventing wider monastic dissolutions and expropriations in the later eighteenth century, in which Catholic regimes unwittingly set precedents for Revolutionary attack on the institutional Church in its entirety. Yet, as is equally evident, a consciously Catholic Christianity survived both Revolutionary and Napoleonic disruption, and in turn developed a conspicuously increased not diminished veneration for the papacy. During the 'long Counter-Reformation', between 1564 and 1789, public loyalty was still manifested rather more to the office than the person of the pope. But the absence of a later style of personal cult did not mean that the pre-eminence of the Apostolic See was unrecognized, even when specific dimensions of Roman authority were challenged. Despite the insistence of some Curial experts on the indefectibility of the Petrine office, in response to regalian or Jansenist criticism, the concept of inerrancy had not yet been developed as a formal and binding declaration of personal infallibility. The achievements of the post-Tridentine popes were indeed not absolute, but they were considerable.

Further Reading

J. Bossy, 'The Counter-Reformation and the People of Catholic Europe', *Past and Present*, XLVII (1970), 51–70.

J. Bossy, *Christianity in the West 1400–1700* (Oxford 1985).

O. Chadwick, *Catholicism and History: The Opening of the Vatican Archives* (Cambridge 1978).

J. Delumeau, *Catholicism from Luther to Voltaire* (London 1977).

A.G. Dickens, *The Counter-Reformation* (London 1968).

E. Duffy, *Saints and Sinners: A History of the Popes* (New Haven, CT–London 1997).

A. Dupront, 'Du Concile de Trente: réflexions', *Revue historique*, CCVI (1951), 262–80.

H.O. Evennett, *The Spirit of the Counter-Reformation*, with a Postscript by J. Bossy (Cambridge 1968).

A. Fliche and V. Martin (eds), *Histoire de l'Eglise*, vols 17–19ii (Paris 1948–60); but compare more recent revisions and expansions of vols 17, 18, 19: A. Galuzzi (ed.), *La Chiesa al tempo del Concilio di Trento* (Turin 1977), E. da Veroli (ed.), *La restaurazione cattolica dopo il Concilio di Trento (1563–1648)* (Turin 1976), L. Mezzadri (ed.), *Le lotte politiche e dottrinali nei secoli XVII e XVIII* (2 vols, Turin 1974–75).

H. Jedin (ed.), *History of the Church*, vols 5–6 (London 1980–81).

H. Koenigsberger, 'Decadence or Shift? Changes in the Civilization of Italy and Europe in the Sixteenth and Seventeenth Centuries', *Transactions of the Royal Historical Society*, X (1960), 1–18.

H. Koenigsberger, 'Republics and Courts in Italian and European Culture in the Sixteenth and Seventeenth Centuries', *Past and Present*, LXXXIII (1979), 32–56.

H.J. Schroeder (ed.), *The Canons and Decrees of the Council of Trent* [1941] (St Louis 1960).

Select Bibliography

Wherever possible the works selected are in the English language. But obviously that possibility is limited on this subject.

CHAPTER 2

D. Balestracci, 'Le confraternite romane fra tardo medioevo ed età moderna nei contributi della recente storiografia', *Archivio storico italiano*, CXLVI (1988), 321–30.

M. Bevilacqua, *Il Monte dei Cenci: una famiglia Romana e il suo insediamento urbano tra medioevo ed età barocca* (Rome 1988).

J. Bignami Odier, *La bibliothèque Vaticane de Sixte IV à Pie XI: Recherches sur l'histoire des collections de manuscrits* (Vatican City 1973).

R. Bonfil, *Rabbis and Jewish Communities in Renaissance Italy* (Oxford 1990).

A. Borromeo, 'España y el problema de la elección papal de 1592', *Cuadernos de Investigación Histórica*, II (1978), 175–200.

M. Caffiero, *La politica della santità: nascita di un culto nell' età dei lumi* (Bari–Rome 1996).

L. Càstano, *Gregorio XIV* (Turin 1957).

N. Del Re, *La Curia Romana: lineamenti storico-giuridici* (Rome 1970).

N. Del Re, *Monsignor Governatore di Roma* (Rome 1972).

C. Donati, *L'idea di nobiltà in Italia, secoli XIV–XVIII* (Rome–Bari 1988).

J.P. Donnelly, 'To Close a Giant Eye: the Pantheon, 1591', *Archivum Historiae Pontificiae*, XXIV (1986), 377–84.

B. Dooley, 'Social Control and the Italian Universities: from Renaissance to Illuminismo', *Journal of Modern History*, LXI, 2 (1989), 205–39.

L. Firpo, *Esecuzioni capitali in Roma (1567–1671)* (Florence 1974).

J.M. Giménez, *Un catecismo para la iglesia universal: historia de la iniciativa desde su origen hasta el Sínodo Extraordinario de 1985* (Pamplona 1987).

E. Göller, *Die päpstliche Pönitentiarie von ihrem Ursprung bis zu ihrer Umgestaltung unter Pius V* (2 vols, Rome 1907–11).

P. Grendler, *Schooling in Renaissance Italy. Literacy and Learning, 1300–1600* (Baltimore–London 1989).

P. Herre, *Papsttum und Papstwahl im Zeitalter Philipps II* (Leipzig 1907), [repr. Aalen 1973].

P. Hurtubise, *Une famille-témoin: les Salviati* (Vatican City 1985).

A. Jacobson Schutte, 'Periodization of Sixteenth-century Italian Religious History: The Post-Cantimori Paradigm Shift', *Journal of Modern History*, LXI, 2 (1989), 269–84.

K. Jaitner, 'Il nepotismo di papa Clemente VIII (1592–1605): il dramma del cardinale Cinzio Aldobrandini', *Archivio storico italiano*, CXLVI (1988), 57–93.

C.M.S. Johns, 'Papal Patronage and Cultural Bureaucracy in Eighteenth-century Rome: Clement XI and the Accademia di San Luca', *Eighteenth-century Studies*, XXII (1988), 1–23.

T. Magnuson, *Rome in the Age of Bernini* (2 vols, Stockholm 1982–86).

J.-M. le Maire, 'L'enquête de 1598 ordonnée par la Congrégation de l'Index relative aux livres conservés dans les monastères et couvents italiens', *Revue française d'histoire du livre*, LIII (1986) [1988], 543–5.

B. Neveu, 'Episcopus et Princeps Urbis: Innocent XI réformateur de Rome d'après des documents inédits (1676–89)', in *Römische Kurie. Kirchliche Finanzen. Vatikanisches Archiv. Studien zu Ehren von Hermann Hoberg*, ed. E. Gatz (2 vols, Rome 1979), II, pp. 597–633.

B. Neveu, 'Politique ecclésiastique et controverses doctrinales à Rome de 1683 à 1705', *Bulletin de la Société d'Histoire Moderne*, Ve série, 10 (1975), 11–19.

B. Neveu, 'Tricentenaire de la fondation à Rome de "l'Ospizio de' Convertendi" (1673): ses hôtes français au XVIIe siècle', *Rivista di storia della Chiesa in Italia*, XXVII, 2 (1973), 361–403.

L. de Palma (ed.), *Studi su Antonio Pignatelli, Papa Innocenzo XII* (Lecce 1992).

G. Papa, 'I primi cardinali prefetti della S. Congregazione del Concilio', *Rivista di storia della Chiesa in Italia*, XXVII, 2 (1973), 171–84.

L. Pásztor, 'Giuseppe Livizzani sul governo pontificio nel Settecento', *Archivum Historiae Pontificiae*, XXIV (1986), 233–72.

A. Prosperi, 'L'Inquisizione: verso una nuova immagine?', *Critica storica*, XXV, 1 (1988), 119–45.

C. Roth, *A History of the Marranos* (New York 1975).

W.H. Rudt de Collenberg, 'Le baptême des juifs à Rome de 1614 à 1798 selon les registres de la "Casa dei catecumeni"', *Archivum Historiae Pontificiae*, XXIV (1986), 90–231; and XXV (1987), 105–261.

V. Spampanato, *Vita di Giordano Bruno* (2 vols, Messina 1921), [repr. Rome 1988].

CHAPTER 3

G. Alberigo, *Cardinalato e collegialità* (Florence 1969).

W. Angelini, *Gli Ebrei di Ferrara nel Settecento* (Urbino 1973).

L'Archivio della S. Congregazione del Buon Governo (1592–1847) [Archivio di Stato di Roma] (Rome 1956).

A. Bellettini, *La popolazione di Bologna dal secolo XV all' unificazione italiana* (Bologna 1961).

S. Boesch Gajano, *Culto dei santi, istituzioni e classi sociali in età preindustriale* (L'Aquila–Rome 1984).

S. Boesch Gajano et al. (eds), *Luoghi sacri e spazi della santità* (Turin 1990).

S. Boesch Gajano, *Raccolte di vite di santi dal XIII al XVIII secolo: strutture, messaggi, fruizioni* (Fasano di Brindisi 1990).

P. Brezzi, 'L'assolutismo statale di Sisto V', *Studi Romani*, XXXVII (1989), 225–34.

G.P. Brizzi, *La formazione della classe dirigente nel Sei-Settecento* (Bologna 1976).

P. Caiazza, 'L'archivio storico della Sacra Congregazione del Concilio', *Ricerche di storia sociale e religiosa*, XXI, 42 (1992), 7–24.

L. Calabretta and G. Sinatora (eds), *Il cardinal Guglielmo Sirleto (1514–85). Atti del convegno di studi* (Catanzaro 1989).

R. Canosa, *Storia dell' Inquisizione in Italia dalla metà del Cinquecento alla fine del Settecento*, vols 1 ff. (Rome 1986 onwards).

M. Chiabò et al., *Le Diocesi Suburbicarie nelle 'Visitae ad limina' dell' Archivio Segreto Vaticano* (Vatican City 1988).

La S. Congregazione del Concilio. Quarto centenario della fondazione (1564–1964) (Vatican City 1964).

J. Delumeau, *L'aveu et le pardon* (Paris 1990).

J. Delumeau, 'Rome: Political and Administrative Centralization in the Papal State in the Sixteenth Century', in *The Late Italian Renaissance 1525–1630*, ed. E. Cochrane (London 1970), pp. 287–304.

F. Diaz, 'Divagazioni sulla nobiltà del Settecento', *Rivista storica italiana*, CII, 2 (1990), 340–57.

L. Fiorani et al., *Riti cerimonie feste e vita di popolo nella Roma dei papi* (Bologna 1970).

S. Giner Guerri, *San José de Calasanz, Maestro y Fundador* (Madrid 1992).

A. Ilari, 'I cardinali vicari. Cronologia biobibliografica', *Rivista diocesana di Roma*, IV (1962), 273–95.

L'Inquisizione Romana in Italia nell' età moderna. Archivi, Problemi di Metodo e nuove ricerche (Rome 1991).

H. Kleindienst, 'Das Apologiemodell einer "Anatomia Aesthetica in Cera" im Zeitalter Papst Benedikts XIV (1740–58)', *Archiv für Kulturgeschichte*, LXXII, 2 (1990), 367–80.

T.M. Lucas (ed.), *Saint, Site and Sacred Stategy: Ignatius, Rome and Jesuit Urbanism* (Vatican City 1990).

G. Lutz, 'Rom und Europa während des Pontifikats Urbans VIII.', in *Rom in der Neuzeit*, ed. R. Elze et al. (Vienna–Rome 1976), pp. 72–167.

F.R. McManus, *The Congregation of Sacred Rites* (Washington, DC 1954).

D. Menozzi, 'Prospettive sinodali nel Settecento', *Cristianesimo nella Storia*, VIII, 1 (1987), 115–45.

Miscellanea in occasione del IV centenario della Congregazione per le cause dei santi (1588–1988) (Vatican City 1988).

W. Monter, 'Women and the Italian Inquisitions', in *Women in the Middle Ages and the Renaissance. Literary and Historical Perspectives* (Syracuse, NY 1986), pp. 73–87.

C. Mozzarelli (ed.), *'Familia' del principe e famiglia aristocratica* (2 vols, Rome 1988).

T. Mrkonjić (ed.), *Epistolae ad principes, II, S. Pius V–Gregorius XIII (1566–1585)* (Vatican City 1994).

G. dall' Olio, 'I rapporti tra la Congregazione del Sant' Ufficio e gli inquisitori locali nei carteggi bolognesi (1573–94)', *Rivista storica italiana*, CV, 1 (1993), 246–86.

S.F. Ostrow, 'Gianlorenzo Bernini, Girolamo Lucenti, and the Statue of Philip IV in S. Maria Maggiore: Patronage and Politics in Seicento Rome', *Art Bulletin*, LXXIII (1991), 89–118.

S. Pagano, 'L'azione antiereticale di San Carlo a Mantova nel 1568', *Studia Borromaica*, IV (1990), 171–251.

G. Penco, *Storia della Chiesa in Italia, II. Dal Concilio di Trento ai nostri giorni* (Milan 1978).

M. Rosa, 'Politica ecclesiastica e riformismo religioso in Italia alla fine dell' antico regime', *Cristianesimo nella Storia*, X, 2 (1989), 227–48.

A. Rotondò, *Forme e destinazione del messaggio religioso: aspetti della propaganda religiosa nel Cinquecento* (Florence 1991).

G. Ruggieri, *Teologi in difesa: Il confronto tra chiesa e società nella Bologna della fine del Settecento* (Brescia 1988).

F.E. Schneider, *Die Römische Rota* (Paderborn 1914).

J. Semmler, *Das päpstliche Staatssekretariat in den Pontifikaten Pauls V. und Gregors XV. 1605–1623* (Rome 1969).

P. Tacchi Venturi, *Storia della Compagnia di Gesù in Italia*, vols I ff. (3rd edn, Rome 1950 onwards).

M. Turrini, *Penitenza e devozione. L'episcopato del card. Marcello Crescenzi a Ferrara (1746–88)* (Brescia 1989).

S. Vareschi, 'Le cardinal Ludovico Madruzzo', *Revue d'histoire ecclésiastique*, XC, 3–4 (1995), 483–92.

M. Völkel, 'Die Sapienza als Klient. Die römische Universität unter dem Protektorat der Barberini und Chigi', *Quellen und Forschungen aus italienischen Archiven und Bibliotheken*, LXX (1990), 491–512.

P. Waddy, *Seventeenth-century Roman Palaces: Use and the Art of the Plan* (New York 1990).

J. Wodka, *Zur Geschichte der nationalen Protektorate der Kardinäle* (Leipzig 1938).

CHAPTER 4

A. Acosta González, *Estudio comparado de tribunales inquisitoriales (períodos 1540–1570 y 1571–1621)* (Madrid 1990).

A. d'Addario, *Aspetti della Controriforma a Firenze* (Rome 1972).

R. Ago, *Carriere e clientele nella Roma barocca* (Rome–Bari 1990).

R. Ajello, 'I filosofi e la regina. Il governo delle Due Sicilie da Tanucci a Caracciolo (I), 1776–86', *Rivista storica italiana*, CIII, 2 (1991), 398–454.

B. Alamos de Barrientos, *Discurso político al rey Felipe III al comienzo de su reinado* (Madrid–Barcelona 1990).

G. Alberigo, 'Carlo Borromeo come modello di vescovo nella Chiesa post-tridentina', *Rivista storica italiana*, LXXIX (1967), 1031–52.

G. Alberigo, 'Studi e problemi relativi all' applicazione del Concilio di Trento in Italia', *Rivista storica italiana*, LXX (1958), 239–98.

A. Antonovics, 'Counter-Reformation Cardinals, 1534–1590', *European Studies Review*, II (1972), 301–28.

J. Bargrave, *Pope Alexander the Seventh and the College of Cardinals*, ed. J.C. Robertson (London 1866) [1867].

G. Benzoni, 'Una controversia tra Roma e Venezia all' inizio del Seicento: la conferma del Patriarca', *Bollettino dell' Istituto di Storia della Società e dello Stato Veneziano*, III (1961), 121 ff.

C.A. Bolton, *Church Reform in 18th Century Italy. (The Synod of Pistoia, 1786)* (The Hague 1969).

P. Bondioli, 'Il mancato ritorno dell' arcivescovo Alfonso Litta a Milano', in *Studi in onore di Carlo Castiglioni* (Milan 1957), pp. 107 ff.

W.J. Bouwsma, *Venice and the Defense of Republican Liberty: Renaissance Values in the Age of the Counter-Reformation* (Berkeley, CA 1968).

J.L. Bouza Alvarez, *Religiosidad contrarreformista y cultura simbólica del Barroco* (Madrid 1990).

L. Braida, 'L'affermazione della censura di Stato in Piemonte, dall' editto del 1648 alle costituzioni per l'Università del 1772', *Rivista storica italiana*, CII, 3 (1990), 717–95.

P. Brown, *Lionardo Salviati* (Oxford 1974).

P. Caiazza, 'L'applicazione del Tridentino attraverso la corrispondenza dei nunzî di Napoli', in *Il Concilio di Trento nella vita spirituale e culturale del Mezzogiorno tra XVI e XVII secolo. Atti del Convegno*, ed. G. De Rosa and A. Cestaro (2 vols, Venosa 1988), I, pp. 57–64.

L. Châtellier, *The Religion of the Poor. Rural Missions in Europe and the Formation of Modern Catholicism, c. 1500–c. 1800* (Cambridge 1997).

I. Chiesa, *Vita di Carlo Bascapè*, ed. S. Pagano (Florence 1993).

Città italiane del Cinquecento tra Riforma e Controriforma. Atti del convegno internazionale di studi (Lucca 1988).

E. Codignola (ed.), *Carteggi di Giansenisti Liguri*, vols 1–3 (Florence 1941–42).

E. Codignola, *Illuministi, Giansenisti e Giacobini nell' Italia del Settecento* (Florence 1947).

P. Corsi, 'Vescovi e comunità greche di Puglia tra XIV e XVI secolo: alcuni esempi', in *Vescovi e Diocesi in Italia dal XIV alla metà del XVI secolo*, ed. G. De Sandre Gasparini et al. (2 vols, Rome 1990), II, pp. 965–99.

G. Cozzi, 'Gesuiti e politica sul finire del '500. Una mediazione di pace tra Enrico IV, Filippo II e la Sede Apostolica proposta dal p. Achille Gagliardi alla Repubblica di Venezia', *Rivista storica italiana*, LXXV, 3 (1963), 477–537.

G. Cozzi et al., *La Repubblica di Venezia nell' età moderna. Dal 1517 alla fine della Repubblica* [*Storia d'Italia*, ed. G. Galasso, vol. XII, 2] (Turin 1992).

G. Cozzi, 'Traiano Boccalini, il Cardinal Borghese e la Spagna, secondo le riferte di un confidente degli Inquisitori di Stato', *Rivista storica italiana*, LXVIII (1956), 230–54.

V. Criscuolo (ed.), *I Cappuccini e la Congregazione Romana dei Vescovi e Regolari*, vols 1 ff. (Rome 1989 onwards).

E. Dammig, *Il Movimento Giansenista a Roma nella seconda metà del secolo XVIII* (Vatican City 1945).

A. Del Col, 'Organizzazione, composizione e giurisdizione dei tribunali dell' Inquisizione Romana nella Repubblica di Venezia 1500–1550', *Critica storica*, XXV (1988), 244–94.

L. Donvito, *Società meridionale e istituzioni ecclesiastiche nel Cinque e Seicento* (Milan 1987).

A. Dupront, *Du Sacré: Croisades et pèlerinages, images et langages* (Paris 1987).

M. Firpo, *Inquisizione Romana e Controriforma: studi sul cardinal Giovanni Morone e il suo processo d' eresia* (Bologna 1992).

G. Fragnito, *La Bibbia al Rogo: la censura ecclesiastica e i volgarizzamenti della scrittura (1471–1605)* (Bologna 1997).

M.C. Giannini, 'Politica spagnola e giurisdizione ecclesiastica nello Stato di Milano: il conflitto tra il cardinale Federico Borromeo e il *visitador* regio don Felipe de Haro (1606–1607)', *Studia Borromaica*, VI (1992), 195–226.

G. Gravina, *Curia Romana e Regno di Napoli. Cronache politiche e religiose nelle lettere a Francesco Pignatelli (1690–1712)*, ed. A. Sarubbi (Naples 1972).

R.C. Head, 'Religious Boundaries and the Inquisition in Venice: Trials of Jews and Judaizers 1548–80', *Journal of Medieval and Renaissance Studies*, XX, 2 (1990), 175–204.

Italia Judaica: 'Gli ebrei in Italia dalla segregazione alla prima emancipazione' (Rome 1989).

M.C. Jacob, *Living the Enlightenment. Freemasonry and Politics in Eighteenth-century Europe* (New York 1991).

A.C. Jemolo, *Il Giansenismo in Italia prima della Rivoluzione* (Bari 1928).

A.C. Jemolo, *Stato e Chiesa negli scrittori italiani del Seicento e del Settecento* (2nd edn, ed. M. Broglio, Naples 1972).

F.M. Jones, *Alphonsus de Liguori, the Saint of Bourbon Naples 1696–1787* (Dublin 1992).

E. Kovács (ed.), *Katholische Aufklärung und Josephinismus* (Munich 1979).

A. Lauro, *Il giurisdizionalismo pregiannoniano nel Regno di Napoli* (Rome 1974).

O. Logan, *The Venetian Upper Clergy in the Sixteenth and Early Seventeenth Centuries. A Study in Religious Culture* (2 vols, Salzburg 1995).

P. Lopez, *Sul libro a stampa e le origini della censura ecclesiastica* (Naples 1972).

M. Mariotti and E. D'Agostino, 'Concili provinciali e sinodi diocesani post-ridentini in Calabria', *Rivista di Storia della Chiesa in Italia*, XLIV, 1 (1990), 69–80.

E. Martínez Ruiz et al., 'La crisis hispánica del 1640', *Cuadernos de historia moderna*, XI (1991).

M. Miele, *Die Provinzialkonzilien Süditaliens in der Neuzeit* (Paderborn 1996).

P. Morelli, 'Osservanza del precetto pasquale e pubbliche penitenze in una parrocchia della Valdera "lucchese" fra Cinque e Seicento (Soiana, 1596–1623)', *Rivista di Storia della Chiesa in Italia*, XLIV, 2 (1990), 451–65.

P. Paschini, 'I monasteri femminili in Italia nel Cinquecento', *Italia Sacra*, II (1960).

A. Pastore, *Nella Valtellina del tardo cinquecento: fede, cultura, società* (Milan 1975).

L. Pásztor, 'L'Histoire de la Curie Romaine, problème d'histoire de l'église', *Revue d'histoire ecclésiastique*, LXIV (1969), 353–66.

P. Pirri, *L'interdetto di Venezia del 1606 e i Gesuiti* (Rome 1959).

A. Pizzati, *Commende e politica ecclesiastica nella Repubblica di Venezia tra'500 e'600* (Venice 1997).

P. Prodi, 'Charles Borromée, archevêque de Milan, et la papauté', *Revue d'histoire ecclésiastique*, LXII, (1967), 379–411.

P. Prodi, 'San Carlo Borromeo e il Cardinale Gabriele Paleotti. Due vescovi della Riforma cattolica', *Critica storica*, III (1964), 135–51.

A. Prosperi, *Tribunali della coscienza: inquisitori, confessori, missionari* (Turin 1996).

G. Quazza, *La decadenza italiana nella storia europea. Saggi sul Sei-Settecento* (Turin 1971).

G. Ricuperati, *I volti della pubblica felicità: storiografia e politica nel Piemonte settecentesco* (Turin 1989).

M. Rizzo, 'Centro spagnolo e periferia lombarda nell' impero asburgico tra Cinque e Seicento', *Rivista storica italiana*, CIV, ii (1992), 315–48.

G. Romeo, 'Una città, due inquisizioni: l'anomalia del Sant' Ufficio a Napoli nel tardo Cinquecento', *Rivista di storia e letteratura religiosa*, XXIV (1988), 42–67.

C. Roth, *The History of the Jews in Italy* (Philadelphia, PA 1946).

C. Russo, *I monasteri femminili di clausura a Napoli nel secolo XVII* (Naples 1970).

D. Sella, *Italy in the Seventeenth Century* (London 1997).

M. Sievernich et al. (eds), *Ignatianisch: Eigenart und Methode der Gesellschaft Jesu* (Freiburg 1991).

G. Signorotto (ed.), *L'Italia degli Austrias. Monarchia cattolica e domini italiani nei secoli XVI e XVII* (Mantua 1993).

P. Simoncelli, 'Inquisizione Romana e riforma in Italia', *Rivista storica italiana*, C (1988), 5–125.

P. Stella (ed.), *Atti e Decreti del Concilio Diocesano di Pistoia dell' anno 1786*, vol. I [Ristampa dell' edizione Bracali] (Florence 1986).

R.A. Stradling, 'Prelude to Disaster; the Precipitation of the War of the Mantuan Succession, 1627–29', *Historical Journal*, XXXIII (1990), 769–85.

J. Tedeschi, *The Prosecution of Heresy* (Binghamton, NY 1991).

A. Torre, 'Politics Cloaked in Worship: State, Church and Local Power in Piedmont 1570–1770', *Past and Present*, CXXXIV (1992), 42–92.

R. Turtas, *La Chiesa durante il periodo spagnolo. L'età moderna, dagli Aragonesi alla fine del dominio spagnolo* [Storia dei Sardi e della Sardegna, 3] (Milan 1988).

R. Turtas, 'Missioni popolari in Sardegna tra Cinquecento e Seicento', *Rivista di Storia della Chiesa in Italia*, XLIV, 2 (1990), 369–412.

F. Venturi, *Settecento riformatore*, vols II (Turin 1976), V, 1 (Turin 1987).

K. Walf, *Das bischöfliche Amt in der Sicht josephinischer Kirchenrechtler* (Vienna 1975).

J.-C. Waquet, *Corruption, Ethics and Power in Florence, 1600–1770* (Cambridge 1991).

J.-C. Waquet, *Le grand-duché de Toscane sous les derniers Médicis: essai sur le système des finances et la stabilité des institutions* (Rome 1990).

S.J. Woolf, *A History of Italy 1700–1860. The Social Constraints of Political Change* (London 1979).

CHAPTER 5

S. Adorni-Braccesi, *'Una città infetta': la Repubblica di Lucca nella crisi religiosa del Cinquecento* (Florence 1994).

G. Alberigo, *Lo sviluppo della dottrina sui poteri nella Chiesa universale* (Rome 1964).

M. Albert, *Nuntius Fabio Chigi und die Anfänge des Jansenismus 1639–51: ein römischer Diplomat in theologischen Auseinandersetzungen* (Rome 1988).

J.F. Alcaraz Gómez, *Jesuitas y Reformismo. El Padre Francisco de Rávago (1747–1755)* (Valencia 1995).

D. Alden, *The Making of an Enterprise. The Society of Jesus in Portugal, its Empire, and Beyond, 1540–1750* (Stanford, CA 1996).

N. Aston (ed.), *Religious Change in Europe 1650–1914. Essays for John McManners* (Oxford 1997).

A. Astrain, *Historia de la Compañía de Jesús en la asistencia de España* (7 vols, Madrid 1902–25).

P. Batiffol, *History of the Roman Breviary* (London 1912).

D. Beales, 'The False Joseph II', *Historical Journal*, XVIII (1975), 467–95.

D. Beales, *Joseph II*, vol. 1 (Cambridge 1987).

R. Becker, 'Aus dem Alltag des Nuntius Malatesta Baglioni. Nichtdiplomatische Aufgaben der Wiener Nuntiatur um 1635', *Quellen und Forschungen*, LXV (1985), 306–41.

Y.-M. Bercé, 'Rome et l'Italie au XVIIe siècle. La dernière chance temporelle de l'état ecclésiastique 1641–49', in *L'Europe, l'Alsace et la France. Etudes réunies en l'honneur du doyen Georges Livet* (Strasbourg 1987), pp. 229–37.

J. Bergin, *The Making of the French Episcopate 1589–1661* (New Haven, CT–London 1996).

J. Bergin and L. Brockliss (eds), *Richelieu and his Age* (Oxford 1992).

M. Biagioli, *Galileo, Courtier: the Practice of Science in the Culture of Absolutism* (Chicago, IL 1994).

R. Bireley, *The Counter-Reformation Prince: Anti-Machiavellianism or Catholic Statecraft in Early Modern Europe* (Chapel Hill, NC–London 1990).

R.J. Blackwell, *Galileo, Bellarmine and the Bible* (London 1991).

T. Blanning, *Joseph II* (London 1994).

P. Blet, *Le clergé du Grand Siècle en ses assemblées (1615–1715)* (Paris 1995).

P. Blet, 'Louis XIV et le Saint-Siège', *XVIIe siècle*, CXXIII (1979), 137–54.

V. Borg (ed.), *Fabio Chigi, Apostolic Delegate in Malta: an Edition of his Official Correspondence* (Vatican City 1967).

W.J. Callahan and D. Higgs (eds), *Church and Society in Catholic Europe of the Eighteenth Century* (Cambridge 1979).

M.M. Cárcel Ortí (ed.), *Relaciones sobre el estado de las diócesis valencianas* (3 vols, Valencia 1989).

M.H. Carvalho dos Santos, *Pombal revisitado* (2 vols, Lisbon 1984).

Coloquio internacional: Carlos III y su siglo (2 vols, Madrid 1990).

E. De Heeckeren (ed.), *Correspondance de Benoît XIV* (2 vols, Paris 1912).

G. Demerson et al. (eds), *Les Jésuites parmi les hommes aux XVIe et XVIIe siècles: Actes du colloque de Clermont-Ferrand* (Clermont-Ferrand 1987).

G. Dethan, *The Young Mazarin* (London 1977).

W. De Vries, *Rom und die Patriarchate des Ostens* (Munich 1963).

P.G.M. Dickson, 'Joseph II's Reshaping of the Austrian Church', *Historical Journal*, XXXVI, 1 (1993), 89–114.

A. Dupront, *L.A. Muratori, et la société européenne des pré-lumières* (Florence 1976).

F. Edwards, *Robert Persons. The Biography of an Elizabethan Jesuit 1546–1610* (St Louis, MS 1995).

A. Fantoli, *Galileo: For Copernicanism and for the Church* (Chicago, IL 1994).

A. Fernández Collado, *Gregorio XIII y Felipe II en la Nunciatura de Felipe Sega (1577–81): aspectos político, jurisdiccional y de reforma* (Toledo 1991).

M.A. Finocchiaro (ed.), *The Galileo Affair: a Documentary History* (Berkeley, CA 1989).

G. Fragnito, 'Cardinals' Courts in Sixteenth-century Rome', *Journal of Modern History*, LXV (1993), 26–56.

V. Frajese, *Sarpi scettico. Stato e Chiesa a Venezia tra Cinque e Seicento* (Bologna 1994).

J.M. García Marín, *Monarquía católica en Italia: Burocracia imperial y privilegios constitucionales* (Madrid 1992).

E. Gatz, 'Das Collegium Germanicum und der Episkopat der Reichskirche nach 1648', *Römische Quartalschrift*, LXXXIII (1988), 337–44.

J.M. Gres-Gayer, 'Gallicans et romains en Sorbonne d'après le nonce Bargellini (1670)', *Revue d'histoire ecclésiastique*, LXXXVII, 3–4 (1992), 682–744.

J.M. Gres-Gayer, *Jansénisme en Sorbonne 1643–1656* (Paris 1996).

J.M. Gres-Gayer, *Théologie et pouvoir en Sorbonne. La faculté de théologie de Paris et la bulle Unigenitus 1714–21* (Paris 1991).

S. Haliczer, *Sexuality in the Confessional: a Sacrament Profaned* (New York 1996).

F. Haskell, *History and its Images* (New Haven, CT–London 1993).

J.M. Headley, 'Tommaso Campanella and the End of the Renaissance', *Journal of Medieval and Renaissance Studies*, XX, 2 (1990), 157–74.

P. Hersche, *Der aufgeklärte Reformkatholizismus in Österreich* (Bern 1976).

P. Hersche, *Der Spätjansenismus in Österreich* (Vienna 1977).

F. Hildesheimer, *Le jansénisme en France aux XVIIe et XVIIIe siècles* (Paris 1992).

F. Hildesheimer, *Le jansénisme, l'histoire et l'héritage* (Paris 1992).

R. de Hinojosa, *Los despachos de la diplomacia pontificia en España*, I (Madrid 1896).

C. Hirschauer, *La politique de St. Pie V en France (1566–1572)* (Paris 1922).

K. Jaitner (ed.), *Die Hauptinstruktionen Clemens' VIII. für die Nuntien und Legaten an den europäischen Fürstenhöfen 1592–1605* (2 vols, Tübingen 1984). *Die Hauptinstruktionen Gregors XV. für die Nuntien und Gesandten an den europäischen Fürstenhöfen 1621–1623* (2 vols, Tübingen 1997).

H. Jedin and P. Prodi (eds), *Il Concilio di Trento come crocevia della politica europea* (Bologna 1979).

B. Joassart, 'L'accueil réservé aux "Acta Sanctorum" à Rome en 1643. En marge d'un anniversaire', *Analecta Bollandiana*, CXI, 1–2 (1993), 5–18.

A. Jordà i Fernández, *Església i poder a la Catalunya del segle XVII. La Seu de Tarragona* (Barcelona 1993).

H. Kamen, *Philip of Spain* (New Haven, CT–London 1997).

D. van Kley, *The Jansenists and the Expulsion of the Jesuits from France 1757–65* (New Haven, CT 1975).

G. Klingenstein and F.A.J. Szabo (eds), *Staatskanzler Wenzel Anton von Kaunitz-Rietberg 1711–1794* (Graz 1996).

R. Knecht, *Richelieu* (London 1991).

L. Kolakowski, *Chrétiens sans Eglise* (Paris 1969).

E. Kovács, *Der Pabst in Teutschland. Die Reise Pius VI. im Jahre 1782* (Munich 1983).

E. Kovács, *Ultramontanismus und Staatskirchentum im theresianisch-josephinischen Staat: der Kampf der Kardinäle Migazzi und Franckenberg gegen Ferdinand Stöger* (Vienna 1975).

A. Kraus, 'Die Geschichte des päpstlichen Staatssekretariats im Zeitalter der katholischen Reform und der Gegenreformation als Aufgabe der Forschung', *Römische Quartalschrift*, LXXXIV (1989), 74–91.

J.R. Kušej, *Joseph II. und die äussere Kirchenverfassung Innerösterreichs* (Stuttgart 1908).

J.M. Lattis, *Between Copernicus and Galileo: Christoph Clavius and the Collapse of Ptolemaic Cosmology* (Chicago, IL 1995).

A. Leman, *Urbain VIII et la rivalité de la France et de la maison d'Autriche de 1631 à 1635* (Lille–Paris 1920).

G. Lutz (ed.), *Das Papsttum, die Christenheit und die Staaten Europas 1592–1605. Forschungen zu den Hauptinstruktionen Clemens' VIII.* (Tübingen 1994).

J. Lynch, *Spain under the Habsburgs* (2nd edn, Oxford 1981).

F. Maass (ed.), *Der Josephinismus. Quellen zu seiner Geschichte in Österreich, 1760–1850* (5 vols, Vienna 1951–61).

J.M. Marqués, *La Santa Sede y la España de Carlos II* (Rome 1981–82) [1983].

A.G. Martimort, *Le gallicanisme de Bossuet* (Paris 1953).

N.G. Martín, 'Secciones, emolumentos y personal de la Nunciatura española en tiempos de César Monti', *Anthologica Annua*, IV (1956), 283 ff.

D.J. Martín Gutiérrez, *La Junta de Hacienda de Portugal* (Pamplona 1996).

P.-N. Mayaud, 'Les "Fuit Congregatio S. Officii in . . . coram . . ." de 1611 à 1642: 32 ans de vie de la Congrégation du Saint Office', *Archivum Historiae Pontificiae*, XXX (1992), 231–89.

T.M. McCoog (ed.), *The Reckoned Expense. Edmund Campion and the Early English Jesuits* (Woodbridge 1996).

T.M. McCoog, *The Society of Jesus in Ireland, Scotland and England 1541–1588. 'Our Way of Proceeding?'* (Leiden 1996).

A. Menniti Ippolito, *Fortuna e sfortune di una famiglia veneziana nel Seicento. Gli Ottoboni al tempo dell' aggregazione al patriziato* (Venice 1996).

E. Michaud, *Louis XIV et Innocent XI* (4 vols, Paris 1882–83).

S.J. Miller, *Portugal and Rome c. 1748–1830: an Aspect of the Catholic Enlightenment* (Rome 1978).

R.U. Montini, 'Aspetti della politica interna e della politica estera all' inizio del pontificato di Clemente VIII', *Studi Romani*, VII (1959), 647 ff.

S.-M. Morgain, *Pierre de Bérulle et les carmélites de France. La querelle du gouvernement 1583–1629* (Paris 1995).

R. Mousnier, *The Assassination of Henri IV, the Tyrannicide Problem and the Consolidation of the French Absolute Monarchy in the Early Seventeenth Century* (London 1973).

C. Mozzarelli and D. Zardin (eds), *I Tempi del Concilio: religione, cultura e società nell' Europa tridentina* (Rome 1997).

B. Neveu, *L'erreur et son juge. Remarques sur les censures doctrinales à l'époque moderne* (Naples 1993).

B. Neveu, *Erudition et religion aux XVIIe et XVIIIe siècles* (Paris 1994).

A. Nichols, *Rome and the Eastern Churches: a Study in Schism* (Edinburgh 1992).

Nuntiaturberichte aus Deutschland, 2. Abteilung, 3. Abteilung, 4. Abteilung; *Die Kölner Nuntiatur* (Berlin and subsequently other places of publication, 1892 onwards).

J. de Olarra Garmendía et al., *Correspondencia entre la Nunciatura en España y la Santa Sede. Reinado de Felipe III (1598–1621)*, vols 1–6 (Rome 1960–66).

J. Orcibal, *Louis XIV contre Innocent XI* (Paris 1949).

G. Parker et al., *The Thirty Years' War* (2nd edn, London 1997).

P. Paschini, 'La Nomina del Patriarca di Aquileia e la Repubblica di Venezia nel secolo XVI', *Rivista di storia della Chiesa in Italia*, II (1948), 61–76.

V. Pitzner, *Justinus Febronius. Das Ringen eines katholischen Irenikers um die Einheit der Kirche im Zeitalter der Aufklärung* (Göttingen 1976).

A. Poppi, *Cremonini e Galilei inquisiti a Padova nel 1604. Nuovi documenti d'archivio* (Padua 1992).

J.M. Pou y Martí, 'La intervención española en el conflicto entre Paulo V y Venecia (1605–7)', in *Miscellanea P. Paschini* (2 vols, Rome 1949), II, pp. 359 ff.

P. Prodi, 'Controriforma e/o riforma cattolica: superamento di vecchi dilemmi nei nuovi panorami storiografici', *Römische historische Mitteilungen*, XXXI (1989), 227–37.

P. Prodi, 'San Carlo Borromeo e le trattative tra Gregorio XIII e Filippo II sulla giurisdizione ecclesiastica', *Rivista di storia della Chiesa in Italia*, XI (1957), 195–240.

P. Prodi and W. Reinhard (eds), *Il Concilio di Trento e il Moderno* (Bologna 1996).

J.A. Pujol Aguado, *La Corona de Aragón en la Cámara de Castilla* (Alicante 1994).

K. Repgen, *Die Römische Kurie und der Westfälische Friede. Idee und Wirklichkeit des Papsttums im 16. und 17. Jahrhundert*, vol. I, 1–2 (Tübingen 1962–65).

B. Roberg, 'Türkenkrieg und Kirchenpolitik. Die Sendung Kardinal Madruzzos an den Kaiserhof 1593 und zum Reichstag von 1594', *Quellen und Forschungen*, LXV (1985), 192–305; and LXVI (1986), 192–268.

R. Robres and V. Castell, 'La visita "ad limina" durante el pontificado de Sixto V (1585–1590)', *Anthologica Annua*, VII (1959), 147–214.

P. Rodríguez and J. Rodríguez, *Don Francés de Alava y Beamonte: Correspondencia inédita de Felipe II con su embajador en París (1564–1570)* (Donostia–San Sebastian 1991).

Saggi storici intorno al papato, Miscellanea Historiae Pontificiae, vol. XXI (Rome 1959).

G. Schreiber, 'Tridentinische Reformdekrete in deutschen Bistümern', in *Concilium Tridentinum*, ed. R. Bäumer (Darmstadt 1979), pp. 462–521.

F.X. Seppelt, *Das Papsttum im Kampf mit Staatsabsolutismus und Aufklärung von Paul III. bis zur Französischen Revolution* (2nd edn, ed. G. Schwaiger, Munich 1959).

P. Simoncelli, 'Galileo e la Curia: un problema', *Belfagor*, XLVIII, 1 (1993), 29–40.

G. Sorgia, *Studi sull' Inquisizione in Sardegna* (Cagliari 1961).

M.G. Spietz, *L'église catholique des Provinces-Unies et le Saint-Siège pendant la deuxième moitié du XVIIe siècle* (Louvain 1975).

B. Steinhauf, *Giovanni Ludovico Madruzzo (1532–1600). Katholische Reformation zwischen Kaiser und Papst* (Münster 1993).

J.W. Stoye, *Marsigli's Europe, 1680–1730* (New Haven, CT–London 1994).

F.A.J. Szabo, *Kaunitz and Enlightened Absolutism 1753–1780* (Cambridge 1994).

A. Tallon, *La Compagnie du Saint-Sacrement* (Paris 1990).

R. Taveneaux, *Jansénisme et prêt à intérêt* (Paris 1977).

A.-C. Tizon-Germe, 'Juridiction spirituelle et action pastorale des légats et nonces en France pendant la Ligue (1589–94)', *Archivum Historiae Pontificiae*, XXX (1992), 159–230.

C. Vivanti, *Lotta politica e pace religiosa in Francia fra cinquecento e seicento* (Turin 1963).

L. Vos (ed.), *La correspondance d'Andrea Mangelli Internonce aux pays-bas (1652–1655)* (Brussels–Rome 1993).

M. Walker, *The Salzburg Transaction: Expulsion and Redemption in Eighteenth-century Germany* (Ithaca, NY–London 1992).

C. Weber (ed.), *Legati e governatori dello Stato pontificio (1550–1809)* (Rome 1994).

C. Weber, 'Papstgeschichte und Genealogie', *Römische Quartalschrift*, LXXXIV (1989), 331–400.

A. Wendland, *Der Nutzen der Pässe und die Gefährdung der Seelen. Spanien, Mailand und der Kampf ums Veltlin 1620–1641* (Zurich 1995).

L. Wolff, *The Vatican and Poland in the Age of the Partitions: Diplomatic and Cultural Encounters at the Warsaw Nunciature* (Boulder, CO. 1988).

E. Wolgast, *Hochstift und Reformation. Studien zur Geschichte der Reichskirche zwischen 1517 und 1648* (Stuttgart 1995).

CHAPTER 6

G. Albion, *Charles I and the Court of Rome* (London 1935).

J. Bossy, 'The Counter-Reformation and the People of Catholic Ireland', in *Historical Studies*, ed. T.D. Williams, VIII (Dublin 1971), pp. 155–69.

J. Bossy, 'Rome and the Elizabethan Catholics: a Question of Geography', *Historical Journal*, VII (1964), 135–42.

L. Bourdon, *La Compagnie de Jésus et le Japon* (Paris 1993).

L.W. Brown, *The Indian Christians of Saint Thomas* (Cambridge 1956).

M. Caffiero, '"Le insidie de' perfidi giudei": Antiebraismo e riconquista cattolica alla fine del Settecento', *Rivista storica italiana*, CV, 2 (1993), 555–81.

P. Caraman, *The Lost Empire: the Story of the Jesuits in Ethiopia, 1555–1634* (London 1985).

M. Cooper, *Rodrigues the Interpreter: an Early Jesuit in Japan and China* (New York 1974).

J.S. Cummins, *A Question of Rites: Friar Domingo Navarrete and the Jesuits in China* (Aldershot 1993).

C. Davey, *Pioneer for Unity: Metrophanes Kritopoulos (1589–1639) and Relations between the Orthodox, Roman Catholic and Reformed Churches* (London 1987).

J.-P. Duteil, 'L'évangélisation et les femmes en Chine au XVIIe siècle: l'adaptation et ses limites', *Mélanges de Science Religieuse*, LI, 3 (1994), 239–53.

J.H. Elliott, 'A Europe of Composite Monarchies', *Past and Present*, CXXXVII (1992), 48–71.

R.J.W. Evans et al. (eds), *Crown, Church and Estates: Central European Politics in the Sixteenth and Seventeenth Centuries* (London 1991).

O. Garstein, *Rome and the Counter-Reformation in Scandinavia*, vols 3–4 (Leiden 1992).

J. Gernet, *China and the Christian Impact. A Conflict of Cultures* (Cambridge 1985).

M. Gervers et al. (eds), *Conversion and Continuity: Indigenous Christian Communities in Islamic Lands, Eighth to Eighteenth Centuries* (Toronto 1990).

M. Goldie, 'The Scottish Catholic Enlightenment', *Journal of British Studies*, XXX, 1 (1991), 20–62.

S. Gruzinski, *The Conquest of Mexico: the Incorporation of Indian Societies into the Western World, Sixteenth to Eighteenth Centuries* (Cambridge 1993).

M. Hane, *Premodern Japan: a Historical Survey* (Boulder, CO 1991).

G. Hanlon, *Confession and Community in Seventeenth-century France: Catholic and Protestant Coexistence in Aquitaine* (Philadelphia, PA 1993).

D.P. Hupchick, *The Bulgarians in the Seventeenth Century: Slavic Orthodox Society and Culture under Ottoman Rule* (Jefferson, NC 1993).

P.C. Ioly Zorattini, *Processi del S. Uffizio di Venezia contro Ebrei e Giudaizzanti*, vols 1 ff. (Florence 1980 onwards).

H. d. La Costa, *The Jesuits in the Philippines, 1581–1768* (Cambridge, MA 1961).

H. Levine, *Economic Origins of Antisemitism: Poland and its Jews in the Early Modern Period* (New Haven, CT–London 1991).

M. Luzzati (ed.), *L'Inquisizione e gli Ebrei in Italia* (Rome–Bari 1994).

J.J. Martin, *Venice's Hidden Enemies: Italian Heretics in a Renaissance City* (Berkeley, CA 1993).

J.F. Moran, *The Japanese and the Jesuits: Alessandro Valignano in Sixteenth-century Japan* (London 1992).

M. Morford, *Stoics and Neostoics: Rubens and the Circle of Lipsius* (Princeton, NJ 1991).

H. Morgan, 'Hugh O'Neill and the Nine Years' War in Tudor Ireland', *Historical Journal*, XXXVI, 1 (1993), 21–37.

D. Mungello, *Curious Land: Jesuit Accommodation and the Origins of Sinology* (Stuttgart 1985).

M. Nédoncelle, *Trois aspects du problème anglo-catholique au XVIIe siècle* (Paris 1951).

S. Neill, *A History of Christianity in India* (2 vols, Cambridge 1984–85).

W.B. Patterson, *King James VI and I and the Reunion of Christendom* (Cambridge 1997).

M. Pernot, *Les guerres de religion en France 1559–98* (Paris 1987).

A. Plowden, *The Elizabethan Secret Service* (New York 1991).

J. Robertson, 'Franco Venturi's Enlightenment', *Past and Present*, CXXXVII (1992), 183–206.

M.J. Rodríguez-Salgado et al. (eds), *England, Spain and the 'Gran Armada' 1585–1604* (Edinburgh 1991).

A.C. Ross, *A Vision Betrayed. The Jesuits in Japan and China 1542–1742* (Edinburgh 1994).

A. Santos Hernandez, *Las misiones bajo el Patronato portugués* (Madrid 1977).

G. Scott, *Gothic Rage Undone: English Monks in the Age of Enlightenment* (Bath 1992).

A. Shishkin and B. Uspenskij, 'L'influence du Jansénisme en Russie au XVIIIe siècle. Deux épisodes', *Cahiers du monde russe et soviétique*, XXIX, 3–4 (1988), 337–42.

R.A. Stradling, *The Spanish Monarchy and Irish Mercenaries: the Wild Geese in Spain 1618–68* (Dublin 1994).

F. Tamburini, 'Una indagine su religiosi e laici del Nuovo Mondo dai registri della Penitenzieria Apostolica (1504–76)', *Quellen und Forschungen aus italienischen Archiven und Bibliotheken*, LXXIII (1993), 418–95.

D. Tollet, *Histoire des juifs en Pologne, du XVIe siècle à nos jours* (Paris 1992).

C.D. Totman, *Early Modern Japan* (Berkeley, CA 1993).

S. Vareschi, *La Legazione del Cardinale Ludovico Madruzzo alla Dieta Imperiale di Augusta 1582: Chiesa, Papato e Impero nella seconda metà del secolo XVI* (Trento 1990).

A. Walsham, *Church Papists: Catholicism, Conformity and Confessional Polemic in Early Modern England* (Woodbridge 1993).

R.B. Wernham, *The Return of the Armadas: the Last Years of the Elizabethan War against Spain 1595–1603* (Oxford 1994).

C. Wessels, *Early Jesuit Travellers in Central Asia 1603–1721* (The Hague 1924) [repr. New Delhi 1992].

J. Whitney Hall (ed.), *The Cambridge History of Japan*, vol. 4 (Cambridge 1991).

B.H. Willeke, 'A Memorandum of Pedro Baptista Porres Tamayo, OFM, on the State of the Missions in Japan (1625)', *Archivum Franciscanum Historicum*, LXXXVI, 1–2 (1993), 81–98.

CHAPTER 7

W. Angelini, *Economia e cultura a Ferrara dal Seicento al tardo Settecento* (Urbino 1979).

A. Antinori, *Scipione Borghese e l'architettura* (Rome 1995).

F. Baldinucci, *The Life of Bernini* (London 1966).

G.P. Bellori, *Le Vite de' Pittori, Scultori e Architetti Moderni*, ed. E. Borea (Turin 1976).

G. Benzoni, 'I papi e la "corte di Roma" vista dagli ambasciatori veneziani', in *Venezia e la Roma dei papi* (Milan 1987), pp. 75–104.

P. Blastenbrei, *Kriminalität in Rom 1560–1585* (Tübingen 1995).

A. Blunt, *Borromini* (London 1979).

D. Butler, 'Orazio Spada and his Architects: Amateurs and Professionals in Late-seventeenth-century Rome', *Journal of the Society of Architectural Historians*, LIII, 1 (1994), 61–79.

M. Caravale, *La finanza pontificia nel Cinquecento: le provincie del Lazio* (Camerino 1974).

D. Chiomenti Vassalli, *Donna Olimpia, o del nepotismo nel seicento* (Milan 1979).

G. Cipriani, *Gli obelischi egizi: politica e cultura nella Roma barocca* (Florence 1993).

G. Cozzi, 'Stato e chiesa: vicende di un confronto secolare', in *Venezia e la Roma dei papi* (Milan 1987), pp. 11–56.

L. Dal Pane, *Lo Stato pontificio e il movimento riformatore del Settecento* (Milan 1959).

A.-L. Desmas, 'Un monument oublié en l'honneur de Louis XV au Latran', *Gazette des Beaux-Arts*, CXXXI (1998), 235–48.

M. Dunn, 'Piety and Patronage in Seicento Rome: Two Noblewomen and their Convents', *Art Bulletin*, LXXVI, 4 (1994), 644–64.

M. Dunn, 'Spiritual Philanthropists: Women as Convent Patrons in Seicento Rome', in *Women and Art in Early Modern Europe: Patrons, Collectors, and Connoisseurs*, ed. C. Lawrence (University Park, PA 1997), pp. 154–88.

I. de Feo, *Sisto V. Un grande papa tra Rinascimento e Barocco* (Milan 1987).

C.C. Fornili, *Delinquenti e carcerati a Roma alla metà del Seicento. Opera dei papi nella riforma carceraria* (Rome 1991).

I. Fosi, *All' Ombra dei Barberini: fedeltà e servizio nella Roma barocca* (Rome 1997).

I. Fosi, 'Justice and its Image: Political Propaganda and Judicial Reality in the Pontificate of Sixtus V', *Sixteenth Century Journal*, XXIV (1993), 75–95.

I. Fosi, *La società violenta. Il banditismo nello Stato pontificio nella seconda metà del Cinquecento* (Rome 1985).

J. Freiberg, *The Lateran in 1600. Christian Concord in Counter-Reformation Rome* (Cambridge 1995).

G. Gabrieli, *Contributi alla storia della Accademia dei Lincei* (2 vols, Rome 1989).

A. Gardi, *Il cardinale Enrico Caetani e la legazione di Bologna (1586–87)* (Rome 1985).

A. Gardi, 'La fiscalità pontificia fra medioevo ed età moderna', *Società e storia*, XXXIII (1986), 509–57.

A. Gardi, *Lo stato in provincia. L'amministrazione della Legazione di Bologna durante il regno di Sisto V (1585–90)* (Bologna 1994).

C.E. Gilbert, *Caravaggio and his Two Cardinals* (University Park, PA 1995).

F. Hammond, *Music and Spectacle in Baroque Rome: Barberini Patronage under Urban VIII* (New Haven, CT 1994).

F. Haskell, *Patrons and Painters: a Study in the Relations between Art and Society in the Age of the Baroque* (London 1963).

M. Laurain-Portemer, 'Absolutisme et Népotisme. La surintendance de l'état ecclésiastique', *Bibliothèque de l'Ecole des Chartes*, CXXXI (1973), 487–568.

M. Laurain-Portemer, 'Ministériat, finances et papauté au temps de la réforme catholique', *ibid.*, CXXXIV (1976), 396–405.

L. Lewis, *Connoisseurs and Secret Agents in Eighteenth-century Rome* (London 1961).

M.L. Madonna (ed.), *Roma di Sisto V. Le arti e la cultura* (Rome 1993).

T.A. Marder, *Bernini's Scala Regia at the Vatican Palace* (Cambridge 1997).

A. Menniti Ippolito, 'Ecclesiastici veneti tra Venezia e Roma', in *Venezia e la Roma dei papi* (Milan 1987), pp. 209–34.

A. Menniti Ippolito, 'Nepotisti e antinepotisti: Pietro Ottoboni, i "conservatori" di curia e i pontefici Odescalchi e Pignatelli', *Studi Veneziani*, XXV (1993), 131–49.

O. Mischiati et al. (eds), *La cappella musicale nell' Italia della Controriforma* (Florence 1993).

M. Monaco, *Le finanze pontificie al tempo di Paulo V (1605–21). La fondazione del primo banco pubblico in Roma* (Rome 1974).

M. Monaco, *Lo Stato della Chiesa*, II (Lecce 1979).

J. Montagu, *Alessandro Algardi* (2 vols, New Haven, CT–London 1985).

A. Morelli, *Il tempio armonico: musica nell' Oratorio dei Filippini in Roma (1575–1705)* (Laaber 1991).

C. Mozzarelli et al. (eds), *L'Europa delle corti alla fine dell' antico regime* (Rome 1991).

K. Oberhuber, *Poussin: the Early Years in Rome; the Origins of French Classicism* (New York 1988).

N. O'Regan, *Institutional Patronage in Post-Tridentine Rome: Music at Santissima Trinità dei Pellegrini 1550–1650* (London 1995).

S.F. Ostrow, *Art and Spirituality in Counter-Reformation Rome. The Sistine and Pauline Chapels in Santa Maria Maggiore* (Cambridge 1996).

B. Pellegrino (ed.), *Riforme, religione e politica durante il pontificato di Innocenzo XII (1691–1700)* (Galatina 1994).

G. Pelliccia, *La scuola primaria a Roma dal secolo XVI al XIX* (Rome 1986).

M. Petrocchi, *Roma nel seicento* (Bologna 1975).

L. Poliakov, 'La communauté juive à Rome aux XVIe et XVIIe siècles', *Annales E.S.C.*, XII (1957), 119–22.

A. Potts, *Flesh and the Ideal. Winckelmann and the Origins of Art History* (London 1994).

W. Reinhard, 'Amici e creature. Politische Mikrogeschichte der römischen Kurie im 17. Jahrhundert', *Quellen und Forschungen aus Italienischen Archiven und Bibliotheken*, LXXVI (1996), 308–34.

W. Reinhard, 'Papal Power and Family Strategy in the Sixteenth and Seventeenth Centuries', in *Princes, Patronage, and the Nobility. The Court at the Beginning of the Modern Age, c. 1450–1650*, ed. R.G. Asch and A.M. Birke (Oxford 1991), pp. 329–56.

W. Reinhard, *Papstfinanz und Nepotismus unter Paul V (1605–21)* (2 vols, Stuttgart 1974).

W. Reinhard and H. Schilling (eds), *Die katholische Konfessionalisierung* (Münster 1995).

L. Rice, *The Altars and Altarpieces of New St. Peter's. Outfitting the Basilica, 1621–1666* (Cambridge 1997).

M. Rosa, 'Curia Romana e pensioni ecclesiastiche. Fiscalità pontificia nel Mezzogiorno (secc. XVI–XVII)', *Quaderni storici*, XLII (1979), 1015–55.

M. Rosa, '"La scarsella di N. Signore": aspetti della fiscalità spirituale pontificia nell' età moderna', *Società e storia*, XXXIII (1986), 505–57.

S.M. Seidler, *'Il teatro del mondo'. Diplomatische und journalistische Relationen vom römischen Hof aus dem 17. Jahrhundert* (Frankfurt AM 1996).

G.R. Smith, *Architectural Diplomacy: Rome and Paris in the Late Baroque* (New York 1993).

E. Sori (ed.), *Città e controllo sociale in Italia tra XVIII e XIX secolo* (Milan 1982).

F. Troncarelli (ed.), *La città dei segreti: magia, astrologia e cultura esoterica a Roma (XV–XVIII secolo)* (Milan 1985).

C. Valone, 'Women on the Quirinal Hill: Patronage in Rome, 1560–1630', *Art Bulletin*, LXXVI, 1 (1994), 129–46.

F. Valsecchi, *Riformismo e Antico Regime nel secolo XVIII: Il riformismo borbonico a Napoli e a Parma. Lo Stato della Chiesa* (Rome 1967).

R. Volpi, *Le regioni introvabili. Centralizzazione e regionalizzazione dello Stato pontificio* (Bologna 1983).

E. Waterhouse, *Roman Baroque Painting* (London 1976).

C. Weber, *Die Territorien des Kirchenstaates im 18. Jahrhundert* (Frankfurt AM 1991).

M.S. Weil, *History and Decoration of the Ponte S. Angelo* (London 1974).

R. Wittkower, *Bernini* (2nd edn, London 1966).

R. Zapperi, *Der Neid und die Macht. Die Farnese und Aldobrandini in barocken Rom* (Munich 1994).

B.G. Zenobi, *Le 'Ben Regolate Città': Modelli politici nel governo delle periferie pontificie in età moderna* (Rome 1994).

Glossary

Arnauld The name of a French family conspicuous in the history of *Jansenism*. The most prominent member was Antoine, 'the Great Arnauld' (1612–94), whose prolific writings included a work which caused *Jansenism* to be associated with opposition to frequent communion.

Augustinianism A theological tradition giving an overwhelming authority to the teaching of St Augustine of Hippo (354–430). This severe interpretation of Christian belief was promoted particularly by the followers of *Jansenism* from the seventeenth century.

Austrian Succession The death without a male heir of the Holy Roman Emperor Charles VI, in 1740, caused a conflict over the succession in the distinct Austrian Habsburg family lands, including those in Italy and the Netherlands. The resulting War (1740–48) among the European powers eventually preserved substantially, but not entirely, the inheritance of Maria Theresa.

Baius, Michel (1513–89) His theological teaching at the University of Louvain in the Southern Netherlands was attacked by other Catholic scholars for its allegedly heterodox presentation of *Augustinianism*. His opponents included Jesuits, at a time when *Bellarmine* was among those at Louvain.

Baronius, Cesare Baronio (1538–1607) He was a leading member of Philip Neri's Roman Oratory, cardinal and writer on ecclesiastical history. His published work was intended to counter Protestant attack on the history of the Catholic Church.

Bellarmine, St Robert Roberto Bellarmino (1542–1621) was a Jesuit theologian and cardinal. After a period at Louvain he returned to Italy, teaching at Rome and publishing extensively on Catholic doctrine and Protestant error.

Bérulle, Pierre de (1575–1629) The French ecclesiastic and cardinal was inspired by Neri's Roman Oratory to found the distinct French Oratory. By this and other means he influenced the internal reform of the Catholic Church in France, after the disruption of war in the sixteenth century. Despite his own loyalty to Rome, some members of his Oratory were later accused of *Jansenism*.

Bossuet, Jacques-Bénigne (1627–1704)   The French bishop was prominent during much of the reign of Louis XIV. Despite his involvement in the evolution of *Gallicanism*, he was concerned to defend the Catholic faith, as by his publications against Protestantism. His conflict with *Fénelon* partly reflected a rivalry for influence at the royal court.

botti   Casks, barrels; in liquid measure.

Bruno, Giordano (1548–1600)   The Dominican friar left Italy for many years and extended his travels as far as Protestant England. On his return to Italy he was taken into custody by the Roman Inquisition. His non-scientific mysticism gave him a sympathy with the heliocentric cosmology of Copernicus but encouraged the pantheism which led to his execution for heresy.

cantari   The *cantaro* was a measure of weight estimated to have been about 100lbs.

Catholic League   During the French religious and dynastic wars in the second half of the sixteenth century (1560–98) a Catholic League was active from 1576, and from 1585 it sought to exclude the Calvinist Henri of Navarre from succession to the throne. From 1590 Philip II of Spain sought to capitalize on this conflict, until Henri finally secured the Crown, as a Catholic since 1593, between 1595 and 1598, at the cost of granting the *Edict of Nantes*. Philip II was also a leading participant in the Holy League, formed by Pius V against the Turks, which won the naval victory of Lepanto in 1571.

During the Thirty Years' War (1618–48) a Catholic League of German Catholic princes was active. It had been formed previously, in 1609, by Duke Maximilian of Bavaria. Its forces were subordinated to the Emperor from 1635.

Congregation   Within the Roman Curia new administrative boards were added, from the mid-sixteenth century onwards, to the existing, medieval departments and tribunals. These new Congregations were headed by cardinals, with the staff of each section of the Curia forming the *dicasteries*.

Consistory   A formal assembly of cardinals, normally those resident in Rome, was summoned by the pope. Such a Consistory, over which the pope presided, increasingly dealt with the more routine aspects of ecclesiastical business, but not, as yet, entirely to the exclusion of more extraordinary affairs.

Convulsionaries   During the evolution of *Jansenism*, a group of adherents focused their attention on the Parisian tomb of a member of the movement, François de Paris, at which miraculous phenomena were supposedly evident, from 1731, a few years after his death. Their enthusiastic agitation was not admired by all, and their behaviour led to this identification.

De Auxiliis   The theological questions involved in *Augustinianism* centrally included problems about the operation of divine grace, not least in relation to predestination and free will. Controversy among Catholic theologians after the Council of Trent, especially between Jesuits and Dominicans, grew, above all in Spain. In an effort to resolve the conflict Clement VIII appointed a special commission 'On the Means of Grace' (Congregatio De Auxiliis), but he had not himself pronounced formal judgement at the time of his death. Paul V attempted to impose silence on the issue.

Dicasteries   The departments of the Roman Curia and their staff.

Edict of Nantes   By this edict of 1598, Henri IV, the ultimate victor in the French religious and civil wars, pacified his former co-religionists, the French Calvinists (Huguenots). The edict and other originally appended royal documents defined the religious, judicial and military rights of the Huguenot minority in Catholic France. After modification of these terms under Louis XIII, the edict was finally revoked by Louis XIV in 1685.

Edict of Restitution   During the Thirty Years' War, a period of Catholic advantage allowed the Holy Roman Emperor Ferdinand II in 1629 to issue the edict, ordering the restoration of Church lands within the Empire occupied by Protestants since 1552. Its inherently political effect proved counterproductive, in that it stimulated distrust of the Emperor's power among the German princes generally, not only the Protestants.

Erastianism   The assertion of the supremacy of the State in ecclesiastical affairs, originally made in the context of the Protestant Reformation, was articulated by the Swiss theologian, Erastus (1524–83).

Febronianism   In German-speaking Catholic Europe of the eighteenth century, an attack on aspects of papal power was advanced in defence of episcopal authority. The initial propositions of von Hontheim (1710–90), influenced by *Gallicanism*, were published in 1763 under the pseudonym of Febronius.

Fénelon, François de Salignac de la Mothe (1651–1715)   The French ecclesiastic and archbishop was for a while influential in royal circles. But in his rivalry with *Bossuet*, he was put at a disadvantage because of his association with *Quietism*. Despite his opposition to *Jansenism* he was critical of some of the French Jesuits, but loyally submitted to Rome when a publication of his was condemned for its allegedly Quietist nature.

Galileo   Galileo Galilei (1546–1642) was the son of an eminent musical theorist. His own mathematical studies won him professorial appointments in Medicean Tuscany and then at the Venetian University of Padua. By the time of his return to Florence his interest in the physics of motion was complemented by his observations of the heavens, using the then new instrument, the telescope. The problems inherent in adjusting conventional cosmology, supported by traditional scriptural interpretations, and new observations drew attention to the heliocentric supposition published in the mid-sixteenth century by Copernicus. An initial encounter with the Inquisition, in 1615–16, seemed to leave Galileo free in his work but circumscribed as to the terms in which he could publish, after the intervention of **Bellarmine**. His final trial before the Roman Inquisition resulted in a sentence of house arrest in 1633. This followed immediately the publication not of Galileo's *Assayer* (1623) but of his *Dialogue on the Two World-Systems* (1632).

Gallicanism   The 'liberties' of the French Church, claiming a privileged position of considerable practical independence from papal supervision, under the alternative protection of the French Crown, were originally articulated in the fifteenth century, in the context of competition between popes and General Councils of the Church. From the end of the sixteenth century they were reasserted by French jurists, stimulated by the crisis over the royal succession. This position was accordingly maintained by members of the supreme legal tribunal, the Paris *parlement*, throughout the seventeenth and eighteenth centuries. Because of the political tensions during that period between the monarchs themselves and the *parlement*, however, royal Gallicanism and *parlementaire* Gallicanism were not necessarily identical, especially with regard to the treatment of **Jansenism**. Despite royal nomination to French bishoprics, the emphasis on the rights of diocesan bishops as against papal authority enshrined in Gallican theory naturally encouraged an episcopal Gallicanism, during the same two centuries, which pursued its own interests, irrespective of the other two versions. At a moment of particular tension between the papacy and Louis XIV, the king prompted an assembly of the French clergy in 1682 to build on an earlier Gallican declaration so as to produce the Four Gallican Articles. These proclaimed limitations to papal power with respect to both royal authority and General Councils of the Church. Credit for the relatively moderate formulation of these Articles was attributed to **Bossuet**. Episcopal Gallicanism was more generally kept within certain limits by French bishops' opposition to the claims of the lower clergy advanced by **Richer**.

Giannone, Pietro (1676–1748)   The Neapolitan lawyer fled to the Austrian Habsburg Court after publishing an historical work critical of the power and wealth of the Church. His thinking and unpublished writings became more radical still, involving fundamental criticism of Christian belief, but after an attempt to return to Italy and a retreat to Geneva he was imprisoned by the Savoyard government until his death.

Hussites   The national movement inspired by the Bohemian Church reformer Jan Hus (*c.* 1372–1415) articulated its aims in the Four Articles of Prague (1420). These included control of Church property and a vernacular liturgy. A prolonged armed struggle (1420–34) failed to prevent division within this tradition, producing by the end of the fifteenth century the more radical Bohemian Brethren, who separated from the more moderate **Utraquists**, also known as Calixtines.

Jansenism   The monumental treatise prepared by Cornelius Jansen, a bishop in the Southern Netherlands, and published in 1640, two years after his death, was an extended exercise in *Augustinianism*, which revived the teachings on grace of *Baius*. Jansen's known criticism of the Jesuits ensured that this posthumous work would be controversial, and he himself had been aware of the difficulty of publishing on divine grace in the light of papal policy during and since the *De Auxiliis* dispute. Defence of Jansen's reputation and the orthodoxy of his treatise was rapidly taken up by some French Catholics, originally emerging from an existing movement of the especially devout, who looked for internal reform of the French Church after the disruption of the sixteenth century. This devout tradition was also critical of the anti-Habsburg and therefore not pan-Catholic foreign policy pursued by Richelieu, a policy criticized also by Jansen in the Habsburg-ruled Netherlands. Richelieu was thus moved to imprison Jansen's friend and initial leader of the French Jansenists as well as critic of the Jesuits, the abbé de Saint-Cyran. After the latter's death in 1643 the French movement was led by *Arnauld*, and was particularly associated with Port-Royal, a pair of linked convents, until the suppression of the original community of nuns in 1709. The literary genius of Blaise Pascal (1623–62), in his attack on the Jesuits, ensured that Jansenism remained a movement opposed to and opposed by the Society of Jesus. Jansenism also became identified by some opponents as politically subversive, in the mid-seventeenth-century crisis during the minority of Louis XIV. But royal disapproval of the Jansenists, in the France of Louis XIV, did not perfectly correspond with papal condemnation of Jansenist doctrine, not least because of the complications of *Gallicanism*. The theologians of the Parisian *Sorbonne* had initially condemned Jansen's publication. But the *Sorbonne* was also determined to maintain its own traditional competence in such judgements, irrespective of papal positions. Similarly, the Paris *parlement* increasingly attempted to defend Jansenists against papal authority, as an exercise in *parlementaire* Gallicanism, in opposition to royal policy on this issue. In eighteenth-century France the nature of Jansenism thus became increasingly politicized, and eventually in this form it helped to produce the expulsion of the Jesuits.

In the mid-seventeenth century, however, the French Jansenists attempted to evade papal condemnation by distinguishing between the 'right' involved in condemnation of heretical propositions and the 'fact' of whether such propositions could be demonstrably found in Jansen's text. But after half a century of manoeuvres the Jansenist movement was reinvigorated by papal condemnation of the teachings, above all on grace, of *Quesnel*. The condemnation of 101 propositions from his work, in the papal Constitution *Unigenitus* of 1713, revived resistance to papal authority exercised in this way on such an issue not only in France but more widely too. Jansenists who left France to escape anti-Jansenist discipline in Church or State added their support to those sympathetic to the memory of Jansen in the Netherlands themselves. From this Netherlandish tradition emerged the schismatic Church of Utrecht in the early eighteenth century. Jansenist criticism of papal authority as exerted in

Unigenitus spread more widely still, to affect and merge with other strands of anti-Roman dissidence in eighteenth-century Catholic Europe, such as anti-Curialism in parts of Italy or the campaign against the Jesuits in the Iberian peninsula. There was thus interaction by the end of the century between such broader Jansenism and other tendencies, such as *Febronianism* and *Josephinism*. But to the last Jansenism itself also stood for an austerity in Christian practice, a rigorism in the sacrament of confession, and a desire for further institutional reform within the Catholic Church.

Josephinism The claims of the secular ruler to impose changes in the life of the Catholic Church within his territories, irrespective of, and if necessary in opposition to, the wishes of the papacy, were put into practice by the Emperor Joseph II, acting as ruler of the Habsburg family lands in Austria, the Southern Netherlands and parts of Italy. But the pursuit of such policies did not occur only between 1780, when Joseph became sole ruler of the Habsburg territories on the death of his mother, Maria Theresa, and his own death in 1790 or that of his brother Leopold, who succeeded him as Emperor, in 1792. The idea that internal reform of aspects of the Church might be imposed locally by the secular ruler was already evident while Maria Theresa was alive, especially once Joseph joined her as co-ruler of the Habsburg territories in 1765. Such concepts in origin owed something to a strand of pro-Jansenist *Gallicanism* fostered in the Netherlands which had also influenced *Febronianism*.

Laxism The consistent opposition of *Jansenism* to the Society of Jesus concentrated in particular on the allegedly relaxed standards applied by Jesuit confessors in the sacrament of penance. Despite the Society's attempts to dissociate itself from the type of propositions, put forward by theorists ('casuists') on the hearing of hypothetical cases in confession, which incurred papal condemnation for excessive lack of rigour, the Jesuits' critics did not relinquish this line of attack.

Mantuan Succession Political control of areas of Northern Italy was crucial for military reasons. Troops being moved from the Mediterranean lands, south of the Alps, into areas of Northern Europe such as the Netherlands or the German lands, needed to pass along routes which hostile powers might seek to occupy or block. This was true not only of an Alpine corridor like the *Valtelline*, but also of the Monferrato, with its fortress of Casale, control of which was challenged by the duke of Savoy in the first War of Monferrato (1613–17). The death of the duke of Mantua without male heirs thus renewed the prospect of war in Northern Italy, since the Gonzagas had ruled the Monferrato as well as Mantua itself. The papacy correctly feared the involvement in such a war of the major European powers, France and Spain, because of the military importance of the territories, quite apart from renewed Savoyard claims. France and Spain backed rival claimants to the succession, and the Emperor claimed the right to adjudicate. During 1628–29 war spread across

Northern Italy, involving Spanish, Savoyard, French and Imperial troops. After the sack of Mantua in 1630 a treaty was eventually agreed in 1631 by which the duke of Savoy made some gains, to balance French conquests in Northern Italy, and the French candidate succeeded in Mantua. But the papacy had thus been unable to preserve the Italian peninsula from what was effectively an over-spill of the Thirty Years' War or to prevent a clash between the rival Catholic powers of France and the Habsburgs, in a prelude to open and prolonged war between them a few years later.

Molinos, Miguel de (1628–96)   The Spanish priest moved to Rome in 1663 and attracted an important following there as a confessor and spiritual director. Despite his social connections he was put on trial by the Holy Office in 1686 and remained in prison until his death. The accusations of personal immorality did not prevent his published work, *The Spiritual Guide* (1675), having a wider influence in the evolution of **Quietism**.

Noris, Enrico (1631–1704)   The scholar and cardinal taught theology in Italy and advocated by his writing an **Augustinianism** which in his mind was obviously orthodox but which critics denounced as reviving the errors of **Baius** and **Jansenism**. Roman rehabilitation of his reputation was complicated by the effective independence of the Spanish Inquisition and Spanish Index.

Olier, Jean-Jacques (1608–57)   The French priest represented the devout tradition of those Catholics in France during the first half of the seventeenth century who looked for internal reform of the Church there but did not necessarily all join the movement known as **Jansenism**. His promotion of a high standard of priestly conduct and improved training of priests through seminary education secured for his Parisian church of Saint-Sulpice a lasting fame and wide influence in France. He himself was influenced by the spirituality of the French Oratory founded by **Bérulle**.

Oriental and Orthodox Churches   The Oriental Christians of the Armenian, Coptic, Ethiopian and Syrian Orthodox Churches were originally known as Monophysites, in reference to divisions over the definition of Christ's nature in the early history of the Christian Church, during the fifth century. For historical reasons the Syrian Orthodox are still alternatively known as Jacobites. In the fifth century, reaction against Monophysite theology, opposed by Nestorius, led to some other Christians becoming known as Nestorians. This latter term was for long applied, however incorrectly, to the Christians now known as the Church of the East, some of whom, since entering into communion with Rome in the sixteenth century, have also been known as Chaldean Christians.

The Orthodox Churches, normally maintaining communion with the patriarch of Constantinople, included the Greek, Russian (and Polish), Serbian, Rumanian and Bulgarian Orthodox Christians, as well as the Orthodox *patriarchates* of Alexandria, Antioch and Jerusalem. Some Christians of many of these Churches entered at various dates into communion with Rome, adhering liturgically to their Eastern rites and forming movements known, however improperly, as **Uniate**. The Maronites of the Lebanon represent an early example of an Eastern-rite Church in communion with Rome. The Eastern-rite Christians of the *patriarchates* of Alexandria, Antioch and Jerusalem were known as Melkites (or Melchites), and this term was increasingly applied to those of them who entered into communion with Rome. Those of the Eastern-rite Christians in Poland, Lithuania, the Ukraine, and eventually parts of Hungary who entered into communion with Rome were historically known as Ruthenians, even if now more often as Ukrainian.

Patriarchate In the early centuries of the Church the title of patriarch was reserved for the bishops of the five most major sees: Rome, Alexandria, Antioch, Constantinople and Jerusalem. The heads of many of the **Oriental and Orthodox Churches** were commonly using the title in the sixteenth, seventeenth and eighteenth centuries, and when such leaders led all or part of their Church membership into union with Rome they might retain this title as head of an Eastern-rite **Uniate** Church. The use in this period of the title for the archbishops of Aquileia, Venice and Lisbon did not carry the same jurisdictional implications, despite the ceremonial privileges acquired by the last of these.

Quietism This form of Christian spirituality advocated complete passivity and abandonment of self, to be achieved by a prayerful state which avoided not only set forms or precise intentions but even conscious meditation. Such teaching seemed to make all conventional devotion and indeed sacramental duties superfluous, and was alleged to make the category of sin dangerously meaningless. Papal condemnation in 1687 of such propositions, from the work of **Molinos**, did not for a while prevent the retention of similar views in France by Madame Guyon (1648–1717). She impressed **Fénelon**, but her eventual condemnation in France was followed by papal condemnation in 1699 of supposedly Quietist propositions in a book he had published two years earlier.

Quesnel, Pasquier (1634–1719) The French ecclesiastic was originally a member of the French Oratory founded by **Bérulle**. He encountered difficulties arising from accusations against him of **Jansenism** and left France for the Southern Netherlands. He was eventually imprisoned there but escaped to the Dutch Netherlands. In the early eighteenth century the papacy issued a condemnation of his views as expressed in a work which he had first published many years before, on the grounds of its reassertion of Jansenist teaching. The condemnation was definitively confirmed by the Constitution **Unigenitus**.

Reductions In the South American interior, specifically in Paraguay (including areas now in Argentina), the Jesuits sought to protect their native converts from exploitation by colonists, by settling Indians in isolated communes, where religious instruction and limited education were provided. These self-supporting communities were planned as model villages, each under Jesuit direction. In the seventeenth century the Portuguese monarchy originally approved these Reductions, to the extent of agreeing that the Indians might be armed for self-defence. When in the eighteenth century opposition to the Society of Jesus in the Iberian kingdoms became strident, the effective independence of the Jesuits' Paraguayan 'republic' appeared objectionable. The expulsion of the Jesuits from the territories of the Iberian monarchs caused the collapse of native communities which had not developed self-reliance.

Richer, Edmond (1559–1631)   The form of *Gallicanism* advocated by Richer argued for the independent rights not just of bishops with respect to popes but also of priests alongside bishops. This was naturally viewed with reserve by French bishops, despite their promotion of their own version of *Gallicanism*. Such Richerism found increasing support among some of the French lower clergy in the eighteenth century, who were opposed to episcopal monopolization of ecclesiastical wealth and power, especially where bishops attempted to discipline clerics for supposed sympathy with *Jansenism*.

rubbia   The measurement of grain was in *rubbia*, but there is uncertainty about the cubic capacity of each *rubbio*. Since different types of grain were lighter or heavier a *rubbio* might weigh more or less than 200kg.

salme   Sicilian measurement of grain, however, was in *salme*. The *salma* is now reckoned to equal 275.1 litres.

scudi   The Roman currency unit was the scudo, divided into ten paoli, each in turn divided into ten baiocchi, worth five quattrini each. The scudo was originally supposed to correspond, in the sixteenth century, to the French écu. But while it was notionally reckoned to be worth slightly less than the ducat, in practice the value of a ducat depended on its place of issue. The intrinsic value of the écu had declined considerably by the end of the sixteenth century, making the official equation of three livres to the écu of little use.

Sorbonne   This college of the University of Paris was used from the mid-sixteenth century as the regular meeting-place of the Theology Faculty. This gave rise to the common use of the name to refer to the Faculty.

Uniates   The Eastern-rite Christians whose Churches are in communion with Rome do not normally favour the description Uniate (or Uniat), but the term has persisted in common historical use. In the period from the sixteenth to the eighteenth century these Churches preserved their distinctive liturgies, as well as features of their own canon law, which permitted married parish clergy, for example. Such Churches were commonly organized under a *patriarchate*.

Unigenitus   The Constitution known by this initial word was a papal bull issued by Clement XI in 1713. In it were condemned 101 propositions extracted from a work which *Quesnel* had published in its original form many years before. Though the work urged lay access to the scriptures, Roman condemnation was inspired above all by the seeming reappearance in it of theological positions central to *Jansenism* but already repeatedly condemned. Opposition to the Constitution was widespread and persistent in France, but continued to increase with time elsewhere too, as in the Netherlands, while throughout many parts of Catholic Europe the whole episode stimulated broader objection to aspects of Roman authority in action.

Utraquists   The Bohemian *Hussites* developed almost as a defining programme of their movement the demand that communion should be administered in both kinds (bread and wine) to all recipients, so that those other than the celebrant should not be confined to communion in one kind (bread alone). Even the more moderate members of the movement thus persisted in this central demand, to which the term Utraquism refers.

Valtelline   The importance for the major European powers of corridors by which troops might be moved across the Alps was evident even before the **Mantuan Succession** crisis. From the very first years of the seventeenth century attention was concentrated on one Alpine route in particular, involving the Stelvio pass. The Valtelline thus provided the most direct link between Spanish-ruled Lombardy in Northern Italy and the territories of the Austrian Habsburgs. There was an uprising of the Catholic population of the valley in 1620 against their overlords, the neighbouring Grisons who adhered to a Swiss form of Protestantism. The resolution of the internal faction struggles of the area, which were also involved in this, complicated a political and religious settlement for the valley itself, and that was also delayed by Spain's need to balance strategic requirements against defence of the Catholics' religion. The papacy was thus naturally concerned by events in the Valtelline from the beginning of the 1620s, but even more alarmed by the prospect of armed conflict over the valley breaking out between the major Catholic powers, France and the Habsburgs, with the likely consequence of the European war which was raging north of the Alps spilling over into Italy itself. It was in such circumstances that the plan was adopted, initially with considerable reluctance, to police the Valtelline with papal troops. After France had expelled the papal garrisons, Cardinal Richelieu nevertheless professed to share Spain's concern for the Catholicism of the Valtelline population, in a treaty of 1626 by which he was effectively compelled to allow Spain control of the valley.

Vico, Giovanni Battista (1668–1744)   The Neapolitan jurist published an innovative study which attempted a wide-ranging philosophy of history. In that sense his work was more profound than that of **Giannone**.

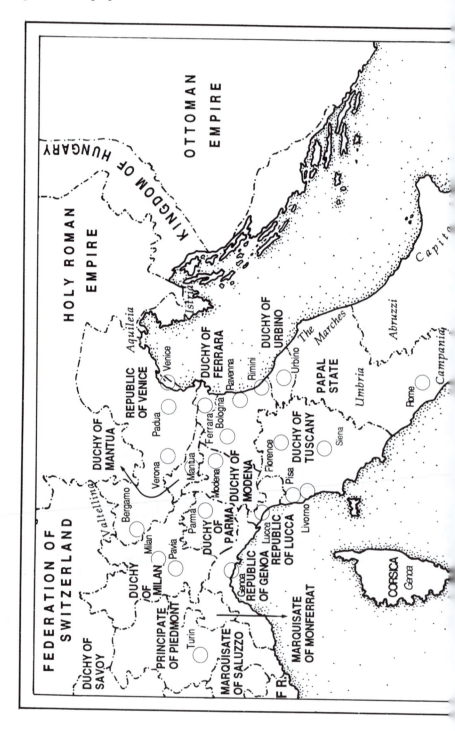

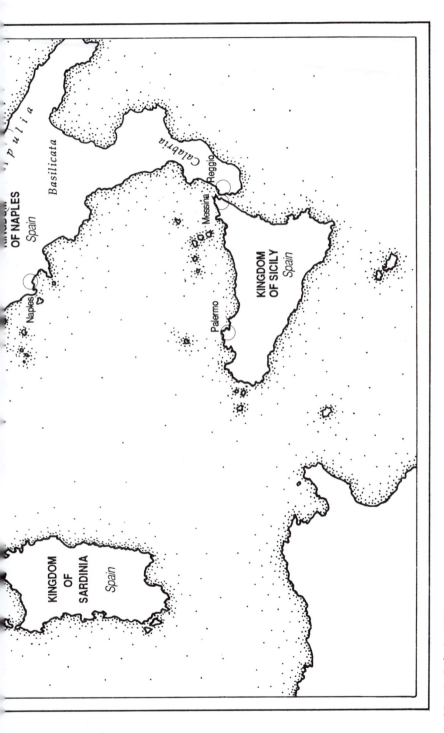

Map 1 Italy in 1564

Map 2   Political divisions during the eighteenth century

Index